UNIVERSITY OF
WINCHESTER

Martial Rose Library
Tel: 01962 827306

To be returned on or before the day marked above, subject to recall.

THE STORY OF
MY PELICAN

ALBERT SCHWEITZER

THE STORY OF MY PELICAN

PHOTOGRAPHS BY
ANNA WILDIKANN

Translated by
Martha Wardenburg

HAWTHORN BOOKS, INC.

Publishers, New York

FIRST AMERICAN PRINTING

H-9020

Lambaréné - Gabon
French Equatorial Africa,
26. 5. 57

Mrs Martha Wardenburg me dit
que vous aimeriez que je certifie
que tout ce que je raconte du pélican
~~si tout~~ dans le petit livre dont elle
vous offre une traduction avec des
photographies, est vrai. Je puis
vous assurer que c'est absolument le cas
Ce pélican était un personnage
remarquable

    Avec mes bonnes pensées
votre dévoué

        Albert Schweitzer

Lambaréné, Gabon
French Equatorial Africa
May 26, 1957

Mrs. Martha Wardenburg tells me you would
like me to certify that everything I relate about
the pelican, along with the photographs, is true
in the little book she has translated. I can assure
you that it is absolutely so. That pelican was a
remarkable personality.

With all good wishes,

Sincerely yours,

Albert Schweitzer

THE STORY OF
MY PELICAN

I AM THE PELICAN, the hero of this book. So it seems to me that I ought to introduce myself and give you some facts about my life. Only a confused memory remains of the days when I was a fledgling. I can recall being with my two brothers in a nest up in a great tree overlooking the river and forest. There we waited with wide open beaks for the food our parents were going to bring us. I have no idea how we came down out of that tree to find ourselves on a sand bank near a thicket of papyrus.

My first real memories date from the time when some black men, shouting and brandishing sticks to frighten off our parents, carried the three of us away with our legs tied up. In the village, they pushed us into a basket where we could scarcely move our beaks.

The next day, two men put us into a canoe and set off with us. On the second day of this journey, we left the river and were paddled into a broad stream. Twice the sun went down and night fell.

In the middle of the third day, the canoe came ashore where there were palm trees and mangoes and many mud huts. The two men climbed up a hill towards a large house. Dogs came bounding and barking out of the compound—I can tell you, we were very frightened. A strong voice was heard and silence was restored. There appeared a man of great height and with him someone dressed in white. I soon learned that it was Dr. Schweitzer and Nurse Emma Haussknecht.

For some time, the Doctor looked over our kidnappers and our basket. Then he said to Mlle Emma, "Three pelicans to feed—that's all we needed!"

At that, silence fell again, finally broken by the Doctor who said to the two men, "Don't you know it's a sin to take little ones away from their parents? How could you have done it? Wait and see, the good Lord will find a way to punish you. Didn't you learn that from the missionary at school?"

The expression on the Doctor's face was

terrifying and the two men looked very uncomfortable. However, they recovered themselves quickly and said, "We thought you'd like
the pelicans and that's why we brought them
to you. If you make us an offer, they're yours.
Otherwise we'll take them to another white
man."

The Doctor's face reddened with anger.
"That's enough. Do you think I'm going to let
you drag those poor creatures, half dead with
hunger, around any longer? What if you gave
them to someone who wouldn't feed them
well? They shall remain here! Now then, here's
some money to pay you for your journey and
for the fish you bought them. All right, off
with you!"

In the midst of this, Mlle Emma had un-
fastened the basket and we managed to get
out. How good it felt to move about! The
Doctor gently felt our wings and feet.

"You're lucky," he said to the two natives,
"not to have broken anything. I would have
given you a bad half hour." Then, turning to

the nurse, "We'll obviously have to feed them for several months. It won't be an easy thing. The dry season is coming to an end. When the river rises, it's going to be difficult to get any fish. But after that, they'll fly off and we'll be rid of them. How I regret having to sacrifice so many fish for these gluttons!"

The two rogues were still there begging the Doctor to give them more. They put forward the expense of feeding us, claiming that young pelicans are never satisfied, that they had given us an enormous quantity of fish bought in the villages we passed through. What lies they told! Why, they scarcely gave us anything! It was no use opening our beaks as wide as we could to soften their hearts. Finally they went off without getting anything more.

Meanwhile more nurses had arrived as well as one they called, "Doctoresse." Looking down at us, she cried, "What a wonderfully stupid look they have! But they are cute with their round behinds still covered with down." They wanted to take hold of us and pet us, but

for the first time we struck out with our beaks in every direction.

"First, I'll have to build a shelter for them," the Doctor announced. "It will take the whole afternoon and I have so many other things to do."

He summoned George the local carpenter, and together they sorted out corrugated iron and planks to make us a shelter between the piles on which the house stood.

"Protected from the wind, they won't be cold at night," he explained to Mlle Emma.

He worked under the house all afternoon, crawling around and not trying to hide his bad humor over all the extra work. I had had no experience with men and I found it quite peculiar that such a kind person could be so disagreeable. Little by little, as the Doctor and his helper went on hammering and sawing, the idlers went off to their own work.

As the Doctoresse turned away, she said, "One of these days, I'll come and photograph them."

Mlle Emma went away, too, but a few minutes later she returned carrying some fish which she proceeded to push down our beaks. What a joy it was for half-starved creatures like us! When there were no more little fish, she said to the Doctor, "They're still hungry! —but there's nothing left but some big carp. They could never swallow them!"

The Doctor's voice echoed from under the house. "Well, try it. You may see a miracle."

The truth is that we finished off the big carp, too. To make them go down, they poured water down our beaks. This was a wonderful change after the treatment we had had from those rascals.

By sundown, our shelter under the house was ready. They spread a soft bed of dry leaves over the ground and we snuggled down into it. We were protected by a coop which the Doctor and Mlle Emma had found for us.

"Above all," the Doctor said, "we must see to it that nobody touches them and bruises a wing. If they're not in shape to fly off some

day, you'll have to feed them fish, day after day, for years!"

"Heaven preserve us from that," Mlle Emma exclaimed.

I found it somewhat embarrassing that from the beginning they were in such a hurry to get rid of us. Still, their intentions seemed better than those of the other two, so I was easy in my mind. Snug in our bed, we had a refreshing nap until sunrise. Then, barking dogs, cackling chickens, noisy geese, and our own hunger woke us up. We were put into an enclosure just outside the Doctor's own room where the mango trees and palms gave marvellous shade. They brought us a wooden tub filled with water and more fish which the Doctor and Mlle Emma divided between us. As they had to push the fish down our beaks and we were clumsy, they both soon had blood trickling from scratches on their arms. "If only these creatures could feed themselves," the Doctor grumbled.

But three whole weeks were needed for that. Then we were able to catch fish tossed to us.

When the rainy season came, the river began to rise and the fisherman no longer brought in much of anything. The good days were over! "Poor creatures!" said the Doctor, after our meagre repast. More than once when the fisherman arrived, I heard him say to Mlle Emma, "Don't have any fish served at the table today. Give it all to the pelicans. They need it more than we do." She took the order gladly.

I remember one morning when they came to get us out of our coop, the Doctoresse appeared with her little box, and said, "I really must take a picture of them." After several attempts, she managed to get into the enclosure. She worked around us from a distance for fear of being pecked.

Because I was the youngest—and also, I must confess—the weakest, I was the favorite of the Doctor and the nurse. My brothers always tried to eat up my fish. When we were fed, they pecked at me to make me drop my share. I was glad that I was protected by the Doctor and Mlle Emma.

With the coming of the Christmas season, we had lost our down and possessed some real feathers. My eldest brother was already waddling around under the mango trees, flapping his great wings. While I was watching him do it, the Doctoresse arrived with her little black box and said once more, "I must take a picture."

One day, my eldest brother, beating his wings hard, swept up into the air and found himself perched high on the fence of the enclosure. All the hospital staff, African and European, hurried to admire him. "There goes one of them who will soon know how to fly. . . ." A few days later, my second brother did the same thing. They stayed up on the fence and would not come down even when they brought our fish. So they tossed them up and my brothers never missed one, even when the aim was too high, or too low, or too far to one side.

"Quite a circus act," the Doctoresse remarked as she watched the performance.

As for me, I had not even managed a few steps, let alone flapping my wings. Mlle Emma was very concerned about me and lamented the fact to the Doctor.

"He is eating," the Doctor told her consolingly, "and when a pelican eats, he always ends up by getting along fine."

I think she was afraid I might not even live.

Soon, my brothers found out how to get down from the fence, go off to the river, and swim near the shore. In the evening, their guardians brought them back to the house. A few days later, they could be seen going down the hill with a sweep of wings. Everyone looked pityingly at me—I, who could not even get to the top of the enclosure.

But in the springtime, at the end of the rainy season, I succeeded in getting down to the river. Not very skilfully, but still managed quite a graceful flight.

"You see," said the Doctor, smiling at Mlle Emma, "he managed it in the end."

So we could all swim and fish in the river.

But what we caught was not enough to fill us up, we needed so much. Luckily, they still fed us in the evening, and that is why we went back up to the house again when the gong rang at the end of the day's work.

I still lagged behind my brothers in one thing—I could take off from the ground quite well with a spring into the air, but not from the water. I tried hard to get myself off the river for a whole week but I could not manage it. One Sunday afternoon, the Doctor was sitting on the shore. He seemed to take pleasure in watching my vain efforts to lift myself from the water, efforts that alternated with returns to the shore followed by fresh take-offs, trying to convince myself that I was about to fly away. The Doctor who usually spent his Sundays writing letters—I knew that well enough because I could look into his office from my perch on the enclosure fence—stayed all afternoon, entertained by the spectacle I made.

"Beginnings are always difficult," he would say to me every time I ran aground. When a

patient came walking by, he said to him, "You see a rare sight there. A pelican who can take off from solid ground but not from the water."

The patient watched, too, and began to laugh with the Doctor. The annoyance I felt at so much stupidity gave me the strength of ten. I rose from the water—and repeated my victory several times over.

"Bravo!" the Doctor cried. "Now we can hope to be rid of you some day, too."

With those words, off he went to work on his correspondence. Luckily, the Doctoresse did not come along with her little box.

At the beginning of summer, the dry season returned. Sand bars emerged and pools appeared between them where fish were abundant. From little side streams, other pelicans arrived attracted by the excellent conditions. Among them were some like us who had been brought up in the hospital and had later flown away, returning now with their own little ones. These old timers could be recognized by the fact that they swam near the shore like us and

came up on the land without fear of mankind
The others—the tourists—as well as the young
of the old timers, stayed out on the sand bars
well away from the shore, flying off when anyone approached.

What a good life we led that first dry season
when we were grown up! It was then that we
began to learn what it meant to fly. Before that
we had only skimmed over the water. But with
the other pelicans, we rose high into the air
describing majestic circles of smooth flight
above the hospital. With them, we went on long
flights into the distance.

When the other pelicans went back to the
lake regions and marshlands at the end of the
dry season, my brothers went with them.

"Good riddance," said the Doctor to Mlle
Emma. "Let's hope the little one will do the
same."

But the little one—meaning me—had decided
not to give them that satisfaction. At the hospital, I was at home. Why go off, far away,
into a life full of strangers?

It was the same thing with we as with the monkeys who grew up in the hospital. When they were big enough to be on their own, some of the nurses went deep into the forest with the boys who carried the gentle creatures. There, they were set free. The nurses, returning home with tears in their eyes, usually found the same monkeys waiting for them under the veranda. They could only get rid of them—for they were getting quite insupportable—by ferrying them to the other side of the river somewhere off in the forest. The Doctor tried to dry the nurses' tears by assuring them that the monkeys would quickly come to appreciate their freedom and that their new way of life would surely please them more than the old.

As for me, I swore that the Doctor would not shake me off so easily. I think I know better than he does what is best for me.

There are several good reasons for my staying here. When the fisherman has not been too lazy, they always give me one or two fish from the kitchen in the evening. This is in addition

to my own catch: so the problem of nourishment is assured. I do not have to go to so much trouble as the pelicans from lakes and rivers.

Moreover, I am so used to the excitement going on in the enclosure and at the hospital landing that I have not the slightest desire to pass my life in the lonely lakes and marshes.

Lady pelicans have several times suggested that I leave the hospital and set up housekeeping in a tree somewhere with them. I have always remained quite reserved, standing pat. I do not want to be like Koudekou, the Doctor's parrot, who was foolish enough to get caught in his old age in the net of a lady parrot. He went off with her after living at the hospital for years as though in his own home. Of course, he was quite free to make the change if he took the fancy. Now he lives with his wife in the hollow of a tree down in a papyrus swamp below the hospital. How could he prefer gathering his own miserable palm nuts instead of being seated by his master at dinner on the back of his chair, having his share of everything that

39

was served? Not to speak of the sorrow his incomprehensible departure caused the Doctor.

So the fact that they could not get rid of me was due to unselfish as well as selfish reasons. Besides, I no longer think they are considering sending me away. If I were gone, something would be lacking.

Little by little, I have become a person of some importance throughout the countryside. For years, of course, other pelicans have lived here for short spells and, in some cases, permanently. But I am unique among them all. No one dares question my status. Once, well in the past, an intruder, a vagabond from no-one knew where—he was not even a descendant of one of the hospital pelicans—tried to do it. When the others went off after the end of the dry season, he stayed on. Because he had a tuft of feathers on the back of his head, the staff called him "The Professor." The Professor very much wanted my position. When the Doctor was down by the river, he went too. Several times he had the effrontery to appear

in the evening to get some fish at the kitchen door. One day when there was only one fish, the Doctor gave it to him, rewarding me with a fine speech on the subject of brotherhood. The blows I administered to that so-called brother would have brought him to reason a long time ago if the Doctor had not treated him with such misplaced kindliness.

The other pelicans, in all decency, would never dream of elevating themselves to my level. It would be a mad enterprise. I am the only one in the neighbourhood to bear the title, "The Doctor's Pelican." When I go off on an excursion perching along the river banks or lakes near a village, as I fly up over the banks, the children cry, "Look, there's the Doctor's pelican!" And they escort me on my way. No, the truth is, no other pelican dares to compare himself with me.

I mention only in passing the silly, quarrelsome white gander who tried to make himself important for a while by walking beside me. He will not think of doing that again. When he

comes down the river on outstretched wings with his two companions, he avoids alighting near me or swimming in my preserves. I taught him a little modesty. I have a pleasant relationship with the goats and sheep. The big ram is a friend of mine. But as for the dogs—that is another story. I am not too proud of that. When I return in the evening and perch in the compound, they usually leave me in peace. Sometimes, the whole pack gets ready to descend on me.

When I manage to get my back up against a tree to protect my rear, I can keep them respectful by pecking at them. When I don't manage to protect myself in that way, I have to rush off as quickly as I can. Many a mean trick they have played on me while I tried to shift positions.

My standing at the hospital is such that I can take many liberties. In general though, I simply swim around the spot where the women clean fish along the river bank. The things they cast out into the water are mouthfuls not to be dis-

dained. Sometimes, a longing comes over me not to be satisfied with scraps but to have a whole fish. I have to join in with one or two other pelicans for a project such as that. My tactics are simple and usually crowned with success. We perch on a canoe and with a very absorbed air, we begin preening our plumage. We busy ourselves with that until most of the women have finished cleaning their fish and returned home. Nothing can be done before that for the whole troop would defend themselves with paddles and machetes. The attack can succeed only against one of two women who remain behind, lulled into a sense of security. Suddenly we rush upon them with loud cries and terrible blows from our beaks and wings. They take flight in terror, and the fish are ours. When mothers are foolish enough to send their children to the river with fish to clean, I need no help to make them give up the prize. The conclusion of these battles takes place at the Doctor's where the women go with their complaints and demands for payment.

They receive it—and I get a scolding. Sometimes though, they make demands out of pure greediness, that are not fair, and I hope they get what they deserve.

I must confess that these pranks do not always end up so well. It has happened that one or another of these intrepid women will defend herself valiantly. Already, I have had two severe blows on the beak with a machete. As for whacks with a paddle, I do not even count them any more.

Twice, with success at hand, I almost died of suffocation. This was because the Africans have a foolish habit of tying up their fish, four or five of them together, with a liana vine passed through their gills. They sell them that way, by the string. Too greedily, I swooped down on a cluster of them, and after swallowing one or two of the fish, dragged the others down my gullet but found I could not swallow them. Every effort to cough them up was in vain. The string of fish stuck there and I was gasping for air. I was saved both times by some of the boys

49

who saw my distress. They ran off to the Doctor's to let him know what had happened and he came quickly, plunging his arm down my throat right up to his elbow, and pulled out the fish. Then he took his knife, cut the liana vine and as I recovered, gave me the fish one by one. To the women, he paid what they asked. But why the doctor does not rise up against this dangerous habit of stringing fish into bunches, remains a mystery to me.

It does not keep me from feeling a deep veneration for him. At night, I love more than anything else to be near where he is and mount guard over him.

After getting my fish from the kitchen, I perch on the door that closes the veranda near his room. Whoever wants to come up on the porch gets warned off by my hissing. If the visitor pays no attention, I hit him hard with my beak from above—European or African, it makes no difference to me.

After dinner, when the Doctor is sitting by the light of a lamp at his work table, I fly to the

door of the enclosure surrounding our old shelter and perch there facing him. When I hiss or click my beak, he says to me, "Dear pelican, dear pelican!"

Sometimes he stops writing and talks softly to me in the night. Those night hours spent with him are very precious to me. When his light goes out, I sleep until dawn, the hour for fishing. If I do not spend the night there for any reason, I perch with the other pelicans on the tall kapok tree down by the river.

The friendship between the Doctor and me gives me the right to be his companion wherever he goes. I walk along beside him when we meet on the hospital street or down by the river. I join in the conversations he has with whites and blacks. I was with him when he discussed the question about repairing the big canoe they had pulled up on the shore, with Basile, the carpenter. When Basile, for whom I have no love at all, started to work with his saw, I showed my disapproval of the whole affair by thrusting about with my beak.

Among all the people of the hospital, I believe that I have only one enemy. That is the Doctor's cook. The Doctor has declared once and for all that when fish are delivered to the hospital, one of them is to go to me. But the cook does not follow these orders. When the Doctor and Mlle Emma asks him in the evening if there are any fish for me, he is quite likely occasionally to reply, "No," even when I myself saw them delivered that day. I suppose he puts the fish aside to eat for himself! He knows better than to come outside while I am in front of the kitchen door, knowing full well that my beak would not let him get away with it. Once in a while when he has gone too far, I slip into the kitchen behind someone else and he has to jump to the top of the table to escape.

How the Doctor and Mlle Emma can be taken in by his report, without even making a careful examination every time to get to the bottom of the matter or at least question the staff to see whether there really are no fish for me, is more than I can understand. Doubtless

they are much too busy, and perhaps they realize that the servants would support each other and cover up for the cook. More than that, they respect him and refuse to believe him capable of the things I accuse him of doing. Then, too, have I been a bit unfair to him myself?

As I say, apart from the cook, I have no real enemy among the people in the hospital. Even the women I steal fish from are not angry with me for long, perhaps because of their ready good nature or because the Doctor pays them well. Anyway, none of them hit out at me with their paddles when our paths cross by the river. The Doctor would never permit that. On my part, I forgive them for hurting me when they were trying to protect themselves.

But I insist that all men, white or black, keep a respectful distance. I allow only the Doctor and Mlle Emma to come near me. Only they have the right to hold my closed beak firmly in their hands and lead me behind them, to lift me up and carry me under their arms just

like the story of "Jeannot le Chanceux", and in general to do whatever they think best. But all the others had better watch out, otherwise —a hard blow from my beak. I do not like poor jokes. One of the nurses, an impertinent little person, once gave me a quarter of an orange instead of a fish. She had better watch herself and keep out of my path! Several black and blue marks already decorate her legs and more may come.

I am always pleased when the Doctor lets visitors and patients alike know right away that I do not want them to get familiar with me. When he says that, they keep their place and I do not have to put them there.

My relations with the Doctoresse are of a special character. To tell the truth, she does not like me. But she finds me interesting. I feel the same and accept her attentions more patiently than those of others!

It took me a long time to understand why she followed me about with her little black box. She gave it away herself one day when she

said to one of the staff who came along as she was following me. "I've got some adorable pictures of him." I knew then what made her stay near me. She was doing to me what she did to the boy Goma with her little box, when he complained later that she had stolen his face. I was just a model.

For very little, I would have broken off our relationship. One day, soon after I realised what she was after, I heard her say to someone, "He loves to be photographed in interesting poses. That's why he holds so still, the vain old chap. . . ." Those foolish words wounded me to the depths of my soul. It is not because of any interest in what she wants to do with the little black box that I let her come near me and keep so quiet, but one of kindness and because she is a part of the Doctor's household.

In fact, one time she wanted to photograph a whole flock of about thirty pelicans where I was sitting with my brothers on a sand bar out in the middle of the river. She thought she could approach without our noticing it. The

paddlers had to handle their oars silently, crouched in the canoe. She was down so low that only the little black box could be seen. The effort was wasted. Before she came near enough to get a picture, the whole flock would rise up in the air and settle down on another sand bar. Chasing us from bar to bar, several times she kept trying to take a picture. When she decided to give up, I was quite moved by the disappointment that I read on her face. I understood then that it was her heart that drove her on to photograph pelicans. I resolved never to give her any trouble but always let her come close to me with her little black box. And when I saw that she wanted me to take some pose or go through some movement or other, I tried to oblige her. Never again did I change my attitude toward her.

I gave proof that I understood her. Perhaps on her part, she came to appreciate me more. Who knows? Perhaps she has already regretted saying the words, "vain old chap," and even now has a feeling almost of tenderness for me.

She will surely miss me when she has gone away, and she will try to console herself for my absence by looking at these pictures. For my part, I will be sorry not to be followed around any more by that little black box.

SELECTED BIBLIOGRAPHY

BOOKS BY ALBERT SCHWEITZER

African Notebook, Bloomington, Indiana University Press, 1958.

Animal World of Albert Schweitzer, Boston, Beacon Press, 1959.

Memoirs of Childhood and Youth, New York, Macmillan Co., 1949.

BOOKS ABOUT ALBERT SCHWEITZER

ANDERSON, ERICA, and EUGENE EXMAN, *World of Albert Schweitzer,* New York, Harper & Row, 1955.

COUSINS, NORMAN, *Dr. Schweitzer of Lambaréné,* New York, Harper & Row, 1960.

FRANCK, FREDERICK M., *Days with Albert Schweitzer,* New York, Holt, Rinehart & Winston, 1959.

JOY, CHARLES R. and MELVIN ARNOLD, *Africa of Albert Schweitzer,* New York, Harper & Row, 1959.

PAYNE, ROBERT, *Three Worlds of Albert Schweitzer,* New York, Thomas Nelson, 1957.

BOOKS ABOUT ALBERT SCHWEITZER FOR YOUNGER READERS

BERRILL, JACQUELYN, *Albert Schweitzer: Man of Mercy,* New York, Dodd, Mead & Co., 1956.

DANIEL, ANITA, *Story of Albert Schweitzer,* New York, Random House, 1957.

FRANCK, FREDERICK, *My Friend in Africa,* New York, Bobbs-Merrill, 1960.

FRITZ, JEAN, *Animals of Doctor Schweitzer,* New York, Coward-McCann, 1958.

MERRETT, JOHN, *True Story of Albert Schweitzer, Humanitarian,* Chicago, Childrens Press, 1964.

SIMON, CHARLIE MAY, *All Men are Brothers: A Portrait of Albert Schweitzer,* New York, E. P. Dutton, 1956.

SINGER, KURT, and JANE SHERROD, *Dr. Albert Schweitzer, Medical Missionary,* Minneapolis, T. S. Dennison, 1963.

THE AUTHOR AND HIS BOOK

DR. ALBERT SCHWEITZER is one of the most honored humanitarians of the twentieth century. A French theologian, musician, physician and author, he is probably best known for his founding of the hospital at Lambaréné, in Equatorial Africa. Dr. Schweitzer has devoted most of his life to Lambaréné and its people and even — as this book so eloquently shows — its animals. He was awarded the Nobel Peace Prize in 1952 for his work at Lambaréné.

But Dr. Schweitzer is also deeply respected for his achievements in other areas. A fine musician, he was organist of the J. S. Bach Society in Paris for eight years, and his rare recordings and concerts, to raise money for his hospital, are eagerly awaited. He has also written many important books, on such diverse subjects as the philosophy of Kant, the music of Bach, the life of Jesus, and his own work in Africa. His writings have been translated into many languages, including those of Asia and Africa, and read all over the world. He has also written books, such as *THE STORY OF MY PELICAN,* which express his rich sense of humor and his simple humanity.

THE STORY OF MY PELICAN (Hawthorn, 1965) was printed by Universal Lithographers of Baltimore and bound by The Book Press of Brattleboro, Vermont. The typeface used is Times New Roman, designed by Stanley Morrison in 1931 for *The Times* of London.

A HAWTHORN BOOK

Sixty Years
A FISHERMAN

The Autobiography of Fishing Legend
John Wilson

GreenUmbrella
Publishing

This book is for my granddaughters Alisha and Lana who through another generation will, I hope, come to love the flora and fauna of the countryside and wild open places as much as their granddad.

This edition first published in the UK in 2008
By Green Umbrella Publishing

© Green Umbrella Publishing 2008

www.gupublishing.co.uk

Publishers Jules Gammond and Vanessa Gardner

Creative Director: Kevin Gardner

Proofread by Rebecca Ellis

Images © John Wilson

The right of John Wilson to be identified as Author of this book has been asserted by him in accordance with the Copyright, Designs and Patents Act 1988.

Printed and bound in Italy

ISBN 978-1-905828-39-5

Contents

Acknowledgements

HOW can I possibly thank everyone who has been influential in my life, which spans more than half a century? It's impossible. Nevertheless a big dept of gratitude goes to my late parents who both gave me immense encouragement and a totally free hand during those all-important formative years. I should also like to compliment James Wadeson for his cartoons, and for the first two thirds of this book (I typed the last third myself) a really huge badge of merit must go to my long-suffering typist, Jan Carver, who was wonderful in turning my terrible longhand and 'Wilsonisms' into readable English. Very special thanks go to my wonderful wife and soul mate, Jo, for putting up with a veritable fishing junkie and my tantrums when the computer wouldn't do what I wanted it to. I wonder if she knew what she was really letting herself in for with those immortal words 'I do'.

Lastly, in addition to seeking absolution from my two children (now adults and approaching 40 years old themselves) Lee and Lisa, who could have seen more of their father during their adolescence but for the fact he was always fishing, I wish to thank all the mates and acquaintances who have become part of my fishing life. I cannot possibly name everyone but the list includes people like my oldest friend John (Jinx) Davey, Terry Houseago, Bruce Vaughan, Andy Davison, Dave Batten, Norman and Martin Symonds, Christine Slater, Martin Founds, Susheel and Nanda Gyanchand, guides Bola and the late Suban from the Cauvery River, Tim Baily, John and Veronica Stuart, the late Trevor Housby, the late Charlie Clay and the late Doug Allen, Dave Lewis, Sid Johnson, Simon Clarke, Keith Lambert, Gary Allen, Nick Beardmore, Andy Jubb, my brother Dave Wilson, my uncle, the late Joe Bowler plus his grandsons, Martin and Richard Bowler, who have all been greatly influential in what you are now about to read.

BELOW
Sunset on Lake
Kariba, Zimbabwe.

Introduction

The intention of this book is not to give an intimate and full account of my life, but I trust you will discover enough detail about my love for fishing which has never left me in over half a century. To feature each and every special angling occasion and every memorable fish I've caught over the past 60 years is of course an impossibility within the confines of this albeit lengthy volume, and I sincerely hope readers, particularly those who have followed my exploits throughout nearly 40 years of angling journalism, will not in any way feel cheated. For this reason the final chapter contains a complete list of all the largest specimens of every species of coarse, sea and game fish I have ever caught both at home and abroad.

It would take a book in itself simply to cover fully the 108 half hour *Go Fishing* programmes I have researched and then presented for Anglia Television, let alone anything else. What I have tried to provide however is a balance of my angling life covering a wide spectrum of interests and subsequent events, be it wine-making, scuba diving, shooting, travel, photography, taxidermy, lake management, or landing the whoppers. My sport has taken me all around the globe to enjoy some of the most exciting adversaries in both fresh and saltwater, from the mighty mahseer in southern India, to the giant lake trout of Canada's frozen Northwest Territories and the Yukon. I've learnt so much along the way and teamed up with some wonderful characters. Fishing has naturally dictated the path of my life and for the past 40 years at least – during my involvement with the tackle trade, television and as a journalist – I have been unable to separate work from play. I enjoy my work so much that they are indeed one and the same thing, which I guess makes me one contented person and a very lucky one.

They say, however, that you only ever get out what you are prepared to put into anything, and following a lifetime's fishing I reckon that's pretty accurate. So, good and bad luck can make all the difference on the day but, overall, things have a way of evening out. No one can always be lucky or always unlucky. For the most part you make your own luck by researching where the fish are, when they feed, and at what depth, and then fish accordingly, hopefully choosing the right bait. Sometimes your luck is in and you beat all the odds of landing a monster hooked on ultra-light tackle when you shouldn't have stood a chance. Then on the very next trip the hook will inexplicably pull free from the very fish you've been after, within inches of the waiting net, when you've seemingly done everything right. But that's life!

John Wilson Great Witchingham, 2008.

ABOVE

Ponies and cart horses were a way of life for rag and bone trader, Granddad Wilson. Although I was just two years old at the time, perhaps he saw me as a budding Steptoe!

RIGHT

As soon as he could walk, brother Dave (left) was as fascinated as me by the sticklebacks and stone loach we netted from Hilly Fields Brook.

Early Days

I was born in 1943 in Lea Road, Enfield in the very same flat where my mother and father, Margaret and Denis Wilson, continued to live for the following 45 years until they eventually moved into sheltered accommodation, also in Enfield. My brother, David – another keen angler and now living in Thailand – was born four and a half years later in 1948.

My Dad's father 'Granddad Wilson' was a rag and bone man, 'Steptoe style', who operated a small family business just half a mile away in Baker Street. Some of my earliest recollections are of sitting up there on the horse-driven cart next to him as he yelled out those immortal words, 'any old iron!' and 'any old lumber!' My late mother every so often would take great delight in reminding me of the time when I fell foul of such a street trader, by exchanging her best Sunday dress for two large goldfish. But that's how things were in those days. Our bread was even delivered by horse-drawn wagon and any old rags or iron were the conditions by which people traded.

Thus living in a north London flat without a garden or easy access to wild open places until the age of 22 when I left home to work abroad, much of my early childhood was spent exploring local park ponds, streams and ditches, first with a net, then with a worm tied by thread to a garden cane and eventually using rod and line. I must have been around three or four years old when Dad first took me netting for sticklebacks at Hilly fields Brook next to Whitewebbs Park in Enfield, about a mile's walk from our home. And it was Nan's old 'Nora Batty' heavy-duty stockings which kept me constantly supplied with nets. A galvanised wire coat hanger was formed into a circle leaving the ends bent at right angles for whipping with Dad's garden string on to a stiff cane, after first threading through the stocking's hem. To finish, a tight knot was tied halfway down the stocking and the remainder below cut off.

Now exactly why I had acquired a liking for frogs, toads, newts and fish at such an early age I can only attribute to Dad, bless him, who being a bricklayer by trade often brought newts home from the old wartime bomb sites where he was working at the time, helping to rebuild Greater London after the war, and as a keen gardener and chrysanthemum grower, encouraged me to potter about looking for creepy crawlies when accompanying him to his allotment at weekends. Apparently I'd play happily for hours on end collecting frogs and toads, but I'm sure those early impressions of fat, silver bellied prickly finned sticklebacks, and especially the red-throated males resplendent in their turquoise livery, lying there glistening like jewels in the folds of Nan's stocking net is what filled my imagination and made me into a life-long angler.

Dad's arms, being significantly longer, could reach far into all the deep, dark and mysterious spots beneath steep banking where young Wilson's could not, to capture the biggest sticklebacks and occasionally a much-prized stone loach or even a bull head. Inverting the net after every scoop, never knowing what was inside, before tipping the catch into the bucket was to me the ultimate in excitement. Netting also gave me a continual lesson in and immediate love of natural history through identifying a myriad of invertebrates like freshwater shrimps, beetles, leeches, dragonfly and caddis larvae, and to a little boy this was far more thrilling than watching chrysanthemums grow. It revealed a wonderful sense of mystery that remains with me to this day and will no doubt continue with me to the grave. My wife, Jo, thinks I would happily fish into a bucket of coloured water providing I couldn't see the bottom. And I guess she's right. Indeed wherever I am beside water, be it a village brook or out upon deep blue tropical saltwater miles off shore that same sense of mystery prevails. I always want to know what lives down there, what it looks like, how big it grows, what it feeds upon, how it fights and how it reproduces. To me fishing provides the consummate challenge.

As my interest in waterside flora and fauna grew I progressed to garden cane rods and the proverbial bent pin stage. Not that I actually recall using a bent pin. My favourite captures were the smooth newt, occasionally even great crested

newts (now an endangered species) and the gluttonous stickleback. They could each be readily lifted from the water once they had gorged half a red worm down their throats. The worm was simply tied on gently around the middle using strong black cotton, with a matchstick float half hitched on two feet above, and 4-5 foot of cotton line tied to the end of a garden cane.

Thus a garden cane became my first makeshift rod and with this outfit I explored all the local ditches, brooks, water-filled bomb holes and park ponds with other young kids from my street. I also pursued newts from some of the local boating pools. They loved to hide up within cracks in the concrete just above water level all around the edges. I was always being chased by 'parkies' (the park keepers) for newting, though I can't think why. The old 'jobs worth' syndrome I suppose. This was the late 1940s. There were no computer games, fancy toys, portable sound systems, play stations, mobile phones, chat lines or karate clubs; everyone made their own amusement. And working-class families in many of the council housing estates around London were lucky to have electricity, let alone a television. In fact our flat was not wired up until I was around 13 years old, mains gas providing everything until then. Seems strange now, doesn't it.

In our road only one family had a car parked outside. Today you can barely drive along Lea Road in Enfield (try it) for the parked cars. In those days however there was but one, an old dark blue Austin Seven owned by a Mr Lucas, who also owned the only television. At Easter or Whitsun he would kindly take some of us kids to the seaside at Southend or Clacton and at Christmas time he had us all in to watch Laurel and Hardy movies on his black-and-white television. It was one of those old polished wooden monstrosities the size of a washing machine with a huge speaker and a tiny nine inch screen. Those were the days! Kids went fishing, bird-nesting and happily played football and impromptu cricket matches down the middle of back streets. I purposely mention bird-nesting (egg collecting) because, abhorrent as it may seem in our conservation-minded, politically correct, nanny state society today, it then actually gave many kids a valuable education in natural history. While collecting birds' eggs from hedgerows and woodland we soon learned in which trees and bushes to find which nests, and identified countless plants, trees and animals along the way. It got kids out into the countryside, into the fresh air, and in addition to getting their wellies muddy, fulfilled part of the primal hunting instinct that is in all men and which modern society unfortunately does its utmost to suppress. Now not for one minute am I trying to condone bird-nesting, especially now that numerous indigenous breeds are declining in numbers with some even on the point of extinction. We do however need to recognise why this decline has occurred. It is certainly in no way due to the kids of my generation, and long before, collecting a few eggs. Usually just one egg was taken from a clutch. It was then pricked with a pin at both ends and blown out prior to being displayed proudly upon fine sawdust

LEFT
Mum and Dad with Dave and me at Warners Holiday Camp, Hayling Island in Hampshire, 1950, where I first learnt to swim and row a dinghy.

in a glass-fronted cabinet. We knew that the lighter-weight eggs were maturing inside and so these were never taken, only the heavier freshly-laid ones. Harsh though it may seem it was part of a youngster's education in the countryside.

The fact is, even if a bird's entire clutch of eggs is taken it will simply produce another. But take its habitat away and it has nowhere to breed. Blame therefore can be laid fairly and squarely upon the shoulders of successive governments who, during the 1960s, decreed that British farmers must grow more wheat (for a mountain we didn't need) and in so doing consequently tore out countryside hedgerows in the creation of unnaturally huge, easy-to-plough and easy-to-reap, grain-producing fields. Pop over to Ireland if you wish to see what much of southern England looked like prior to the 1960s. There you will find lovely wind-protected little fields of no more than a few acres apiece, bordered by thick hedges of blackthorn and hawthorn – all full of breeding birds. So the lack of chiffchaffs, chaffinches, greenfinches, goldfinches, hedge sparrows, song thrushes and the like in England today is down purely to government policy through farming practices. Nothing else. Please understand this.

To put it simply, if you destroy its habitat, you ultimately destroy the animal, be

it a songbird which has nowhere to build a nest, an orang-utan which finds its rainforest home being felled all around it, or a man without a house. The result is exactly the same. I mention all this because sadly a complete and successive lack of government legislation required to protect our inland waterways has led directly to the destruction of many once fast-flowing and habitat-rich rivers where fish used to breed freely and prolifically. The uncaring actions of Margaret Thatcher selling off to the highest bidder the country's utilities, especially our water companies during the 1980s, was one huge nail in the coffin of British natural history. I have never been in favour of selling off to another something which the country (that's all of us) already owns. But selling off natural resources tops the lot and will no doubt go down in history as one of the biggest blunders ever made by a British government. And I choose to vote Tory. You can live without a telephone, without electricity even, but you cannot exist without fresh water. Think about it!

Why should a French conglomerate for instance, Lyonnaise Des Eaux, own Essex and Suffolk water? It is scandalous. The entire subject of water, our most important and valuable natural resource by far, has never been properly addressed by any British government. In the years since the last war both Labour and Conservative administrations have put commercial interests before the existence and maintenance of the country's natural resources. Yes, I do have the bit between my teeth especially as far as water abstraction is concerned, having witnessed the destruction of so many sparkling brooks and streams around north London and in Hertfordshire where I first learnt to fish. This is a subject I shall come back to again and again throughout this book. But let's return to those early years.

ABOVE
Catching this (then) reasonable roach from the New River in Enfield made me a roach fisherman for life from an early age.

Minnows were not silly enough to gorge upon a worm long enough for lifting out, neither were young roach and the likes of gudgeon and dace. So young Wilson, who must have been around six or seven at the time, spent his pocket money on some size 20 hooks tied to nylon, 10 yards of green flax linen line and a small tin of 'gentles', as maggots were commonly referred to in those days. I also invested in a brightly coloured 'Day-Glo' bobber float. Few of the fish we caught in those days, though we didn't realise it at the time of course, had the physical strength to pull such bulbous floats under when sucking in our bait. Hence the term 'bobber floats' I suppose, because all they ever did was 'bob'. A cheap and noisy 'clicker' (centre pin) reel was fixed with insulating tape to my designer 'garden cane' rod which Dad furnished with rod rings made from safety pins. With this outfit I happily caught tiddlers from Whitewebbs Park brook in north Enfield and the New River which then flowed swiftly, sweet and pure, right through Enfield and around the Town Park known as the 'loop'. Created in Hertford with water taken from the rivers Rib, Lea, Mimram and Beane, the New River still is in fact north London's drinking supply. Though mostly private and patrolled by guard dogs, certain stretches are fishable and way back in 1907 an 18lb brown trout was caught from the river at Haringey by Mr J Briggs. It remained the British record for many years and was proof to the quality of fish living in the New River.

During the late 1940s and 1950s, the New River was my only local river, and many a fat goggle-eyed perch I caught on trotted worm from the dark mysterious water beneath Enfield Town Road Bridge. It was a wonderful training ground for many young anglers. Some bright spark on the local council however decided that the New River could be pumped straight to Winchmore Hill from Enfield Town without flowing around the Town Park, and so part of the very river where I first seriously learnt to fish was actually filled in to become a car park. Can you believe it? While the rest of the river that meanders around Enfield has since become stagnant, full of urban rubbish, fishless and a thorough disgrace to the community. Where the children of Enfield learn to fish nowadays I dread to think. Perhaps they simply don't!

Formative Years

O ne of my favourite locations was the outflow brook which ran from Wildwoods private lake through Whitewebbs Park and golf course in north Enfield. How we kids never got hit by a golf ball I'll never know, but we certainly topped up our pocket money by selling golf balls back to the very golfers who had just lost them in the brook. Though naturally, not on the same day. We weren't that silly. We even acquired little curly wire cups which golfers in those days used to retrieve balls from the water, or simply took our boots and socks off and got in to feel around in the silt if we couldn't actually see where their ball entered the brook. By now most of those golfers must surely have passed on into that big 'golden green' in the sky, so I'm sure they'll forgive the white lies of little boys who had them searching all over the place – everywhere except where we knew their balls had really gone. Yes, fishing and ball collecting proved top pursuits throughout those long school holidays.

Fishing for minnows and roach along the Whitewebbs brook also taught me how to obtain free bait. As we couldn't always afford maggots, and what with Matthew's tackle shop in Enfield Town being a mile's walk in the opposite direction on top of the mile walk from home to Whitewebbs, we used worms or caddis grubs most of the time. Complete in their portable homes made of twigs and pieces of gravel, as every angler knows or should know – though I doubt as many as one in a thousand uses them for bait nowadays – caddis can be found easily in shallow water clinging to the undersides of large pieces of flint or crawling along sunken branches. You simply squeeze the rear end of its casing so that when its head and legs appear at the front the greyish white succulent grub (of the sedge fly) can be gently eased out using thumb and forefinger.

Most caddis grubs are noticeably longer than the biggest shop-bought maggot and marry perfectly with a size 16 hook. What's more, in half an hour enough can be collected for a morning's float fishing; reason enough, even today, for me to carry on driving if I suddenly realise I've left the bait at home on the way to a summer river session. Caddis are always abundant, and free to those who look. Incidentally, baiting the hook with a large caddis grub or two, whilst loose feeding shop-bought maggots, is a great way of sorting out better quality roach and dace.

It may seem strange to you that here was a young Wilson from the age of six or seven upwards, setting out with other kids of his age and often on his own to boating ponds, rivers and lakes unaccompanied by an adult. In today's climate of mega media hype I guess it would appear totally irresponsible; that is if you believe there are more flashers, kidnappers and rapists about now pro rata than there were 60 years ago. Personally I doubt it. I can remember as a young footballer over at the local recreation park always seeing the same so-called 'dirty old men' in proverbial grey raincoats and had been forewarned by our parents never to take sweets from or even talk to them, so we stayed well clear. Dad also made sure I could swim at an early age.

When it must have seemed that his young nephew, now around eight years old, wouldn't be too much trouble, my Uncle Joe (the late Joe Bowler) invited me out for a day's serious fishing at the Barnet Angling Club pit and stream complex in London Colney in Hertfordshire. Here we fished with real Mr Crabtree-type 11 foot rods comprising three sections: the first two of whole cane and the top of built or 'split cane' to give it its more commonly used name. Reels were centre pins of the 'flick 'em' type and the float rigs we used were all carefully stored on six section wooden winders, having been made up and shotted correctly by Uncle Joe, especially for the smaller river we fished. Auntie Girlie came along because she too liked to fish, but as I recall she spent more time untangling my tackle than fishing herself. From garden cane to a large float rod was too much for young Wilson to accomplish in one day. But the seed was sown and shortly I was tapping Dad for a real rod. My first rod was constructed from an old army tank aerial and though sloppy its nine feet aided line pick-up enormously compared to a short garden cane.

Now aged around 10 and armed with my new rod, I visited all the local ponds and lakes, occasionally making a trip by the number 107A bus over to Enfield Lock and the canalised River Lea which became my training ground for several years. To catch roach (in those days the river was full of them) stewed hempseed was the magical bait during the summer months when the fish could easily be seen 'flashing' for the seeds in the clear upper water layers. Using maggots only attracted the dreaded bleak which weren't interested in stewed hempseed. The distinction was such that a handful of hemp resulted in just roach and the odd good dace flashing through the clear water over cabbages, whilst a handful of maggots ensured hundreds of bleak plus small dace hitting the surface within seconds. Rivers were certainly 'fish full' in those days. Even a handful of gravel from the towpath would raise a few roach and I've even had them flashing simply to the movement of an empty hand. Honestly. Broxbourne in Hertfordshire was my favourite venue and the first eight inch roach I ever caught on hempseed was taken home and fried in batter by Mum, which I ate apparently. Yuk!

I was so keen that, with a rod strapped to the crossbar of my bike, I even used to grab an hour either before or after completing my paper round, depending upon the lake or pond in question. One location was a small man-made lake in front of the old hall at Forty Hill Park in Enfield, not too far in fact from my last paper delivery. During the summer months I just loved fishing there in the early morning before the park keeper got up. It was so stuffed full of common carp – that old 'wildie' strain first brought over by German monks during the fifteenth century and easily identified by a long, lean, powerful body and immaculate scales – that sport was usually both instant and hectic. This was just as well really because I rarely enjoyed more than half an hour's fishing at this shallow, pea-green carp haven before an old gander owned by the park keeper started honking away noisily. Geese are great burglar alarms.

Having hidden my bike amongst the rhododendrons about half a mile away and despite a long walk up a steep hill from the opposite direction of the hall, it was nevertheless always worth the effort. I could usually account for at least three or four carp to around 3lbs on float-fished lobworm, before the park keeper could stand it no longer and lights went on in the lodge house opposite. He was a tall man with unusually large ears that stuck out and which were even noticeable from 60 to 70 yards away across the lake, and as he started walking around the lake towards my position I reeled in, returned the carp and disappeared post-haste over the fence and down through the long grass across the field towards my bike.

Though I fished the lake for a couple or three seasons I never did catch a carp from there of over 5lbs, something which I couldn't understand. I read all the books, particularly the writings of the late Dick Walker, who was my hero, and those of the Carp Catchers' Club. I tried floating crust during the hours of darkness, plus balanced paste and crust baits, all to no avail. The plain truth however was that, as with many 'wild carp only' fisheries of that era, there were simply no large carp in the lake. This was borne out during the big freeze in the winter of 1963 when the lake remained frozen over for several weeks. Like so many shallow, overstocked lakes that winter, from which the decomposing gases could not escape, the entire stock of fish, from the smallest gudgeon to the largest carp, perished. The local council collected four lorry loads of bloated carcasses for burial, once the

lake thawed out and the grisly facts were revealed. The largest carp weighed barely 8lbs.

I never did fish the lake again following those early morning paper round days, and was later sad to hear about all the carp dying. But some 40 years later, Dad came up with some revealing information about Forty Hill Lake. Jo and I were in Enfield for the day having travelled down from Norwich to see Mum and Dad who now, in their mid 80's, lived in sheltered accommodation. We were enjoying a conversation about the good old times when Dad suddenly said, 'Old Bill Walker passed away last week, John. You know him with the big ears who used to see you in the morning over at Forty Hill Lake.' Now Dad wasn't aware of my early morning poaching sessions, or so I thought. So I said, 'How did you know I fished there?' 'Well old Bill always told me when you'd been fishing,' says Dad, with a chuckle. 'But whenever he came over for a friendly chat you were always gone by the time he'd walked round the lake' Boy, was I gob smacked!

One day during the summer holidays of 1954, whilst buying goldfish from a pet shop along Green Street in eastern Enfield, I met a lad slightly older than me, one Tony Morgan, who lived but a few yards from a pretty little lily-covered lake called Lakeside, near Oakwood tube station at the end of the Piccadilly Line. I accepted his invitation to fish for the stunted roach and crucian carp it contained and in a much bigger lake at the bottom of his road called Boxers Lake. I learnt to catch the crafty shy-biting golden-coloured crucians up to almost 2lbs using a flour and water paste, coloured and flavoured with custard powder which Mum used to make. But I lost touch with Tony after a few years. Then some 30 years later, having arrived at a mutual friend's party in Taverham where I then lived, close to Norwich, the first guest I bumped into was none other than Tony Morgan who to me hadn't changed facially one little bit over the years. I said, 'You're Tony Morgan aren't you? We fished together when we were about 10 years old back in Enfield.' He thought it was a wind-up and just couldn't accept what I said for quite some time afterwards. Now we often laugh about the coincidence, though he hasn't fished since those childhood years.

My fascination with fish and other pets continued throughout my childhood, including budgies, pigeons, mice and lizards, and has not waned to this day. I simply adore animals. In fact Jo and I currently have two dogs, a 13 stone French mastiff called Alfie and a West Highland Terrier called Bola, plus Cheeko, an African Grey parrot, six budgies and two love birds. Not forgetting all the fish in our two lakes of course. Way back in the 1950s however, living in a London flat merely stretched to a cat and an old galvanised 50 gallon water tank full of fish on the veranda. I could never have a dog though I was for ever pestering Dad who always said, 'We'll see'. It was his favourite saying and one which once I grew up I swore I would never use with my own children. But you can guess what my favourite 'get out of it' phrase was when my own two children came along. (Exactly!).

Amongst the more regular pets at Lea Road was an assortment of lizards, slow worms and snakes. Young Wilson was always first in putting his hand up when the biology teacher enquired who would like to look after the laboratory's exhibits during the school holidays. Hence poor Mum suffered tanks of frogs, newts, lizards, slow worms, toads and once a large grass snake. Unfortunately this particular snake's life ended rather unceremoniously when it escaped from the makeshift vivarium and wound its way along Lea Road via the guttering of several flats, only to have its head separated from its body by a brave Mr Bullock who thought it was an adder and deadly poisonous. This necessitated Mum accompanying her son to Chase Boys School, once the new term resumed, to recount the unfortunate snake saga.

It was with much pride that Jo and I accepted an invitation back to my old school over a decade ago to give a leaving address and lecture to the sixth formers, most of whom seemed too young and spotty-faced to have gained so many A levels. In my day no one at Chase Boys took A levels, and few were clever enough to pass any GCE examinations. I based my lecture upon a future life where you can either live to work or work to live. Naturally, being a workaholic who loves his work, I recommended the former and by the approving look on the faces of mums and dads present the message got through to both parents and pupils. I emphasised the point that life can be explained by three eight hour segments each day. You sleep for eight hours and are not conscious so that leaves but two eight hour segments – or two halves of your life – one for work and one for play. So if you think about it, if you don't thoroughly enjoy your work, half your life could be a lost opportunity.

It would perhaps seem rather strange to the young anglers of today that back in the early 1950s there was little choice of inexpensive fixed spool reels. Thread line and spinning reels were the names given to early top-of-the-range models such as the Ambidex and Mitchell. Those of us using the old 'clicker' centre pins made from cheap bright steel had to pull yards and yards of line from the reel and lay it down on the ground if a long cast was required when ledgering, resulting often in unbelievable birds' nests as bits of twig and leaves clung to the coils as they tried to flow through the rod rings. Trotting in rivers therefore became my favourite technique (and still is) because by now, in addition to owning a three-piece 11 foot float rod which replaced the tank aerial, I had invested in a quality reel from Matthew's tackle shop. it was an old Trudex centre pin complete with an integral line guard, marked up at the bargain shop-soiled price of £2.19s.6d.

This reel lasted for many years and actually started me upon the road to float fishing fulfilment. This also resulted, I am proud to say, albeit over 40 years later, in the very same company, J W Young and Sons Ltd of Redditch, producing a modern exceptionally free-running centre pin of my very own design. Named the John Wilson Heritage centre pin and marketed through Masterline with whom I have designed

At the tender age of 13, I proudly accepted the Enfield Town Angling Society's Challenge Shield for top junior in the club during the 1955-56 season.

fishing tackle now for over 20 years, this 4½ inch diameter, ¾ inch-wide model has a multi-position line guard made from stainless steel and the centre pin itself benefits from two ball races.

The first couple of fixed spool reels I owned, because they were cheap, were absolutely awful. Then at 13 years of age, I decided to spend my paper round money on a Mitchell 300, arguably the world's best ever fixed spool, simply light years ahead of its time (as we all realise now) which cost £7.19s.6d by mail order from Bennett's of Sheffield. And those eight monthly postal order payments were certainly worth it. That particular reel finally came to grief 15 years later having served me splendidly all around the world in both fresh and saltwater, when I dropped it on the concrete pier at Dakar in French West Africa and the stem snapped.

I guess fellow anglers over the age of 40 will also fondly remember the British-made Intrepid range of reels which, though satisfactory, in no way came close to the French-made Mitchell's. It's really all about what's available at the time, and the sheer choice in expertly engineered fixed spool reels currently available is staggering; even more so is their low retail cost.

Much the same can be said about modern rods, especially lightweight carbon float rods. Yet prior to the mid 1970s we all managed happily (or unhappily if you were a long trotting enthusiast and suffered missed bites through arm ache) with hollow fibreglass. Back in the early 1950s however hollow glass was in its infancy and float fishermen used built cane, or Spanish reed rods, which had a built cane tip spliced into the top joint. I can remember mine snapping off like a carrot six inches above the handle when punching a float out too enthusiastically into a strong facing wind.

At the tender age of 13, or I could have been a year younger, I attended the inaugural meeting of what was to become the Enfield Town Angling Society. So I was among the first members of a club which, due to its monthly coach outings to lakes and river systems all over southern England, broadened my knowledge considerably.

In the early days there were just four or five of us juniors and some of the older members took us individually under their wings on club outings so we could learn the ropes. Dear old Bill Saville, Bill Poulton and Denis Brown, bless 'em, now all passed on, were each instrumental in their own way in encouraging me. Denis especially, who was the local barber, took my regular fishing pal, Doug Pledger and me, in his old Austin Atlantic to venues not visited by the club, like the River Lark at West Roe and King George VI reservoirs near Chingford where we ledgered during the winter months in the hope of catching specimen roach. We also went to the Suffolk Stour at Bures, Great Henny and Lamarsh, all fabulous roach hot spots if you fished hemp and berry. I can vividly remember taking a catch of roach from the Stour at Bures at the famous 'Rookery Stretch' numbering around 150 fish to around 1¼lbs with at least half of them 'goers', meaning they measured larger than eight inches. Sadly I couldn't match such a haul nowadays from anywhere I fish even if my very life depended upon it, such is the extent to which silver shoal species in our rivers have been depleted by cormorants.

All the clubs in and around the London area fished to London Angling Association size limit rules in those days. Bleak and gudgeon were not even considered worth weighing in at the end of our club outings. So if you didn't have a dace over seven inches, a roach over eight inches, perch over nine inches, bream over 12 inches and so on... you couldn't weigh in. Few clubs now bother with these rules which is a pity because it meant that as most of the fish caught were under size, they never spent all day in a keep net and didn't have their tail spread out on a fish rule which we all carried.

Among the great baits in those days were elderberries which I used to bottle when ripe in September (preserved in a weak solution of formalin) specifically for winter use. Fished in conjunction with loose-fed hemp, berries always sorted out the quality fish – just as casters do today really. This was a tip passed on to me by one of the older club members. In fact one of the great advantages of being a club member was that knowledge was freely passed around. We junior members learned so much about a whole variety of alternative baits to maggots.

Another great bait, though only effective during the summer months, was stewed wheat. You put a cupful of wheat into a vacuum flask and topped it up only to within three inches of the top with just boiled hot water. The gap was to allow for the expansion of the wheat which could easily shatter the glass insides of the flask. If left overnight, the following morning the now perfectly prepared wheat, with just enough of the white insides showing against the golden corn husk, is tipped out into a bait tin and any surplus water drained off. The nutty aroma of this superb bait is both unusual and attractive, especially to dace, roach, chub, tench, bream and particularly carp. Try it.

Stewed wheat was my favourite summer bait of all and I used it to good effect against the older members on outings to Cambridgeshire's rivers Cam, Granta, Lark, Old West and throughout the Great Ouse. One of my favourite locations was the Old Bedford Drain and River Delph at Mepal,

BELOW
Yes, I'm the baby-faced teenager on the extreme right of this group of ETAS club members (over half of whom have passed on, I'm sad to say) at an annual dinner-dance and prize-giving during the late 1950s.

where specimen-size rudd could be readily caught 'on the drop' using a single grain of wheat presented without shots beneath a matchstick float attached to the line with a band of silicon. Using an old bamboo roach pole with the 3lb test line simply tied to the end via a whipped-on loop of 20lb line (no elastic in those days), the single grain of wheat was accurately lowered into small gaps in the lilies which in parts virtually covered the surface of these narrow drains from one bank to another. If you found a hole the size of your hat or larger, it was a swim. It was a situation where no other technique would work. I remember one particular early morning about half an hour after our club members had settled into their respective swims, a Sheffield club turned up on the opposite bank. Within minutes they deemed the Old Bedford totally unfishable and climbed back into their coach. Where they went I don't know, but I recall coming amongst the 'bob a nob' prize money that day (everyone put a shilling into the hat) by weighing in several sizeable rudd to nearly 2lbs.

Many anglers today probably associate the effectiveness and popularity of pole fishing with European innovation, and as far as the current, super-light super-long carbon models are concerned including internal elastication etc, it is. But pole fishing was born on the rivers Lea and Thames. The famous London firm of Sowerbutts constructed the best bamboo poles made from carefully straightened, tempered and drilled Tonkin cane. Most were around 19 feet long and comprising five sections each heavily varnished over black decorative whippings, the top three of which fitted into the 48 inch bottom two. The tip was of spliced-in finely tapered built cane to which a float rig was attached via a small loop. A couple of the old dodgers in the Enfield Town Club incidentally sometimes used an elastic band between loop and rig, if big fish were on the cards. Was this pole elastic 40 years ahead of its time? I'm tempted to say it was.

Of course the technique of sensitively presenting a light float rig directly beneath the pole tip on just a few feet of line for maximum control and instant striking is no less valid today than 50 or even 100 years back. The main difference is one of weight. And with precision-turned brass ferrules those poles of yesteryear weighed an absolute ton. So in no way would I like to turn the clock back. Actually I caught my first ever 4lb tench on a bamboo roach pole and it led me a merry song and dance through the weed beds of a Lea Valley gravel pit. I managed to land barbel on the pole too (fixed line remember) and though a walk along the towpath was required to keep in touch with anything over 2lbs, it was great fun.

Those early years along the Lea Valley and other rivers like the Thames and Kennet visited by the club on regular monthly outings, always fishing to size limits, certainly influenced me. I found larger fish more interesting to pursue and thus more exciting and satisfying to catch – values that have not changed to this day, incidentally. So wherever possible if bigger and consequently much harder fighting specimens are on the cards, then I want some of the action.

At 15 years of age I left school and the very next week started an apprenticeship as a ladies' hairdresser at Fior Hair Fashions in Palmers Green, north London. Why a hairdresser? Well, all I can remember is that I'd heard young hairdressers could earn as much as £20 a week – a very good wage back in 1957.

This strange environment with its perfumed shampoo, ammonia-based perm solutions and female gossip was pretty alien to me but I stuck with it nonetheless and, as you will discover, I have much to thank my career in hairdressing for. I had in fact joined a fashion profession immediately before the swinging 60's and I enjoyed everything that came with it, including a regular supply of attractive girlfriends.

My boss, John Horne, in conjunction with an analytical chemist, one, Bibby Vine, had perfected a hair-straightening cream for Negroid hair which, under the microscope, is one really tight curl after another. One of the most famous piano players of that era, Winifred Atwell, was amongst our customers, together with an exceptionally attractive black jazz singer whom I shall not name, because Wilson was responsible for making her bald as the proverbial coot. I had left the (then extremely strong) cream on too long after brushing the hair straight and during the final rinsing the plug hole in the basin started to clog up. Within 30 seconds her entire head of beautifully straightened long hair lay in the sink. It had snapped off within a millimetre of the scalp, leaving her head looking for all the world like a black egg with a day's growth. I guess my hairdressing days could have ended there and then but those were pioneering times. Instead I got a bollocking and our jazz singer got a wig, compliments of Fior Hair Fashions.

During the school holidays when the salon wasn't that busy, I was given the miserable job, not a lot of fun for a 15 year old, of taking John Horne's son, Nicky, a precocious little kid of around five or six years old, to various exhibitions in London's West End including the Schoolboy's Own Exhibition. To get my own back, whenever he came into the salon I used to pick him up and sit him six feet off the floor in the staff room on a shampoo bottle shelf and leave him crying and yelling for his dad.

Nicky Horne is now well known as a DJ and television presenter, and back in the 1990s he asked me to appear on his *Tight Lines* angling phone-in programme for Sky TV then hosted by Bruno Brooks. Being too young at the time to remember, he had no idea that he had previously come across me when he was little, let alone been the object of teenage Wilson's adolescent mischievousness. So when I came out with this live on the programme, Nicky was speechless and just sat there open mouthed.

My regular fishing mate, Doug, and I fancied fishing further afield from our local River Lea – where we would stand a chance of catching really big roach and bream. We answered an advertisement in *Angling Times* and had a week's fishing holiday at the Watch House Inn (now no longer) in Bungay, Suffolk which was just a short walk from the then magical River Waveney. We joined the Bungay Cherry Tree Angling Club which controlled much of the fishing and, employing simple trotting tactics, caught mountains of quality roach from both the main river and the many streams using stewed wheat. Even the tiniest drainage dykes were so full of roach it was staggering and I think there and then I vowed one day to live amongst the roach-rich rivers of Norfolk and Suffolk. Now ironically that reason for living in East Anglia no longer exists, thanks to cormorants, abstraction and farming policies, subjects I shall cover shortly. From the deep and swirling Falcon weir pool in the centre of Bungay I even caught my first ever 2lb roach, also on a grain of stewed wheat. As its massive head-shaking shape came up through the clear water I just couldn't believe roach grew that huge. I can still picture it now lying on the landing net, immensely deep in the flank, with shimmering scales etched in silvery blue and fins of red. All 2lbs 2oz of it. It made a 15 year old a roach angler for life.

During the holiday was also the first time I ever set eyes upon a coypu. This giant South American rodent which, having originally been imported for its pelt (though also nice to eat) escaped from the rearing farms to cause destruction throughout East Anglian river systems. The network of wide sub-surface burrows made by the coypu unfortunately created massive bank erosion and you saw them everywhere when fishing, the adults being fully two feet long and weighing between 10 and 20lbs. Quite some rat, believe me. When they dived in the splash they made could have been created by a small dog.

My first encounter was during a break from roach fishing at the Falcon pool when I crept into the old galvanised eel trap, long since replaced with a modern sluice. An old dog coypu was in one corner munching away happily on a clump of lily root (they are totally vegetarian), but when it saw me at close quarters it felt threatened and reared up on its hind legs displaying a nasty pair of long orange-stained front teeth and hissing menacingly. Needless to say young Wilson made a hasty retreat.

Coypus have now finally been eradicated from East Anglia through many years of persistent trapping. Yet in a strange way I miss their busy, early morning and late evening goings on. They were very much part of those early impressionable years spent fishing the rivers of Norfolk and Suffolk.

From the two mile stretch of the Waveney between Wainford Maltings and Ellingham, both Doug and I took several bream to over 5lbs massive specimens to the young Londoners. Trouble was, the most productive bream swim, a 12 foot deep bend lined with a thick bed of reed along the far bank, was situated halfway along a field where bullocks grazed. It seems funny now to think we should have been frightened, but whenever the herd started running our way, as inquisitive bullocks do, the two townies grabbed all their gear and high-tailed it over the nearest fence. This completely ruined the chances of us ever amounting any decent bags of big bream.

Then, on the very last morning of our week's holiday, with the bream feeding ravenously, and having again just vacated the swim due to charging bullocks (or so we thought), a couple of kids who couldn't have been more than five or six years old – the farmer's sons in fact – came walking merrily across the field we had just left. We looked on in absolute horror as what must have been 40 or 50 Friesian bullocks galloped at full charge towards the helpless children. When the herd was

about 30 feet away both kids yelled at the top of their voices and actually ran towards the approaching bullocks, which all instantly about turned and belted off away up the field. Doug and I looked at each other in absolute amazement. Had we been missing out on the biggest bream catches of our young lives due to a herd of mindless bullocks? We had indeed.

At that time I met a Bungay lad the same age as me, one John ('Jinx') Davey who worked in the local printers and we have remained close friends to this day. Jinx unselfishly put me on to so much superb fishing in and around Bungay that I shall forever be in his debt. My book *Where to Fish in Norfolk and Suffolk* (now in it's seventh reprint) is dedicated to Jinx with whom I cannot ever remember having a cross word. Except perhaps for one occasion when we decided to drive my Hillman Minx convertible illegally across Bungay Golf Course in the early hours of the morning to avoid the long walk around the common which the Waveney skirts for over four miles. Instead of catching big roach at the crack of dawn we found ourselves well and truly stuck in a bunker. What the first golfer thought who saw us I can't imagine. We were frantically digging for over an hour to get the car's rear wheels moving and by the time we'd finished, the bunker had doubled in size and gave the impression that perhaps a

ABOVE

My life-long friend John (Jinx) Davey (right) and me with a pike he caught from the Waveney in Bungay. Sorry about the gaff. The word conservation wasn't associated with angling in those days!

dinosaur had deposited its eggs beneath the yellow sand.

Jinx's dad, the late Jim Davey, whose lovely old double-barrelled 'Bond' 12-bore I have proudly clipped in my gun cabinet, was for most of his life the carpenter at nearby Earsham Mill. Like my own father he was a skilled tradesman of the old school and someone I really respected. I can remember receiving a letter from Jinx (no phones for the likes of us in those days remember) telling me that his dad had witnessed the removal of a colossal chub taken out alive from the eel trap one morning at the mill. It weighed over 9lbs and was returned into the Waveney.

The following weekend saw young Wilson, complete with a bucketful of live bleak from the Lea, driving up to Earsham Mill in order to attempt to lure the monster. Boy, I must have been either keen or fanatical in those days. But neither I nor anyone else ever saw or heard of that huge chub again. I can only assume it was one of the original adult stock fish introduced during the 1950s from Norfolk's River Wissey which had quickly grown fat on the Waveney's rich aquatic food larder. Prior to that era there were no chub in the river, whereas today the Waveney possibly still has record potential, a monster of 8lb 2oz being caught at Bungay in 1993 by P Heywood.

Today much of the Upper Waveney in these diminutive upper reaches is sadly but a memory of its former self. Entire stretches which were once swiftly flowing roach-rich swims, four to six feet deep with clumps of quivering bulrushes sprouting from clean gravel and long sandy runs, are now half the depth, flow at half the pace and the bottom is for the most part covered in blanket weed. What a pitiful legacy we have left our grandchildren. Only the odd group of, albeit large, chub living over clearings beneath overhanging alders and willows, where light cannot penetrate, seem able to fare well in this over-eutrophic, abstraction-riddled river.

If you think I am exaggerating about the modern scourge of abstraction, compare these two photographs of exactly the same spot on the River Waveney at Bungay. One I took in the early 1960s, the other in 1998. In fact shortly afterwards Jinx

BELOW
Here's photographic proof that water authorities kill rivers through abstraction. On the left is the Waveney between Earsham and Bungay in the late 1950s where my brother Dave and mate, Tony Bayford (foreground), are long trotting for roach. On the right, the very same spot 40 years on. Need I say more?

and I were discussing the sad situation at a once favourite swim along Bungay Common called 'Toby's Hole', then a deep junction where a carrier joined the main flow, creating a great 'winter eddy' and popular summer swimming spot where all the local kids used to run and dive in. 50 years ago! Funnily enough, despite all the commotion in those days, I always managed to tempt roach to over 1lb whilst trotting close to the bottom of this deep eddy. It is now less than two feet deep at summer level and barren.

Part of this modern dilemma is also due to government policy and the over-production of cereals. This leads to over-enrichment of the river from nitrates and phosphates continually leeching in from the land, encouraging over-prolific growth from the wrong kind of aquatic plants. Blanket weed, in particular, strangles the river, covering and restricting light to runs once inhabited by dace and roach. Now the weed carpets all slow-moving areas of the river bed; not only of the Waveney but every other East Anglian river including my local River Wensum, which during the 1970s produced more specimen roach than any other watercourse in the UK. But that's all history I'm afraid. Blanket weed really is the kiss of death because even if, by some act of God, roach were suddenly reintroduced by the thousand, they would have nowhere to live. Shoal fish will not tolerate blanket weed where sand and gravel should be. It's as simple as that.

Water abstraction however, and the dreadful way in which water authorities have been allowed to suck the very life blood from our river systems during the past 60 years, is actually a reversible situation. Ponder for a moment what the consequences would be were government legislation to ban all forms of abstraction along a river's course from source to sea, allowing water to be taken only once it has completed its journey and tips down over the last weir into the tidal reaches. Then, and only then, should the water required by water authorities, farming and industry be abstracted and pumped back along its course via a large bore pipe set beside the river, below ground or short-cutted across farmland, or even sunk in the river itself along one margin. The river would then be as swiftly flowing and as deep as nature intended throughout its entire course. Think seriously about this. Cost apart, I cannot see why such a project or one along similar lines cannot be implemented by government because ultimately water abstraction is the worst killer of all.

Dramatically culling cormorants would help enormously in re-establishing healthy stocks of silver shoal fish throughout clear watered lakes and gravel pit complexes and numerous stretches of rivers. But considering running water as a whole, unless something is done within the next couple of decades to reverse water abstraction, we are not going to have many rivers left to save.

During the late 1950s and early 1960s whilst in my teens, I witnessed the start of a slow death to my local rivers in north London and in Hertfordshire, such as the rivers Ash, Ver, Beane, Rib and Mimram, through abstraction. This resulted eventually in my forsaking the south and coming to live in Norfolk. And now I can see it happening all over again here.

In the 1960s if you lived in areas suffering in their river fishing like London or Sheffield, you only contemplated one spot to go fishing on holiday: the fabulous Norfolk Broads. Now in this new millennium and the first decade of the year 2000 with the Broads sadly in decline and not even a shadow of their former selves, those same anglers cross the sea to Ireland, Holland or to Denmark if they want to experience prolific sport with roach, rudd, perch and bream. I wonder where we'll all be trotting off to in another 30 years.

Due to the interest instigated by the Enfield Town Angling Society's monthly coach outings to venues further afield, on my sixteenth birthday I purchased my first motorbike. One of the members, Les Minton, was selling his 125cc BSA Bantam complete with a pair of gauntlets and crash helmet for the bargain price of £40. That little bike took me everywhere within a radius of about 60 miles from home. Lying flat on the tank going down a steep hill the speedo just about clipped 50 miles per hour but it wasn't really speed I was after, simply accessibility.

I could then fish many of the same rivers that we had visited on our Sunday coach outings, but during the middle of the week on my day off when the banks were less crowded. Our club fielded a team of six to compete in the then most prestigious London Anglers Association matches which were usually held on the Thames and the Great Ouse. And all were 'rovers', never pegged down. In fact why small clubs insist on pegged-down competitions has always puzzled me. It is much quicker, instead of waiting for a steward to knock a load of pegs in, to put the same amount of numbered tokens into a hat and the angler who draws the highest sees everyone off. He then simply holds the hat whilst number one puts his token in and walks off along the river or around the lake (closely followed by number two and so on) until he stops at a swim he fancies fishing. Then the rest can overtake and select their spots accordingly.

After all, who wants to sit all day in a piece of the countryside they are not happy with? Rovers allow each angler to utilise his skill or watercraft – call it what you will – in selecting his particular swim as long as he doesn't overtake the man in front. Consequently, everyone starts fishing immediately and there are never any moans about drawing a bad peg or being unlucky.

I caught my very first barbel from the Old Lea at Wormley where the river divides at Kings Weir to become both canal and fast-flowing 'backstream', as it was known in those days. I remember on one autumn afternoon catching no fewer than 22 barbel (all small) plus a 2lb chub on ledgered cheese paste from just one swim. I can also remember a painful experience that occurred during the first hour of darkness when I loaded up the BSA Bantam for the ride home.

As a short cut to the 'backstream' I used to drive down a narrow lane and across a farmer's field which more or less took me straight to the lock behind which were some of the best swims. A swift and painful belt across the mouth came from nowhere out of the darkness as I popped along at around 20 miles per hour back along the lane towards the main road. Suddenly I was sitting on the deck in a daze. The bike, which had carried on, was still revving like mad several yards away in a ditch. So I got up to turn it off, when 'Bang!' – something clouted me over the head again (thank heavens for crash helmets). I fell back to the ground, this time

snapping the rod ends protruding from the holdall across my shoulders. My face was one bloody mess, and I could actually feel several bottom teeth protruding through a gaping hole beneath my lower lip but everything else seemed to be in working order. Slowly I attempted to get up again and felt what appeared to be a steel scaffold pole in my way. Indeed it was. Someone – the farmer I suppose – must have put the pole right across the lane about five feet off the ground, to stop the cows from roaming. Trouble was, the totally useless dipped headlight on my old Bantam (no quartz halogen bulbs in those days I'm afraid) had not picked it out and, being more concerned about my tyres and the pot holes, my eyes were of course directed downwards. Had it not been for the Perspex windscreen which was completely shattered because it hit the scaffold pole first and instantly slowed the bike down, I might well have been decapitated. There but for the grace of God, eh?

Whilst contemplating strange occurrences, it was around this time when young Wilson experienced one of the most embarrassing moments of his life. One day, with the Bantam hidden amongst roadside shrubbery, I was enjoying an afternoon's free lining for trout along a strictly private beat of the lovely little River Ash, near Ware in Hertfordshire. The banks were marvellously overgrown with bushes and mature trees and as I always crept about stealthily exploring each likely-looking hole and deep run with a lively lobworm, with my ex-Army parka blending into the greenery perfectly, nobody ever saw me.

On this particular afternoon, I'd already accounted for a couple of pound plus brown trout and a deep-bodied roach of fully 1½lbs (a superb catch for such a little river) when I saw a car pull up alongside the hedge where my Bantam was hidden. Suddenly the doors flew open and out climbed three women all around their early 30's who passed through a gap in the hedge and ran straight across the ploughed field towards the huge weeping chestnut, whose lower branches almost touched the ground and beneath which I stood leaning against the wide trunk as though a part of it. The deep run beneath was in fact one of my favourite roach swims. Surely it was impossible for them to know I was hidden there poaching (though I always returned everything I caught of course) so why were they making a beeline for my tree? Suddenly and without more ado, certainly before I could clear my throat and say, 'Er, excuse me ladies', it was a case of knickers down and them peeing and farting away to their heart's content, not yards from where Wilson was doing his best impression of a chestnut tree trunk.

But my ploy didn't work. Quite suddenly the closest woman fixed her eyes upon mine and let out an excruciatingly loud manic scream, whereupon all three pulled up their knickers and went running across that field as fast as they could. Can't say I ever want to experience anything like that again!

From the BSA Bantam I progressed first on to a 225cc James and then to a

Loading up after a day's fishing on the Great Ouse at Godmanchester. Our BSA 350 motorbikes took my friend, Doug Pledger (right), and me to rivers and lakes all over southern England.

lovely old British motorbike (now a classic of course), a BSA 350cc single called the B3l. Lavishly appointed in maroon and chrome, it had double crash bars through which my rod holdall passed, enabling me to sit astride the rods as opposed to having the strain of the strap across my shoulders.

I visited many southern rivers on the BSA like the Kentish Stour near Canterbury, the Kennet at Burghfield, and numerous spots along the Thames from Appleford all the way downstream to the tidal reaches at Richmond. I very nearly came a cropper one morning, though, on the way to Richmond for a roaching session. I was heading for a spot just in front of the ice rink where, from between the moored boats, superb bags of winter roach could be taken on trotted maggots. On this particular foggy morning (those living and working in London during that period will indeed remember them with little sense of affection) I was chugging along through Enfield Town at around six o'clock opposite the Roman Catholic Church, when completely from nowhere a nun walked across the road right in front of my bike. One minute she was there, the next she was gone and disappeared from view in the grey fog. It happened too quickly for me to brake, swerve or react in any way. And had I not been opposite the church at that time I might have even considered the event a hallucination!

I would also regularly trundle the 100 or so miles from Enfield to Bungay, even during the winter months, just for a day's roach fishing. And I'm sure that old bike would still be ticking over now with that lovely throb of a big single, had I not chopped it in for my first car, the Hillman Minx convertible.

Despite the slow decline of my local rivers, I learnt a tremendous amount from stalking individual fish from one small haven in particular – the River Rib at Wadesmill in Hertfordshire. It passes beneath the A10 road bridge at the bottom of a long steep hill at Thunderidge just outside Ware (though don't bother walking its course today, it's heartbreaking) and whilst my mates could be fishing in next to no time by visiting their local River Lea, I chose the extra distance of the River Rib because I knew the fish I would catch there were far larger than those of the Lea. I guess I had a leaning towards specimen hunting even then at the age of 17. Due to the overgrown banks and crystal clear water, however, extracting sizeable specimens from the diminutive River Rib took much cunning and creeping about stealthily on all fours. Once I had seen the inhabitants' reactions to a careless footfall or my shadow over the water, I soon developed a cautious approach which of course I use to this day wherever I fish. Those days were a wonderful education for me.

This was also the time I became seriously interested in colour transparency photography. I had been disappointed with the quality of black-and-white photos taken using Dad's old pre-war Brownie box camera and by several equally useless cheapies. I therefore purchased a 35mm Halina camera from Boots. This was later superseded by a German Super Frankarette and then a few years later by a single lens reflex, a Minolta SR7 with a Tokina 135 telephoto lens in addition to the standard 55mm. I enjoyed immensely recording all the locations visited and regularly gave slide shows to the Enfield Town Angling Club.

Full of crayfish, brook lampreys, huge dace, and roach to over 2lbs and prolific in chub between two and 3lbs, the sparklingly clear River Rib was a joy to fish. I free lined bread flake, large lumps on a size 8 hook direct to a 3lb line to lure the roach and dace, and fared best with the chub by using crayfish, though big lobworms and cheese paste also produced. So rich in crayfish was this charming little river that my brother, Dave, and I decided to start the new season at Wadesmill on 16 June after chub and actually left home without any bait. Who would have the bottle to do this nowadays? But we did, and in an hour of darkness prior to dawn breaking, using a powerful torch each, we gathered enough two to three inch crayfish from beneath large pieces of flint and sunken logs to keep us in chub baits until we headed for home in the late morning, having accounted for close on 20 sizeable chub and walked over three miles of river. Being five years my junior I was until now rather reluctant to take Dave fishing. But from around the age of 13 he started to become quite serious and we have been regular partners to this day.

For several years the River Rib became my training ground for practising the art of concealment, stealth and observation, where through polarised glasses I was able to watch most of the fish I caught actually suck in the bait. Such close-range stalking of a diminutive, overgrown river also demanded the utmost skill in tackle control, using the flow to work a free lined bait downstream into a certain lie, or skate casting fat slugs or crayfish beneath overhanging branches to the chub hiding below, using nothing more than an underarm flick of the rod. I learnt to crawl on all fours where necessary and always to keep my silhouette low to the ground. I carried the absolute minimum of tackle and thus roamed happily for miles learning a new trick or overcoming a particularly difficult swim or problem around each and every twist of this enchanting little river.

One incident in particular portrays how shy and sensitive to bank side movements those fish were. I had taken fully several minutes on all fours to worm my way beneath blackthorn bushes into a position high above a deep bend. There I plopped in a fat slug a couple of feet upstream from where five nice chub, the best pushing 3lbs, were enjoying their afternoon siesta beneath an old willow whose lower limbs shaded the surface on the opposite bank. I knew I hadn't made any detrimental movements, but, with the slug in mid flight and yet to touch the surface, those chub suddenly turned tail and shot downstream as though scared by the devil himself. Had the sun hit the varnish along the rod and created a 'flash'? Had my arm movement caught their attention? No, neither. A minute later all was explained as a large man, sweating profusely from the heat wave conditions, carrying a wicker basket and rod holdall plus rod and landing net already made up, crunched through the undergrowth, uttering those immortal words ... 'Any luck, mate?' For him I doubt the penny ever dropped, despite a pitiful look in his direction from the teenager emerging from the marginal entanglement. The point is, those chub had heard the vibrations of this 17 stone 'chuck it and chance it' long before I did and it's a lesson I've never forgotten.

I often used to fish on into darkness during the summer and autumn, because when the light has all but gone, that's when bites from the biggest roach and dace become extremely confident. Sensitive quiver tips and luminous beta light elements were not around in those days of course and I simply touch ledgered by pointing the rod tip more or less directly at the bait, with the line hooked over the tip of my forefinger. It's such a super-sensitive way of feeling for bites in the dark whilst ledgering or free lining at close range. I even use the technique when I am float fishing for big fish like carp and tench during the daytime when my eyes might, for a few seconds, wander away from the float. It's that sudden tightening of the line over the ball of the forefinger that brings an instant response with a hard strike. Try it yourself and see. This can only be accomplished, however, if you hold the rod handle with your four fingers split around the reel's stem. Your right forefinger will then be perfectly placed to pick up the line directly from the bale arm roller which should be wound close up to the rod handle. The same finger will then also be ideally positioned to apply pressure to the side of the spool when playing big fish.

Touch ledgering is of course equally effective whilst holding a quiver tip rod in a strong current with barbel and chub in mind. Again that tightening over the tip of your forefinger instantly puts you on 'red alert'. Whilst in my late teens I spent many a dark evening touch ledgering for barbel on a lovely streamy and weedy stretch of the Old Lea at Enfield Lock behind the Royal Small Arms Company factory. In fact I rarely ever arrived until an hour after dark because by then the barbel had usually left the weediest, snaggiest swims and moved immediately upstream to feed upon the shallows where less than two feet of water covered the clean gravel. After loose feeding in a few lumps of cheese paste, it wasn't long before a barbel snuffed up

ABOVE

Outside 32 Lea
Road in Enfield,
North London,
where I was born,
and spent the
first 22 years of
my life, with the
perfect fishing
jalopy of that era –
an A35 van.

mine and tore off downstream, virtually hooking itself. So I needed neither torch nor rod rest, simply the line hooked around my forefinger. The sheer suspense of waiting for a bite in the dark is electrifying, especially when a fish rolls in the swim or approaches the bait from the side creating a gentle 'plink' on the line as its pectoral fins momentarily catch it.

My rod then was an old 11 foot, three-piece built cane 'Octofloat' which, though it bent alarmingly in conjunction with a 6lb reel line, managed to subdue barbel to just over 9lbs. I never did succeed in catching a double from the Lea, and had to wait over 20 years to achieve that goal with a 10lb 14oz fish from the River Wensum at Drayton, near Norwich, in 1981. This very same fish incidentally (easily identified by fin disfiguration) I caught again a few years later from the very same deep run immediately downstream from an overhanging willow, weighing exactly 12¾lb, which was my largest barbel for many years. Little was I to know then however, that a massive near 17lbs fish would come my way on a ledgered halibut pellet boilie over 20 years later. Another coincidence is that on both previous occasions I was float fishing stret-pegging style. Yes, those teenage years were much inspired by the barbel and chub of Izaak Walton's old River Lea, the wonderful Waveney in Suffolk and through crawling along the overgrown reaches of Hertfordshire's River Rib, not to mention countless lakes and rivers all over southern England visited through the Enfield Town Angling Society's monthly coach outings. Reading the *Angling Times* (the only paper of its kind then) also fired my imagination, especially the articles written by my hero of the day, the late Richard Walker, surely the motivator of many a specialist angler today whether they are too young to remember him or not.

The Swinging Decade

The swinging 60s, as they are affectionately named by those of us fortunate enough to have experienced young life during this period, were indeed a revelation. It seems now as if I went from the age of 17-27 in a flash, though on reflection a great deal happened to affect my personal life and fishing during this impressionable decade.

Sadly it started with me not being able to afford the steep monthly payments on the Hillman Minx convertible and so I took Dad's advice and, in 1962, chopped it in for what turned out to be a far more practical fishing vehicle – an Austin A35 van. This left me with no outstanding debts, though I had indeed paid the price for trying to look flash as youngsters do (image came at a price even then) and it's a lesson I've never forgotten.

Together with my cousin, John, who had a Morris Mini van, I fished all over southern England and from then on over the next three to four years we took it in turns using each other's vehicles both at weekends and summer holidays to visit the Broads, the Dorset Stour at Throop Mill and many spots along the Great Ouse system. We even combined courting with fishing by driving up to Norwich and spending Saturday night at the Samson & Hercules – 'the' night club of the area – followed the next day with some roach fishing on the River Waveney at Bungay or flattie fishing in the harbour at Great Yarmouth if we didn't score!

I have already mentioned that it was my Uncle Joe, John's dad, who started me fishing seriously, but John never became an ardent angler and within a few years had sold all his gear. Ironically two of his four sons have become extremely fine anglers. In their early teens, Martin and Richard Bowler used to come and stay with me in Norfolk to catch carp from my two lakes (Martin has since caught more big carp than I've had hot dinners), and nowadays I like to join them every so often along their local stretches of the Great Ouse above Bedford after big perch. With their help during the mid 1990s for instance, I accounted for rudd to 3½lb, perch to 3¾lb and barbel getting on for double figures live on camera during the filming of my *Go Fishing* television series. So you could say it has taken 50 years for an angling family to go full circle since I first gave their granddad's tackle a bashing. Dear old Uncle Joe.

During the early 60s, in my later teen years, I used to relish all-night bream bashing sessions on the middle reaches of the Great Ouse. By today's standards they

LEFT
With my cousin, John Bowler (left), on Bournemouth Pier in the early 1960s. Though John never became a serious angler, over 40 years on I now regularly fish with his two sons, Richard and Martin.

were very modest-sized bream, averaging perhaps 2-3lbs a piece with the occasional 2lb plus hybrid thrown in for good measure. But what the Ouse lacked in quality it made up for in quantity. By ledgering bread paste or flake eels were avoided and in favourable conditions bites could be expected consistently throughout the hours of darkness, following heavy ground baiting with a mixture of mashed bread and bran.

The St Neots to Little Paxton beat was my favourite, particularly St Neots Common where a flood dyke joined the main stream. I have a precious memory of something hilarious that happened one morning when a group of us young Enfield Town Angling Club members trudged wearily back to our old bangers (all of them classic cars today of course) after a good bream haul. It seems crazy now but we regularly descended upon St Neots in the early hours after a Saturday night's bash at the Locarno in Stevenage. With all the breaming gear and a change of clothing stashed in the cars, we simply drove to the Ouse whenever the dancing finished, with a warming fry-up at an all-night transport cafe en route. Anyway, there we were all covered in bream slime, weary but happy and hoping, as always, that the cars would start. An idiosyncrasy of the 60s was that ignition systems were not always obliging in damp, foggy conditions.

One of our gang, Howard, a tall slim lad, spent week upon week painstakingly hand-painting – yes, hand-painting – his old Morris Oxford. He made a really nice job of it too, carefully smoothing out all the brush strokes with cutting-down compound and finishing off with Brasso and then polish. It really did match any baked-on spray job at a fraction of the cost, though it took hundreds of hours to complete. Trouble was, nobody told the bullocks on St Neots Common. They obviously liked the taste of Howard's paint because that herd of Friesians almost completely licked his car paint less during the latter part of one night. We just didn't know what to do – laugh cry or look the other way and pretend we hadn't noticed. So we did the sort of honourable thing any gang of mates would do and

SIXTY YEARS A FISHERMAN

split our bellies laughing. Poor old Howard!

At the tender age of 20 I became engaged to my first wife, Barbara. We had met as hairdressers at Fior Hair Fashions and planned within a year or so to move to Norfolk where I would eventually seek employment in the printers where my friend John (Jinx) Davey worked. Detached, three-bedroom bungalows backing on to farmland were at that time selling for between just £2000-£3000 in East Anglia, (difficult to believe eh?) and we so much wanted to vacate the claustrophobia of foggy London for the charm of the countryside. So in 1964 I made a career change, having become somewhat disgruntled with hairdressing, and started as a trainee lithographic printer at Waltham Abbey Press in Hertfordshire. Then after a year of being engaged we drifted apart and Barbara found someone else (although we did meet up again and eventually marry four years later) and I found myself in a trade without a reason, which although I stuck at it and became quite proficient, was not what I really wanted.

However, I struck up a firm friendship with my boss in the printing department of Standard Telephones and Cables (my third and last printing employer incidentally within a two-year separation from hairdressing), one Les Wright. He got me really interested in sea fishing. During the next two summers we regularly drove south to Beachy Head in Sussex in search of bass and picked our tides carefully so we could dig for lugworm and collect peeler crabs from Eastbourne, before making the long pilgrimage along the steep cliffs to Burling Gap where we climbed down. We then fished all of the flood tide up and some of the ebb throughout the hours of darkness before we could safely leave our chosen ledges and climb back up again for the arduous walk back to where we'd left Les' old Morris Countryman. One of the tricks at Beachy Head, where long fringes of rocks reach out to sea, was literally to place your bait by hand in a sandy area amongst a cluster of rocks at low tide and then walk backwards up the beach paying out line as the tide came in.

BELOW
Yes, that's me on the left – young Wilson, the printer – with two workmates at Waltham Abbey Press during a short career change from hairdressing.

This sometimes produced a good bass, once the bait was covered by several feet of water. Generally however, having gone through all this palaver, a fat pouting would find it first.

I also did a bit of beach fishing for cod during the winter months at Dungeness, which was 'the' south coast hot spot at that time, and enjoyed boat fishing out from Bournemouth after thornback rays and tope. Had I been living closer to the sea I would have gone more often I'm sure. But I later made up for this, as you will discover.

Career-wise printing was finally kicked into touch and in 1966 I made a return to hairdressing at a salon in St John's Wood High Street in northwest London, called 'Boris and Andre'. It was only a short walk from the London Zoo where I frequently spent my lunch hour admiring the late Dick Walker's then record 44lb common carp caught from Redmire. Though decidedly lean in the body, after so long in captivity, its huge frame literally dwarfed all the other specimens in the long tank and had a mesmerising effect upon every angler who paid to see it. I doubt Dick ever received a penny from the Zoo but he certainly should have been on a lucrative commission.

My new workplace had amongst its influential clientele numerous top flight models from the fashion industry. It was an exciting world which Wilson now found himself playing – sorry – working in, with regular invites after work to way-out bashes in London's West End including those thrown by Harrison Marks, one of the top nude photographers of the day. At these parties it was not unusual to rub noses with many of the fashion world's top models, some of whom were wearing nothing else but painted-on illustrations from head to toe, which left absolutely nothing to the imagination. My part in the 'swinging 60s' had indeed begun. I'd traded the old van in for a sporty new Mini and was at the time dating an airline hostess who worked for Pan Am. Life in the fast lane was fulfilling, hectic, extremely demanding, but above all exciting. Yet strangely there was still something missing – I felt footloose despite my enjoyable everyday commitments.

There was in me at this time what I can only describe as an explorer trying to emerge, and travelling abroad to work, play and fish seemed the obvious course. Within a year of answering adverts in foreign hairdressing magazines I was given the opportunity of a position in a busy salon in the USA in Kansas City, Missouri. What the fishing was like I never found out unfortunately because I was then advised that anyone entering the United States on a work permit would be first in the line-up for drafting out to Vietnam!

Along with several other London stylists I then put in for what seemed like a fantastic position in Dar es Salaam in Tanzania, managing the salon in the famous Kilimanjaro Hotel, only a cast away from the Indian Ocean on Africa's prolific east coast. What with a large salary, my own apartment in the hotel and big game fishing boats on tap close by, this was the job of all jobs. And hey presto! Within a few days the agency confirmed that I had been selected for the position and suggested I book flights immediately as the hotel wanted someone within a few weeks.

Well, talk about being excited! I was absolutely over the moon and quickly sold the car, then booked a one-way passage to Dar es Salaam. The Enfield Town Angling Club presented me with an engraved reverse taper Moncrieff-style beach caster and I said farewell to all my friends. However as it turned out, I was counting my chickens. I was not particularly politically motivated at this time so I didn't know that the Tanzanian government had decided to break off diplomatic relations with Britain out of sympathy for Rhodesia (now Zimbabwe). This was because our prime minister, Harold Wilson, would not pressurise Rhodesia's Prime Minister, the late Ian Smith, into giving the country black majority rule. This meant that this Wilson could not obtain an entry visa and work permit, even though I had a job arranged. I even pestered the Tanzanian staff at Australia House into which their embassy had retreated. But it was all to no avail: Wilson wasn't going big game fishing on Africa's east coast after all.

Actually as it turned out, I rather think being unable to get that work permit changed my life for the better because just a few years back whilst researching the Rufigi River in Tanzania for the catfish and tiger fish with fellow angling journalist, Dave Lewis, I found myself in Dar es Salaam with time to kill between flights. So Dave and I had lunch at the Kilimanjaro. It was not what I had expected at all, now being rather run down and not at all the glamorous colonial-type hotel I had imagined!

Anyway, let's return to the latter part of 1966 because whilst in town trying unsuccessfully to secure an entry visa I decided on impulse (you know the slogan – 'Run away to sea with P & O') to pop into the Peninsular and Oriental Steam Navigation Company's offices to see whether there were any hairdressers' jobs going aboard their passenger liners. It was no secret amongst hairstylists that working on the ships and seeing the world unlocked enormous possibilities because you were likely to meet all the 'right people'. I was interviewed by a Mr Crawford, who must have been impressed because he put me on P & O's list of future possibilities for cruise ship work. He suggested that I take a medical there and then in case a position suddenly arose but as he couldn't guarantee anything, it was still a case of 'don't ring us we'll ring you'.

So it was back to racing across north London every morning and evening from Enfield to St John's Wood and back again, which are only slightly more than 10 miles apart as the crow flies. Yet rarely could I make the journey in less than an hour and a quarter. It all changed for the better however when, around three months later and barely a month before Christmas when the salon was getting madly busy, I received a telegram. It read: 'Hairdresser leaving SS Oronsay when it berths in two weeks. You can sail New Year's day. Urgent reply required. Mr Crawford, P & O lines.' Incidentally, all shop and hairdressing staff were contracted to sign on 'articles' for one voyage at a time, most of which were mail-run sailings going west to east lasting three and a half months, plus the occasional five-month trip which incorporated either Australian or Mediterranean cruising. As it turned out I loved the life so much I was to stay on board for two years.

Wilson's door had been opened at last, but there was so much to arrange. For starters I'd told Crawford that I could handle both ladies 'and gents' hairdressing and, despite what your local unisex stylist tells you, the two skills are entirely different. If you doubt what I'm saying, ask your ladies' hairdresser for a crew cut. Although on second thoughts – don't! So I asked my cousin, Terry Webb, who ran a barber's shop in Enfield, to give me a crash course. He sold me some Forfex electric clippers complete with three different cutting heads and I arranged for a group of my Dad's mates to come round to our flat for a free 'back and sides'.

Then I attended a shaving course in the West End at a hairdressing training school, as the credentials from P & O lines insisted on their hairdressers being able to shave their passengers if they so wished. Not once incidentally, during the two years I spent on *SS Oronsay* did anyone ever ask for a shave. Frankly who in their right mind would ask for a shave with a cutthroat razor on a rocking ship? But I wasn't to know that then, and together with several female would-be barbers – lady barbers were just starting to become fashionable in the West End – I joined a one day shaving class. This included the entire works, from preparing hot scented towels to working up a good lather of soap in the shaving mug and of course sharpening cutthroat razors. Our training started with balloons which were blown up to head size and well lathered, then shaved. All went perfectly well in the morning but after lunch it was the real thing a human skin. A number of unsuspecting, filthy dirty drunks had been brought in straight off the street. Though eager for a clean shave, they were about to experience rather more than they had bargained for. On lathered balloons the girls had no qualms. Yet once they approached real flesh, their razor hands started to visibly shake. Within seconds the drunks' faces started to look for all the world like strawberry truffles, with blood welling up through the pure white shaving lather in a glorious whirl of colour. It was modern art almost, and when the girls had wiped off the remaining lather each drunk owned an amazing array of bleeding slits, cuts and slashes, plus missing moles and warts. Even sizeable chunks of skin had been gouged out!

Together with several mates from the Enfield Town Angling Club I spent New Year's Eve enjoying a riotous send-off in London's West End, in and out of the fountains at Trafalgar Square and getting completely paralytic. I cannot ever remember being so drunk, either before or since. I can recall one of the lads, on leave from the Marines (so I guess he had to look tough) who stood up on a table in one of the numerous bars we visited, peed into an empty pint mug and, downed the lot in one. And how I made it on time the following morning to join *SS Oronsay* I'll never know.

Dad drove me to the dismal Tilbury docks for eight o'clock in the morning on 1 January 1967. Everything was various shades of grey, grey and grey; even the weather was foggy and drizzling. Dad parked right beside the towering presence of the steamer ship *SS Oronsay* and said, 'Well John, see you in five months'. I looked upwards and wondered what lay ahead. We shook hands and I staggered up the crew gangplank with suitcase and beach caster into an entirely different world.

Named after a Scottish island, *SS Oronsay* amounted to 28,000 tons, had seven decks, a crew of 600 (half European and half Goanese Indians) and, with both first-and second-class accommodation completely full, had a capacity for 1,600 passengers. Some were on short voyages to a particular country; some were on a lengthy cruise or round-the-world tour, whilst others were on their way to a new

LEFT
P & O Liner, *SS Oronsay* (my home for two years), tied up in the picturesque natural harbour of Pago Pago (American Samoa), one of the most evocative locations I have ever fished, allowed me to travel the world and really enjoy the swinging 60s.

life in Australia via the then £10 assisted passage deal. To say that the ship was similar to a village or small town even, with its associated galaxy of social problems, indiscretions, joys and aspirations is an understatement. It was a travelling institution and the biggest learning curve of my life.

I was introduced to the shop and hairdressing staff including shops manager, Roy Lee, and spent the following week going nowhere humping heavy cardboard boxes around from where a crane had deposited them on the forward deck, to lockers all over the ship. Shop staff, under which I came with the strange title of junior leading hand (whatever that meant), had to be back on board five days prior to sailing in order to load up with confectionery, toiletries, medicines, clothes and soft goods – in fact everything passengers would buy during our five month voyage. No one had told me that part of my job when I had finished hairdressing each day – which I did from eight in the morning to six in the evening – was to replace all that had been sold in the shops that day from various lockers. I was about to work the hardest I have ever worked in my life, often not finishing until gone 10 o'clock or sometimes much later. But then I made certain I played hard too.

This first voyage – which was the longest I ever made – included Australian cruising for six weeks out of Sydney to such exotic places as the Great Barrier Reef, Fiji, Tonga and the Samoan Islands. Even better, for one of those cruises a convention of no fewer than 300 young, female schoolteachers was on board. So with half the crew being Goanese and not permitted to mix with the passengers and half the 300 European crew being rampant gays, that left us heterosexual males outnumbered by young schoolteachers at a ratio of 2:1. Need I say more!

As shop staff we did not have officer status like the engineers and electricians, so we didn't have our own cabins at passenger deck levels. This made womanising a continual problem, because we had to dodge back and forth, up and down decks from tourist to first-class accommodation in the early hours of the morning to evade the two Masters at Arms. But on the positive side we did eat extremely well on our own table in the passenger dining rooms and had virtually the same amount of time off in port as the passengers.

I initially found all the rules and regulations difficult to handle, like having to wear 'whites' when in the tropics and 'blues' when in temperate climates. I'd often climb the numerous staircases from my cabin five decks down, up to the hairdressing salon for instance, only to find I was in whites and the order of the day was blues, or vice versa, and a change to the correct colour was mandatory. (Quite simply, as *Oronsay* cruised at over 20 knots and could cover 500 miles in a day, we passed from one temperature band to another very quickly). I soon learned to keep my head down and realised that as a barber a free haircut could get me almost anything on board, from an empty first-class cabin for the night when wanting to wine and dine, to enough blood and best raw steak from the butcher to enjoy a day's shark fishing.

This brings me to a particular occasion in the Mediterranean when *Oronsay* had anchored well off shore in deep water at Palermo. Most of the passengers had gone ashore via the life-boat shuttle service together with most of the deck crew who enjoyed nothing better than irritating the local Mafiosi, so I decided on a quiet session at the aft end of the ship just above the laundry. This was actually an isolation deck, with a lock-up cell where anyone extremely infectious or aggressive was put, and so rarely used. And it became my favourite spot when fishing from the ship at anchor or in port, despite the deck being 20 feet above the waterline. Anyway first things first, and a visit to the fish chef was required but he was nowhere to be seen. So I helped myself to a few whole herrings and a tray of large peeled Pacific prawns, no doubt prepared for first-class starters that evening.

To cut a long story short, after liberally scattering all the prawns into the deep blue void and watching them spiral straight down to the bottom during slack water, I lowered a whole herring on a wire trace to the bottom and was rewarded an hour later with a conger eel of around 30lbs, which put up a great scrap. The Goanese Indian crew, some of who were keen anglers themselves and ardent fish eaters, were always around whenever I caught anything. Whatever it was – and I've eaten curried sailfish, stingray and conger to name but a few dishes – was instantly taken down to the galley and cooked. My conger was therefore immediately grabbed and I never saw it again, though there were strange and dire consequences.

Whilst down in my cabin getting ready for dinner once we had pulled anchor and were under way (the ship's screws turning over became a noise as familiar as one's front door bell ringing) there was a loud knock on the cabin door. I opened it and there stood the imposing figure of ship's chef, Lou King, with an angry look on his red face. From behind his back a huge hand appeared and slowly opened to reveal three partly digested peeled prawns. 'Can you explain how my peeled Pacific prawns got into the stomach of a Mediterranean conger?' asks the chef. All I could think of saying was 'Er, how about a couple of free haircuts, Lou?' He smiled and said 'Yeah OK! But keep your bloody hands off my starters in future!'

The rod I used to catch that unforgettable conger eel was in fact the top joint of my beach caster fitted into a short handle I made up, having purchased a duplicate set of ferrules before joining the ship. Though it seems strange now, it was all brass reinforced ferrules in those days. Together with the full-length beach caster plus

ABOVE
I caught this 65lb
eagle ray (its
pointed wings
are folded back),
from the harbour
entrance during
darkness at Port
Adelaide in South
Australia.

a two-piece nine foot ABU heavy spinning rod, I could cope with most situations wherever *Oronsay* docked around the world.

I landed several silver catfish to over 10lbs whilst we were tied up for refuelling in Aden, followed by a small guitar fish and a 65lb stingray from the shore in Adelaide in South Australia. I looked forward to catching leopard sharks to around the 30lb mark whenever *SS Oronsay* berthed in San Francisco opposite the old prison on the island of Alcatraz. Which, incidentally, looked just as foreboding as in the Clint Eastwood movie, *Escape from Alcatraz*. I also once unintentionally foul hooked a dolphin when *Oronsay* was berthed in Bombay harbour and because of the religious value of these friendly mammals I nearly caused an international incident. Workers were running about screaming and gesturing in my direction all over shore side. Fortunately for me the small hook pulled free before I was lynched. That's how I read the situation anyway.

Which brings me to Italy and Naples in particular where, for the price of 200 cigarettes, you could walk back on to the ship with an armful of wrist watches. These were then swapped in Bombay for leather suitcases which were sold on to passengers at a later date. We worked a similar ruse with coloured coral which could be bought by the basketful quite cheaply in Fiji, but only in Fiji. The white, sun-bleached pieces of coral were put into hot springs full of various coloured dyes and the result looked most exotic. We could have got our money back purely on the raffia baskets the coral was sold in. We waited until Fiji was not on *Oronsay's* itinerary before getting the coral out for sale. There were other money-making schemes, of course, that I shan't go into. So back to the fishing.

Every now and again, usually when tied up in tropical deep water harbours and presenting fresh fish baits on the bottom, I became attached to unseen monsters which just kept on going, despite all the pressure I could apply with a 40lb reel line. When nothing was left on the Penn Long Beach multiplier, one of two things usually happened. Either the hook snapped or the brass ferrules on my beach caster bent at right angles immediately prior to the line cracking off like a pistol shot. Whilst fishing from the rocks in American Samoa on the island of Pago Pago, however, I watched my rod break in half for the last time as an unseen shark or ray made off for the horizon. I finally decided to do something about landing these unstoppable monsters.

I wanted an outfit with real big-time stopping power, or at least slowing-down power, and so in Honolulu, where I repeatedly lost leviathans in the harbour, I purchased a six foot, 130lb class, hollow glass marlin tip together with an extra-strong boat rod screw-reel fitting in heavily chromed brass, plus top-quality roller tip and butt rings, and enough intermediates to construct an eight foot custom whopper stopper, once I had added a two foot hardwood handle. I also purchased the ideal partner in a Penn 9/0 Senator reel which held around a quarter of a mile of 80lb monofilament. I still have that reel incidentally, and occasionally use it in warmer parts when sharking.

On our next voyage when berthed in Auckland in New Zealand, where I usually enjoyed charter boat fishing for red snapper and yellowtail 25 miles out near the heads, my new outfit was well and truly put to the test. *Oronsay* was berthed alongside an old wooden pier under which I had, on previous visits, lost huge, unstoppable stingrays fishing from the aft end, and I was more than keen to see one of the monsters at close quarters. There are in fact many different species of stingray around the globe and the two species liable to be caught from British shores, *Dasyatis pastinaca* and *Myliobatis aquila* (eagle ray) are typical of the two shapes which seem to dominate the stingray kingdom which, incidentally, even includes freshwater species such as those found in the mighty Amazon river system in South America and in several rivers in Thailand.

That stingrays attain monstrous proportions there is no doubt. But because comparatively few anglers bother to specialise in catching them, even on a worldwide basis, very little is known of their ultimate weight potential. Something approaching 1000lbs is far from unrealistic in my opinion, and what an awesome creature that would be.

Anyway, back to North Island, New Zealand and to Auckland harbour with *Oronsay* tied up to the pier. One afternoon I lowered half a fresh herring mounted on a strong 5/0 tuna hook to 100lb test-wire trace down to the bottom beside the aft end. Due to there being next to no tide I used just an ounce bomb above the trace and, allowing a little slack line from bait to rod tip, put the 9/0 Senator out of gear after flicking the ratchet on. After about an hour or so, the reel suddenly clicked a couple of times (just like the big-game reel in the film *Jaws*) then screeched into life like a stuck pig, as something powerful made off, fortunately not towards the pier (something I was afraid of) but across the wide harbour in the direction of where *Oronsay*'s sister ship, *SS Orsova*, was coincidentally also berthed.

I stuck the rod's long handle under my crotch, steadied myself against the handrail and flipped the reel into gear having already preset the clutch to a firm setting. Yet still I was not prepared for the awesome animal power which came vibrating through the arched marlin tip, as the hook made purchase. It was like connecting my line to a lorry on the M25. The ray, and somehow I instinctively knew that this was a huge stingray by the way it kept close to the bottom, instantly doubled its speed and roared off across the harbour going deeper and deeper. And there in the middle of the harbour between the two ships, first kiting one way and then the other, it stayed for what seemed an eternity. The 80lb mono sang loudly in the wind, while I strained every muscle in my body to pump back line whenever I could. I was much lighter in those days – I can remember weighing in for one of the boxing matches, regularly held on the crew deck up forward, at just 10 stone 13lb. So I had little weight to lean against this obviously huge fish, For close on two hours the ray battled away, but my stand-up big-game outfit eventually proved its worth and I was able to pump my adversary back to directly below the ship where it sulked for a while, until it finally lay exhausted on the surface close beside SS Oronsay.

It was absolutely monstrous, as wide as a car, two feet thick and with a tail root as large as a man's calf, thrashing its sting positioned halfway along the tail frantically from side to side. At this stage I was shaking with nervous exhaustion and pumped up on pure adrenaline, though quite near to the point of not caring whether I landed it or not, which is a period anyone who has ever experienced blue water game fishing always goes through. The light was fading fast and the time was getting closer to the Oronsay's departure from Auckland. Because of this the captain, generally a most obliging chap to those of us who fished, couldn't really hold up the scheduled departure by putting a lifeboat down just because one of the crew had by far the largest fish of his life waiting on the surface to be gaffed. After all it was a passenger ship.

BELOW
(Left to right) Jim, Phil (the plumber) and I in 'blues' on Oronsay's port side back in Southampton Docks.

Anyway the best I could do was to let some mates try and rope-gaff it, but from over 20 feet up this proved impossible and not a little dangerous. Then suddenly there came a real chance of turning the now ridiculous situation around, which unintentionally had become a floodlit spectacle for both passengers and their loved ones on the quay waving goodbye. Thankfully a tug had arrived alongside early in order to push us off and the obliging crewmen, realising my predicament, picked up the two gaffs thrown down to them. Unfortunately they couldn't hold the beast even with a gaff in each wing and once it started to dive one of the gaffs bent straight, leaving the ray thrashing about on the other. The trace was then severed below the swivel as it became tangled up in the confusion, leaving two New Zealand tug men trying to haul something like 500lbs over the side of their craft on one gaff head. Needless to say they didn't make it, which brought a pained 'oh' from the gallery of spectators on the upper decks.

A rope was then dangled down to the tug to retrieve my two now useless gaffs and I slowly packed up the big-game outfit, numb but thankful that the ordeal was over. In a way I was glad that my ray was not killed simply to ascertain what it weighed. But I still wonder – even now.

I once spent what turned out to be a most infuriating day fishing in Kobe harbour in Japan. Despite a good supply of fresh bait in the way of prawns and sardines, compliments of the fish cook, not a single twitch or nibble did I have with all three rods out over the side. But the penny quickly dropped in the late afternoon when our local English-speaking agent asked the shops manager why I was bothering to fish in a harbour that had been polluted for years. Boy, did I feel stupid!

It was upon leaving Japan on one of our many visits there, with the next port on the itinerary being Hong Kong, that a most harrowing experience came to all those working and travelling aboard *SS Oronsay*, somewhere in the middle of the Taiwan Sea. At the time I was relaxing next to the swimming pool on the tourist sundeck at lunchtime. I overheard a woman asking a young officer what was the fine trail of smoke coming from a hole in one of the hatch covers. He opened it slowly and whoosh, up it all went. A huge hold that you could drive dozens of double-decker buses into was full of toys, radios and other plastic goods that apparently had been smouldering away for a couple of days since we left Japan and suddenly ignited into a veritable fireball.

All colour instantly drained from the officer's face as he slammed the cover down and ran off to hit the alarm. Within the next couple of hours complete pandemonium had broken out. All of both E and F decks in tourist accommodation, which amounted to several hundred cabins, were flooded with sea water to stop the bulk heads from melting, leaving most passengers owning little more than what they had been wearing on deck. Cameras and hi-fi systems purchased in Japan, plus money, valuables and everything else left in their cabins became immediately irretrievable to hundreds of passengers.

SS Oronsay was within a short space of time put on 'abandon ship alert' and, in truth from those in the know, I was given the impression that for a day or so at least it was indeed touch and go whilst crews worked unceasingly to prevent the intense heat from spreading. My mum must have had a fit when listening to the news back home. Most newspapers ran the headlines '*SS Oronsay* ablaze in Taiwan Sea'. The truth however was that visible flames were never seen by the majority of both passengers and crew.

My most vivid memory of the occasion, bizarre though it may seem, was that within a few hours of crew alert, at every embarkation lifeboat station, there suddenly appeared from the bowels of the ship hundreds of sewing machines and bicycles, property of the Goanese Indian crew who, laden down with these valuables, were all life-jacketed up and ready to go. Where they thought they were going I'm not sure, but they sure as hell weren't going to let their prize possessions go down with the ship.

Fortunately the internal fire was kept at bay and the old man made the decision of going into our next port of call, Hong Kong, with *SS Oronsay* still technically on fire. It was quickly made safe on arrival however and everyone enjoyed an extra week's leave in this truly magical city while Lloyd's insurance delegates flew in from London to estimate the cost of the damage.

Much of the damaged cargo was in fact simply heaved over the side in Hong Kong harbour but a quantity of salvageable goods, novelty radios in particular, somehow found their way into the cabins of *Oronsay*'s wheeler dealers. No, not me, but my fishing buddy, Phil the plumber (with whom I have kept in touch ever since), came by an assignment of these which were dried out and sold a few weeks later on the west coast of Africa when we berthed in Dakar. Saltwater had achieved the obvious, however, resulting in those who bought them only ever hearing a crackle and buzz, regardless of battery strength. Phil handed out a cock-and-bull story about not being able to hear anything in port due to *Oronsay*'s aerials interfering with the radio channels, which seemed to pacify his unsophisticated customers. And he promised that once *Oronsay* had departed, the radios would work perfectly.

Needless to say the next time we tied up in Dakar several months later, where the fishing can be exceptionally good from the harbour entrance piers, there was a reception committee all on the look-out for Phil. This didn't stop us fishing though, because we smuggled Phil out with a hood over his head down the galley gangway straight into a waiting taxi. But it was a bit hairy. Those tall, French-speaking West Africans in their fezzes would have lynched him given the chance.

Phil and I fished together all over the world once the screws had stopped and *SS Oronsay* was tied up. Australian ports were amongst our favourite and when on leave in Sydney we'd sometimes get a taxi up to the Hawkesbury River at Bobbin Head and hire a 20 foot boat on which we lived for a couple of days whilst exploring the fascinating maze of saltwater channels north of the City. One night Phil swore I was snoring so loudly that a wild boar up in the hills close to where we were anchored in a deep channel was answering me. What codswallop! At night the deep, crystal clear water was continually lit up by millions of moving particles of luminous green phosphorus. It was indeed an eerie experience whilst fishing when anything could turn up from flatheads to sharks.

Mention of the wonderful city of Sydney reminds me of an occasion when *Oronsay* was tied up at Circular Bay and I was fishing from the rocks at famous Bondi Beach. It almost ended in tragedy. Mine. I was casting from a high rocky plateau way out beyond the waves crashing on to the rocks below, hoping for grouper, and holding my beach caster up high to stop the line from being dragged in. I had just asked a mate standing a fair way back behind my precarious perch what he thought of the two birds sitting upon a large rock around 100 yards away (which were actually bronze statues and a local landmark) and as I turned back to watch the rod tip all I could see was a gigantic column of water accompanied by a loud roar. It was one of those freak waves (every forty-ninth some say) and it completely engulfed me. For what seemed like an eternity it was as though I had been put in a washing machine.

I was in fact being bowled backwards head over heels, over and over the jagged, limpet-covered rocks from which I had been casting by the enormous force of water. I managed fortunately (and this probably saved my life) to hold on to my beach caster with both hands. When the sea receded the draw was immensely strong, and had it not been for the rod sticking fast amongst the crevices I would have been drawn over 20 feet down and smashed against the lower rocks.

Then came my only experience of the famous Australian lifeguards, a group of whom were posing with muscles pumped up at the top of the beach by the main road. When I came hobbling along in a half-concussed state, sporting numerous rather nasty open wounds on my back, elbows and legs which were all bleeding profusely, I received a curt 'There's a chemist down the road, Mack'.

Whenever *Oronsay* was berthed for a week or more in Sydney, probably the most picturesque natural harbour in the world, I took the opportunity of travelling

BELOW

Having nearly been smashed to death by a freak wave the previous day, here I am, patched up, fishing from the same rocks at the famous Bondi Beach, near Sydney, Australia.

inland and seeing something of Australia. One of the relief Australian hairdressers, Fred, invited me back to share a few days with his wife and kids in the town of Yass close to the Burrinjuck Dam near the Blue Mountains. Here on spinners we caught brim (a brownish, unstriped version of our perch), rainbow trout and small Murray cod, in a most enchanting flooded valley where only the bleating of grazing sheep could be heard in an otherwise completely silent environment.

In one of the rivers, called the Goodradigbee, we fished for rainbow trout and I actually set eyes upon a duck-billed platypus in the wild – which is something even most Australians haven't experienced. It suddenly popped up to the surface right beneath my rod tip, all black and shiny with that strange-looking flat head and tail combination, and was actually much smaller than I had imagined, being no more than 20 inches long. It looked directly up at me for a couple of seconds and dived out of sight in a flash. Every so often along the valley, we caught sight of sulphur-crested cockatoos and huge flocks of budgerigars. It actually seemed kind of strange to see them in the wild.

The rainbow trout were totally preoccupied feeding on grasshoppers which, due to a strong wind, were continually landing upon the surface of this extremely fast-flowing river (it reminded me of Derbyshire's River Derwent). They would look

at neither worm nor spinner, so Fred and I set about catching some live hoppers. For a container we used an empty beer bottle and following an hour's toil chasing these unusually large and fast insects through waist-high grass, we were streaming with sweat and close to exhaustion, having captured just two. Sadly even one of these appeared dead. It mattered not however to those rainbow trout; for we caught an unbelievably hard fighting rainbow apiece, both over 3lbs, within mere minutes of trotting our hoppers downstream beneath a bubble float.

Judging by the number of aggressive swirls on the surface, the river was full of trout and all of them were large, wild rainbows. When I think back to that day the memory still frustrates me because we packed up shortly after that brace of trout, unable to capture any more grasshoppers. We needed to be on our way in any event due to the long drive back into Yass, and before we left the river where the track veered upwards and across the next valley, I saw an old man with long grey hair flapping either side of his bush hat, in the middle of a meadow beside the river behaving in a most unusual way. Fred stopped the shooting-break and we sauntered through the long grass to say 'hello', passing a trailer van in front of which was a large pile of prime rainbow trout in the 3-6lb class all ready for gutting. At least someone had the answer to catching enough grasshoppers for bait.

This canny bushman was not chasing after them however. Once he spotted the grasshopper he wanted (and he politely showed us exactly how to do it) he raised his hands above his head and from a few yards back simply waved them about in a sort of mock karate display, slowly moving closer and closer. This he said confused the grasshopper's two long antennae which could then not focus on any one point (rather like a modern auto-focus camera lens hunts when it is aimed at a moving object) and simply by swaying his hands from side to side he could quietly walk right up to any grasshopper and pick it up. Fred and I looked at each other in despair at what might have been. A drawstring cotton bag around the old man's neck was twitching away, full of dozens of live insects, so he wasn't kidding us. And I can assure you that this ruse works all over the world for catching grasshoppers. You can literally see their two antennae crossing over each other trying to obtain an accurate bearing. But of course by then they are bait.

I caught my very first shark, an 80lb black-tipped spinner shark, whilst Pacific cruising out from Sydney in the warm blue waters off the islands of Fiji. A Swiss passenger and angling fanatic, Jacques, and I had struck up a firm friendship and we hired a 15 foot water-skiing boat for the day with a local guide. Upon returning to the marina with the shark, which unfortunately had swallowed the hook and 3lbs of raw steak (compliments of the butcher), its belly suddenly started to move. Although this female was well and truly dead on arrival, the four live pups inside, complete with umbilical cords connected to food sacs, swam straight away when returned to the sea. This, in part I like to think, vindicated my catching it on rod and line.

Later that trip when berthed in Acapulco, Mexico, Jacques and I teamed up again and talked David, a young hairdresser, and Barry, who worked in the ship's shop (both non-anglers), into sharing the expense of a big-game boat for the day to see if we could catch a sailfish. With pelicans following overhead we left the harbour and allowed the two non-anglers to sit on the rods, thinking that nothing would grab hold until we hit blue water. What a mistake! Within minutes out whizzed one of the outrigger lines presenting a fresh whole mullet, and non-angler Barry was fast into a bloody great sailfish, which went absolutely berserk, repeatedly jumping all over the place on a ridiculously inadequate rod and reel combination. Consequently it took ages to bring to the boat.

Fortunately the ocean off Acapulco was at that time a veritable sailfish haven and we boated no fewer than three, despite our inexperience at blue water trolling. Each was around 80-90lbs, and one of these we took back to the ship and from the

fishing boat hauled it up the side of *Oronsay* by rope to the afterdeck. After the photographs I'm ashamed to say that this magnificent creature was subsequently curried. But in those days conservation was a rarely used word.

We were taking a big risk as it was, because if the old man had seen an eight foot sailfish being hauled on to his ship, we'd all have been in deep trouble. Sadly Jacques was the only one of the group who didn't hit a sail, but he made up for it by boating a big bull Dorado.

Acapulco was a most colourful resort which typified third-world countries at that time. Plenty of showcase, plush hotels and westernised facilities, but always just away from the commercialised sector people lived in squalor, literally on the poverty line in houses made from cardboard boxes. On the face of it, it seems little different from tourists coming to London and seeing the down-and-outs and winos dossing down for the night along the Embankment and in shop doorways. Again, in makeshift cardboard shelters. But in third-world countries, for such a large proportion of the population, it is their way of life, and I think witnessing this all over the globe whilst *SS Oronsay* took its passengers to some of the most elegant resorts really opened up my eyes to the reality of life in third-world countries and made me feel both humble and thankful for my own roots. It also blew my childish belief that British was always best. I guess being brought up in London just after the war, at a time when we still had colonies and much of the world atlas was subsequently coloured in pink and under British rule, this belief was perhaps excusable. Naturally I also gained a clear impression of what the rest of the world thought of us, which really opened my eyes – for it, was not always complimentary.

I have already hinted at the swinging 60s attitude towards sex on *SS Oronsay*. It was indeed one floating hotel for the hot-blooded folk of the world and I can

SIXTY YEARS A FISHERMAN

only explain this by the way in which the so-called fairer sex totally change for the better, as far as rampant males are concerned, particularly the young Wilson, as soon as they are taken away from a socially controlled environment where their family and friends know both them and their position within the local community. To say inhibitions go straight out the window would indeed be a gross understatement!

Even the chastest of women change from demure, hard to chat up housewives and lovers and turn into vociferous predators, after a few days out on the ocean waves. Scientists no doubt put a label on this phenomenon, but the young Wilson never tried to understand what was happening, he simply enjoyed it.

As tourist hairdresser for the greater part of my two years aboard *SS Oronsay*, you could say that just about every female travelling tourist class, plus some of those who filtered down from first-class, passed through my hands. Perhaps mention of that immortal film, *Shampoo*, starring Warren Beatty, might provide an idea of what life as a hairdresser on board a P & O liner was like during the latter part of the 1960s. Suffice it to say that I always felt knackered. I hope memories of the following two clandestine meetings give a sufficient clue.

I became particularly involved with a first-class passenger, an attractive blonde in her late 20's, whom I shall call Carol from Oregon. I first met her in the salon whilst *Oronsay* was in Fort Lauderdale, Miami (all the hairdressers took it in turns to be on duty for the morning only whilst in port). Each evening Carol would leave her cabin door on the latch while she drank with some of the young officers, all of whom were dying to get her into the sack, so I could let myself into her first-class cabin up on A deck once my duties were finished and wait for her return. To be frank, she was a bit of an artist, probably worse than me, and usually three parts to the wind, but was a wonderfully warm person and once I'd belted down a few whiskies (she would always leave a bottle and some ginger ales on ice in her cabin) we were soon on the same level. Anyway, one particular evening Carol didn't arrive back in the cabin at the usual time of around midnight and I must have dozed off. Because at 2 o'clock crash bang went the door and into the cabin fell Carol completely bombed. Great, I thought, no nookie for Wilson tonight, and pushed the door shut (still on the latch) before heaving her from the floor onto the bed and removing her clothes. She threw up a couple of times and immediately started dry retching. Nevertheless I dragged her completely naked from the bed towards the shower, supporting her dead weight with my arms lightly locked around her waist and was just in front of the cabin door when solid footsteps and gentle, but concerned words from the tall, ginger-haired officer whose voice I recognised, whispered, 'Are you alright Carol? Are you alright?'

There I was, a junior leading hand (the lowest of the low) and not supposed to be anywhere near passenger accommodation, particularly first-class, doing my best to stop the woman that same officer had been plying with drinks all night and thinking no doubt he had cracked it, from sliding to the floor. I'd also stripped off to hold her up in the shower, so was standing stock still, bollock naked, just two feet from the mahogany door which separated us, still on the latch, unable to free a hand to put the lock on.

Fortunately at that precise moment, which seemed like an eternity (I could picture Wilson being hanged from the yard arm), fate took a positive turn in the form of a couple of passengers who must have returned to their cabin nearby, because there was a polite exchange of words and the lanky young officer walked away slowly down the passageway.

About a week later Carol decided to risk the journey (passengers were not allowed to walk from one class to another class, and would be asked to return to their own section if caught) and visit me in the tourist salon for a hairdo. Now to cut a long, complicated story short, I ended up in a strange situation with three women under dryers all at the same time, each of whom I had been carrying on with during the preceding weeks. My problem was how to get the first out from beneath the dryer, brushed out and away from the small salon before the other two switched off their dryers. Women cannot hear under the dryer (though some were masters at lip reading) due to a headful of rollers covered in a net with cardboard covers over their ears so they don't burn. I worked frantically away simultaneously trying to look nonchalant, whilst arranging the next rendezvous with one, while the other two exchanged curious glances every so often. It was indeed a most precarious tightrope I walked in those days. But I loved every minute of it.

I did however get my come-uppance a few months later whilst trying to woo a particularly attractive woman from America's Deep South, called Mary Lou. Just about everyone had tried it on with this striking woman whose high cheek bones and vivacious looks were not totally unlike those of the actress Mary Tyler Moore. But in no way was she getting into the sack with anyone not holding out a wedding ring. She was, you might say, the exception to just about every unattached young woman travelling on board *SS Oronsay* that time, and as such posed a magnificent challenge. In fact to Wilson it was the ultimate challenge and I decided on the 'cool' approach by suggesting we play chess one evening, to which she actually agreed. Yes, chess!

My good pal, Geoff Wedge (now settled in Melbourne) who worked in the purser's department, nicked a key to an unoccupied cabin (as he regularly did) in tourist accommodation on F deck for the occasion. In truth Mary Lou and I spent a really pleasant evening – she was a cute chess player – but I got absolutely nowhere. I was in fact on the point of calling it a night and conceding defeat at around two o'clock in the morning when there was a loud authoritative banging at the door. I knelt down and looked up through the grill at the bottom of the cabin door to a most unwelcome scene: there were the staff captain, chief steward, the master at arms, plus several young officers who each no doubt relished the chance of doing Wilson down and being along at the kill. A bedroom steward must have heard our voices or seen the light on in what should have been an unoccupied cabin and reported it.

By the following morning stories of the fiasco had spread throughout the ship like a forest fire and I was a laughing stock. My penance included a dressing-down from the old man himself who tried to keep a straight face while I stood in his office upon the Union Jack (an obligatory act) lined on both sides by sniggering young officers. I also lost a day's pay with the inevitability that Crawford in London would get to hear about my wrongdoings, which could result in Wilson not joining *Oronsay* on its next voyage. (Actually Crawford was informed, but being a good hairdresser with a clean record, save for this one indiscretion, I suffered his caustic remarks and innuendoes in silence when *Oronsay* docked in Southampton, and that was the end of it.)

Several months after this little episode Geoff Wedge said 'goodbye' to us all on board and emigrated to Australia where, as far as I know, he still lives. But before he departed he threw a party at his parents' large house in Brighton (they were on holiday). This necessitated hiring a car from a firm based just outside Southampton Docks where *Oronsay* was berthed. Being younger than me, both Geoff and Jeremy, the ship's chemist, rented a new Ford on my licence and took turns in gunning it along narrow coastal roads between Southampton and Brighton where we picked up three obliging young ladies from Geoff's local pub to take back to the party. On the way back during the early hours of the morning (we had to get back to *Oronsay* for departure that day) I experienced the weird dream of spinning round and round, followed by falling heavily. In fact I had, straight on to the floor from a prone position on the rear seats, while Geoff completely lost control at the wheel and promptly razed to the ground the low front walls of at least two terraced houses. He then crashed back onto the road and continued the journey as though nothing had happened.

As the mangled Ford was taken out on my licence I had to drive it the last 200 yards back into the car hire compound, which was in fact the only occasion I sat behind the steering wheel. The blonde behind the desk should never have been sweet-talked by Geoff into hiring it out on my licence (but she fancied him) and I saw her clutch her head in disbelief and horror as I chugged the forlorn-looking Ford around the corner into the yard. But there was more to come.

Unknown to us at the time, although we saw them at the party, a spanking new pillar-box red Hillman Imp taken out by Bruce, a self-confessed driving wizard, who was said to be on first-name terms with Lotus boss, the now late Colin Chapman, and Kevin, the laundryman, arrived back a total write-off. Somehow they had managed to wrap it around a tree on the outskirts of Southampton and

then just about limp back. At least ours only needed a new front end plus passenger and driver's side doors!

Hiring cars whilst on leave between trips was never my strong point. Take for instance the Triumph Herald convertible I hired from Edwards of Epsom in Surrey. It was a lovely little car to drive. It was white with a black hood, and the soft top was a real boon in the particularly hot weather we were experiencing that week.

I had chosen to visit a favourite haunt on the Great Ouse in Holywell where for several years I regularly rented a punt during the winter months for piking from the late Tom Metcalf Arnold – one of the few people at that time still making eel traps from reeds. Only being midsummer, my thoughts were with the tench and bream inhabiting the deeper water about half a mile downstream from Tom's house, and he kindly opened the farm gate allowing me to drive right down to within 10 yards of the river. It was a lovely spot with a raised bank behind to break the wind and comfortable swims cut into thick beds of sweet rush and reeds. There was a good depth close in and I quickly got amongst the bream by laying on with bread flake over a carpet of ground bait. I had left all the hustle and bustle behind, and my mind was completely relaxed by the serenity of being alone and at peace with the river.

Then I heard a most peculiar sound. It was quite indescribable really, but I can remember thinking at the time that it sounded like heavy munching. It went on for several minutes before curiosity got the better of me and I stood up to look over the high bank from behind which it seemed to be coming. Nothing out of the ordinary, from my angle of view, just picturesque open countryside and the Triumph convertible with a horse's head inside.

Inside the car! What the bloody hell was a horse's head doing inside the car?

SIXTY YEARS A FISHERMAN

What happens to my own jalopies is one thing but what happens to a hired car is something else. I'd lose my deposit for a start. I flew up the bank clutching the landing net. The entire car shook and off bolted the horse leaving behind a gaping two foot hole right in the middle of the black leatherette roof. When I rang Edwards of Epsom that afternoon enquiring about mitigating circumstances in insurance claims, I first said to the girl on the phone, 'now you're not going to believe this, but …' 'Try me,' she said. After my story she said, 'You're right I don't, it's a bit far fetched isn't it? I am afraid you will have to forfeit your deposit, Mr Wilson.'

By far the largest thing I ever hooked during those two wonderful years on *SS Oronsay*, which included several east-to-west mail runs around the globe lasting three months apiece, was a police launch. How? Well we were lying at anchor in deep water off Bermuda at the time with most of the passengers having been taken ashore in the lifeboat shuttle service. This was the perfect combination of circumstances for Wilson to partake in a spot of serious shark fishing which necessitated collecting a big drum of fresh blood from the butcher (who saved it up for me) and emptying the lot over the side from the afterdeck by the isolation hospital. One of the shop's staff, a likeable Geordie called Andrew, fancied a go at fishing and so I made him up a light outfit baited with thin strips of raw steak in the hope of him catching a reasonable-sized snapper or grunt to use as live shark bait. (Incidentally wherever you find yourself in tropical blue waters around the world without bait remember that strips of raw steak will catch most species from catfish to sharks. It's the blood which is the attractor of course, and this soon washes from the steak, necessitating regular bait changes).

Then I put together my heavy whopper-stopper outfit with the Penn 9/0 reel, and on to the cable laid wire trace and duo of size 10/0 hooks went a huge slab of best beef steak simply dripping with blood. A balloon was tied on the 80lb reel line several feet above the 10 foot trace and this I used to drift the bait slowly down tide with the ratchet on and the big multiplier out of gear.

Emptying blood over the side usually resulted – and often in a ridiculously short time – in several sharks following the trail up to the ship. But this time action came from an entirely different quarter. I suddenly heard Andrew croak loudly and turned around to see him crash backwards against the steel door of the isolation hospital – gripped firmly around the throat by a pair of large black hands reaching through the iron bars. Unbeknown to us a Goanese crew member, who was delirious and completely off his trolley, had been locked up for the night in the isolation deck cell. He was ranting and raving exactly how you would expect a madman to with Andrew's face turning redder by the second.

He was on the point of passing out when I finally managed to prise the lunatic's fingers from around his throat and we settled back down to the fishing again, several feet in front of the cell door with the incarcerated man still shouting and

raving. With the amount of blood spreading below I was expecting a shark to show up at any minute. In the distance there came the sound of a motorboat. It was the Bermuda police launch circling *Oronsay*, no doubt to see that no one was engaged in any kind of smuggling. Trouble was it was heading straight towards my shark line, so I yelled at the top of my voice and waved exaggeratedly at the copper to get out of the way and gestured towards my balloon float. But he obviously could not hear and simply waved back cordially.

By now there was insufficient time for me to retrieve the shark rig, and so the inevitable happened. Suddenly the put, put, put of the engine stopped as the wire trace wound around the propeller. Wilson was fast into a 20 foot police launch drifting downwind begrudgingly against a heavily set drag on the 9/0 and slowly taking line. The copper came out of the wheelhouse, looked at my 80lb line angled up from his stern to the rod I was holding and shook his fist angrily. It was no time to argue whose fault it was and without further ado he stripped off to his underpants and, grabbing a pair of pliers, plopped over the side beneath the boat. With so much blood in the sea (if only the passengers knew what went on) the farce could well have turned into *Jaws 4*.

I couldn't look; I simply bent my back into the police launch trying to stop it from going further down tide with the 80lb line so tight that it sang in the wind. After what seemed an age that included several dives beneath the launch, the copper finally managed to unwind the 200lb wire trace from his prop and clambered wearily on board, again shaking a fist in my direction. But Wilson was long gone, having packed up in record time to make a hasty retreat back to the sanctuary of his cabin before the irate copper could kick up a fuss with the master at arms at embarkation deck level. An hour after we pulled anchor, a bell boy knocked on my cabin door and said, 'here's your trace back, compliments of the Bermuda police force.'

I honestly think I could fill a whole book with weird and wonderful tales experienced on board *SS Oronsay*. I could relate the time in Horseshoe Bay, Vancouver, Canada, for instance, (little did I know that 40 years later I would be sturgeon fishing near Vancouver) when my hired boat was nearly mowed down in thick fog by the Victoria Island ferry, and on the very same day how I almost became attached to a sea eagle which grabbed a fish bait in full flight during the cast. Fortunately the hooks came clear. I could provide more womanising stories but I was really no different from any other red-blooded unattached male in his early 20's. Besides, there then came a complete change in direction for me when, on leave between trips back in north London, I met up again with my former fiancée, Barbara, in a local night club.

Having sown my wild oats, I was ready to settle down and get married. During the intervening years since we last met, Barbara and I had both lived life to the full. With the prospect of marriage there also came the additional opportunity of starting a new life, managing a chain of hairdressing salons together in the West Indies on the island of Barbados.

I had been informed of this position by one of my clients on board *Oronsay* and when I was next on leave, Barbara and I went to see John and Veronica Stuart (our eventual bosses) at their house in south London. We struck up a friendship immediately (which lasts to this day) and at the beginning of December, Barbara and I were due out in Barbados to take on the extra workload in the hairdressing salons at the start of peak tourist season which ran through until April.

BELOW

This picture taken in 1970, is the beautiful tropical shoreline of Barbados near its capital, Bridgetown, between the Hilton and Holiday Inn Hotel, where I ran the hairdressing salon, skin dived and spear fished every day for three years.

It was certainly a whirlwind December for us in 1968. Within five days of saying farewell to all my friends and two fantastic years on board *SS Oronsay*, Barbara and I were married in a church close to where she lived in Muswell Hill, northwest London, and two days later the VC10 from Heathrow touched down in Bridgetown, Barbados. Another chapter of life and fishing had begun.

Measuring just 25 miles long by seven miles wide, Barbados is the most easterly of all the Caribbean islands. The rugged east coast receives a constant battering from the full force of the Atlantic whilst the quieter west coast faces the Caribbean Sea, lined with hotels and condominiums. As the population at that time was 97 percent black, living on the island as a resident as opposed to a holidaymaker – two entirely different things – gave me first-hand experience of what it feels like to be the minority race. And the West Indians and Asians living on the outskirts of London, or any ethnic minority living in any country, have my sympathy.

Although Barbara and I worked in the Miramar, Colony Club and Discovery Bay hotels on the west coast and in the Holiday Inn, catering for a westernised clientele (the largest segment coming from the USA's eastern seaboard, particularly New York), we lived in a small wooden house on the beach surrounded by local people. Coconut and banana trees grew wild around the house – which in Britain would amount to little more than a garden shed – from which a pebble could be thrown underarm into the warm, clear blue Caribbean Sea. So we went to sleep with the restful sound of the surf rolling up on to the white coral sand. It was that close, and for a while it was absolute paradise, just like the Bounty Bar television adverts. With best-quality local cane rum costing just £1.50 a gallon (yes, a gallon), how could you not be happy? We enjoyed numerous parties in that little cottage, with bottles of Coke being the most expensive items.

For the first time in my life I had my own house (albeit rented) and a garden, so we bought a pair of young Labrador puppies, one black and one golden, which we named Bonnie and Clyde. It seems strange, I know, but there were so many coconuts in the palms high above the garden all around the house that I regularly had to pay a young local lad to climb up and cut them down, in case they fell on the dogs.

Before long I started to explore all the local creeks and tidal channels entering the Caribbean Sea between the numerous hotels. I can remember vividly my first encounter with a tarpon one morning when I was armed with a spinning rod and small diving plug.

The 60 foot wide swamp was festooned along both banks with impenetrable mangrove roots and ran inland for about 200 yards into dense tropical vegetation. It was in fact separated from the gently sloping beach of white coral sand by a giant mound of grass-covered sand with the Caribbean Sea no more than 30 yards away. I was later to find out that most of these drainage swamps and dykes were actually flooded open once a year by high spring tides, allowing the fish they contained, which had grown fat on a rich diet of crabs and small fishes, to swim out and a new consignment of both young snook and tarpon to swim in.

Anyway back to my first tarpon. The only spot I could comfortably stand to make a cast without sinking up to my knees in black, foul-smelling mud was at the sea end. And as I crept up several long, dark, slow-moving shadows could be seen just beneath the surface of the decidedly green water. This was such a vastly different world from the sparklingly clear ocean only a stone's throw away. I was tingling with excitement as I threw the small yellow plug out under the bushes to my right, not really knowing what to expect.

That very first cast made me a tarpon fan for life, because as the plug jittered and fluttered along the surface at the start of the retrieve, there was an instant bow wave in its wake. I reeled in faster and faster as the bow wave followed until, quite suddenly, there was an almighty 'boil' at my feet and a giant silver fish of 40lbs plus and fully five feet long cavorted six feet into the air, shaking its huge head from side to side, soaking and almost hitting me before it crashed back into the swamp snapping the line like cotton. I stood there dumbfounded, plug less and shaking like a nervous fruit jelly as the tarpon went charging along the dyke, leaping every few yards to rid itself of the plug which was stuck in its jaws. It was still jumping and thrashing about some minutes later when I finally regained my composure and tried to puzzle out what had actually happened.

My next visit to the little dyke later that evening proved more fruitful and although I couldn't induce a take by lure fishing, I managed to tempt an 18lb fish into accepting a soft crab twitched below a bottle cork which put up one hell of a scrap on the 10lb line. I immediately noticed those bevelled jaw hinges,

BELOW

Using my old Minolta SR7 35mm camera I actually managed to photograph this 40lb tarpon tail walking and crashing through a shallow inland swamp, whilst playing it.

abrasive and sharp, and thought myself lucky that the monofil had not parted. It is the hard bony jaws and sharp hinges that make hooking and landing a tarpon so difficult, because as it leaps and shakes its head while tail-walking, even a stout wire trace is sometimes severed, unless you can quickly lower the rod tip and give line instantly.

After taking a dozen or more fish up to nearly 30lbs from the little dyke, I soon managed to locate other such swamps on the island. One in particular was not unlike the Norfolk Broads where much of my present-day fishing is done. It was quite extensive – about 40 acres – and completely covered around the perimeter with huge irregular beds of marsh grass and reeds, which sometimes formed little bays and lagoons. I came across this veritable tarpon and snook haven whilst exploring along the southern coast.

In an eerie way it was a piece of colonial Barbados forgotten by time. All around were the dilapidated remains of duck-shooting hides built on wooden stagings that reached through the reedy margins into open water (they made great fishing platforms) and in the centre of the swamp, reached via a gravel track, was an old wooden pavilion with a galvanised sheet roof. Inside were wartime posters of dance bands and coming events still pinned to the walls. I could almost hear the music of Glenn Miller come whispering through the rotting tongue-and-groove planking. I felt a little uneasy even being there on my first visit. But the gate was open and as I walked down to the pavilion all along the site of a creek to my right was the chicken wire framework of duck breeding pens.

In an old sink sunk into the ground to provide a drinking trough were a dozen or so tilapia of ideal size which I took for bait. However, unbeknown to me they were observed and fed daily by an old boy from the village who had been paid a pittance for many years, via a UK account, to look after the entire swamp complex. Now it is a posh marina – a fishing swamp no longer. But then, in 1969, it became my favourite tarpon location once I had the approval of its curator. Every so often I bribed him with a fish for his supper, and he finally forgave me for taking his family of tilapia to use as live baits.

It was at this time I purchased and learnt to use a cast net which procured enough tilapia for bait in mere minutes. I also made fish traps from one inch diameter chicken wire that I baited with bread scraps and lowered into several of the dykes close to our beach house. Thus I was never short of bait.

The water in the swamp was never more than four feet deep or less than two feet, being connected to the ocean via drainage locks, and was always gin clear. Due to their extreme caution in such clear, open water I could only catch tarpon by carefully stalking (carp-fishing fashion) through the reeds. As soon as a group of fish came patrolling round I offered a six inch tilapia on a small treble to two foot of 18lb wire, reel line being 12lb on my battered old Mitchell 300 on a 10 foot carp rod. When the lead fish saw or sensed the bait it would make a beeline for it, sometimes engulfing the fish in those huge jaws and occasionally even batting the bait right out of the water and grabbing it in mid air. They really are the greatest acrobats among fishes and quite unpredictable. Tarpon can twist, somersault, swap ends, leap while running and run hard whilst leaping. They make the most agile trout look positively senile. They can wallow in shallow water like a bream, run faster than a tope and hit live bait harder than any bass, but sometimes – and thank goodness it is only sometimes – they can be as discerning over a fly or an artificial lure as the salmon.

I have had them jump high into bank side trees, go crashing through the branches and make off the other side with a free line. One good fish, I remember, actually jumped out on to a hard bank and snapped the line over a rock as it jumped back in again. There are even stories of huge tarpon – which can weigh anything up to 300lb – jumping into the boat on top of the angler playing them; and, in two known incidents, actually killing the angler in the process. I can well believe it!

Tarpon are members of the 'bony' fish family to which the herring is related and perhaps the best way to describe one would be to imagine a colossal herring, or better still a six foot long bleak. They are deep bodied, with compressed flanks covered in vast silver scales just like a mahseer. (It is customary in fact, should a scale come adrift, for the angler to write on it the fish's weight and date of capture, once dried between the pages of a book. Incidentally, I would put these two species at the top of my all time best fighting fish list, with mahseer first and tarpon second – although perhaps I am being unfair to the tarpon for I have yet to catch one in flowing water). Tarpon are also equipped with large, extremely powerful fins and a huge extendible bony mouth which, together with very abrasive jaw hinges, makes hooking them extremely difficult.

It is a great pity that tarpon are such warm water lovers and could not tolerate our colder climate, for they would suit the beach caster, the boat angler, the salmon spinner, the fly fishing fraternity and the live baiter. They are just about every fresh and saltwater fisherman's dream fish rolled into one. Mind you, it's perhaps just as well we haven't got them in our waters. Who'd fish for salmon?

Though I accounted for snook to around 10lbs and tarpon to over 40lbs from the swamp, I soon realised that to contact those 50lbs plus tarpon I would need to leave the swamps – interesting though they were – and fish in the ocean proper. Due to the shallow, incredibly clear water this necessitated fishing from the beach at night despite irritating bites from sand flies. I smoked in those days however, which usually kept them under control. But from the sand jiggers there was no respite. These tiny burrowing worms lived in the dead sand just above high-water mark and all too easily penetrated your feet. You could even follow their route around your foot by a fine white line just beneath the skin. Usually a hatchet job

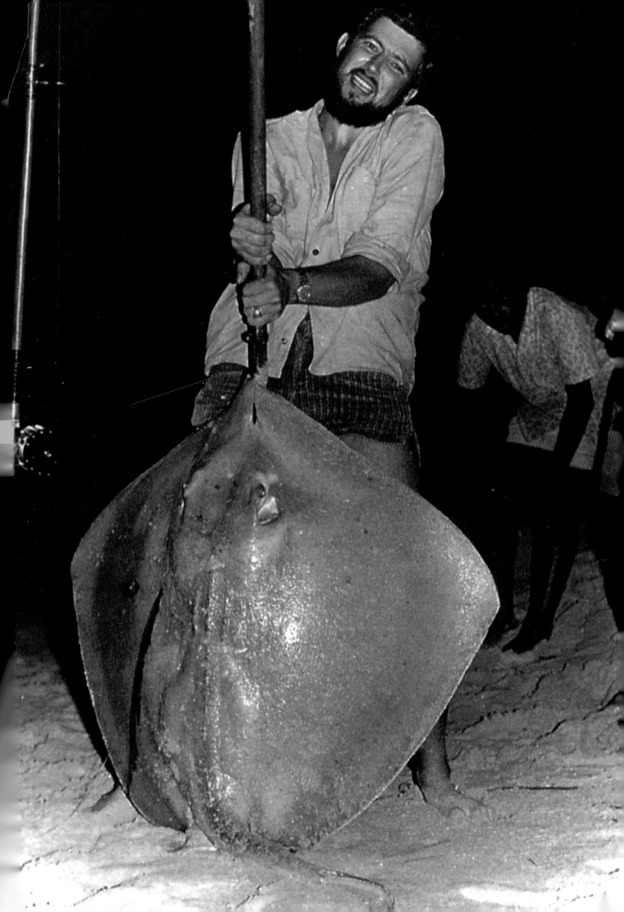

with a razor blade had the desired effect. Even so I still had a jigger in my big toe when we returned to the UK – but it didn't last long in our colder climate.

When fishing at the top of the highest spring tides I usually found a pod or two of nomadic big tarpon working close in shore. But when one came along – just like my first encounter in the swamp – it was really more by chance and it happened most unexpectedly. One evening I was concentrating my efforts on stingrays using a whole, fresh flying fish (cheaply bought from the markets). I lobbed 50 yards into a gulley between two reefs at Discovery Bay Hotel which was as far as my metal-spooled Penn Delmar would allow with 18lb line without overruns and with just a 1oz bomb to hold the bottom (there are no real tide problems in shore in the Caribbean). Having taken stingrays on this set-up to over 100lbs a few weeks before, I felt confident of beaching almost anything. It was surprising what the average British reverse-taper beach caster (popular at that time due to the lay-back casting technique developed by shore-fishing guru, Leslie Moncrieff, back in the 60s) could handle.

Then I hit into something which ran and ran and ran, and then jumped high into the air. I could see its shape caught by the hotel spotlights which shone out over the bay and at once I knew it was a really big tarpon – perhaps 150lb plus. Unfortunately I never stood a chance with that fish and after just two more jumps I reeled in a frayed 50lb wire trace. So up in strength went the trace wire to 80lb (cabled) and I swapped the Penn Delmar for a Long Beach 67 holding 350 yards of 25lb mono, still keeping my 12 foot reverse-taper 'Dungeness Special'. Being a keen spear fisherman I speared fresh squid and octopus (tarpon delicacies) a few hours before dark and swam out to place them in the sandy gulley for the tarpon to find (little tides, remember). Few other predators would take these free baits except tarpon and stingrays because I fished midway between the two reefs and nuisance fish like moray eels and lobsters rarely left the reefs, even at night. I found the fairly high spring tides most productive (if you can call a rise and fall of around five feet high) and usually at high water, which gave me a depth of about nine feet where the bait was lying, I expected runs!

Perhaps 'run' is the wrong word to use. I know how hard tarpon hit a plug, or a big streamer fly like they use in the Florida Keys, but they pick up a dead bait like it is the only one left in the sea. If you connected your hook to a speedboat you might understand the velocity of the take. Unfortunately you always lose far more than you land. In fact in two and a half years of serious big tarpon fishing from the beach at night I had more than 60 good runs, hooked into about 40 for a few seconds (and occasionally for a little longer) and beached the grand total of three! The best was pushing 100lbs but I lost several fish of twice the size. One such fish caught me off balance as I ran back up the beach to keep in contact as it sped towards the shore. It suddenly changed direction and made for the horizon, dragging me down on to the sand. Can you imagine anybody being towed on his belly through the sand whilst trying frantically to release the drag, with the sickening sight of a 200lb tarpon leaping away on the end of his line some 100 yards away? I soon learned to accept such times as part of the crazy world of tarpon fishing.

Earlier I mentioned stingrays, for which the warm shallow beaches along the west coast of Barbados were a real haven. Although I haven't sought stingrays since I left the West Indies nearly 40 years ago, I was once a stingray fanatic. I am therefore a little puzzled why the British record stingray of 68¼lb has not been increased substantially, as the same species in the Mediterranean reaches weights of around 500lb. I cannot accept that only small stingers frequent our coastal waters and I rather suspect that the main reason for 100lb plus stingrays not being caught is because they are simply not landed. They are most certainly hooked, if all the stories you hear of immovable, unstoppable fish from beach anglers – who had their reels stripped of every yard of line before parting company – are true.

Such encounters are invariably attributed to seals or oversize tope, conger or even sharks. An argument against the presence of large stingrays might be put forward on behalf of the charter and keen off shore boat anglers. They would expect to encounter the odd big one among their usual thornback and tope hauls, especially on the generally heavier gear used for boat work and where running out of line like the shore men is a rare event. However, as stingrays in general prefer quite shallow water over a sandy bottom, which is not the usual boat angler's choice when he leaves harbour, it is hardly surprising that few big rays are taken off shore. Unless of course someone has been keeping very quiet! No, big stingrays are certainly present around our shallow coastlines and I predict that if enough thinking anglers seek them out on gear sound and are man enough to beach something of 70-80lbs plus, the present 68¼lb record could be obliterated.

There are actually two separate species of ray to be caught around British shores although both are considered to be sub-tropical and tropical species. The first, *Dasyatis pastinaca*, is usually called the plain stingray and is the most commonly caught Atlantic stingray. It is of a uniform shape following, if anything, the thornback lines, but in complete contrast to the thornback it is immensely thick in the body (at least twice as thick as any other ray) and has a long, thickish tail. Its back colouring can range from grey-green to brown (depending on the ground over which it is caught) whilst underneath it is a dirty shade of pale grey. There are a few denticles along its mid back travelling towards the tail, and here, halfway along, lies the lethal serrated spine or sting. The *Myliobatis Aquila*, or eagle ray as it is frequently called, differs vastly in its appearance from the plain stingray. This ray has a pronounced hump-shaped head and long triangular wings, which in fact render it almost a miniature copy of the giant manta ray of the family *Mobulidae*. But here the similarity ends, for whilst the manta is a plankton eater, the eagle ray, being true of all stingrays, is a flesh and crustacean muncher. Colouration is generally on the dark side and there are often many lightish flecks or spots over the wings. A tiny dorsal fin is situated at the junction between tail and body and immediately below this protrudes the sting, which is a rather weak affair considering its location compared to most species of stingrays. The tail is very long and quite round, rather like a whip.

The sting, which can cause acute pain accompanied by hallucinations and possibly temporary paralysis, is a hard, porous, stiletto-shape bone projection covered in a dark, jelly-like poisonous secretion. This bevelled spine has mini serrations along both edges which are actually barbs that grow downwards towards the base where it is literally part of the tail. These would make the sting's removal from a victim excruciatingly painful and would cause much flesh-tearing, but the sting itself is rarely left behind. Usually only the poisonous jelly remains.

The truth is that few sea anglers outside Europe really consider fish like congers and rays worth catching. Or rather, I should say the International Game Fishing Association (IGFA), based and organised in the United States, does not consider them game enough. Why anybody worries about claiming records from the IGFA, which is geared just about 100 percent to accepting fish only found off the USA coastline as worthy adversaries and everything else to be just trash fish, amazes me. (British Record Fish Committee, please note: you are not the only record body to be knocked). However there are a few Americans who show a little interest in the stingray. Down in Florida, for instance, where they hunt them across the shallow flats with bow and arrow. Who knows, perhaps they have bow and arrow records for rays! But catching rays by this method has nothing on how a friend of mine once beat one. Have you ever heard of a stingray landed by a Mini-Moke? Then read on.

It was during our stay in Barbados that a friend of mine, George Lyons, an American who owned a scenic waterfront property near Bridgetown, invented a unique way of long-lining stingrays from his patio which overlooked a beautiful clear water shallow bay. Day and night George always had a hand line over the patio wall baited with a whole dead flying-fish for anything that happened along and as the depth alongside the wall was usually between six and eight feet (little tide drop in the Caribbean, remember) almost everything did. We occasionally saw a pair of eyes which we took to be sharks and once a huge manta ray flung itself clear of the surface just 100 yards out from the house. It was at a party round at George's however that I first found out about his craving for hand lining.

A crowd of friends was gathered on the patio in the warm evening air, talking quietly over the local rum cocktails, when all of a sudden the drinks table lurched forward a foot or so and then went careering across the patio and nearly over the wall before there was a loud 'crack' somewhere out in the ocean. George went charging after the runaway table, swearing about losing another ray. This was the point where I joined in the hunt, becoming firm friends with George as soon as I mentioned my mania for catching stingrays from the beach at night, only half a mile down the coast from his beach house.

From that moment on Barbara and I were weekly guests of George in a sort of drinking-cum-stingray-fishing way, and week by week George increased his tackle strength from a 200lb hand line to a huge drum of nylon cord with a breaking strain of 750lb to which was added 20 feet of 500lb cable laid wire and an 8/0 hook, should a fish reach the reef before he could slow it down. For several evenings it seemed that every stingray (attracted to George's bait by a wicker basket full of rotten flying-fish rubby-dubby slung over the wall into the sea) must at some time or another have been hooked and lost. It appeared that even sea fish learn not to repeat their mistakes and the only action for quite a while was my being bitten by a large centipede whilst sitting on the patio wall waiting for a run. Within minutes my left leg started to feel very warm indeed and blew up to at least one-third larger, but George came quickly to the rescue with half a bottle of whisky which he poured over the bite. What a waste! Anyhow it had the desired effect and within a few hours my leg resumed its usual size, so we carried on the long wait. (Incidentally, having been bitten twice by scorpions in India whilst mahseer fishing, its worth mentioning that the bite of a centipede is far more painful. Both, however, are not recommended – believe me.)

George had the most unusual arrangement of bite detection in the form of two empty tin cans tied on the line and resting on the patio wall. (He discarded his table idea after nearly losing it.) Above these were more cans as the line swept upwards over a pulley which was raw-plugged into the wall just below the bedroom window on road level, high above the patio. Then the line ran around another pulley below the adjacent garage and finally disappeared through a drain pipe to be tied to the bumper bar of his Mini-Moke.

This probably sounds like the best cock-and-bull story you have ever heard but I swear that it is all perfectly true. There were several yards of slack line from bait to bumper bar used in the hope that a ray would hook itself and be stopped when it had straightened out the line. Funnily enough George was right, and late one evening the phone rang and an excited voice blurted out that a ray had been landed – or driven perhaps. For when I arrived at George's the following morning after breakfast there, dangling from the garage wall was his first stingray – a female of about 160lb.

A few weeks afterwards while night fishing, I landed an even larger ray – which I estimated at over 200lb – from my favourite sandy beach behind Discovery Bay Hotel. Fortunately it had sucked up the fresh flying-fish bait on my whopper-stopper rod Penn 9/0 reel outfit loaded with 80lb test and it took a good 45 minutes to

SIXTY YEARS A FISHERMAN

subdue. Small wonder a ray of similar size cannot be handled on a standard British beach outfit. Its power was phenomenal, even without any appreciable tide to help. It was so immensely thick, a good 20 inches or more, with a pair of substantial serrated bone stings halfway along its tail, and after a few photos I dragged it back into the-gentle surf. I did in fact hook into a much larger, far more powerful creature one evening but I rather think it was a big shark.

Holiday-makers were known to go skinny dipping at the very spot where I placed my bait (in just five feet of water) once they were full of rum cocktails and in partying mood following a late dinner. They were obviously completely unaware of the dangers. How no one was ever ravaged whilst bathing after dark along the west coast amazes me.

Anyway, I stuck into what I thought initially to be a big ray. This monster whatever it was had not the slightest intention of slowing down against a firmly set clutch with fully 200 yards of line gone from the reel. It never jumped which ruled out a big tarpon, and simply kept on heading out to sea against everything I piled on, in long powerful surges. There was simply no way I could slow it down and I guess the end was inevitable. When it reached the first large coral reef with over a quarter of a mile of 80lb line on the 9/0 now gone and just a few turns remaining, two things happened in quick succession. The hardwood rod handle snapped just below the reel and a split second later (otherwise I would have lost the lot and been left with a stump) the 80lb monofilament severed over the reef. The word 'awesome' simply cannot describe the power of that huge fish which could only have been a very large shark – probably a tiger shark, the predominant big boys throughout the West Indies.

There is a rather gruesome postscript to this encounter which came about through my love of spear fishing along the west coast. In fact there was hardly a day for the best part of three years when I didn't spend at least two or three hours exploring the colourful coral reefs either directly in front of our cottage or out from the Holiday Inn Hotel near Bridgetown, where I ran the hairdressing salon. Apart from the occasional local client there was little to do until around three in the afternoon when the ladies started to leave the beach or pool and have their hair done in readiness for the evening entertainment. So Wilson made the most of the best job he had ever had by skin-diving and returning with spear-caught squid, octopus and lobsters.

I made the mistake of spearing a big stingray once, which actually towed me for some distance over the reefs into a deep blue void. So discretion being the better part of valour, I let go of the spear gun. On another occasion, probably the closest shave of all – and I have experienced a few – I nearly drowned through spearing a big moray eel that lived in a huge clump of brain coral. Unfortunately the spear went through both eel and coral and so I dived down to unscrew the removable head

in order to pull the shaft free. Trouble was I needed to come up for a gulp of air midway through due to the tight fitting spear head. However when my head was within just a foot or so of the surface, my ascent was stopped abruptly. Looking down I could see that the strong nylon cord connecting spear gun to the eel and clump of brain coral had somehow knotted around one ankle. I carried no knife then, so at the point when my lungs were about to burst, and craving for air, I had to exhale and dive down to undo it. The very next day I went out and purchased the best diving knife I could find.

One of my regular diving companions was a local Bajan of around my own age called Frank who worked as maitre d' at Discovery Bay Hotel where Barbara ran the hairdressers. He was so fit he could free dive and sit on a clump of coral 15 to 20 feet down on the sea floor and actually wait for up to a minute for a grouper or parrotfish to come out of its hole, while I trod water above wondering how on earth he could hold his breath for so long. When diving alone Frank's little terrier would follow him along the beach as he methodically worked his way through various routes in the never-ending maze of coral reefs, spearing rock hind, trigger fish, lobsters and octopus for the pot.

Then one afternoon, only two days after I had lost the huge shark and just an hour or so before Frank was due to put on his tuxedo for the evening's restaurant duties, he did not return when expected. His wife went down to the beach and found their terrier standing rooted to the spot, looking out to sea and whining continually.

At this point I must say there was another factor to consider. A lot of quarrying was done on the island to produce blocks of white coral stone for building, and as a result far too many people had access to explosives. It was common knowledge that indiscriminate poachers used explosives to obtain basketfuls of marketable reef fishes. In fact in shore sport with sizeable reef fishes was virtually non-existent all along the west coast due to years of constant dynamiting – hence my preferring to fish after dark when big fish ventured close into shore. Today incidentally, I'm told that around Barbados, there is no fishing allowed for one mile from the beach.

Was the fact that Frank could stay so long underwater the very cause of his disappearance at the hands of indiscriminate fish poachers? They might have thought the area was clear of witnesses when they threw in their detonators. And if so, surely they must then have concealed the body. I have already mentioned that there is little tide flow in shore on the west coast, so a body would not drift far overnight. Then again had Frank been unlucky enough to meet the same marauding shark which (as I was later to find out) had been spotted on several occasions within that same week? It was skirting the reefs between Sandy Lane Hotel and the Colony Club – a distance of only a few miles.

By the following morning everyone in the hotel business was aware of Frank's disappearance, and there was soon a police launch from Bridgetown patrolling up and down the west coast. As I knew Frank's route along the local reefs better than anyone I eventually persuaded Trevor, assistant manager to Mike Beckley at Discovery Bay Hotel, to accompany me on a wide search of the area as the police launch had come up with nothing.

Now I am not by any means over glorifying the situation but once we were out there, several hundred yards off shore in water so deep you could hardly make out the coral on the bottom, we were absolutely terrified – we felt completely vulnerable to attack. We only had my one spear gun, a powerful three rubber champion model, but it was no match for a man-eating shark. Initially we covered every route in shore through a network of coral reefs that Frank might have taken. Then we ventured seawards over depths of 50 to 60 feet, but all to no avail.

The idea of suddenly coming upon a friend's dismembered body is bad enough, but when you think you could well be the next victim, your nerves get the better of you – believe me. Boy was I glad when we eventually entered shallow warm water again after two hours of searching. But just before I pulled off my face mask I saw a head rolling about on the sand in the little furrows made by the waves. For a minute I thought I was going to be sick, and then reality sank in. It was only a doll's head, and it had blue eyes and blonde hair – nothing at all like Frank! Everything appears around one-third larger than it actually is when viewed through the glass of a diving mask, so for a split second my heart was in my mouth.

I am sad to say there is no happy conclusion to this story, but the incident was hushed up so the tourists didn't become alarmed. Immediately following Frank's disappearance six of us got together for a 'retribution fish in'. We decided to stage an all-night vigil from a 30 foot yacht owned by one of the hotel managers, moored in 40 feet of water 100 yards off shore from the Colony Club, in the hope of contacting the rogue shark. We rowed out in the yacht's tiny plywood dinghy late in the afternoon complete with my big game outfit, extra-strong commercial long lines, several gallons of fresh blood, compliments of Bill the chef at Discovery Bay, and enough food and booze – obligatory in the Caribbean – to last until dawn.

Little happened during the night, other than everybody getting paralytic, and by two o'clock in the morning, having caught nothing but snappers on our light outfits, with not a murmur coming from the shark baits, general opinion was for us to call it a night seeing as all the booze and food were gone. Then the reality of the situation dawned upon us. With so much blood around the anchored yacht, to risk the six of us paddling back in a tiny dinghy with just a few inches of free board was not such a good idea. So we stayed until dawn. The shark was never seen again and neither, I am saddened to say, was my friend Frank. Some said he had just left everything and gone to live on another island. But with the financial security that his job provided, plus a lovely wife and a young son whom he adored, it was most unlikely and completely out of character. In fact nothing of what happened that afternoon ever surfaced, right up until we left the island a year or so later, but I'm convinced a big tiger shark was responsible for Frank's disappearance.

Strangely, something occurred several months later which got me thinking how vulnerable you are when snorkelling alone. A whole group of hairdressers, hotel managers and chefs were larking about on the east coast near Bathsheba on a Sunday, using foam boards to body surf in the strong waves, having taken a barbecue along for the day. I was standing waist deep and laughing at someone falling off their board when suddenly I couldn't breathe. I could neither inhale nor exhale. It was as though my throat was paralysed. I indicated to Barbara to bang my back which she did and eventually, not long before I passed out, I was able to cough, be sick and breathe again. Now, had this freak occurrence happened whilst snorkelling over deep water bingo! It would have been a case of 'goodnight nurse'. So I went along to my doctor who said that just a single drop of water had hit the tip of my larynx and literally paralysed it. And if it ever happens to 'you' while swimming, get your feet on to firm ground immediately.

In addition to my lunchtime spear fishing jaunts and at least one weekly night-time fishing vigil from the beach after stingrays and tarpon, I crewed each Thursday on my afternoon off aboard a 42 foot sports fishing boat owned by an ex-pat, Charles Angelus, who had settled in Barbados many years before and opened a furniture factory near Bridgetown.

We trolled up and down the west coast following the outer reefs using drone spoons on monel metal line (horrible stuff to fish with but it got the lure down fast and kept it there) in depths of 40 to 60 feet and took some good hauls of jacks, plus barracudas and the occasional Wahoo. On several occasions we hooked sailfish (and once a small marlin) on flying-fish presented away from the boat on outriggers but for various reasons we never landed any. In fact it was always a joke at parties that Wilson seemed to catch bigger fish from the beach than when out in Charles' expensively imported sports fishing cruiser. And the truth was they were right!

Incidentally, here's a simple, extremely 'tasty' treatment for frying one inch thick cutlets of round (in cross section) pelagic saltwater species like Barracuda and Wahoo etc, as used in Barbados, called 'Bajan' fried fish. But there is no reason not to enjoy coldwater species such as cod, bass, coalfish or pollack, or even freshwater fish such as pike and especially zander, prepared and fried in the same way.

ABOVE
The late Charles Angelus, on whose sports fishing boat I crewed once a week, with a hard battling blackjack caught trolling along the west coast of Barbados.

Start by gutting and de-scaling a large fish. Remove the head and tail, including the tail root and narrow part of the body. Then carefully cut the fish into inch-thick cutlets. Place the cutlets in a large shallow dish and squeeze in enough juice from fresh limes (you will need somewhere between 12-20) to a depth of half the cutlets. After an hour, turn the cutlets over and leave for a further hour. This process not only par-cooks the flesh and turns it from pink to white, but also dries it in texture.

Remove the cutlets and carefully dry off upon kitchen paper. Now make two or three deep cuts on each side of the cutlets and gently fill with finely chopped onion. Heavily sprinkle both sides with, coarse, freshly ground black pepper, and a little salt, and then lightly dust with corn flour before frying for four to five minutes on each side in hot oil. The resulting taste is delicious, although some prefer to add a little 'hot pepper' sauce.

Daily life on the island at the end of the swinging 60s was, I suppose, as close as you could get to the perfect existence. By then Barbados had the best infrastructure of all the Caribbean islands. It was the place to be seen. We ate extremely well and drank a great deal, we played hard and we received invites to all the best parties going. Hosts usually incorporated grass into some of the dishes, so we couldn't help having a great time, and quite often various celebrities of the day would show up. These included people like the late Natalie Wood, and the late Oliver Reed, plus David Bailey, who at that time was producing some unusual photography for *Vogue* and *Tatler* magazines with the help of an equally unusual-looking model, Penelope Tree. Being fashion hair stylists, Barbara and I were in the thick of it and enjoying our life tremendously. Barbados then was indeed the up-and-coming island, still with an old fashioned charm all of its own. It is certainly different today.

A Tropical Start

After a while we thought about starting a family and began looking at life on the island of Barbados as a permanent thing. Returning to the cold winters of Britain was not appealing at all, though eventually, and it seems strange now, I know, heading up towards when we finally left, I used to crave a pint of cold milk (no fresh milk on the island) and really missed the seasons.

With her first pregnancy Barbara unfortunately miscarried at five months. However after much rest, life carried on and a year later on 28 October 1970, our son, Lee Stephen Wilson, was born. I still remember sitting up all night in the waiting room listening to the wailing and screams of several dozen local women (I was the only husband there) until one of the nurses suggested I rest on a spare bed until they called me.

At sometime between three and four in the morning I was woken up, told to put on a green gown and face mask and led into the delivery room. My instant reaction was 'I don't want to be here'. Ultimately the whole experience was, and remains, one of the most wonderful moments in my life.

With a family now started Barbara and I were considering investing in a plot of land and having a house built, preferably on the beach overlooking the sea, just like our little rented cottage. Our boss, John Stuart, had hinted he would like us to think about a partnership, and our future on the island seemed to have a ring of permanency about it. But within a short space of time two events were to change the way we felt about settling down in paradise.

The first was when I picked up the phone in the salon one morning to take what I thought was a hairdressing appointment. The male caller said, 'Is that John Wilson?' and I replied 'Yes'. He then said in a flat tone, 'I'm going to put a bullet through your head' and then put the phone down. Instantly the hairs on the back of my neck stood up and that cold sweat feeling of fear came over me. It obviously wasn't a joke and I discussed the situation with John Stuart who immediately called the police. Following a few sleepless nights and days of constantly looking over my shoulder, the call was traced back by the police to the disgruntled boyfriend of one of our female staff, a girl whom I had had the displeasure of sacking only a couple of weeks before because she was stealing.

This event quickly blew over however and life returned to normal. But then something happened which instantly made our minds up about returning to Britain and deciding against raising our family in Barbados, no matter how idyllic life appeared to the holiday-maker. John and Veronica Stuart who owned a superb property on Bamboo Ridge, near Holetown, along with other beautifully designed ex-pat homes, asked Barbara and me if we would move into their house for a few weeks and look after it while they went back to Britain on holiday – which we agreed to do. What they forgot to tell us was that this would be the only occupied house in the entire group of several luxurious designer properties during their absence, everyone having gone back to Britain for their summer holidays whilst trade in their island boutiques, hairdressers and hotels was extremely quiet.

On the second night after moving in, just when we were starting to enjoy the facilities provided by John's cook, Viola, and a house girl who came in for a few hours each day, I suddenly noticed through the dense canopy of trees surrounding the house that the courtesy light in one of the cars had come on. Now I don't know why, but I instinctively felt very uneasy. It was pitch black outside and Barbara and I were in the master bedroom (where John Stuart's safe was installed) which, like all the other spacious rooms, was independent of the lounge and kitchen, being secured with louvre doors and connected only by gravel pathways and mock Spanish wooden screen work, densely overgrown with tropical palms and vines.

As no one ever locked their cars on the islands (the furthest a thief could go was 25 miles) I wasn't worried about the car being stolen but word had obviously been passed around – possibly via one of the house servants – that we were alone with all the week's takings from the hairdressing salons and boutiques in the house. Quickly I locked the four louvre doors and then the phone rang. Barbara answered and by the look on her face it was an obscene caller – who wouldn't hang up. This was obviously a ploy to keep us occupied because while Barbara was lying back on the bed trembling with fear and totally incoherent, I could make out the noise of several feet walking around the bedroom towards the louvre doors. I tried slapping Barbara's face to bring her back to reality but it was no use. I picked up the phone and could understand why she had entered into a nervous stupor. The guy at the other end had no intention of stopping his foul-mouth intentions nor of putting the phone down which would allow me to ring the police. I was on my own. I even feel shivery now, over 35 years on from that night, just writing about it.

I sat on the end of the large double bed sick with fear, tingling with pure adrenaline with my powerful three rubber champion spear gun loaded. What was going round in my head at that point was that I was going to take the first bastard out regardless, knowing full well that afterwards I could have been killed and Barbara most certainly raped, not to mention what could have happened to our newborn son, Lee, who was fast asleep in his cot. For what seemed like an eternity, though it could have been no more than a minute or so – during which time I could see in the light from the patio eyes peering up at me through the lower half of those

SIXTY YEARS A FISHERMAN

LEFT

Barbara and baby son, Lee, beside the rugged east coast of Barbados, near Bathsheba, where the full force of the Atlantic Ocean provides marvellous surfing and shore casting.

flimsy louvre doors – it was as though our idyllic world stood still. I could hear much shuffling about and low murmuring whispers but I couldn't make out what they were saying. I expected the doors to be kicked in at any moment. And then, as if by some miracle, the dark menacing figures melted slowly away into the humid night air and we were left with just the sound of the crickets. Perhaps they saw my spear gun and didn't fancy four feet of quarter inch steel through their gut after all. I tried the phone again. Now it was free and within minutes we saw the headlights of two police cars racing up Bamboo Ridge towards the house.

Whoever they were, they were never caught. But they convinced me of one thing – that we should return to England. Barbara and I, together with our son, Lee, now just six months old, were going home. Consequently it wasn't long before I wrote to John (Jinx) Davey back in East Anglia (I had kept in touch with him throughout my years abroad both in the Merchant Navy and whilst in the West Indies) asking him to send me the local Norfolk and Suffolk newspapers. Barbara and I had discussed whether we should sink our savings into a hairdressing salon when we returned home, or a fishing tackle shop which had been my life's ambition. As Barbara would be restricted at home for some while (we wanted more children) and I really didn't fancy being a hairdresser for much longer, a tackle shop it was – preferably somewhere in Norfolk where property was still affordable and where I had enjoyed such wonderful roach fishing during my late teens.

Week after week of thumbing through Norfolk and Suffolk papers, kindly sent out by Jinx, produced just one possibility: an old existing tackle shop in Bridewell Alley in the middle of Norwich, run for 30 years by the late Bill Cooper. Unfortunately it had also been run right down and there was little stock left because Bill was about to lease it out (he owned the freehold) to a delicatessen. This transaction could only be halted by my cheque to put down a deposit by post from Barbados. Bill, bless him, obviously wanted it to remain a tackle shop and I figured that he couldn't have been losing money for 30 years. So off went the cheque and we booked our flight home. We had purchased our first business site, unseen. I wouldn't want to do that now, but I was just 28, and the thought of failure didn't even enter my mind.

During those last few weeks prior to our leaving the island, many of our friends made during the previous three years wanted to take us out for farewell dinners. The trouble was I suddenly started to suffer chronic stomach pains and so we could not take anyone up on their kindness. My doctor said it was nerves. I thought it was far more serious than that, but he was obviously right because once on the plane I suffered no more.

John and Veronica Stuart, who had been both employers and wonderful friends, came round to the cottage early on the morning of our departure with a gift of a cine camera. I still have the footage John shot of my last walk along the beach dipping six month old Lee in and out of the waves. Many years have passed since that walk and now he's getting on for 40 years of age six foot two inches tall and 15 stone of muscle, due to his sport of bodybuilding.

I can remember our homecoming extremely well for two reasons. We were met by Mum, Dad and brother Dave, at Heathrow and I asked to drive Dad's Morris Traveller home. It promptly stuck in first gear at the first set of traffic lights. 'What did you rest your hand on the lever for?' said Dad, as if I was to know about his car's peculiarities! So we drove the entire way home to Enfield, in north London, in first gear. How strange it was to be back in the old country again. The first thing I did at Mum and Dad's was down two pints of milk straight from the fridge.

The second event came two days later when, having purchased a second-hand Mini van, Barbara and I drove to Norwich. As we walked slowly up Bridewell Alley the shops seemed to be getting narrower and narrower. And there it was, Bill Cooper's, (or rather our) tackle shop. It was the width of a London cigarette kiosk. It was tiny. I think, had we not put money down, we would have happily walked away there and then, but while we were wondering what we had let ourselves in for, Bill's wife, Terry, came from behind the counter and said, 'You must be John and Barbara Wilson.' She put the kettle on and in a very short space of time, judging by the number of customers asking to purchase items which weren't in stock; I realised that we were going to be able to make a success of it. If you stood in the middle of the incredibly narrow sales area (which is now a wine shop) and stretched out both arms, you could touch both walls, honestly. But it was our first

SIXTY YEARS A FISHERMAN

stab at the retail trade and I was going to make it work, though what happened when we took over the shop two weeks later made me wish I had never got involved. After paying the deposit of a month's rent on a small terraced cottage along the Aylsham Road (which is now Smarts Auto Parts), we had slightly less than £2000 left to purchase the goodwill and what stock Bill had left, which was not a lot. To say money was tight was indeed an understatement. In fact, during those first few months, I can remember actually covering a dozen of the tall, round maggot tins with wallpaper to form supports for chipboard (also covered in wallpaper) to make bookshelves for an alcove in our cottage.

So now for my favourite maggot story. Late Friday afternoon before our first Saturday of business, I took delivery of 16 gallons of both coloured and white maggots in sawdust. Bill said I probably didn't need anywhere near that many but the last thing I wanted in a new business was to refuse custom. So they were all taken out back to the coolness of a stone floor where Bill said they should be fine until the morning (he only had a small fridge anyway). OK, so I know it was the first week in July and I should have known better, but I didn't. Next morning I arrived early at the shop – now called John's Tackle Den – at around half past eight and eagerly unlocked the door in readiness for what I hoped would be a busy Saturday. I immediately caught sight of a couple of maggots on the floor as I switched the light on, followed by another and another as I walked through the shop. Before I had time to go out the back to see if many more had escaped there was a loud banging on the thinly partitioned wall and an angry voice from the barber's shop next door.

Bill, the barber, had seemed such an amiable fellow when Bill Cooper introduced me to him only a few days earlier, but as I opened his front door he was like a man possessed. 'Look at this place,' he screamed at the top of his voice. 'I've never had anything like this before. I'm getting the public health people in to sort you out.' Great, I thought, though he did have a point. There were maggots everywhere – big time. In fact probably the greater part of my 16 gallons were now the wrong side of the partitioned wall which was constructed from tongue-and-groove planking. (Apparently the two shops had been one many years back and the carpenter hadn't been too bothered about ensuring a tight fit with the floor).

There were maggots in Bill's soap dishes, in his gowns and towels, in his shaving mugs and between magazines. They were coming out of his shampoo nozzle and the floor was one seething, wriggling carpet of white, red and yellow. (Bronze maggots weren't popular as yet). As maggots always travel towards the light and Bill had left a bulb on overnight, he virtually had the lot. I rushed back into my shop and ran outside to the 16 tins. All were empty save for foul-smelling froth all down the sides, proving conclusively that maggots can easily climb vertical sides once they start to sweat in their own juices. Talk about a stink of ammonia!

Fortunately I managed to calm Bill down after a while and stop him from ringing the environmental health people. I think the mention of a free rod and reel did the trick (him being an angler too) and I set about the task with dustpan and brush of reclaiming my maggots. I actually recovered less than half of the 16 gallons, and boy, were there some wonderful hatches over the following weeks.

Only a few weeks after this Bill Cooper popped into the shop to see how I was getting on and to collect some old things he had left in the shop's attic. 'Terry's asked me to take her mother's china home,' said Bill and without more ado climbed the narrow stairs. Now I just knew there was going to be a problem because during the weeks in between, friend Jinx had come up to Norwich to look over the shop. While rummaging through a load of junk in the attic (which I had naturally assumed was mine to dispose of), we came across a stack of old blue patterned plates and jugs. Jinx asked if he could have them for his front garden wall, a mammoth project started by his father: two feet thick and completely fronting their large roadside property in Bungay (friends actually referred to it as the Bungay Wall). This eight foot high wall incorporated all sorts of strange building materials such as flowerpots, pipes, sinks, even old loos, and crockery. Once it was grown over by rockery plants like aubrietia etc, it looked attractively different.

Bill came almost running down the stairs with a look of horror on his face. 'Where's all that china gone to, John? It was in that old galvanised bath. It belonged to Terry's mother and it's priceless.' 'Oh dear,' I said, 'I am afraid it's now in the Bungay Wall.' Bill, I am afraid, never really saw the funny side of the story. Nevertheless his influence and good will of running the shop in Norwich for three

decades were of enormous help in those early years. I never guessed then, however, that I would be a tackle dealer for almost as long.

With the help of a few friends, I organised a kids' fishing match along the River Wensum in the middle of Norwich, and with just a couple of small ads in the local paper, I arrived at Foundry Road bridge opposite the railway station to find over 200 young anglers eagerly awaiting the match. How I wish it could be the same today. But with the wealth of televised and computerised distractions at their disposal, small wonder only a small proportion of today's youngsters get to experience the joy of angling, which is rather sad.

With every penny ploughed back into stock (so extensive advertising was out) I set about making a name for myself by catching specimen fish, which I hoped would draw fresh custom into the shop. I revisited many parts of my old stomping ground along the intimate, roach-rich parts of the Upper Waveney around Bungay that were so productive during the late 1950s. I hoped that things hadn't changed too much and I was excited at the prospect of using light float-fishing tackle again. I was disappointed to find that certain favourite swims had visibly shrunk in both width and depth, as I have described earlier, but others were thankfully as prolific as ever. I quickly familiarised myself with the bream again along the two mile reach between Wainford Maltings and Ellingham, taking some fine hauls with specimens to over 7lbs – big bream in those days.

By walking the Waveney's clear-flowing upper reaches extensively that first summer we were back and searching for roach shoals through Polaroid glasses, I was able to pinpoint the whereabouts of numerous shoals of quality fish, each of which contained specimens to over 2lbs. I then set about catching them on trotting tackle during the winter months, capturing several beauties, the best scaling 2lb 7oz. This opened up opportunities of writing about my exploits both in the local paper, the *Eastern Evening News*, and in the *Angler's Mail*, which had in fact published a story I sent whilst in Barbados called 'Stingrays in the Moonlight'.

At around the same time, Jarrold Publishing, which is based in Norwich, enquired whether I should like to bring up to date a 'where to fish guide' written by Bill Cooper and now hopelessly out of date. I agreed on the condition that I would write a totally new book complete with photos and diagrams. So that's how a Londoner came to write his first book with the imaginative title *Where to Fish in Norfolk and Suffolk*. I really worked at that book. At weekends and before opening the shop, I visited and photographed everywhere I wrote about. I literally walked all the upper reaches of my local rivers – the Tas, Tud, Wensum, Yare, Bure and Waveney – from source to their tidal reaches and fished as many meres, lakes, gravel pits and Broads as I could. I wore Barbara's patience and tolerance down to the bone, often leaving her and young Lee alone for long periods each Sunday in order to gather the information required for the book. Friends like Bill Cooper and Nobby Clarke of Norwich, now both sadly gone, and my old mate, Terry Houseago of Gressinghall, helped enormously on local issues and, when seeking details about fisheries deep in Suffolk, George Alderson and the late Len Head came to the rescue in addition to Jinx Davey.

Eventually many local anglers, who had probably jeered behind my back when I first arrived on the scene, started coming into the shop and asked me where to fish. I felt that I had indeed arrived. That same book has now been in print for 34 years. It has been updated and reprinted no less than seven times. It must be one of the longest surviving angling books in the UK.

Once settled in Norfolk, with the shop doing well, we managed to obtain a house mortgage. I borrowed the deposit off Dad, and Barbara and I left the cottage for our own property, a detached three-bedroom bungalow (costing just £6500,

RIGHT
Start 'em young, that's what I say. A (1999) photo of my daughter, Lisa, and granddaughter, Alisha, and me, enjoying the rudd fishing on our own lakes in Norfolk.

SIXTY YEARS A FISHERMAN

which seems ridiculous now) in Taverham, a nice little village on the point of expanding (it has now fully exploded) on the outskirts of Norwich, just six miles west of the city.

Within a year of enjoying my own house at last, with a garden in which I quickly built a pond, Barbara gave birth to our daughter, Lisa. She grew up to become more interested in going fishing with Dad than Lee. Now over 30 years on I take great pride in taking her own daughters fishing. In fact my two 13 and four year-old granddaughters, Alisha and Lana are even more fascinated by water than their mother. So unless either of my children eventually produce a grandson to continue the craze, I'll put all my bets on them. With just a little help from Granddad, Alisha for instance has already caught numerous small roach and rudd, plus the odd double figure carp on float tackle from our own lakes. She is absolutely mustard.

Unfortunately I made the cardinal mistake when taking young Lee fishing in allowing him to catch the specimen-size roach, bream and tench that I was enjoying at that time. So he virtually bypassed that bent-pin-cum-mystery stage in which I served my apprenticeship amidst the park lakes and brooks of north London. With Dad, Lee, for instance, actually struck and landed, single-handedly, tench to almost 6lbs when only six years old. That was a big tench back in the mid 1970s. I should have weaned him on sticklebacks and 2oz roach. But so it goes.

It was around this time, the mid 1970s, that another interest became important to me. Allow me to refer back to Barbados for a moment, because it was there that I first became interested in taxidermy. This came about through my spearing really large puffer fish and handing them over to an old lady in the village for preserving. This she did simply by making a slit from throat to vent, removing the insides which, considering their size (between 16 and 24 inches long) amounted to just a handful of guts, and stitching them up again. She then made a cardboard funnel and filled the entire puffer fish up with dry sand through its mouth. This stretched the puffer out to the expanded size it reaches as a defence mechanism against predators. Finally the entire sand-filled fish was sprayed with formalin, to preserve and harden the skin, and hung out in the sun to dry.

About a week or so later the sun had done its work and the sand could be emptied out. And hey presto – you had a unique lampshade complete with puffer fish prickles fully erect. It was taxidermy at its most basic but I was intrigued and bought a book on the ancient art. This resulted in my buying a few of the basic chemicals required and actually setting up some of the weird and wonderful fishes I speared over the coral reefs. These I brought back to the UK and arranged in a display case along with pieces of coloured coral (from Fiji, collected during my two years on SS *Oronsay*) and various sea fans, shells and sea urchins. The arrangement is a wonderful reminder of those exciting three years skin diving the reefs along the west coast of Barbados.

I was so pleased with the result of my Caribbean display that I decided to have a go at freshwater species, my first attempt being a 7lb zander. This was followed by a pike, then a carp from Redmire that was found dead. I later restored a big pike found virtually falling to bits in someone's damp garage, originally preserved by the famous firm, Gunns of Norwich, followed by a brace of unwanted grayling from a chalk stream trout fishery and then a couple of 2½lb perch which died through being hooked in deep water. These I found three days after catching and releasing them back into a large clay pit near Newmarket. Had I not returned and come across them dead in the margins I would have sworn they were released none the worse for being caught. I was so concerned that I rang the late Dick Walker, whose catches from the depths of Arlesey Lake during the 1950s were legendary, and asked him if he had ever noticed repeat catches, before sport with the big stripies inexplicably dropped off after just a couple of productive seasons. Dick said no, and hinted that he too suspected many he returned could have suffered what scuba divers know as the bends. The fish have excess air in their swim bladder that cannot escape and which can lead to their death unless they are taken immediately back down to the depth at which they were caught.

In recent years I have experienced similar problems with the huge Nile perch inhabiting Lake Nasser in Egypt, where certain fish hooked on the troll in depths of 30 feet or more have 'blown', or 'gassed up', to quote the phrase best used to describe their problem. Using a heavy weight to lower these monsters back down to somewhere approaching the depth at which they were holding has achieved a high success rate, incidentally. Quite how you get big British perch back out into the middle of a deep clay or gravel pit without the use of a boat is another

problem. I guess it can only be solved by not fishing for them at great depths in the first place. This brings me back full circle to the brace of perch which I decided to preserve so they were not entirely wasted.

Not for one moment am I suggesting in today's world of catch and release that specimen fish should be killed to be stuffed. There are precious few whoppers to go round as it is. A colour photo on the wall can provide equal memories, and the fish like it better too.

However as jumbo-size rainbow and brown trout are now bred in such vast quantities to be caught and killed for the table, no one is going to give you a hard time for preserving the skin of a particularly large or beautifully marked specimen as an art form. Similarly should you come across a well-proportioned, freshly dead specimen of any species that has died through natural causes (everything has to die at some time) what's the harm in having a go at preserving it for others to enjoy? There are several specialist books available covering the fascinating art of taxidermy, and it's surprising just how quickly these new skills can be acquired, particularly for those who are artistically minded and enjoy modelling or painting.

The last fish I preserved was a monstrous 39½lb pike caught locally in the village of Lyng from a then gravel pit trout fishery (now a carp fishery) by an old friend, Dan Leary. I didn't really want to take on the responsibility of such a magnificent specimen but Dan talked me into it nevertheless. Two years later, following goodness knows how many hours of painstaking work, particularly in colouring and constructing the bow-fronted glass case, I felt rather proud finally presenting Dan with his trophy. But it's not something I want to take on ever again.

Around 1973-74 I started writing for the prestigious *Angling* magazine edited by Brian Harris, which was later sold to Burlington Publishing to become *Coarse Fishing Monthly*, edited by Sandy Leventon and Bruce Vaughan. Since then Bruce has been one of my best fishing buddies. The same magazine was then sold on to Emap and became *The Coarse Fishing Handbook*, then later *Coarse Fishing Today*. All in all I survived too many editors to name and ended up writing for more or less the same publication (despite its four different titles) for over 20 years when Emap finally stopped the last title in the early 1990s.

But back to those early *Angling* days. The magazine was much loved by traditionalist anglers such as me who enjoyed all three disciplines of game, sea and coarse, plus fishing in foreign parts. In fact some of what I have already mentioned about my exploits in the tropics with stingrays and tarpon appeared within the pages of *Angling*, plus my experiences when scuba diving my local lakes, gravel pits and rivers. Though I had skin dived virtually every day whilst in Barbados, I had in fact never scuba dived before. Then one day Sid Johnson popped into John's Tackle Den to buy a new float rod and happened to ask if I fancied joining him diving for bottles in a few of the local mill pools. Being a commercial diver in the North Sea, Sid was a great teacher and I soon became fascinated by being able to appreciate many of my local clear water fisheries from a sub-surface viewpoint.

Sid and I quickly became firm friends, as we are to this day, and we dived regularly together during the summer months for over 10 years. Initially I borrowed one of his old neoprene wet suits, but once the bug had got a hold I bought my own singlephase demand valve, an aluminium bottle and a lead belt. I even decided to make my own wet suit.

A company in Southampton specialised in DIY wet suits made from top-quality 6mm neoprene and cut the required pieces exactly to fit, once body dimensions

had been measured and sent off. All I had to do when a parcel full of numbered pieces arrived two weeks later was glue them all together and then glue yellow tape over and along each join. Everything was provided including several heavy duty zips plus a large screw-top tin of black, evil-smelling adhesive. I can remember Barbara saying, 'You're not going to do that in the middle of the carpet are you?' But I was. Besides, I had spread several old newspapers all around the lounge over which I laid all the numbered parts. It was kind of like painting by numbers really and I soon had my new wet suit resplendent with a rich red lining taking shape. You simply butted the two edges together after coating them in adhesive and then left them for a minute until almost dry. Then you couldn't pull them apart. I took great care in assembling the wet suit and finally adding the yellow (easy to see under water) tape over each join.

I was almost on the home straight with just a few lengths of yellow tape left to glue on, when I accidentally knocked over the tin of adhesive. I looked round in horror to see a football-size patch of black Evo-Stik slowly spreading out even further over the gold-coloured carpet. Barbara was not a happy bunny.

With my new DIY wet suit complete, and not a bad fit, I was raring to go. As a specimen hunter opting then to study the quarry from beneath the surface whilst scuba diving in addition to bank side fish spotting, I was often asked how diving could help to catch more and larger fish. The obvious answer, of course, was that within a short dive it's possible to assess the potential of most small waters fairly accurately, providing visibility is good. However seeing and even being able to

My diving buddy, Sid Johnson (right), and me in the mid 1970s preparing to scuba dive the River Wensum at Costessey Mill Pool near Norwich, in search of earthenware bottles, and to play with the barbel.

touch, say, a 3lb roach in the water bears no comparison with putting that same fish on the bank via a baited hook. Yet many people are under the impression that if you have located a big fish under the surface, catching it is a mere formality. I wish!

Actually I was often amazed whilst diving a section of river which, from bank side experiences, I thought I knew well, that there were far fewer fish around than I had imagined. This is a common occurrence; because we all prefer to believe there are far more, and far larger, fish in a water than have ever come out of it on rod and line. It's part of our inherent eternal optimism as anglers. Yet it's surprising how much water (and this applies to most fisheries) is, for the most part, totally barren of fish. We nearly always assume fish are 'off' the feed when a bite less session occurs but the reality is that they are often simply just not there. Miniature, shallow, weedy rivers are probably among the few exceptions and, to the square foot of water, invariably contain a larger proportion of specimen fish than any other type of water.

After diving dozens of my favourite swims at varying times throughout a period of over 10 years I was surprised on just a very few occasions. The surprises were usually fish which shouldn't have been there, like a double-figure brown trout in a pike hot spot, perhaps finding plenty of crayfish in a tidal river, or the sheer number of eels in a big weir pool which would reach a bait long before the tiny percentage of specimens present. This was a real eye-opener which swayed my attention from rivers as potential big eel locations.

Understanding the fish's silent underwater world from its own point of view with regard to fluctuations of water flow, displacement of silt throughout the year, gravel bars, weeds, snags and predators is the reward when diving. Furthermore you can choose angling tactics accordingly and decide where a bait should be placed for optimum results.

When seen from the bank side, surface movement – especially that of running water where much of my diving was done – can be very misleading. You may often pass by a boiling or turbulent swim, such as weir hatches and sluices, and overshoot pools, simply because the surface deviations suggest the current is far too powerful to hold fish or to present the tackle easily. Yet immediately you dive a few feet below the 'white water' visibility increases and in nearly all cases – particularly if there is a goodish depth below – the current is quite slow, providing a larder for both the fish and the food they eat. With a little more forethought all but the most turbulent of swims may be fished, provided you present enough line over-depth to allow the bait and lead to rest on the bottom of the hole, while the float (capped top and bottom) lies flat and sways alongside and within inches of the bank – stret-pegging style.

Fishing 12 feet deep in a five foot hole may seem out of the question, but for the float man it is the way to succeed in turbulent water, for a float will create that valuable 'slack', particularly when fishing directly downstream – something the ledger cannot do. Even non-turbulent, purely fast water glides, requiring several swan shot to float fish, are so much slower close to the river bed. Here lies the reason why excessively light tackle so often fails in such a swim: the bait is whisked away along the bottom, much faster than the loose feed around it, whereas the heavier float and lead allows the bait a more natural passage. I often think that if anglers could only see their terminal tackle in action below the surface they would pay much more attention to its design and be more inclined to experiment if bites were not forthcoming.

All anglers appreciate the advantages of having that all-important tinge of colour to the water prior to fishing. To the diver, of course, it works in reverse and I always hoped for good visibility whenever I dived. I was often amazed, however, just how clear beneath the surface even apparently quite coloured water actually is. Even in near flood water conditions, given a fairly bright day, the diver has some 18 inches of good visibility. This being the case, the fish must have it too and so are quite capable of seeing, for instance, the bait, line and shot, or an angler walking too close along the banks of a flooded river. The angler, remember, is looking down into darkness whereas the fish is looking up into brightness.

A phenomenon I sometimes encountered, particularly in the summer time and especially in tidal rivers, was that at the point of entry the river appeared heavily coloured and until I neared the bottom it was, but the last two feet down to the bottom were curiously really clear. Silt washed up by water craft, for example, appears suspended in the warmer upper water layers. For the angler this means problems if he has geared his tackle and tactics to the apparent colour of the water he can see. This is indeed a point well worth remembering.

Now on to monofilament lines which, despite the makers' claims to the contrary, are seen only too easily by our quarry. Even to my eyes a 5lb line looks like a hawser beneath the surface and, in clear water sunny conditions, the shadow of it thrown on the river bed is giant-size. Indeed I deem it a blessing, whether it is through sight or their radar system, that fish are aware of our lines at night as well as during daylight. Just imagine the number of frustrating line bites that would occur if the situation were otherwise! As it is we usually only suffer from line bites when bream are in a feeding frenzy or when some species, such as carp or tench, are spawning and oblivious to everything else.

However you can minimise the number of line bites when free lining or ledgering by soaking the line with washing-up liquid so it sinks quickly and clings to the contours along the bottom. Because fish are used to weed fronds bending as they swim into them, they are in turn frightened by anything which is stiff and doesn't give to their body or fins, or the flow of water. Hence the lighter the line the more it gives, and it subsequently imparts a more natural appearance to the bait. Obviously the softer and the suppler the line the better – when fish are shy it produces more bites.

The most important lesson learned whilst diving some of my favourite river haunts was how vastly different most undercut bank swims actually are compared to how I imagined them to be. Take, for instance, those typical chub swims where overhanging alder and willow trees shade the surface. I once thought there simply existed a big cavern into which the chub retreated when danger seemed imminent, and I rather pictured the cavern stretching from just below the surface right down to the river bed. But how wrong I was! Certainly a little way under the surface the bank has usually eroded away inwards a little into a sort of half circle, but in nine cases out of 10 the cavern itself is a long, low, flat tunnel starting from the bottom up some six to 12 inches, and often reaching far into the bank.

Several swims into which Sid and I regularly dived had caverns cutting as much as 10 feet into the bank, with entrances so narrow that the chub and barbel inhabiting them were forced to lie over on their sides to swim in. There is obviously no good reason to expect a ledgered hook length to drift into these undercuts and even if it did I doubt whether the bait would be taken, because it always seemed to me that those caverns were resting places, the darkness being such that even with a powerful diving torch you only caught glimpses of bodies slowly, sleepily and almost aimlessly drifting about. The occupants always seemed to be anything but in a feeding mood.

It is the very existence of these caverns that gives the impression that a river is devoid of fish when the water is gin clear and everything or nothing may be seen through Polaroid's from the bank side. Even to the diver there sometimes appear to be few fish about, and one such occasion – when Sid and I were diving Trowse Mill pool on the River Yare on the outskirts of Norwich – really had us puzzled. Visibility was excellent, helped by a nice sunny day, as we entered the deep pool from the shallow water downstream with the sun's rays filtering down through the unbelievably clear water. However there appeared not to be a single big fish present, apart from a huge shoal of roach in the middle of the white water in the operative sluice. We knew that big chub, trout and barbel inhabited the pool and we were at a complete loss to their whereabouts until we stumbled upon the one and only resting place in a cavern under the roots of a huge chestnut tree.

To view its occupants I had to lie flat on the river bed, moving as little as possible lest the silt clouded the water, and stretch my arm plus torch into a six inch crevice. The cavern opened up inside to about the size of a coffin and there, all in a semi-dormant state, were three barbel to about 8lbs, a huge brown trout looking all of 7lbs plus and a dozen or so chub from 3lbs upwards. A lone biggish perch was resting suspended on its side between two exposed roots and there was another smaller brownie at the far end of the hide-out, which must have gone back for at least seven feet into the clay bank. All the fish seemed to be in a semi-torpid state and the largest barbel actually allowed me, gently to pull him backwards out through the entrance, but once outside in the light he soon woke up and promptly shot off.

Barbel certainly are by far the most amiable of fishes that I have experienced underwater anywhere in the world – and that includes both salt and freshwater. With the exception of the prickly puffer fish which blows itself up as a defence mechanism and so cannot get away fast, I have yet to come across anything comparable to the closeness one can experience with barbel. Through diving I discovered why it is that you often get a 'sandpapery' feeling up the line just before a bite. The explanation is simply that the barbel's barbules 'pluck' over the line as it gently swings its head from side to side – but in an agitated fashion – to locate the bait with it's under slung mouth. The barbel cannot quite see what it is about to eat right at the last moment, so it 'feels' for it instead. We humans have relatively flat faces so we lose sight of our food only a split second before it enters our mouths. Just hold a cup to your lips and then imagine a mouth situated beneath the cup. This should help you appreciate just what a snout the barbel has to put up with! No wonder it was blessed with such enormous barbules.

I think the most fascinating sub-surface encounter Sid and I shared whilst diving was when we were exploring beneath one of the huge rafts covering an overhanging goat willow immediately downstream from the mill pool at Costessey, near Norwich on my local River Wensum. As we moved slowly and carefully between the entangled roots and accumulated debris, keeping our bodies at an angle of 45 degrees, the water pressure kept us pressed to the bottom. I clung to the handle of an old bucket lying on its side buried in silt. We waited, perfectly still, while our pupils grew accustomed to the low light values, then we noticed the barbel swimming all around us. There were a dozen or so sheltering among the roots, several with markings or peculiarities well known to us, for we had shared their dark, silent world on many occasions in the past.

Ever so slowly we moved our free hands to touch the barbel grouped in twos and threes and resting on the bottom between us and the point where the silt shelved up to the bank. Sid watched while I gently lifted a fish of around 9lbs off the bottom and cradled it in my arms like a baby. I twitched its whiskers slowly. The barbel sensed no danger but I encouraged it to return to the others as the current washed me downstream and almost out of the cavern. I crept slowly back, half swimming and half pulling myself upstream along the water weed. Sid was making friends with the barbel too. They allowed him to stroke their fins and run his hand along their flanks and backs, their eyes restful, their dorsal fins lowered.

In this mood, provided your movements are slow and friendly, barbel will remain approachable for as long as you care to stay. I am even tempted to say that they enjoy friendship. On this occasion we spent a full 15 minutes with a pair of fish, taking it in turns to caress and hold them in our arms. My emotions as an angler had been stirred as never before. We had shared a rare and quite remarkable encounter and come as close, perhaps, as it will ever be possible to come to the fish in its wild

environment. It was an unforgettable experience and afterwards, when we came up for a breath of fresh air and a quick rest, Sid pulled a long hank of blanket weed from his mask, took out his mouthpiece and said, 'How on earth do you explain that?' He didn't even swear – most out of character.

Whilst learning where some of the largest specimen-size roach, chub and barbel used to hide up in several stretches of our local rivers, the Bure, Yare and Wensum, Sid and I simultaneously enjoyed collecting old ceramic beer bottles and marmalade jars, some of which had lain in the silt undisturbed for 50 years or more. I guess it's a similar buzz enjoyed by those who go metal detecting and subsequently find ancient coins and other items. Then one evening whilst diving one of our favourite locations at Hellesdon Mill pool where the Wensum starts to enter the city of Norwich, we really thought we had struck gold. The bottom of the pool was quite literally littered with hundreds of little red jewellery boxes containing rings, earrings, necklaces etc. I could see Sid's eyes lighting up even through the thick protective glass of his diving mask, and like me he instantly assumed someone had dumped the spoils of a robbery in the pool to avoid being caught.

We filled the inside of our wet suit jackets with booty until the zips could cope with no more and swam over to the private side of the pool to surface beneath a canopy of overhanging willow branches to inspect our haul. Sid was smiling like a Cheshire cat. But when he rubbed the pearls the paint immediately came off. We had simply come across the dross of a heist, so it was back to barbel and bottle spotting until our compressed air ran out.

I was not the only angler/diver putting pen to paper about sub-surface experiences during the 1970s in *Angling* magazine. Polish angler/diver, Tadeusz Andrzejczyk, was also filling in many parts of the underwater puzzle and years later, in February 1998 to be exact, I had the privilege of actually meeting 'Ted' whilst attending a tackle exhibition in Warsaw. We had so very much in common to talk about and a signed copy of his excellent book, *Wedkarsturo Jeziorowe*, covering every aspect of Poland's vast lake lands, stares down at me from a bulging bookcase as I write. First written in 1978, it contains many superb underwater photographs that would more than do justice to any magazine printed today.

During the heat wave year of 1976, I wrote a book entitled *A Specimen Fishing Year* which was a factual diary-type account of my fishing for that year whilst in pursuit of specimen fish within Norfolk and Suffolk. The book started as a labour of love, but by the end of 1976 I found myself more than looking forward to putting the pen down. Writing about each and every trip as soon as I got home was all very well after a red letter day when I was all hyped up but very demanding, to

say the least, after a series of blanks or miserable weather conditions when little had materialised.

Prior to contacting publishers I asked my good friend Nick Fletcher (then of the *Angler's Mail*) to read the manuscript. He immediately gave it the thumbs-up, but publishers were not so enthusiastic and after negative reactions from a couple, I was on the point of breaking it down into separate chapters, thus enabling Brian Harris to give it a monthly spot in *Angling* magazine, when A & C Black, to whom

I had also sent the manuscript, confirmed that they would indeed like to publish my diary. By its very nature of being a diary it quickly became out of date and has been out of print now for several years. So much has changed in our fishing within the past 30 years that I am compelled to make comparisons between what happens today and how it all was then.

Remember 1976 and that heat wave? It was a time without sophisticated electronic bite alarms and boilies, thermal one-pieces and two-man bivvies. There were no carbon, boron or Kevlar wrapped rods on the market, although I did actually test fish that year with one of the first prototype carbon trotting rods ever produced. But we did have one precious asset which for the most part is not there today: roach in our rivers. Personally, I would much prefer to go back to those days of less gadgetry when you could trot a swim which not only looked like a roach swim, but actually had roach in it. But that's life, ain't it?

My diary book started in January 1976 with what can only be described as a mountainous glut of incredibly large roach, because the clear-flowing upper reaches of Norfolk and Suffolk rivers were as prolific with quality roach then as they are barren today. For instance, my diary entries for 4 January 1976 – despite a severe overnight frost and snow showers – included two big roach of 2lb 9oz and 2lb 10½oz from the River Wensum at Taverham in the 'rushes' stretch. Both came long trotting too. On 5 January I caught one roach of 2lb 2½oz plus a string of others over 1lb. On 7 January I achieved a huge bag including five over 2lbs, the best being 2lb 13oz. The next day I got a roach of 2lb 3oz followed, on 11 January, by a 2lb 1oz and a 2lb 7oz. Then I caught a 2lb 4oz on 12 January. Many of these beautiful roach actually came in very short sessions fitted in before I had to set off to open the shop and also whilst long trotting maggots. It was fairy-tale fishing; it was just too good – unreal almost.

Rod sales over the tackle shop counter were not of designer long-range carp poles but 13ft trotting rods capable of picking up 20 to 30 yards of line and setting the hook at that distance. There were no production carbon rods then, remember. All the winter talk was of big-river roach when anglers got together. With friends like Terry Houseago, Jimmy Sapey, Jimmy Henry and John Bailey I concentrated on the Wensum from Bintry Mill all the way downstream to Taverham. It was a wonderful period, with the River Wensum rightly hailed as the finest roach river in Britain – a crown it held for over a decade.

In the 1974-75 season I caught no fewer than 49 river roach over the magical weight of 2lbs from four different rivers. You can only guess how many there must have been below 2lbs to produce the whoppers. I simply lost count and even became blasé, I regret to say. The roach fishing was that unbelievably good. And yet even then I made the occasional reference in my diary book about the future of the upper rivers, particularly the Wensum. I was obviously worried because it was easier to catch 10 roach over 1lb than five of just 6oz. Without a healthy pyramid containing myriad lesser fish to follow on from the shoals of specimen roach, I could see no way the river could continue rich in roach once the biggies died off. And that is exactly what has happened.

It was during the mid 1970s when the late Doug Allen, who was to be my regular weekly companion for over 10 years, first came into the shop. Doug, who had been a fighter pilot during the Second World War and was exactly 20 years my senior, was known locally for catching some big pike from several Bure-fed Broads to which he had access. But he had never landed a roach over 2lbs. So we got together: my wish was a pike over 20lbs, his a 2lb roach. With each other's help we both achieved these life-long ambitions. Amazingly my first ever 20lb pike was one of a brace taken on the same day whilst fishing with Doug on a shallow, strictly private Broad. I had waited for so long to see a 20 pounder come sliding over my waiting net and then I went and caught two of 22lb and 23lb during the very same session. But that's fishing!

Doug and I shared so many catches of big pike together. We travelled up to Loch Lomond in Scotland for pike and to the River Isla for grayling, a species we both loved. We caught pike to 25lbs from the River Waveney at Beccles, plus dozens of specimens to over 30lbs from all over Broadland, but allow me to recall one particularly memorable occasion on a Bure-fed Broad.

We had in fact been lucky and picked a cracking day with big pike potential. Dawn greeted us with a good southwesterly blowing – super weather for fishing dead baits – and with the sky nicely overcast we looked to be in for a treat. What's more the track running round the outside of the spinney where the boathouse is hidden was fairly hard, which meant that I could drive my Mini Traveller (couldn't afford a Volvo cross country or Audi Allroad estate which is what I drive today, back then) to within a few yards of the boat instead of lugging all the gear on a long walk across newly ploughed fields from the lodge house.

The Broad was well coloured from the heavy winds, with a visibility of just a foot or so, and literally within minutes of putting down the mud weights in the centre of a four foot deep bay, the action began. Before I could get the second bait out the first float-fished static herring had been snapped up and line was fairly hissing from the old '300'. It's a lovely feeling watching a sliding float sneaking upwind across the waves and even better when the rod goes over on the strike and stays there! A long, lean fish boiled on the surface 20 yards out, and to be honest, it stayed on the surface while I reeled it in. I thought that any second it would see me, the boat, the net or all three and then make a last-ditch dive around the anchor rope. But it didn't, it simply lay on the surface throughout the 20 or so seconds from striking to netting. It was a really thin fish of 18¼lb but nicely spotted and in super trim despite its lack of lustre.

Still some pike don't fight and at that time I was eager for another after returning it. I was not disappointed. The second fish snapped up the herring on my second rod almost as quickly as the first but it felt decidedly heavier and was really fighting. There was nothing spectacular though, just a few runs powerful enough for me to hear the magic of a slipping clutch (yes, I've always been a traditionalist at heart) plus a heavy boil, head-shake and dive close in after which the fish went straight into the net. A long beautifully marked pike that pulled the dial scales round to 24lb 2oz – at that time a personal best. Talk about being over the moon – over 40lbs of fish in just two casts, and the day had only just begun...

Then Doug started to get in amongst them and hit into pike on four consecutive casts – all on free lined herring. They ranged between 9lb and 16½lb and put up

SIXTY YEARS A FISHERMAN

far more of a show than either of mine. It was really a mad spell and, like all mad spells, it was over far too quickly.

I can remember the 16½lb pike well, due to a ghastly gaff wound (the odd elderly angler still used a gaff in those days) under its chin through which protruded its tongue. In fact from more or less the same spot around a year later Doug caught exactly the same pike again, which we affectionately called Stumpy, now weighing nearly 18lbs. A year later it turned up again almost touching 20lbs, again to Doug's rod. Then for two years it didn't show, until one freezing cold day at the end of February.

Doug had just landed a superbly conditioned specimen of exactly 24lb. In fact he was still unhooking it when one of my static dead baits was away and I struck into what felt like a heavy fish. It was too; it was Stumpy now also weighing exactly 24lb. What a brace!

But back to that memorable occasion and what seemed a perfect day where we sat for the rest of the session with just one small fish apiece late on into the afternoon. What a session to remember! It was the kind of day when we were actually glad to put down the rods and enjoy packing away the gear and cleaning out the boat because Lady Luck had been so very kind. Even the drive home was to be savoured, with much talk about the day's events. And to top it all, to give us that extra feeling of inner warmth, within seconds of bundling all the gear into the back of the Traveller, after a completely dry day, rain started to lash heavily against the windscreen. We had missed a storm literally by minutes. 'Thank goodness the rain held until now, otherwise the track might have softened up and proved difficult' said Doug. What an understatement! On went the headlights and wipers and away we went along the track towards the lodge, the rain absolutely bucketing down.

At the first bend where a huge pile of cut pines trespassed on to the track, I kept well over on the other side close to the field not realising the depth of recent

tractor ruts. Doug's prophetic; 'Keep left or we'll get stuck' came too late. I felt the Mini's sump give a thump as the front wheels dangled into a pair of deep ruts. 'Never mind, we'll bump it out,' says Doug. So out into the storm we went, not anticipating the gravity of our plight, and became drenched within minutes. Our waterproofs had, of course, been taken off and packed away for the drive home and I had even swapped my Wellington boots for carpet slippers. What a muddy mess they soon became and naturally the Mini just wouldn't budge. Our 'perfect day' was changing rapidly.

Unfortunately the car battery wasn't up to much and had been playing up for weeks so my turning the engine off for five minutes but leaving the headlights on while we surveyed the situation, hardly did it any good. In short it was knackered, with the inevitable result of refusing to turn the engine over. We would, however, be able to bump start her easily if only we could lever the front end out of the ruts and back on to the track, so I didn't worry unduly at this stage.

It was by now pitch dark, getting a bit chilly, raining at a steady inch an hour, backed up by at least a force eight gale, and so without a torch we set about finding a couple of suitable logs to move the Mini over. The pile of cut pine logs was like a gift from heaven and we soon found a couple of thick ones to lie along one side of the car with another to act as a lever. 'We'll soon have it out,' said Doug with authority, choosing to do the levering while I strained to lift the front end and bounce the sump over the rut. 'One, two, three lift!' For a second the front end rose a little and began to move over but suddenly it slumped back again to the sound of a muffled crunch from somewhere inside the car. Doug opened the driver's door and there sticking up through a jagged gaping hole in the floor was the end of a six inch pine log. That was enough for me. I suggested we trudge along to the lodge and use Mrs Dodd's phone to ring the farm for a tractor. I was about to find out the hard way that secluded private estate waters are all right unless you become stuck miles from nowhere because it just did not occur to me that Mrs Dodds might not be on the phone.

'My husband does have an old bike though' says Mrs Dodds, 'but you'll have to be careful with the chain, it sometimes comes off.' Doug looked at me, I looked at him and he said, 'you're the youngest, John.' So off into the rain along the track went Wilson. There were no lights on the bike – a boneshaker from the 1930's – so how on earth I navigated between the potholes and missed the dykes on both sides of the lane on the mile-long pedal to the farm, I'll never know. But make it somehow I did and found Henry, the tractor driver who, bless him, bolted down his supper to come and drag us out. At the first attempt off came the front bumper complete with number plate. Henry apologised, mumbled something about rusted brackets and reshackled the towing chain somewhere around the rear end while I threw the bits into the car. This time the chain slipped and, in addition to one half of the twin rear bumper, most of the exhaust system was wrenched away. It had actually cracked off at the manifold. Round to the front end went the chain now that my wrecked heap was out of the ruts and like a lame dog it was dragged unceremoniously along the track, now an absolute quagmire of mud, back to the lodge. Miraculously it started first pull and as the headlights were still intact, Doug and I continued the drive home to our worried wives, three hours later than expected.

It was around this time, during 1977, that I moved my John's Tackle Den business from Bill Cooper's old shop, in which turnover had become impossible to increase due to its diminutive size. I was also finding my day-to-day existence somewhat claustrophobic. I was becoming more and more frustrated by potential customers peering in through the window and walking away because they thought I was too busy, when actually the shop was full of local anglers hanging around and swapping stories whilst buying tackle. This is a problem faced by small tackle shops the world over. Location was in fact solved overnight by Colin, who ran the gent's outfitters next door, telling me of his imminent bankruptcy and saying that if I wanted his shop I should ring the landlord. I had previously mentioned my liking for his unit should he ever decide to call it a day.

This was a shop unit with three times the floor space I had been used to with much larger store rooms and a huge attic. There was a back yard large enough for me to construct a cold house for the maggots, and it was exactly what I needed. So I visited the landlord and secured a lease. The trouble was, once Colin had departed several weeks later, I was left with the daunting task of completely fitting out the new shop on my own. This I decided to do over a period of six weeks during the close season in the evenings, with a view, once complete, to swapping everything from one shop to another, literally overnight. Thank goodness it was next door.

Frankly I could never have completed on time had I not been helped by my friend Nigel Thomas, a local copper who, due to his shift work, gave me a few hours' hard work every evening. And if I say so myself, for a couple of non-professionals the new John's Tackle Den didn't look at all bad when we had finished.

Moving shops to some degree prepared me for what now lay ahead on the home

front, because after spending five years in our first bungalow with children, Lee and Lisa, now six and four years old, plus a large German Shepherd called Guy, it too seemed awfully small. So Barbara and I started looking for a larger property in Taverham. We found a pre-war bungalow, albeit needing much work, with a third of an acre of garden, and it was quite close to the local schools and shops. So we put our bungalow up for sale and quickly clinched the deal, although had I known the extent of the work I had let myself in for that summer, I might have thought twice.

Plans were passed for a roof conversion to construct two large bedrooms with dormer windows so Lee and Lisa could each have their own room, and downstairs I decided to knock through from the tiny drawing room into the kitchen. Being a retired builder, Dad came up to help for a few weeks during which time we sorted out most of the structural work and even built a brick wall separating the garden from the long drive.

Then about one year afterwards I set about building the biggest garden pond Barbara would allow. From as early as I can remember I always wanted a large pond, from my childhood in north London – when a 50 gallon galvanised water tank was all the veranda to our tiny flat would allow – to the previous bungalow where I had built a small pond.

Our predecessors in our new home had kept over 30 greyhounds with the garden divided up into pens and runs and bordered at the rear by brick kennels. My first job throughout the winter was to clear and level the entire plot. I then planted a few fruit trees and shrubs for screening, before setting about the most enjoyable part of all, actually sitting down one evening with a pen and paper to design the sort of pond I really wanted. Little did I know then that within five years we would be moving again and I would own my own lake, and have a second excavated to my own design!

Anyway, within a year the huge garden pond – complete with wooden bridge across – was finished, nicely stocked with tubs of plants from the wild and an assortment of both natural and ornamental fish, from golden tench to double-figure carp. I then became particularly interested in biological pond filters and in carp culture, and dug two more ponds for growing on the fry of various species. This incidentally led to my writing a series of articles for *Practical Fish keeping* based on my experiences. I even went into selling a few home-bred carp and goldfish, having converted the previous occupant's old kennels at the end of the garden into a huge fish house complete with filtration units. Barbara must have had the patience of Job... though I was always pushing it too far.

I then became fascinated by what everyone refers to these days as ghost carp.

ABOVE
The finished
result: my garden
pond stocked
and planted with
both ornamental
and wild fish
and marginals
complete with
a double-figure
carp rolling in the
middle.

At that time these beautiful variants were offered for sale in *Practical Fish keeping* as 'metallic carp' (a name I still prefer to use) by a Mr Villis (Latvian for Bill) Michaels of Newhay Fisheries in Selby, Yorkshire, who crossed a male Japanese white ogon koi carp with a German Dinkle spula naturally coloured table carp. This produced stunningly coloured little carp etched in various densities of silver and white, of which I purchased 400. They were barely four inches long and the entire batch fitted into one large poly bag. (Bill, incidentally, who was born in Eastern Europe where the carp culture is a way of life, was one of the first importers of Japanese koi into the UK).

I also purchased a dozen or so of his original unusually coloured grown-on metallics, all of around 1½lbs a piece which, together with a few of the four inch metallics, all went into my garden pond. The remainder I sold on to some local clubs and these same carp still live in their waters, having grown to weights well in excess of 20lbs over the years. Due to their durability these (metallic or ghost) carp really are a splendid strain for stocking as you will discover when I later discuss the creation of my own lake. I have now been monitoring the development of some of these individually recognisable metallic carp in both pond and lake using photography for identification purposes for close on 30 years. But more of this later.

Referring back again to my 1976 roach-rich diary book for a moment, it is painful for me to state that today 95 percent of the River Wensum is devoid of roach. For me and all other roach lovers it is a crying shame. I actually came to live in Norfolk because I wanted to be near flowing rivers where I could long trot for quality roach, for I am and always will be a roach angler before I am anything else.

As far as I can fathom, the only common denominator that exists between the rivers that have declined is the escalating use of farming fertilisers, phosphates, nitrates, fungicides, pesticides and insecticides. I am not alone in believing that intensive farming methods and the subsequent increase in chemicals leaching into our river, systems have an awful lot to answer for. I am sure that things like unsympathetic weed cutting, winter run-off, better drainage, water abstraction and even the endemic roach diseases are also major contributing factors to there being fewer roach.

Throughout much of the Upper Waveney, for instance, the concentrations of ammonia leaching into the river from slurry created by intensive pig farming units is one of the identified causes of pollution and subsequent fish losses. With the Wensum, however, the loss of roach stocks is perhaps more complex and puzzling. It could be attributed to any number of invisible toxins and pollutants in what is generally a clear-flowing river, even if it is somewhat over-weedy and choked with dark-green blanket weed during the warmer months. I personally think that the levels of toxins created from chemicals leaching into the rivers from the huge amount of land that is given over to intensive fanning are what affects fry survival and the ultimate existence of roach in actual shoal numbers. Such levels could affect the young fishes' respiratory systems and/or the food they eat. Minute algae, for instance, which are needed for fry-growth in their early stages, may well be eradicated by these chemicals and/or they may even affect the crustacean foods like daphnia, assellus and shrimps. I truly believe that within the next few decades, just as lung cancer was eventually associated with smoking (and it took some time), a correlation between farming chemicals and the inability of silver shoal species to maintain their numbers will come to light.

It is a peculiar thing however that while roach are in decline at present the chub is having a field day. They have colonised much of the Upper Wensum as they have also done in most other Anglian rivers and streams, the Suffolk Stour being a prime example. And while they are not the reason for the roach decline, as many would have it, their presence will certainly hamper roach trying to re-establish themselves, because they occupy all the best roach-holding areas.

I cannot therefore really foresee any immediate improvement in my local upper rivers in so far as the smaller shoal fish like roach and dace arc concerned.

But abstraction and farming are not totally to blame. What about the cormorant phenomenon? This incredibly voracious, predatory seabird has destroyed an endless list of inland still water and river fisheries throughout the British Isles. It achieves this by consuming vast quantities of dace, roach, perch, young bream and chub – not to mention both salmon and sea trout parr which the country's game rivers can ill afford to lose, plus of course stocked rainbow and brown trout which were once introduced into all our man-made reservoir trout fisheries at perfect swallowing size. Nowadays of course, due to the 'black death' trout are stocked at a much larger size, resulting the following year in far fewer beautifully matured, silver trout that have over-wintered nicely. Bars of silver, we used to call them.

Take Rutland Water for instance, the pride of Anglian Water's reservoir game fisheries and the largest man-made lake in Britain. There are no fewer than 200-plus pairs of breeding cormorants living in the nature reserve and cocking two fingers to all. Goodness knows how much money in swallowed trout and coarse fish they have cost the fishery's management and of course ultimately the consumer, who is supplied and charged through his tap by Anglian Water. So inevitably their presence affects every man on the street – not just anglers.

At the bottom of my garden is a lake – someone else's fortunately – which over the past decade has been totally depleted of its once unbelievably prolific roach and rudd stocks. This is a private, seldom fished, well-matured, clear water gravel pit covering eight acres. Every morning I have witnessed through binoculars up to 10 cormorants flying from their roost in the top of a tall birch tree, which is 100 yards from the house, to gorge on stocks. If I had not witnessed it I would never have believed it. But like many a frustrated fishery owner, I have observed what the 'black death' is capable of achieving at first hand. And I rate cormorants as the main problem to any kind of shoal fish renaissance, particularly in East Anglia which is the first area to suffer from cormorants coming across the channel from Europe.

Sadly, we should have had a national cormorant cull organised by the then MAFF and National Rivers Authority, both of whom were supposed to be 'protecting' our inland fisheries, 20 years ago. When you consider what an adult cormorant can put away, even at the conservative figure of 1½lbs of fish per day, (RSPB figures no less) you don't need to be a genius to work out that in a year just 10 cormorants can remove getting on for three tons of fish. In roach stocks that is equivalent to 30,000 7-8 inch roach. Phenominal statistics, aren't they?

Whether it's three tons of roach or rudd or trout! That's an investment of several thousand pounds at least. Small wonder then that so many clear water club fisheries are not worth a cast and that all the members' hard work over many, many years has been for nothing. But worse still, because both his job and income have been hit, is the plight of the fishery owner who has had to close down due to cormorant activity. I wish I knew where it was all going to end. I wish that someone up there in the godly realms of government departments such as the Ministry of Agriculture and Fisheries, now conveniently re-named DEFRA (in case we all pay too much attention as to exactly 'what' this government department is supposed to be doing) would wake up to the fact that we have all but raped the North Sea through over fishing, which of course is the reason why cormorants have been driven to find easy pickings in our clear watered rivers, gravel pits, lakes and reservoirs. As pigeons, rats, crows, squirrels and rabbits are put on the vermin list in order to conserve our farming industry, isn't it about time we put cormorants on the same list so they can be legally shot (without the need for a silly licence) to reduce their numbers dramatically? The problem is a national one and should be taken away from angling clubs, individuals and fishery owners.

I'll bet if the cormorant turned vegetarian and turned into a four foot high rabbit, which took to chewing its way steadily through ploughed and seeded fields, attitudes in Westminster would change overnight, and there would be a law in place within weeks. At present only a handful of game and coarse fisheries are granted licences to shoot cormorants, because most fishery owners, me included, do not wish to go through the paraphernalia involved in securing a licence. Personally, I just shoot them anyway. Sadly, as a sport we are so fragmented, and poor old freshwater fishing in Great Britain has to suffer continually. I just wonder for how much longer.

The trouble is in the meantime freshwater fishery owners all over the UK have to sit back and watch their life's work destroyed. Also there are other far-reaching consequences. For instance, while the dear old, 'head in the sand' RSPB is totally against the culling of cormorants, it happily sanctions the culling of the North American (blue-beaked) ruddy duck in Britain, which dares to breed with the Spanish white-headed duck, not I might add even in Britain, but in Spain. How about that for hypocrisy. I wonder if they have considered the plight of grebes, kingfishers, herons and the like which, due to a serious lack of small silver shoal fishes to eat, in some areas find their natural food larder (thanks to the cormorant) unnaturally bare. Are we really going to wait until indigenous water birds suffer near starvation as a direct result of cormorant predation upon their daily diet?

But there is an even more sinister consequence yet, one I have unfortunately witnessed in recent years, not 50 yards from the house at the bottom of my garden. In the spring, with little left in the way of silver shoal species to eat, what do you think the lake's pike population prey upon? Yes, that's right, a much larger proportion of young ducklings, goslings and coot or moorhen chicks than they would normally take. In fact I have witnessed more young waterfowl disappear in ferocious swirls during the past 10 years than in my entire life before. The pike patrol purposefully along the margins for new clutches of youngsters fresh from their nests. And they have a field day.

Now I have said this many times before and I will say it again. Although I would sooner be trotting for roach than any other form of fishing, I would sooner be catching carp from an attractive well-stocked lake than catching absolutely nothing in a river. I do have a few personal reservations about modern carp fishing, however. I dislike the pressure of round-the-clock fishing on many waters and the subsequent harm it can do in terms of the repercussions for the state of bank side foliage and acute pressure on fish with lines permanently in the water. And I feel sorry for youngsters who come straight from snooker table or table tennis bang into the cult of modern carping and who, because they see everyone else doing it, misguidedly think that sitting inside a bivvy all day with a pair of matched bolt rigs out near the horizon is what carp fishing is all about. Because it ain't. I have on all too many occasions seen newcomers become disillusioned with our sport and drift on to another. Just look through the tackle ads and you'll see what I mean. Look at all the complete designer carp-fishing outfits there are for sale. I would love to see more carp anglers become all-rounders and learn the craft of catching other species on numerous methods and different baits. Then they could return to carp having served an apprenticeship. They would be much better for it and go on to enjoy catching carp when the situation arises, using a variety of techniques, instead of just one. Unhappily for many anglers today, when the bolts and boilies fail to score they simply have nowhere to go.

Although the pressure syndrome which affects carp fishing is comparatively quite new, it has of course crept into the pursuit of other species, tench and barbel in particular. 30 years ago I used to think I was uptight and fishing heavily when I put in two or three early morning pre-work sessions during the summer weeks, or maybe an all-nighter plus one early morning – and I still opened my shop six days a week. But compared to the sort of hours some anglers are now prepared to put in, these efforts would hardly seem worth it. Each week we read reports of tench, bream and carp anglers finally achieving success after 10, 20 and even

BELOW
Back in the mid 1970s tench were considered specimens from 5lb upwards. I took this bag on long-range feeder tactics while ledgering a shallow Norfolk estate lake. Note the red, fast taper, hollow glass rods. Carbon fibre was not yet available.

30 consecutive bite less all-night sessions. Even the thought of someone actually spending anything up to a week in a river swim, as some do nowadays after species like barbel, would have been mind boggling just 15 years ago.

Freshwater fishing certainly has entered new realms as far as catching big fish is concerned and I am not altogether sure it is a good thing. Once upon a time you could relate to another man's achievements because everyone had more or less about the same amount of leisure time to put into their sport or pastime. Which is not the case now, in these obsessive times. There is so much in today's fishing that simply does not really mean anything; the farcical record fish lists for one. But that's life. I shall now continue with the happenings throughout the 1970s of yours truly.

Something I haven't yet really covered concerning the 1970s is the way in which anglers bent on catching larger and larger specimens got together to pool their knowledge and formed specimen and specialist angling groups. In my area we formed the (now long-since disbanded) Broadland Specimen Group and were, amongst other things, perhaps best known for developing long-range feeder fishing techniques to capture the then specimen tench from Norfolk's silt-rich shallow estate lakes. We caught our fair share of big Broadland pike too, and one of our members, Pete Stacey, was for several years active in the big carp syndicate at famous Redmire Pool. All this is of course by the by now because things have moved on beyond all expectations.

Nevertheless, such groups played an important and pioneering part in formulating fishing techniques within the British Isles as we have come to accept today. In those early times big fish were thin on the ground and consequently hard earned by those willing to devote long hours by the waterside developing baits and specialised terminal rigs, some of which have now been accepted as standard.

One of the most interesting modern phenomena to have occurred during the last quarter century is the way in which tench have on average grown to much larger sizes all over the country. You might put this down to the sheer numbers of HNV baits tench now consume and, in certain waters, no doubt this is fact. Yet monsters over 12lbs and countless doubles have come from undoctored waters, like the reservoirs at Tring in which the bream and tench grow to huge proportions on zooplanktons and bloodworms alone. The tench growth phenomenon is certainly one hell of a modern mystery, because back in the mid 70s when those of us in the Broadland Specimen Group were taking huge numbers of six pounders plus the odd seven from the Marsh Lake in North Norfolk, our catches were highly rated countrywide. But today seven, eight and even nine pounders are regular catches in a whole string of fisheries up and down the country. These weights seem even more incredible when you consider the tench record stood for many years at 8½lb and prior to that in the early 1950s at just 7lb. Now it's over 14lbs. Could it be that gravel pits dug during the Second World War, which produce many of the largest tench today, have only reached their peak in food potential during the 1980s and 1990s? Have modern techniques and baits made more of an impact than many of us believe? Are tench simply holding more spawn when they get caught because our summers start later and is it simply an effect of global warming? Well, you can put all these arguments into the computer and every time out will come the same answer: one big mystery. Though I think that cormorants are also responsible in part, because in many fisheries where the likes of bream, tench, barbel and carp etc once shared the natural food larder with strong concentrations of silver shoal fish, they now have that food source all to themselves. For instance, during the last decade I have taken several tench all exceeding in weight the once British record on simple offerings where high protein baits are never used. So they haven't increased in weight by 30-40 percent due to anglers baits. Indeed, the only common denominator, apart from longer summers, is that those tench have not had to share the rich natural larder of aquatic insect life with dense shoals of roach or rudd. Cormorants have had them all leaving the tench the dominant species.

What about the way in which the bream and barbel record keeps leaping ahead after sticking at 13½lb and 14½lbs respectively for so many years? This too looks set to be another peculiar phenomenon, with both 20lb bream and barbel now required to get you into the record books.

I should also perhaps mention how nowadays we seem to recognise so many of the individual big fish we catch. This was something totally alien to many anglers in the 1970s when more, albeit smaller, specimens were about. We recognise repeat captures not only of carp and pike, but of tench, chub, bream and barbel – even big roach. It just goes to show how few large fish there are actually about, how often we put pressure on them, and how much we should value their existence for continued sport.

The 1970s were certainly an exciting time for everyone on the cutting edge of the big fish scene. As a keen photographer I was starting to demand more impressive results for my efforts which aroused my interest in medium-format cameras. Up until a few years ago of course prior to the digital revolution, film emulsions were so good, with the entire photography and printing industry geared to producing unbelievably sharp colour plates from 35mm transparencies, that eventually there was little need for the expense of larger formats. Back in the 70s, however, magazine and newspaper editors were not only more impressed with, but far more likely to accept and use the larger 2¼ inch (6 x 6cm) format transparency for their colour work than the significantly smaller 35mm, particularly for front covers. It was a lucrative field which only a handful of angling writers were then into, probably due to the high initial cost of a quality medium-format camera.

Until now I had been relying on my old 35mm Minolta SR7 plus a couple of lenses purchased whilst on board *SS Oronsay*. So I decided to go up the ladder carefully by first buying a Yashica 630, twin-lens reflex 2¼ inch square camera. This almost paid for itself with my first front cover on *Angling* magazine. However being of the upright Rolleiflex style with two lenses (hence the term 'twin lens'), one for focusing and one for taking the actual photograph, it was rather old fashioned and completely useless for close-up photography, though I loved the size of the transparency and the fact that the square format could be cropped to produce either a landscape or portrait picture.

While ledgering for tench in the Marsh Lake at Wolterton Hall (now private) in north Norfolk with fellow writer, Kevin Clifford, I had a good look at his Bronica S2A 2¼ inch square single-lens reflex camera. It produced excellent results and I immediately decided to buy one. When I got home in the late morning after the tench fishing, I scanned the adverts in *Amateur Photographer* only to find that someone in Bristol was selling a complete second-hand Bronica S2A outfit with both wide and telephoto lenses in addition to the standard. Luckily he was in when I rang a few minutes later and we agreed on a price of £420, which then was probably more than my Mini Traveller was worth. Barbara thought I was mad. Nevertheless we arranged to meet at Liverpool Street station a few hours later to clinch the deal. When our two trains arrived, to the amazement of fellow passengers, this chap sat counting out my fivers while I carefully inspected the large aluminium photo case full of Bronica goodies. Obviously everyone thought some sort of shady deal was being transacted. It was in fact one of the best investments I ever made because it started me on the road to more 'thinking' photography.

Unfortunately the S2A also became rather limiting in that exposure still had to be calculated by a hand-held meter (an old Weston Master) and that due to the large film transportation handle the camera had to be taken down from the viewing eye in order to wind on. This obviously precluded any action photography. And so after a few years I sold the S2A (for £100 more than I paid for it, incidentally) and bought a Bronica ETRSi 645 which, though slightly reduced in format to a 6 x 4.5cm transparency, produced 15 frames on a 120 roll film to the 6 x 6's 12 shots. But more importantly the 645 was coupled to a lever wind handle and had an automatic exposure system. It could therefore be used in the same way as any 35mm camera and produced stunning transparencies. It was not light, however.

So eventually I sold my two ETRSi Bronicas plus several lenses in favour of lighter camera equipment and nowadays whether making long-haul flights or simply walking for miles along the Wensum stalking chub, I stick to the lightness of a 35mm sized single lense reflex digital camera. A Nikon D200 to be precise, plus a small press and point digital which pops into my top pocket. I have almost as many different-size camera bags as I have cameras, in order that I can take along exactly what is required by the excursion in hand.

I am not a great lover of automatic everything and totally computerised camera systems. Well, I've got to exercise my brain on something! For quite a few years now I relied on a pair of Nikon 301 cameras which had a built-in motor drive and an excellent auto-exposure system. The additional lenses I used went down to 24mm at the wide end – so

essential for boat fishing – and up to 300mm telephoto for wildlife shots. But unquestionably my most useful Nikon for many years – and I still have two of these – (though seldom used) is the 35mm auto-focus/all-weather compact. These have now long since gone out of production but if you should ever come across one second-hand in good order, snap it up straight away.

Many of the thousands of colour transparencies used in my books and articles during the past 30 years have been taken with this wonderful back-up camera. It has a great fill-in flash and can take sub-surface shots down to 14 feet. Whilst capturing mahseer action shots in India, for instance, I simply used to sling both Nikon compacts around my neck, get just downstream from both the angler and the fish about to be landed and jump in. Similarly whilst boat fishing either in heavy rain or with sea spray coming over the side, the little Nikon compacts were invaluable. There was never any worry of malfunction or damage should it become swamped with saltwater or even dropped in the mud. A rinse over with freshwater and that was that. What more can a man ask of any tool, especially a camera? I shall certainly have to start looking around for the equivalent in an all weather 'digital' equivalent.

During the summer of 1978 I was pointed in yet another direction by an invitation from Mike Fuller, of the now defunct local BBC Radio 4 station in Norwich, to accompany him on a series of 'roam about' fishing programmes. Mike asked me to choose topics for six 10 minute weekly programmes to run consecutively and I came up with a bait-gathering session for the first. The idea was then to lead in on the second programme by using the crayfish, grubs and so on that we had collected from a small stream in the first programme (the evening before) while in search of early morning chub along my local stretch of the Upper Wensum. For the other programmes that followed, I chose roach, carp, lake trouting and pike, and a bit of summer plugging to finish which would, I thought, go down quite nicely with lots of jacks thrashing about – but how wrong can you be?

Anyway, throughout the series the format was to be both informative and light-hearted. This is exactly how it went because Mike and I quickly became friends and built up a definite rapport. Now some 30 years later we have also taken similar routes, in that Mike is now a television producer based in Hampshire. But back to those radio days. Quite simply Mike asked the questions while I tried to produce the goods. While I suppose anything can be botched in the studio or end up on the cutting-room floor, once involved in the programmes it became imperative to both of us that the true 'feeling' of fishing and one's thoughts in relation to any number of things which may or may not have occurred as a result of being by the waterside, really came over. And for my part there were the personal rewards to be gained from doing the series, quite apart from the laughter and actually putting some good fish on the bank.

Through thinking deeply about what I was going to say into the microphone (and this applies equally to my *Go Fishing* and other TV programmes) so that listeners could relate to what was happening, I found that I became more acutely and consciously aware of all the beautiful things which surround my fishing – things which must still be there even when I blank. Wild flowers, for instance: their perfume, their colours, their habitat, their abundance. Or grasses, reed mace, sedges, birds, amphibians, flies, caterpillars – the list goes on and on, dictated only by how much you really want to see. And while I was aware of such things before I started the series, and always have been when actually mentioning everything by name, their importance now to me seemed to be amplified. Consequently the enjoyment of that particular plant, insect or fish became greater.

Other curious but certainly beneficial side-effects sometimes came about when I stayed longer in a swim than I would normally, or made more casts than seemed necessary. When attacking a favourite location during the early morning chubbing programme a huge weed raft gathered over trailing willow branches

BELOW
In 1978 Mike Fuller (left) and I teamed up to make a series of fishing programmes for the then local SSC Radio 4 station in Norwich. It proved great fun and, though unbeknown to me at that time, a valuable experience for me as a television presenter.

harbouring at least 20 chub. Mike repeatedly recorded all the subsequent noises such as the casting sounds – bale arm clonk, the 'plop' and the reeling in. All good audible stuff but no chub! I told him that as a chub hadn't hit the crayfish on either the first or second cast, the chances of catching one now on the seventh or eighth time of lobbing it out and going through the motions in water as clear as gin were just about wham! Yes, there was a chub about to break all the rules – a long, lean fish of 4lb 9oz which should have weighed more (that's the trouble with summer chub). It hit the bait at a time when, had Mike not been there shooting tape; I should have been at least three more swims along the bank. Just goes to show doesn't it? Patience, Wilson, patience!

For the roach programme Mike said, 'What about a blank, John, so we can concentrate purely on dialogue about the Wensum and roach chat in general?' I agreed and deliberately walked a remote part of the river I had never seen before, let alone fished, and found a good-looking swim which three or four years before might well have produced several big roach. But the roach fishing on the Wensum had started to deteriorate and many of the big ones which made headlines in the mid 70s had naturally died off. It was really an all-or-nothing session and we settled in the thick rushes at the upstream end of the swim half an hour before dark to quiver tip bread flake downstream on 3lb line and size 8 hook after putting in a couple of handfuls of mashed bread.

Two hours later I returned a chub of 4lb 1oz and a roach of 1lb 12oz, having missed two other bites, while Mike had enough tape to treble the programme's time limit even if he did have the recorder switched off when the chub took! By now we were really feeling cocky as a two-man radio team, and programme number four seemed another dead cert, especially as I had arranged to fish a wildie pond where fully-scaled commons between 1-2lbs normally did their level best to crawl up the rod, even in the worst of conditions.

We baited up with trout pellet paste, put up three rods on the bite alarms and sat back waiting for darkness. An hour after dark, however, I feared the worst. We had but one 12oz wildie to show for our efforts when runs should have been coming every couple of minutes. And that fish was to Mike's rod – the only run of the evening. I just could not understand it. Perhaps a heat wave was on its way, or the air pressure was too low, or pea silage had fouled the pond ... I had no explanation for Mike who, due to my ramblings on how easy it was going to be on the way there, had obviously built himself up into a fever pitch about carp fishing. It's funny how within only a few trips an almost complete novice can become addicted to the fervour of fishing.

Anyway we did have enough tape about the history of the pond, how the carp got there and so on. All interesting stuff, plus the bite alarms bleeping away to the one and only run. So really we were reasonably happy with the programme material and ready to call it a night at 11 o'clock when a set of headlights appeared at one corner of the field and over the bumps came Stephen Burroughs, owner of the water, in his farm truck. Well at least we should now find out what Stephen had been catching recently and why sport was now so bad. Perhaps he'd gone barmy on the protein baits and 'pellet' was blown.

'Hi Stephen,' says I, introducing Mike. 'It's been a useless night.' 'I'm not surprised,' said Stephen, pointing to the ground where several thin pieces of string were disappearing into the pond which I had failed to notice on arrival in the half light. 'I would have told you earlier on' he continued, 'when you rang, had I not been out. We put some fish traps in there this afternoon to get rid of some of those bloody little crucians and wildies.' He picked up the nearest string and pulled slowly, while 20 feet out in the pond (exactly where our baits had lain all evening) a huge 8 foot by 4 foot fish trap slowly rose to the surface like the back of a whale. 'I've got four of these out there,' he said. 'It's a wonder you didn't get caught up.' 'Wasn't it,' I said.

I made sure I picked a 'dead cert' venue for the trouting programme. Curiously, in terms of sheer sport and action it proved the most spectacular. We visited a new gravel pit fishery in west Norfolk where rainbows fight like stink, and I quickly took a 2¼ pounder and then a larger fish within minutes of each other, but then I went through a succession of lost fish including one of at least 4lbs as darkness loomed over the valley. Then, quite suddenly, as the surface went silver, the mar-gins all along our bank started to erupt with rising trout. It was a beautiful sight, and I took another two nice fish on successive casts both on a Corixa.

There were some beautiful pieces on this programme of my giggling away while trying to subdue a thrashing rainbow before Mike's last reel of tape ran out. And unfortunately the fact that rainbows fight for several minutes (although it doesn't seem as long when you are enjoying the fight) restricted the use of further dialogue in the short space of the 10 minutes allocated to each programme. The result was that this particular programme, although entertaining, never really flowed and unfortunately sounded clipped or edited.

When we set off on our last programme I was not just a little sad because, as I stated earlier, I had re-taught and re-explored for myself a few of the basic moods of fishing. It was like catching that first goggle-eyed perch on a penny hook as a six year old all over again. I had indeed explored old values, forgotten feelings, and my only regret was that I would fall again into the modern trend of only caring about the end result and only wanting to catch the biggest fish when the programmes were completed. I am still very much aware of this thought, thank goodness, all these years later.

Plugging for pike on the Upper Wensum close to home is great fun. It's really easy in the summer. The jacks will even grab flake and crust as its wound upstream against the current, and worms, when twitched, are fatal. But for some reason, known only to Wensum pike, on that particular day my Shakespeare 'Big S' plug might not have existed. I even found myself apologising to Mike for the lack of interest and, for fear of blanking on the very last outing, we moved twice to new parts of the river – each time to no avail. I blamed the wind, the sun and the fact that we could only make the session at midday. 'We should have arranged an evening stint,' I said. Then I made a snap decision an hour before the pubs opened and started the car yet again, making for another part of the river.

On the second bend downstream, we struck gold. 'I'm in;' I yelled into the microphone, as what felt like a reasonable fish chugged away close to the bottom. There was no tail-walking or surface fighting, which seemed curious, but I didn't care. It was a summer pike on a plug and that's what we had set out to catch. As the fish neared the net Mike remarked that it didn't look much like a pike – and he was right. Those old rubber lips I knew so well. It was a 4lb chub and what a surprise! It seemed that throughout the series I just couldn't get away from them.

Half a mile downstream the 'Big S' attracted a peculiar swirl as soon as I twitched it. I missed this take but two casts after the culprit made its mistake. Yes, you've guessed it – another chub. This second chub went 2½lb and would have had great difficulty in swallowing the 'Big S' but grabbed it anyway. It was a terrific end to a particularly interesting sextet of fishing stints, shared with Mike Fuller, who had and still has that rare ability to ask just the right questions, the answers to which as I said earlier on can, if you think about it enough, portray the real 'stomach' of fishing.

Writing about chub reminds me of oh so many sessions I spent in search of that 'then' elusive six pounder during the late 1970s. I've since taken more six pounders than I can remember, including two over 7lbs in recent years, but these were unwanted close season captures (so I don't count them) caught whilst trying to extract a particular carp from a friend's ornamental lake. And besides, as already mentioned, many species today, including chub, are growing much larger. So a six pounder now means much less than it did to me over 20 years ago when they were less attainable. You make your own challenges!

At that time I decided to devote an entire year to catching a whopping great chub and walked many miles of the Upper River Wissey in northwest Norfolk during the summer months simply fish spotting. In so doing I came across the moat circling nearby Oxborough Hall, which at that time looked to be stuffed full of monster chub running into double figures. But it was too good to be true and close inspection revealed they were in fact grass carp experimentally stocked by Anglian Water. But the two species do seem so very similar and for a few moments I thought I'd located chub heaven.

I also spotted along miles of my favourite Upper Waveney, and naturally along

the Upper Wensum close to home where I had accounted for some superb winter chub to within just an ounce of 6lbs. Then I eventually struck gold one mild February evening as dusk fell by catching a monster Wensum fish of 6lb 7oz on floating crust, not from the river but from a tiny overgrown adjacent gravel pit into which it had apparently been introduced from the Wensum a few years previous. It measured exactly 24 inches in length and coughed up the remains of a large toad into my hands as I removed the size 4 hook. So much for fish not wanting – as folklore has it – to eat toads or toad spawn because of the bitterness!

Something I also found out that winter when several weeks of ice covering my pond had thawed out was where frogs get to all winter through. I knew toads hibernated on land, as do newts, beneath old logs and other objects. But I must admit I had not consciously pondered on the whereabouts of frogs; at least not until I pulled some of the larger tubs of marginal plants from the pond (which had been under ice for three weeks) to trim around the edges. The disturbance caused numerous large frogs, all now nutty brown in colour (from the peat-based compost they had been lying in) to jump from the tubs. So that was it, quite simply frogs hibernate under water, absorbing oxygen through their skin.

It was during the following summer that I made the mistake of promising my mate, Doug, a few wildies for an ornamental pond. Doug was an ice cream salesman and parked his van just inside the gates at Kilverstone Wildlife Park (now closed unfortunately) owned by Lord and Lady Fisher, who at that time thrilled visitors with their miniature horses. Doug even sponsored one of the monkeys at the park. Anyway I obtained a dozen or so wildies averaging around 1lb a piece for Doug to put into Lord Fisher's ornamental lily pond around which visitors sat and ate their lunch. Lord Fisher had cleaned out and refilled the pond with clear water after trimming back the lilies. I left the wildies in my huge, aerorated live bait tank in the garage complete with net and a transportation tub and told Doug to collect them sometime in the morning while Barbara was in. This he did and rang me in the tackle shop to thank me. 'I didn't know they were going to be that big,' says Doug, 'but thanks ever so much. Lord Fisher will be pleased.'

Now this had me rather puzzled but the matter was soon to be clarified. Within the next half hour another friend (who shall have to remain nameless) rang and

SIXTY YEARS A FISHERMAN

told me that he had finally managed to get hold of a couple of nice grass carp, scale perfect and around 3 and 5lbs a piece. He had put them in the tank. Oh no! Doug had taken the grass carp! Now at this time grass carp were not supposed to be for stocking Wilson's pond, being a totally experimental alien species (that's why I can't say where they came from) and I couldn't risk them being seen in Lord Fisher's goldfish pond and their presence being traced back to me. I just hoped Doug hadn't put them in yet. But he had, and a heated row broke out over the phone. So in the middle of a hot summer's day when visitors were flocking through the turnstiles at the park Doug had to roll up his trousers and wade through the large ornamental pond with his pan landing net trying to retrieve my two grass carp.

Unfortunately this failed and it cost Doug half a day's lost ice cream sales. It took all afternoon to have the pond pumped out sufficiently low to recapture the aliens. This was an escapade we often laughed about over the following years whilst fishing the Broads together. (What I hadn't the heart to tell Doug a few weeks later was that I arrived home one evening to find the largest grass carp – which he'd so carefully retrieved – lying on the paved garden path beside the pond, as stiff as a board. It had jumped completely out of the pond and asphyxiated itself.)

Looking back I guess the latter part of the 1970s was a rather busy time for me. I updated and revised the second edition of my book *Where to Fish in Norfolk and Suffolk*, wrote chapters in other books entitled *The Big Fish Scene* and *Zander*, and started writing for Marshall Cavendish Part works. Edited by Len Cacutt (first editor of the *Angler's Mail* incidentally) this started with the *Fisherman's Handbook* and then the *Handbook Advanced Guide* published weekly as a continuation of the original handbook. This was followed by the *Fisherman's Weekly* magazine, and later in 1982 with four volumes of the *New Fisherman's Handbook*. Considering the sheer number of my colour transparencies consumed by these weekly all-colour publications, my earlier investment in professional camera equipment had more than paid off. Moreover the need for 'how-to' angling literature amongst Britain's army of up-and-coming anglers had well and truly been established by Marshall Cavendish, then the part works experts, which was something the general angling press at that time simply could not grasp. In addition to this I was of course also contributing my regular monthly articles to *Angling* magazine and periodically writing features for *Angler's Mail*, plus working six days a week in the shop, fishing either before or after work and on Sunday mornings when family life permitted.

There are so many hours in a day and workaholics never count them. I have purposely never drawn a line beyond which I am not prepared to work, fearing that if I do I will also be drawing an indelible line marking where my standard of life can advance no further. However, my preoccupation with everything to do with fishing (which happens to encompass both work and hobbies) must have put enormous strain upon my family at that time. It's a real Catch 22.

Television Calls

The 1980s started pretty much how the previous decade had ended, extremely busy. I added the German magazine *Fisch und Fang* and the Swedish *Fiske Journalen*, plus *Practical Fish keeping*, to the list of publications for which I contributed monthly material. I also produced chapters for the *Angler's Mail Guide to Basic Coarse Fishing* and the *Angler's Mail Annual* – both IPC magazine publications. It was in fact most gratifying to have the editors of all these and previously mentioned magazines and part works contacting me not only for copy but for my comprehensive library of colour transparencies. This library has now grown to immense proportions; I have around 200,000 transparencies, most of which are catalogued. There are, for instance, several thousand on fishing in India alone.

But as busy as I was in the shop, trying to steal enough hours before work in order to catch big roach, barbel or chub which I would then write about, finding time for scuba diving with Sid, being father and husband, and keeping the garden and pond in order, there was even more work and responsibility coming my way. I was on the point of digging yet another pond in the garden, which had been extended by purchasing from the lady next door the last third of her plot, when I heard that just the place I had been looking for was coming on to the market. Like many a fisherman, the thought of actually owning my own fishery, undisturbed by the actions of others, had always appealed. I guess the constructing of so many ponds was simply building the stepping-stones in that direction. Now the opportunity had finally presented itself.

This place was part of a large estate in Lenwade, some 11 miles west of Norwich, owned by a friend, Richard Barry, who after having it on the market for over a year without a single enquiry, decided to split the 60 acre sporting estate into five lots. Lot two was the one I could just about afford. It comprised a spacious three bedroom bungalow with six acres of surrounding woodland including a three quarter acre gravel pit. Ah, seclusion at last!

Barbara and I went and viewed the bungalow immediately and the next day rang with an offer that was accepted. But over the months ahead there were those terrible times when everyone feels so uncertain and we were kept on tenterhooks right up to the moment of signing contracts by both the couple purchasing our house and the second buyer responsible for purchasing the remainder of Richard's estate. Naturally he wanted to sell all the lots at the same time, so had the larger

LEFT
This 35lb 15oz catch of bream and a single chub from the tidal reaches of Hampshire's famous Royalty stretch of the River Avon decided the three-match outcome between Dick Clegg and me in the winter of 1989.

buyer pulled out, our sale would have been held up. Fortunately it was not, and in October 1982 the Wilson's moved lock, stock and barrel, including the cat, two German Shepherds, a Labrador, Cheeko, our African Grey parrot (who is garbling away as I write this), Lisa's rabbits, Lee's snakes, plus tank upon tank of golden tench, orfe and carp various, plus Barbara's mother Nora into our new lakeside home.

Having moved Lee and Lisa, now 12 and 10 years old, from the environment where they grew up and away from their friends, we had to drive them around a bit, but I'm sure this was compensated for by their new quality of life. They had six acres of woodland where they could do as they liked. In fact within months of moving in I bought both of them motorbikes and they were soon zooming up and down through the woods loving every minute.

Extraction had last taken place in the woods – which are bordered by an eight acre lake (privately owned) along our northeast boundary – during the Second World War and most of the gravel and sand was taken away by Atlas Aggregates for the nearby airfields at Weston Longville. It left our three quarter acre pit with depths to 14 feet now nicely mature in its own right with a stock of rudd, roach, gudgeon and small tench. To this I added all the various carp, golden tench and orfe from my garden ponds.

Over the following months I arranged to have our lake netted and most of the prolific rudd and roach stock removed. These I swapped for some common carp, and I also purchased a quantity of both mirrors and commons in the 6-12lb range, together with a handful of grass carp (now allowable). During the winter of 1982/83 I also introduced a few chub averaging 3-4lb from the nearby River Wensum in the hope that they would help to keep down the stock of rudd and gudgeon. Under two years later, incidentally, one of those chub was caught. It weighed 5lb 5oz.

Several customers and friends who used the shop suggested they would be

SIXTY YEARS A FISHERMAN

interested in joining a syndicate should I form one to fish my newly acquired lake. So we had a working party to clear a path through the steep bramble-covered banking which restricted access to much of the perimeter, creating a dozen fishable swims. We didn't go all the way round, but left a jungle area where no one could fish – always a wise decision on any fishery, this.

During the summer of 1983 I planted white and red ornamental lilies and the common yellow lily with its cabbage-like sub-surface leaves. In addition I introduced a good margin coverer, the dwarf pond lily, which has tiny round pads and buttercup yellow flowers. As much of the little lake shelves immediately down from one foot in the margins to eight, 10 and 12 feet, this little plant is ideal for a marginal covering; however it does tend to go rampant in lakes which are shallow all over. And I now wish I had not in fact introduced it.

In June that year I contacted Atlas Aggregates asking them to consider future gravel extraction from the wooded valley running parallel to the little lake. I could easily visualise how beautiful the area would be with a lake running throughout its entire length. From digging down deep to plant shrubs, it became apparent to me that the whole area had not been dug and back-filled and all the gravel removed, as I was led to believe by everyone who was familiar with the property. The top six to 10 feet of good quality gravel had simply been skimmed off and the whole area left to grow up in birch shrub. There was more gravel underneath several feet of sand.

As Atlas already owned the mineral rights to an acre of the land anyway (due to a transaction years ago with the previous owner) I was more than hopeful that something could be worked out. The company was in fact excavating a pit just half a mile away at that time, so it would be ideal simply to move the machinery along when they had finished that job, providing there were enough gravel deposits. So we left it that a test digging would be completed in the months ahead and things would go from there.

In the autumn of 1984 Atlas Aggregates sent in their local site manager, Bernard Housden (who by coincidence lived just a few hundred yards down the road), to test dig for gravel potential. After hacking down a few tall, thin birch saplings to make a path for the JCB with an enormous telescopic bucket, Bernard made five test digs over the low level of the valley down to a depth of 18 feet. The water table was around six feet deep and water could be seen gushing in to fill the hole as the sand and gravel were removed and stacked in enormous piles beside each gaping hole. Things looked good right from the start. There was enough sharp sand, building sand and gravel (called stone in the trade) to make reworking the site worthwhile. And whilst a polybag of gravel from each pile was taken away for full analysis Bernard assured me that it was now just a formality and that they would probably start excavating in the New Year.

To a very large extent the future of totally controlled good-quality coarse fishing in the UK relies on continual excavations of sand and gravel. As both minerals are in constant demand for the construction of everything from motorways to houses, the scope to create new fisheries from exhausted pits is enormous. Some pits, of course, remain dry and these are invariably back-filled by the local council and top soiled for agriculture. But as most sand and gravel deposits were laid down along river valleys during the last ice age, most new excavations soon fill up from the local water table. Thus new recreation areas suitable for sailing, windsurfing and angling are continually being made available. What's more, anglers need not wait up to 20 years for these new waters to mature, which has often been the case in the past. Even during digging, provided anglers are consulted, there lies the opportunity of creating numerous features, such as islands, with the option of immediate tree planting to attract wildlife and to make the finished result visually a more beautiful place to behold. Provided various marginal plants, shrubs and trees of the correct types are introduced straight away, a quick transformation from a barren flooded pit to a beautiful, well-stocked lake can result in a handful of years – as indeed I was soon to discover.

All that was left now was to arrange a deal which suited both parties and we settled on a simple arrangement. My gravel – plus all the soil and unwanted poor-quality sand – was to be removed from the site, in exchange for a lake as large as possible dug and landscaped exactly to my design. No money changed hands; there was no contract, simply a handshake. How I wish all business could be done like that. And Atlas Aggregates' then local manager Peter Charlton and I have been firm friends ever since.

The chance of creating my very own water, with total control of the future fishing potential, had arrived and during the autumn of 1984 I started to plan the fishery. This was not easy because until excavation starts no one really knows what depths are possible. Nevertheless I played around with lots of ideas. Should I have one large lake by joining the new one with the existing lake or should I have two separate lakes? I settled for one. The nice thing as far as I was concerned was that I could design on paper more or less how I wanted the shape of the new lake to be. I didn't have to put up with the veritable hole in the ground with monotonous bank side contours and awkward spots to fish from, as many ex-gravel workings turn out. I wanted a lake with an interesting, inviting bank side, deviating every few yards from peninsulas to little bays and inlets occasionally, offering a variety of

swims where anglers would not be aware of the guy in the next swim. With the help of Barbara, Lee and Lisa I started to clear the valley floor of the tall birches. Poor Lee, I'll wager few 14 year olds get a bow-saw for their birthday!

October onwards saw us using it on birch trees. We stacked the cut trunks for future swim-making where step downs would be required due to the steep sides which would surround the new lake. I enjoyed the exercise of bow-sawing immensely and Sunday after Sunday for week upon week, whatever the weather, we gradually cleared the area. We had a great bonfire to dispose of all the brushwood on 5 November with more than 30 friends round. One couple said they thought the entire woods had gone up, as they could see 30 foot columns of flames from the main road prior to driving down the narrow track to our bungalow. Had me worried for a while, too!

By January much of the valley had been cleared and Bernard helped by chain sawing down some of the larger trees. Heavy snowfalls then covered everything and for a few weeks nothing could be done. But at the beginning of February 1985 a Massey Ferguson front loader with tyres six feet high and a 2½ ton capacity shovel arrived. This made short work of widening our drive to take the huge lorries required for gravel transportation, because no processing was to be done on site. All minerals were to be transported to Atlas Aggregates plants either at Swanton Morley or Costessey, both five miles away.

Huge piles of soil, sand and gravel were heaped opposite the house and quite suddenly the property took on the look of a working gravel pit. It is truly amazing

It didn't take long for the heavy machinery to turn scrub woodland into a working gravel pit, taking off top soil and sand to just above the water table where the richest gravel deposits started.

ABOVE
Dragline operator, Barry, skilfully scoops out a steep pathway from the lane in front of the house down to the lake level, while behind him Albert fills up a 20-ton lorry using the massive 2½-ton capacity shovel on his Massey Ferguson front loader.

what one piece of heavy machinery can do in just an eight hour day! I assured Barbara, however, that within a couple of years the beauty of our secluded setting would return – all the better. She didn't believe me! The kids of course loved the huge piles and steep levels of aggregate and sand all over the woods and zoomed through on their motorbikes. They never really wanted the digging to end.

After three weeks of clearing by the Massey Ferguson, the dragline arrived by special loader. Bernard also brought in the site caravan, portable loo and even an old boy from the village complete with dog, whom they had inherited from their previous site. Gravel was spread over the drive all the way from the main road, as the first batch of lorries taking away minerals badly cut up the track. Bernard also had our drive levelled and shingled in front of the house – a most useful by product of the digging.

Although the Massey Ferguson had totally changed the look of our land by removing in places up to six or seven feet of poor quality sand down to gravel level which started more or less at the water table – what the dragline was able to achieve in just one day was unbelievable. I came home from the shop, stopped the car and just gawped at this enormous, lovely hole with sheer sandy sides. The water may have been brown and frothy but I didn't care – it was the start of our lake.

Planning permission had to be obtained from the local county council before gravel extraction and the formation of a wet pit as a fishery could be carried out. Fortunately most councils are sympathetic towards the construction of anything to do with leisure, nature reserves and fisheries, provided heavy vehicle access and subsequent transportation of minerals for months possibly years on end does not inconvenience the owners of adjoining properties. I had no trouble in securing planning permission due to the fact that Atlas Aggregates already owned mineral extraction rights to some of my land, coupled with the plan that the new lake was to be joined to an existing one.

After a couple of days digging, Bernard, the site manager, decided that as most of this new lake would not be much deeper than between four and six feet, due to the gravel seams running quite shallow above a heavy belt of blue clay, he would not bother with the pumps during extraction. Now as far as gravel companies are concerned, to pump out the water as it pours in when minerals are taken out means far more precise digging in comparatively dry conditions. The gravel then doesn't have to be stacked to dry out before being loaded on to 20 ton lorries and taken to the processing plant. It can be dug and carted away immediately, which saves time and allows more space on site. However my pit was easier to dig wet. It was allowed to fill up from the water table and reach its own natural level while the dragline removed the sand and gravel.

This resulted in a rather uneven bottom due to the scooping action of the dragline shoe, which I was not bothered about. But more important, by being dug wet, it meant that I could immediately start organising planting of the margins and building swims – something impossible to achieve when a pit is dug dry, because there is simply no way of guessing where the eventual water line will be to the nearest foot all the way around the perimeter. Within a week of the dragline arriving and starting to dig along the southeastern boundary during March I was able to start planting. That I appeared to be planting as quickly as he was digging actually became an ongoing joke with Barry, the dragline operator, who I swear could have iced a cake with his machine despite its massive 1½ ton capacity shoe, such was his skill in operating. I would ask for a flat, level bank in a particular spot with perhaps two feet of marginal shelf, followed by the drop-off, and, lo and behold, it would be done by the time I arrived home from work.

I really enjoyed our early morning planning talks. We were literally creating the lake features based on paper drawings on a day-to-day basis. Due to the low water table, the only feature no one could do anything about was the incredibly steep sides of the new lake, in places some 15 feet above water level. But as they shelved down from the woodland all the way round, I could easily picture what a beautiful valley it would eventually become. 'Vision' is, I believe, the word I used to convince Barbara that one day the upheaval would all be worthwhile.

For angling access I had to build numerous step-down pathways. These I constructed from the birch logs during the early mornings, evenings and on Sundays throughout the spring. They blended in wonderfully with the hundreds of birch trees left on the higher level but were back-breaking to install. Each step required two holes, each two feet deep, to accommodate the support logs which were chocked in with large flints and then topped up with sand. Rather than nail the horizontal (stepping) logs in, I simply picked one or two fairly smooth thick ones and held them in position by back-filling. This was so that they could be replaced easily, which was just as well really because birch rots all too easily, and I had to replace most of the logs with oak within the first year. That was a lesson well learnt. So if you are planning any home construction work, never put birch in the ground.

Starting the excavation at the southeastern boundary close to the house allowed me systematically to plan and construct log pathways down the steep banking once it had been top-soiled. I was also able to plant both shrubs and marginals as work progressed northwestwards along the site towards the old lake where the two would eventually be joined a few months later. But before Barry's dragline left the house and I had a small pond dug some 25 feet across and four feet deep, with just a narrow pathway between it and the lake. It has turned out to be very useful, and is now a lovely wild pond, used by newts, frogs and toads as well as dragonflies.

Obtaining shrubs and plants to cover the banks of a newly-dug lake could well cost a fortune at a garden centre. By asking around, however, it was surprising what turned up. For instance, my friend Chris Newell, over the other side of Norfolk at Downham Market, happened to be clearing an island on a fishery he runs. It contained some ancient dogwood, that lovely shrub whose bark turns bright red and glistens in the winter sun. The tops of the original shrubs had dropped down into the water and actually rooted on the bottom, which provided me with hundreds of ready-to-plant stems once they had been cleared. It was a job I was only too pleased to lend a hand with.

In addition, the estate game-keeper donated dozens of young rhododendrons which had self propagated in the rich peaty soil. In one day by the late afternoon Barbara and I had planted out a good 60 yards of steep banking with dogwood, hoping the spreading rootstock would help stabilise the slope.

A few weeks later fishing buddy, Steve Allen, mentioned that a close season working party was on at a lake near Norwich and that lots of yellow iris beds were due to be cut back. After an enjoyable evening's work I was 18 bin liners full of iris tubers to the good, with a promise of more should I require them. I was very worried about the car's suspension on the way home though! By offering to clean up a friend's little carp pit which was overgrown, I obtained mountains of common reed, reed mace and common sedge, plus a bucketful of frog spawn which went in the wild pond.

From an overgrown water meadow beside my local River Wensum, the farmer was only too pleased for me to thin out numerous roots of reed grass and reed sweet grass (often called sweet rush). The word soon got around that Wilson was after plants and all sorts of offers came pouring in. I cleared out friends' overgrown garden ponds, farmers' drainage dykes and ditches and tidied up swims around a small club lake. Eventually so much was on offer I had to start declining. I was collecting in the evening and planting it all in the morning before work, day after day.

It is really puzzling just where a whole estate car full of marginal plants disappears to in a natural setting. You will know exactly what I mean if you have popped along to your local nursery or garden centre and spent £50 or even £100 on shrubs which, when planted, are hardly noticeable. Planting a lake is exactly the same, on a larger scale. The plants seem to go absolutely nowhere. However

I stuck to my goal of planting every foot of the lake's perimeter with exactly the variety I wanted, so that undesirable plants could not take hold. For instance, only in one spot, where the marginal shelf drops immediately down to over eight feet, did I plant reed mace. In a new lake which has depths under four feet, should this marginal – often wrongly called bullrush because it sports cigar-like seed heads – start self seeding, soon large areas of the margins could be ruined. The good thing about marginal plants is that you can choose exactly the right one for a specific area and for a particular reason. For tall close-in cover where the shelf dropped quickly away I installed either common reed or reed grass, a similar though slightly shorter reed type, whereas in the shallow areas I opted for the visual beauty of yellow iris which will not spread outwards into the lake and can easily be cut back by paring the tubers with a spade. It has no creeping rootstock and provides a wonderful splash of brilliant yellow flowers throughout June.

Water gardening is the same, be it a tiny pond or a lake. You can spend the first couple of years waiting impatiently for everything to double its rootstock and grow large, and then the rest of your days are spent cutting it back trying to keep the vegetation under control, as I have now been doing for the past two decades. As Barry and Albert, who worked the Massey Ferguson front loader, moved quickly along the site piling up great mounds of gravel which were taken away with equal speed by a succession of lorries, I decided where the first island should go. I decided it should be straight in front of the house so Barbara could have her favourite rhododendrons hanging out over the water within view of the kitchen. I had to make a few concessions, didn't I!

ABOVE
The lake, now almost half excavated, takes shape. On the right I had a small growing-on pond dug (now a wildlife haven for newts, frogs and toads) prior to the first island being made. Note how the bank in the foreground has already been planted with yellow iris and various shrubs.

Bernard, the manager, said that during the 30 years he had been digging pits in Norfolk no one had ever asked for an island to be made, and he reminded me that I would have less water for the fish. I then explained that in my comparatively small lake the last thing I wanted was anglers casting over each other's lines and going after the same fish, as is the problem these days on many popular heavily fished waters. And if there was a narrow, tall island in the way running lengthways down the lake they would not even be able to see each other.

So an island it was (the first of three) made by utilising a great deal of poor-quality sand plus blue clay, which otherwise would have been disposed of, with a good layer of top soil to finish. I then planted it out over a weekend, totally with evergreens including rhododendrons, cotoneaster, pyracanthas, laurels, leylandii, plus a blue cedar and my favourite conifer, the beautiful *Cedrus deodara*. I then asked Barry to leave a gap of around 15 yards before starting on the second island, which I wanted quite flat with gently sloping banks to accommodate water birds. On this second island I planted five Lombardy poplars, a few dogwood roots, some mixed dwarf conifers, and evergreen shrubs including *elaeagnus* and *stranvaesia* which both sport berries during the winter. Also planted, using Barry's dragline, were two large tree roots – one crack willow and one alder – both lifted from where the old lake would eventually join the new.

Originally I had planned on having no deciduous trees anywhere near the waterline of the new lake due to its overall shallow contours. I feared that eventually it would silt up as a direct result of leaf fall, so most shrubs and trees are evergreens. But with the poplars, willow and alder I cheated a little. Along the margins of the island I enjoyed mixing cultivated varieties with plants from the wild, amongst them the purple flowers of water mint and the golden yellow of marsh marigold, the deep blue of hybrid irises and the pinky-white flowers of bogbean, sea club rush and water forget-me-not, plus various sedges and variegated irises. Between the shrubs on the islands I mixed the orange tones of montbretia and day lilies with the yellow of St John's Wort. But this is not meant to be a garden catalogue so I won't list them all. I can't remember half the names anyway! Suffice to say that throughout the calendar year there is always something in leaf, in bloom or in berry, because although the lake is now first and foremost an angling water, it still remains my front garden.

I enjoyed rowing out to the islands in a little dinghy every evening to plant out. It was exciting just being there on this totally new piece of water, always muddy from the disturbed clay bottom, but which over the weekends soon turned almost crystal clear. Like all newly dug gravel pits it had that lovely blue-green clarity that only lasts a few weeks until Mother Nature has stocked her larder. Actually, long before the excavations were finished and the two lakes joined, the fly life cycle was turning over very quickly, with shrimps colonising the bottom strata... so I thought I'd try a bit of an experiment.

One morning Barry suddenly stopped the dragline's diesel motor and came rushing over to where I was walking the dogs. 'Hey, I've just seen a goldfish' he said. 'Yes,' I replied, 'I put in 5,000 yesterday evening.' The look on his face was absolutely magic; a mixture of total disbelief and simple sufferance. After all, who'd be nutty enough to introduce fish into a small lake while it was still being worked? As it turned out the goldfish were a sound investment and trebled their size in 12 months, helped along by a regular supply of floating trout pellets. As the lake was not going to be fished for a year or two until the banks and margins had matured, the goldfish, along with some carp, allowed me both to enjoy and monitor the new lake which by June – after just four months of excavating – was almost complete. Then on the last knockings Barry struck a large area of blue clay at waterline level which Bernard was keen to make into a car park. But the deal was the removal of gravel, sand and blue clay, and so a special machine was brought in for moving the clay across to the opposite side of the site where it could be hidden in a large natural depression in the woods. Although the area was little larger than a tennis court, and resulted in just two feet of water, I felt that a pretty bay full of lilies was more desirable than extra car parking. As it turned out this area is used by the carp at spawning time and the warm shallow water plays host to huge shoals of roach and rudd fry throughout the summer months. The beauty of numerous varieties of water lilies is yet another bonus.

At the beginning of June I donned a wet suit and visited my local club lake where I usually have the job of thinning out the massive beds of common yellow lilies which grow much too thickly if not kept in check. This particular year they were not thrown on the bank to rot but put to very good use. Using a well-sharpened bagging hook I hacked from the thick bottom silt over 200 large crowns, each with flower buds and pads intact and with massive tubers as thick as my arm. After distributing half between committee members of three local clubs for planting in their lakes, I just about managed to cram the rest into the car. Even curled gently in dustbin liners the odd stalk snapped off, but three hours later they were all replanted in the new lake at various spots around the islands and along the margins in depths of three to four feet as cover prior to the shelf dropping away. Not one was planted in open water, only along the bank side shallows. Patches of lilies out in the open can create problems when playing fish, which get snagged in them. I wanted to avoid this especially and the resulting parrot-mouthed carp which result from being hauled through lily roots on bolt rigs and heavy leads. There was no possibility of planting each tuber in its own container with loam as I would have preferred; there were far too many. I simply pushed a spade into the bottom strata, mostly blue clay topped with sediment, and wiggled it back and forth to open a large wedge-shape crevice. Each tuber was then trodden into the wedge with the stalks pointing upwards, as the spade was wiggled out. This proved most satisfactory as only two of the very buoyant roots popped up to the surface and needed to be replanted. After eight hours in the water working in a wet suit I awoke the following morning with aches and pains from muscles I never knew I had – but it was worth it.

One week later I installed another batch of lilies, this time a large white hybrid from a lake in the village owned by a good neighbour. He helped me to fill over

SIXTY YEARS A FISHERMAN

20 bin liners, in addition to accepting the temporary destruction of his beautiful beds. These went into slightly shallower margins than the common yellow variety, in depths between 18 and 36 inches, and were planted in the same way. I have subsequently added many more varieties of beautiful lilies including reds and pinks. In total I have over 20 different varieties and what a wonderful splash of colourful cover they provide throughout the summer months. Ironically the one variety I have not been able to obtain is the original white water lily *Nymphaea alba*. I am quite aware that many water-garden centres call all their white lilies by this name but they are usually, in fact, hybrids.

Back in the late 1800s a Frenchman called Joseph Latour Marliac used *Nymphaea alba* (then very common) to crossbreed so many of the beautiful hybrids which today bear his name and grace ponds all over the country. *Marlida albida*, *Marlicia camea*, *Marlicia chromatella* are the names of just three of over 70 varieties created by Marliac. Strangely the world's most gifted lily hybridiser took all his secrets to the grave when he died in 1911 and as yet no one has come anywhere near to achieving similar success. Today because Marliac's robust, large-flowered hybrid lilies exist in just about every pond, pit and lake throughout the country, the true, original *Nymphaea alba* cannot be found. Even my local Norfolk Broads, once crammed with original white water lilies up to the 1920's and 1930's, contain them no longer. Incidentally, whilst fishing the River Shannon at Meelick a few years later, I came across some white lilies that could well have been the true wild *Nymphaea alba* – but I didn't fancy diving down eight feet to obtain a root. Perhaps it's simply down to the general change in water quality which has effectively made this particular species extinct (just like the burbot). But enough of lilies. At least that's how I felt throughout June and July 1985 having physically removed from source and replanted over 300 large roots!

Once the new lake had achieved its final shape, joining it with the existing one meant a tricky job for Barry. He had to swing the dragline shoe between some mature alders literally only three or four yards apart and scoop out a five foot deep channel that would be spanned by a bridge. Back into the wet suit again, and beneath where the bridge was to go, I installed a sheet of one inch steel mesh, reaching from above the surface right down to the bottom. This was to stop the carp in the old lake from swimming through while the new one matured, and was removed a year later when I allowed fishing in both lakes. Ironically, while the mesh stopped most of the carp from passing through, what I had not bargained for was the goldfish – remember the 5,000 I had put in the new lake to grow on? – swimming through in droves. The syndicate members made a few humorous if somewhat cynical comments about how suddenly, from nowhere, just when the carp were on top taking floaters, up would come swarms of goldfish and devour everything. Fortunately everyone seemed to take their presence in good part, with the promise that the orange devils would be netted out at the end of the season. Barry put the finishing touches to the new lake by gently sloping the bank from the lane down to the water's edge, following up with some top soil. Work for both the dragline and the Massey Ferguson front loader had ended. The following morning I was not woken by the noise of their diesel engines roaring into life and, if the truth be known, it was something I actually missed after close to five months of excavation work. I also missed nattering to Barry and Albert every morning about how the shape of the lake would progress that day and then arriving home in the evening to see it. As it had more or less come to the end of its working life and could no longer be safely towed, the old site caravan was donated by Bernard, the manager, as a club house for the new fishery. He left it exactly where it had stood for five months beneath a clump of silver birch just three yards from the lake. Once painted matt leaf green, it blended in beautifully with the trees and provided refuge to the anglers during foul weather and a place for them to get their heads down during a cold night. This, incidentally, has long since been replaced by a cedar wood summerhouse.

Throughout the summer various shrubs and trees, both deciduous and evergreen, were planted near the pathways and step-downs to separate each swim so the anglers would feel content in their own little environment. Mostly the swims were neat and rather small, with an attractive birch log set horizontally, and two front supports at water level to minimise bank erosion. In a few swims which were low to the water the same objective was achieved by allowing the common fox sedge to form a thick mat-like bed. These have turned out to be great stalking spots.

In only a couple of swims did I leave enough room for a bivvy to be erected. I simply hate those huge patches of bare muddy bank – now unfortunately a common sight on most popular carp fisheries – where flowers and grasses once concealed the stealthy angler. I felt that with more than a generous stocking policy of carp in all weight ranges, scaleage, colour and shape, most of the syndicate members should be able to satisfy their fishing needs sufficiently from even short pre or post work sessions in addition to daytime plus the occasional all-night stint. What's more, I wanted anglers to be able to enjoy the sight of wild flowers, marginal plants and grasses without having to beat them down, and then feel the need to cast to the opposite bank because their cover had been destroyed.

The laborious work of collecting the seeds of numerous wild flowers, including some old favourites like foxgloves, Himalayan balsam and willow herb, has proved most worthwhile. Gorse and broom already existed in the sandy soil in abundance and have subsequently self seeded along the steep banks creating a profusion of yellow. In addition, just about everywhere along the margins and slopes – even along the high ridges between the birches – enormous clumps of soft rush (which looks not unlike a mini-bullrush, with onion-like dark green stems) have self seeded. I'm

SIXTY YEARS A FISHERMAN

certain the seeds must have been lying dormant in the enormous ridge of topsoil first stacked during wartime excavations. Then, 40 years on, they sprouted when the ridge of top-soil was used for landscaping.

I felt that some willows and conifers would really help to achieve that 'valley look', from the marginal growth up the steep slopes to where mature birch stood on level ground along the top ridge. In August 1985 I got a job lot of over 100 mixed conifers, mostly quick-growing leylandii with a few Lawson's, from a local nursery and we planted these 18 inch trees mostly along the northeastern slope which had received a good layer of top soil. Planting out this many young conifers was easier said than done. The sandy soil around the woods is absolutely riddled with rabbits, so after firmly treading in with a good peaty mixture and support cane, each sapling had to be protected – rabbits just love to chew the bark at ground level – by a two foot diameter protective sleeve of chicken wire, two feet high. I really thought I had beaten the rabbits after this little lot, and so didn't bother with chicken wire around the evergreens on the islands. Rabbits would never swim out there, would they? No, but they have no trouble walking across the ice whenever the lake freezes over, the crafty little devils. Their tell-tale paw prints going straight across the lake are clearly visible after a layer of snow has settled on the ice. Nevertheless most of these conifers are now well in excess of 30 feet high and most beautiful, providing a distinct 'Canadian look'.

The last planting job around the new lake was installing some 300 willows along the high southwestern ridge to help stabilise the banking. Dad and I set to and got most of them in and staked, complete with rabbit protectors, during the Christmas break. And the poor chap thought he had come up from London for a

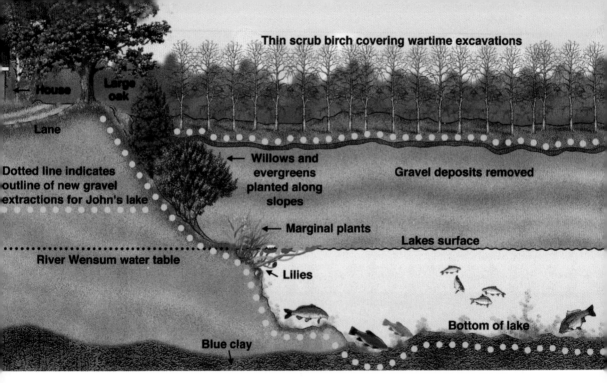

Thin scrub birch covering wartime excavations

← House

Large oak

Lane

Dotted line indicates outline of new gravel extractions for John's lake

← Willows and evergreens planted along slopes

Gravel deposits removed

← Marginal plants

Lakes surface

River Wensum water table

↖ Lilies

Bottom of lake

Blue clay

rest! We planted over 20 different varieties in all, which is nothing compared to the 200 listed in the Edgar Watts Ltd of Bungay, Suffolk, catalogue who specialise in willows, particularly cricket bat willows. I always imagined there were the standard types, like the weeping, crack, white and goat with those lovely fluffy catkins and which we lovingly call 'pussy willow'. But no, you can get willows with coloured barks, coloured catkins or leaves and special varieties with large fibrous rootstocks for consolidating steep banking, which was just what the doctor ordered for the job in hand. The two varieties of *Salix purpurea* and *Salix riminalis* were used along the steepest slopes. Every so often we popped in the odd evergreen between the willows; some Christmas trees, pines, cedars and leylandii. Evergreens dotted here and there look really nice in the winter, especially when there is a little snow on the ground. Incidentally, after planting the willows, I had a dozen or so weeping willows left over, so I pushed my 10 foot dinghy onto the roof rack of the car and took them along to the local lake in Lenwade that was dug just before Bernard moved all the machinery round to my place, and rowed across to the large island (still rather bare) and planted them. Today they are massive and truly beautiful, as anyone who fishes the first lake on the right of the Common Lakes Fishery will see.

Going back to June – the third to be precise – all the carp in the old lake spawned, with water temperature at 66 degrees Fahrenheit. I removed a mass of fertilised spawn, complete with the submerged willow roots it was stuck to, and introduced it to various spots around the new lake, and into the little pond which was by then nicely green with planktonic growth and ideal for fry survival. This resulted, one year later, in over 100 three to five inch carp from the little

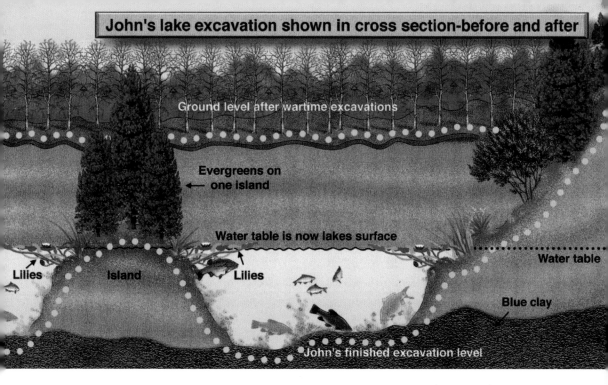

Ground level after wartime excavations

Evergreens on
← one island

Water table is now lakes surface

Water table

Lilies

Island

Lilies

Blue clay

John's finished excavation level

growing-on pond, and an unknown number in the new lake. Although it was not to be fished for at least a year (and that was providing things went well), I couldn't resist introducing a few more fish into the new lake. It's the same with a garden pond. Whoever waits for several weeks for the pond to become established like all the books tell you? You want to see fish in it straight away. I'm no exception, so in with the goldfish went 1,000 small metallic carp (koi/king carp crosses). The plan was to net out the majority of these the following spring, retaining a few to complement the stock of big metallics that had been in the old lake for three years and were then approaching double figures. Things worked very well when netting time came around.

To increase the food for planktonic growth still further, I purchased a hundredweight bag of triple super phosphate in granule form, and distributed it from the boat by hand all along the margins. It was just an hour's job, easy compared to the alternative and organic way of fertilising by shovelling in a ton of well-rotted manure.

From the outset I deliberately did not plant any soft weeds, which would seem to go against the general picture most anglers have of the perfect fishery full of aquatic vegetation and thus full of food. With the high stocking density of carp I had envisaged for the lake, a soft weed environment would not have survived anyway. When their metabolic rate is high during the summer months, feeding fish churn up the sediment in the new lake by rooting for shrimps and those little red men, bloodworms. Contrary to popular belief, a fishery does not need to be clear and prolific in soft weeds to feed a large number of carp. Green-pea farm ponds with

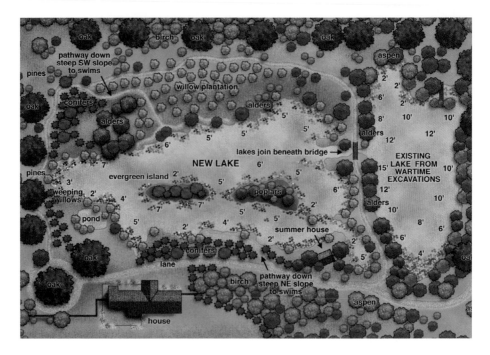

Within the image (map labels):
oak · birch · oak · oak · aspen · pathway down steep SW slope to swims · pines · willow plantation · 2' · 2' · 6' · 2' · conifers · alders · oak · alders · 5' · 8' · 10' · 10' · 5' · alders · 12' · 12' · 6' · 5' · 5' · 5' · lakes join beneath bridge → · NEW LAKE · 6' · EXISTING LAKE FROM WARTIME EXCAVATIONS · 7' · 15' · 5' · 10' · pines · evergreen island · 2' · 5' · 3' · poplars · 6' · 12' · weeping willows · 2' · 4' · alders · 10' · 10' · pond · 7' · 7' · 2' · 8' · 5' · 5' · 4' · 5' · 6' · 2' · summer house · 2' · 2' · 6' · conifers · 5' · 4' · lane · birch · pathway down steep NE slope to swims · oak · oak · aspen · house

not a sprig of weed in sight are prime examples. Area for area and pound for pound they are the richest fish producers of all waters. Carp seem just as happy in coloured water which, from the angling point of view, is more desirable in a lake of limited proportions. Catching them on simple tackle close in to the margins is one of the benefits to be gained and of course the carp still have the protection and the insect food source afforded by extensive lily beds and thick growth of marginal plants.

Before it was even dug, my lake was to be carp-biased with all sorts of shapes, sizes, scale patterns and colours, even the odd koi, some big crucians and a sprinkling of grass carp – where incidentally they do very well without soft weeds to eat. To complement odd batches already introduced throughout the winter of 1985/86 I purchased selected carp when available in preparation for the season ahead when I planned to lift up the retaining grill beneath the bridge allowing the fish to move freely from one lake to another. In went a dozen or so nice commons and mirrors into double figures plus several dozen pretty, smaller fish in the 2-7lb range. I wanted neither bream nor tench which cannot live in small communities with carp, and opted for 20 or so adult eels up to 4lbs and catfish. It makes sense really: being predatory, chub, catfish and eels do not compete on the same level with the carp and all are caught on baits such as luncheon meat or mussels. Introducing predators which help to keep down the enormous population of gudgeon, small roach and rudd, which are continually breeding in the lakes, allows anglers the chance of catching three different hard-fighting species which grow to specimen proportions in addition to plenty of carp. This is better than catching half-starved tench or bream on carp tackle.

SIXTY YEARS A FISHERMAN

The Danubian Wels catfish is not an easy fish to obtain a licence for stocking. In fact all river authorities treat the stocking of an alien fish with suspicion and indeed have good reason since the zander controversy starting back in the 1960s. However, providing the water where they are to be introduced is totally enclosed and complies with the conditions set out by the Ministry of Agriculture, Fisheries and Food, (now DEFRA) there is at least a chance of a licence being granted. Obviously only isolated lakes or pits far enough away from a river system without inlets or outlets, or low-lying banks which flood every so often, even get through the first round. There must be no chance whatsoever of the catfish accidentally going elsewhere and a map of the water concerned complete with its Ordnance Survey grid reference has to be supplied together with the application for a licence.

Before all this becomes possible however a batch of healthy young catfish from a disease-free stock bred in this country has to be found. Fortunately in the autumn of 1986 I was lucky to obtain 30 three to four inch cats, bred by a member of the Catfish Conservation Group. Several of these baby cats were forfeited to the local Water Authority for examination, which in my case then was Anglian Water in Huntingdon. They were cut open and inspected for various diseases, and duly certified as suitable. I was rewarded with an official document called an A30. This was then sent to the Ministry of Agriculture, Fisheries and Food and fortunately I was granted a licence for the catfish to be released. However simply releasing the young cats into a new and possibly hostile environment did not seem a particularly good idea, especially as the licence did not arrive until December.

A high survival rate was imperative and I didn't fancy having the little whiskers gobbled up by the large eels and chub already stocked or by one of the three herons which visit the lake every morning. So I decided to grow on half of them indoors in a large heated aquarium throughout the winter months and put the other half into the growing-on pond where they could take their chances in food stocks. There was an enormous supply of tiny carp, roach and gudgeon fry to see them through so it was up to them.

Much to Barbara's displeasure I set up the tank in the kitchen with one under-gravel filter grid, plus two internal power filters. As catfish are very sensitive to light and invariably seek seclusion in the darkest areas, several lengths of black plastic drainpipe were laid on the gravel. Within seconds of being introduced the baby cats took up residence in the pipes and unless being fed or the lights were turned out, that's where they preferred to be. It was great fun to observe their often comical reactions, especially when bumping into each other. It seemed to me they have very poor close-range vision, relying to a large extent on touch from the two long feelers. Such tiny eyes suggest they hunt more by feel, smell and vibrations than by sight.

The temperature of that tank was thermostatically controlled and after varying

Accompanied by my faithful German Shepherd, 'Buzzy' (now long passed on) I find good use for the remaining mature birch trees by tapping their sap for wine making. A recipe for this tangy wine appears towards the end of the 1990s chapter (see page 205) together with a photograph of how the lake has matured (see page 208).

it to several different temperatures between 55 and 76 degrees Fahrenheit, around 70 to 72 degrees Fahrenheit seemed to suit them best. Their metabolic rate was drastically reduced when temperature was decreased to 60 degrees Fahrenheit or below, which would seem to fit in with in-the-wild experiences of most fishermen. As an experiment and to see how they would co-exist with another species of similar size, I netted out a four inch home-grown metallic carp from the small pond and was pleased to see that in no way, at least on a size for size basis, could they compete against or dominate a king carp. In fact the carp probably had the lion's share of the granulated salmon fry crumbs which were introduced twice daily. The little cats took but a day to find this rich food source and would gorge till their bellies were full before retreating into their drainpipes.

When most of the tank's occupants had reached six to seven inches I supplemented their diet with inch-long gudgeon fry netted from the lake's edge after dark. The carp also took a fancy to gudgeon – as carp do to little fish in the wild – often taking the first three or four before the cats got a look in. As they grew their food size was increased to larger gudgeon, baby carp and roach fry. Once an average length of eight inches was reached I dispensed with the pellet food and went over to a completely fish diet, gudgeon of between two to three inches being the norm which were eagerly devoured by a quick, violent sucking motion from those ear-to-ear jaws – sometimes head first, sometimes tail first. Once a meal touched the front feelers, it was a goner. The carp too carried on munching a diet of live gudgeon.

In late May when water temperature in the lake reached around 60 degrees Fahrenheit, I released the cats, having first taken 10 days to reduce tank water temperatures. The carp, now a beautifully coloured pond fish with plates of gold and silver enamel, was given to a mate for his garden pond. It weighed close on 1lb. Since that first batch I have reared on and stocked a few dozen more Wels catfish, some of which go to 20lbs plus. Most however run much smaller and provide a thrilling tussle and the occasional surprise to those carp fishing.

My initial decision to base the fishing on a prolific head of carp of all shapes, sizes and colours with the additional back-up of eels, chub and cats has proved most popular with my syndicate anglers. It offers the chance of latching on to specimen

SIXTY YEARS A FISHERMAN

fish of several different species, whilst at the same time enjoying old-time carping which doesn't necessitate sitting out all night to get a run. To achieve this calls for a delicate balance because, compared to most, the two lakes would seem to harbour more carp than is healthy. But as the lakes are literally my front garden allowing me to walk around regularly, there is no better opportunity for close monitoring things such as disease, overcrowding, oxygen starvation and so on.

I was of course still fishing as much as possible during the mid 1980s despite the extra labour of love involved in the creation of the new lake. I also updated my book *Where to Fish in Norfolk and Suffolk* during 1984/85. In fact life had taken yet another direction even before lake excavation was started with the opportunity of making some video pilots for television. I was introduced to Independent Television producer, Peter Akehurst, by a mutual friend, Jim Forte, who now lives in Canada, and we shot three pilots during the winter of 1984/85. The first was pike fishing on Rockland Broad, the second was roach fishing on Norfolk's River Tiffey and the last was on my local River Wensum after chub. These were sent out to television companies all over the country (fishing was scarcely represented on television in those days, remember) and luckily for us the tape eventually landed on the desk of Anglia's then head of production, Phil Gamer, who decided (as he told me later) to provide us with a budget for a new series because he particularly liked the way I presented pike fishing on Rockland Broad.

Peter Akehurst went on to direct the first four series of *Go Fishing*. The first two of these were produced in-house with Anglia TV crews and the second two independently for Anglia by Peter's own company, Wizard Productions. Then things turned rather sour between us and I suggested he find another presenter. Within

ABOVE

Well, someone's got to do it, haven't they! In this case it was a photo call publicity shoot organised by Anglia PR where I teamed up with Page Three girl, the lovely Suzanne Mitzi, who squeezed into a mermaid outfit for the occasion on the Serpentine in London.

a few months Anglia's programming commissioner, Colin Ewing, invited me to continue with *Go Fishing* independently as Peter had not come up with a replacement, and so I teamed up with one of the cameramen, Paul Martingel, as director and his producer friend Gelly Morgan, who was all set to produce *Go Fishing* series five through her own production company, Pretty Clever Pictures. However I told Paul that this would be the last series I made without being in total control. This resulted in the formation of Kazan River Productions – named after the most glorious fishing venue in Canada's Northwest Territories – one year later. Paul and I then produced a further six series before he left Kazan to go his own way.

The first six part series of *Go Fishing*, using the first compact Betacam video system installed by Anglia Television (now superseded by Digi Beta), was shot during the summer of 1986 within the Anglia viewing region and screened in 1987. Fortunately it proved to be an instant success and was given rave reviews throughout the angling press. *Angling Times* in particular really warmed to the series and this led to my writing regularly for EMAP magazines (then Emap Active, but now the Bauer Publishing Group) which continues up to this day. (Under my company, Kazan, I also made specialist angling videos for Emap Active, but more of this later.)

Actually, it was during the first couple of years of being involved with *Go Fishing* that I met Sarah Mahaffy who founded Boxtree Limited, then an independent publisher of television and media related titles, now part of the Macmillan group, and Martin Founds of Anglers' World Holidays: two people who were to greatly influence the direction I took within television. I wrote close on 30 titles under the Boxtree imprint and I shall be forever grateful to Sarah and her then co-director, David Inman, for their vision in wanting me to write that first all-important book, *Go Fishing*, which described the ins and outs of putting fishing across on television back in 1988. I had in fact already put a book together before I met Sarah because I could see the marketing potential. Unfortunately, neither Anglia TV nor *Angling Times* shared my view. Without Channel Four agreeing to take the series – which at that time they had not – nobody wanted to commit themselves and so I started chopping up what I'd written into articles for magazine use. But Sarah decided to take my book anyway. Within a few months her loyalty had been rewarded:

Channel Four had decided to screen *Go Fishing* nationwide after all.

Anglers' World Holidays, the leading angling holiday operator in the UK, is owned by Martin Founds, who provided me with a wealth of exciting locations for filming in *Go Fishing* three and four, and also series five, a 12 part international series. Sadly, although probably best remembered by many viewers, series five along with series six (both international series) were not I thought likely to be repeated due to the fact that *Go Fishing* was there after (right up to it's end at series 17) produced on budget money allocated for local programming. Filming locations being restricted to within that same viewing area. Things had become even more complicated for my *Go Fishing* series during those early years in that having been bought out by Meridian Television; Anglia TV was then taken over by United News and Media. As a consequence Channel Four refused to screen *Go Fishing* third hand, so my programmes went back to being filmed in both the Anglia and Meridian regions only, and subsequently shown only in those viewing areas. Sadly, anglers nationwide did not get the chance of watching them, but the programmes were extensively sold on to the satellite channel, Discovery Home and Leisure, who later were to provide budgets for a 12 part international *Fishing Safari* series, and 15 part *Dream Fishing* series. But more of this later on.

It is around this time (the mid 1980s) through their then marketing manager, my good friend, Bruce Vaughan, that I became involved with Ryobi Masterline, and I have subsequently endorsed and designed tackle for them for the best part of 25 years. Bruce went on to become co-owner of Wychwood, the well-known clothing and tackle manufacturer, and was replaced by Andy Orme, who then went on to form his rod manufacturing company, Seer Rods. Chris Leibbrandt then took over as marketing manager for the following 10 years. Ryobi Masterline became Masterline International Ltd in 1999, and a new range of specialist reels, rods and sundry items was designed by me carrying the Wilson logo.

RIGHT

The *Go Fishing*
crew about to
leave Ferguson
Lake Lodge for
Nueltin in Northern
Canada. (Left to
right) Me, Martin
Founds, Paul
Martingel, Melissa
Robertson, Keith
Sharpe and Henry
Marcuzzi. Our
transport: this
ancient 1943
Norseman float-
plane. Was it
hairy!

But let's return to the days of researching and filming abroad in the late 1980s. I researched several Irish locations with Martin, mostly along the River Shannon where we caught mountains of bream and specimen rudd. We caught carp and trout in Austria, sea trout and the strikingly coloured golden ide in Sweden, roach and bream in Denmark, sharks and barracuda in The Gambia, plus barbel, mullet and carp from the Rio Ebro in Spain. In Canada we visited the bountiful province of Manitoba for channel catfish and carp in Winnipeg's Red River, steelhead trout and dolly varden in British Columbia and huge lake trout, northern pike and grayling from the remote Northwest Territories. And what fabulous locations they were! It really opened my eyes to the fishing available elsewhere and I couldn't wait to share those experiences with my viewers. I particularly enjoyed our escapades in Canada's far north, and chronicled a great deal of this in my *Go Fishing Year Book* which included much of the detail about putting the international series five together.

One of the stories included in the *Year Book* illustrates the unbelievably good sport Canada has to offer. It all started innocuously enough when our crew of six finally left Rankin Inlet on the edge of the Hudson Bay (an old mining town full of rather merry Inuit Eskimos) having been fog bound for almost four days and was deposited at Ferguson Lake Lodge. This took three separate trips in the small Cessna float-plane with much grumbling from the joint-smoking pilot, Harvey, a Vietnam vet. I can remember vividly on the first flight across those deserted wastelands, which comprised half land mass and half water, when, with a map on his lap Harvey suddenly turned to me and said in all sincerity, 'Do you know where we are, John?' Having never seen the Northwest Territories before, let alone fished there, I obviously hadn't a clue. This didn't help Harvey who was simply matching the shapes of the river junctions and lakes below us with those on his map, flying by compass being totally out of the question due to minerals in the rocks giving false magnetic readings. So it was sight flying or nothing else (hence the reason for us waiting for the fog to disperse) and Harvey was looking for what appeared to be little more than a garden shed – Ferguson Lake Lodge – beside a huge lakeland and river complex. We were literally hundreds of miles from nowhere, the closest bit of civilisation being some 400 miles away at Baker Lake. So it was Ferguson or bust. Making fishing programmes for television had suddenly taken on board a new facet – danger!

The jovial 23 stone, Keith Sharpe, who settled in the Northwest Territories to avoid alimony payments to his first wife back in Birmingham over 23 years previously, met us at the dock and organised his troop of nine (yes, nine!) children to stash all the gear into the cabins reserved for our stay. Keith had remarried to Alma, an Inuit, and was in the process of putting the Ferguson and Kazan River fishing for giant lake trout and huge arctic grayling on the map, deserted as it was and bisected by the 63rd parallel.

Once Harvey had brought the entire crew over from Rankin Inlet we settled down to a sumptuous dinner of caribou steaks. Then I made the mistake of asking Keith whether we had two boats for the next day's filming. 'Oh dear, no,' said Keith, 'but I do have a spare one left on an old outpost camp not far away.' (The 18 foot hull had in fact been left since last summer turned upside down with an assortment of supplies beneath.) Keith said we would have to make a short trip after dinner in the Cessna, followed by an overnight stop at his new camp situated close to where we would be filming on the Kazan River. We could even enjoy some spinning for lake trout en route 'to get my hand in' so to speak. I was certainly up for it, as was Martin Founds. Director Paul Martingel didn't fancy splitting the crew up but Keith assured him we would all meet up again the following morning. Keith then muttered something about an ice floe, but I was so excited I wasn't listening.

30 minutes later, Harvey skimmed the Cessna down alongside the small island and Keith, Martin and I prepared the aluminium boat for fishing. The 30 horsepower Yamaha engine we'd brought along fired immediately and with darkness but two hours away the Cessna headed back to the lodge while we set off towards Keith's outpost camp at Yathked. That's where the mighty Kazan River merges with the Ferguson immediately above Kazan Falls; a maelstrom of white water so charismatic I named my production company after it. It contains mountains of two-to 3lb grayling and some of the world's largest lake trout which grow to 60lbs and more.

Though we were about to experience the most terrifying time of our lives, for the first half hour the lake was completely clear and I had time to catch several sizeable lakers up to around 15lbs on large spoons cast from a small island. Then we could see what lay ahead, an enormous band of ice stretching seemingly over the entire horizon. Keith's prophetic words, 'I didn't think it would be this big', still failed to dampen our enthusiasm. Anyway we had no option but to press ahead in the direction of Yathked camp where we were to spend the night.

There was in fact more than a mile of pack ice between our boat and clear water on the other side due to the particularly late 'ice out' that year. In Canada's far north the ice melts by July but the rivers and lakes ice over again by September. It is an incredibly short summer which is why everything breeds so prolifically – the mosquitoes and black flies in particular. As dusk started to fall so the flies appeared from nowhere. With the plane now long gone back to Ferguson, it was a case of dragging the boat over the ice floes or perish from exposure. And while yours truly was wondering whether we go around or across it, Keith ran the bows of the 18 foot aluminium hull right up on to the ice, which he guaranteed was perfectly safe to walk on and a good one foot thick. So we all got out and started to pull. Despite the hull weighing over 600lbs plus planks of timber, pots and pans and even a portable loo, which had been left with other sundry supplies beneath the boat all winter, the aluminium boat slid quite freely over the ice. It even looked for a while as though we would soon be in the warm at Keith's outpost camp. Little did we know!

After an hour of pulling and pushing, dark areas of thin ice became far more numerous and we needed to make long detours to stay on the firm, bright white parts. Midnight came quickly and went, though of course we could easily see because it never really gets totally dark that high up during the summer months. Did I say summer? It certainly didn't feel much like summer. Our hands were becoming painfully cold and we were starting to feel exhausted. We could see the clear water beyond the ice still a tantalising way off so we had no alternative but to plod on into the unknown.

Whenever the ice could be felt cracking beneath our feet we immediately transferred most of our weight on to the boat by leaning across the gunnels. On the first occasion the ice actually gave way, Martin got his feet soaked, which kind of served him right for only bringing trainers on a fishing jaunt, but he carried on without a murmur. With Keith at the front pulling and me and Martin pushing on each side, everything went well again for a while. Then quite suddenly the formidable hitherto reassuring figure of Keith Sharpe, who was constantly giving orders from up front, disappeared through the ice with a crash that would have done a bull elephant proud. The boat lunged forward after him, while Martin and I jumped in and grabbed his collar. He managed to roll over into the boat at the first attempt, completely drenched in freezing water. It was a very close shave indeed because without Keith, Martin and I were goners, and without us so was he.

Not knowing if the next footstep would take us under the ice or keep us on it we became more and more anxious about our plight, especially when we saw the number of gaps now appearing between the ice floes. Keith, however, even had a

remedy for this problem, and showed us how to use the boat as a bridge, pushing it across from one chunk of ice to another, then pulling it on to firm ice once we had walked across. In areas large enough we actually pushed the boat in and used both paddles and engine for a few yards. Then Keith would run the boat up onto thicker ice and we could continue on our way. Throughout we were treated to a truly beautiful sunset, as the great shining globe sunk beneath the horizon fusing the icy background into a multitude of yellows, reds and purples.

At around two in the morning a strange thing happened. I had always naively associated mosquitoes with stagnant water and the Tropics, so I was surprised that here we were in the freezing cold being bitten by more mosquitoes than I had ever seen before, or since, incidentally. Like all nightmares ours eventually came to an end when, totally exhausted and almost frozen to the bone, stinking of dried sweat and wondering whether we would actually make it, we finally broke through the last of the ice floes into clear water. What a relief it was! We hooted and whistled like three kids at a funfair. There was then just half an hour's journey to Keith's basic outpost camp at Yathked where we had to wake up Rob, a young American who guided for Keith all summer, to sort us out some bedding. After a brew of strong tea and a warm up over the spirit stove we finally got our heads down shortly before four in the morning, completely knackered and not just a little lucky to be there at all.

What did we eventually catch? Well the lake trout fishing certainly lived up to Keith's promises with everyone in the crew catching lakers of 20lbs plus on both spinner and fly, and even from the shore. We managed to wrap what we wanted in filming action within a day and a half – which was just as well really because that's all the time we had.

The year 1987 was a particularly busy one for me because I travelled from Norwich by train to London once a week as a consultant on the angling part work *Catch* published by Marshall Cavendish. Fellow consultant was my old mate, the late Trevor Housby, and we enjoyed a riotous time together helping with page layouts, correcting copy and captioning the photos. It was a known fact amongst the staff that Trevor and John needed to have the current part work put to bed before everyone went to lunch. Because they couldn't get much out of us in the afternoon once we'd hit the red wine at 'Break for the Border', a Mexican restaurant around the corner. Those were fun days and for me they were not only, great weekly breaks from the tackle shop, but a wonderful experience too.

We even found time to venture away from the office periodically on prize-winner days out. I remember one trip to Nythe Lake in Arlesford, Hampshire (now closed), where two prize-winners were accompanied by all the *Catch* staff for a fly fishing day out after rainbow trout. Unfortunately the sport proved dire due to an uncharacteristically cold and chilly day for May. At lunchtime our two guests had caught nought.

After lunch however Trevor pulled out his trump card and suggested they try the tiny lakes (the stews) behind the lodge where, of course, they couldn't go wrong! We were lucky to get away with it but, as Trevor said, 'Hey, they've come for a day's fly fishing, haven't they?' How could I disagree?

I warmed to everyone on that project, several of whom became firm friends, and respected and valued their professionalism. Simply seeing how my own copy and colour transparencies were used within the part work was of enormous future help.

When I bought my tackle shop in Norwich back in 1971 after returning from Barbados, along with the stock I inherited from my predecessor, the late Bill Cooper, was a large cigar box full of unsaleable junk, amongst which were some enormous size 8/0 treble hooks. The label read, 'Mahseer Trebles 2/9d'. Weren't they those huge fish that inhabited the rivers of India? I had read a little about these legendary monsters – the great *Barbus tor* – but never thought that one day I would actually be catching them. As chance would have it, in 1980 I was asked to write a piece for the British ABU Tight lines tackle catalogue and was sent the previous year's issue by editor, the now late, John Darling, for guidance. It was full of the ABU-sponsored transatlantic overland expedition made by three English guys in a jeep and how they caught mahseer to 90lbs. The pictures were awe-inspiring and left an indelible image on my memory. The mahseer then cropped up the following year when Paul Boote, another English angler, wrote a fascinating series of articles in *Angling* magazine about his exploits in search of mahseer in southern India.

By now I was straining at the bit, but I had a wife, two children and a tackle business. Swanning off for several weeks to the depths of India was, at that time, simply not on, so I did the next best thing and read some books about the monster fish – the standard work on the subject by H S Thomas, entitled *The Rod in India*, and others by Skene Dhu and Jim Corbett, recounting wonderfully those early days of the British Raj in India when mahseer fishing was out of this world all over the country. Unfortunately however since the late Forties, due to indiscriminate dynamiting, poaching and netting of all the major rivers, the mahseer had become non-existent in all but a handful of protected locations, mainly in the extreme north and south. I feared it would all be over long before Wilson got attached to a whopper.

After my initial desire to do battle with the mahseer in the early 1980s several years elapsed during which time little was heard in the angling press of this enigmatic species. I was by now starting to feel the pressure of both shop and television commitments and fancied a diversion. The decision finally to do something about mahseer fishing actually came about when friend Andy Davison and I were at a clay pigeon shooting club annual dinner in Dereham near Norwich, feeling decidedly worse for wear. Quite suddenly the subject came up, and there and then we decided we had to go. Andy drove down to Bristol to meet Paul Boote for some advice, and I spent week upon week collecting maps of the famous Cauvery River in the state of Karnataka, where historically many of the largest mahseer had been caught, including those by Paul Boote and by the ABU-sponsored transatlantic overland expedition. We were going in search of mahseer and that was that. We allowed ourselves a five-week holiday during which time Barbara agreed to look after the tackle shop. And so it was, following over a year of painstaking research and putting together what we hoped would be suitable tackle combinations, that in the middle of February 1988 Andy and I boarded an Air India flight from Heathrow to Bombay and on to Bangalore, there to meet Colonel Naidu of the Wildlife Association of South India.

Spending an entire five weeks in the company of just one person necessitates that he should be one hell of a good friend. The previous occasion that Andy and I shared a fishing holiday was some 10 years back touring along the Tay Valley, in Scotland, grayling fishing. We were cooped up in a caravanette with two other friends, Ron Wells and Doug Allen, both of who have now sadly passed on, and although the trip was enormous fun for a week, it did make us all realise that no matter how good the bond of friendship, eventually you get on each other's nerves. Stuck in that tiny caravanette along with damp, stinking nets and tackle, not to mention smelly socks and maggots that were for ever escaping, brought out the worst in us all.

It resulted in Doug and Ron, real 'meat and two veg' merchants, usually content with tinned meat pie and peas every night, being totally revolted at the eating habits of Wilson and Andy. We were not prepared, however, to allow the remoteness of Scottish grayling rivers to affect the quality of our cuisine. On one particular evening, for instance, we served up chilli can carne and beef-filled enchiladas with lashings of hot garlic bread, all washed down with two large bottles of Chianti.

The enchilada cases I made from seasoned flour and water, rolled out on the flip-up table top with a Heinz tomato sauce bottle (no rolling pin on board) and for a while there was flour and black pepper everywhere, much to the disgust of Ron and Doug who departed for the nearest pub long before we had the gourmet meal bubbling away on the tiny stove. And there they stayed until last orders were called and the aroma within the van had subsided. Doug swore he could still smell chilli over a week later when he cleared up the van before returning it to the hire firm. Truth is, I believed him too!

I wouldn't recommend to anyone the hassle of arriving at Bombay International Airport and clearing customs before attempting the switch-over to the domestic terminal for the final flight to Bangalore. The amount of unnecessary red tape (left by the British) anyone carrying cameras or fishing tackle has to endure is outrageous. Nowadays there are flights straight through, fortunately, but then I guess it was all just part of life's rich tapestry. Anyway before long we had checked in to the West End Hotel for our first night in India. We left for the river in Colonel Naidu's broken-down Jonga the following morning complete with sufficient supplies for our five-week stint which included a dozen live chickens. No freezers in the Indian jungle!

I'm tempted to say at this point that until you've travelled on Indian roads, you have never experienced the pain, heat and exhaustion of third-world travel. 60 miles of being bumped about, plus the continual blast of hot air mixed with dust from the narrow roads was almost choking. Yet this was at the same time utterly fascinating. We passed troops of monkeys, mud hut villages and the most stunningly dressed Indian girls gathering water from remote village wells. The peasant women dressed in colourful saris had fresh flowers in their ebony hair and wore a kind of pride not seen in the West these days. We passed the simple kilns and workings of brick and tile manufacturers, had a ride on an oxen cart and spent an interesting half hour with a group of road workers, mostly women, chipping and brushing away at the gravel road in readiness for laying tarmac. Goodness knows how many rolls of film Andy and I got through on that first memorable drive from Bangalore to the Cauvery (or the Kaveri) valley at Sangham.

As we motored down the steep hill via several hairpin bends towards our final-goal the Cauvery was every bit as magical as we had imagined. Strewn with boulders even in

BELOW

If there is one place on this planet I have come to love enough to think of as my second home, it is the majestic Cauvery River Valley in the state of Karnataka, southern India.

midstream, some larger than a car, the entire centre channel ripped forcibly over more boulders, through a series of rapids and deep swirling pools. This was where we had come to do battle with the mighty mahseer. With steep, thorn-scrub-coated hills picking out the route of the river along both banks we followed the flow upstream, through dry creeks and ravines until we reached what was to be our camp at Gari Bora where a huge rock of granite, half the size of a house, presides over the Cauvery River.

We met guides, Bola and Suban, and camp cook, Ivan, and a most interesting hunter by the name of Don Anderson, whose father, the late Kenneth Anderson, was one of the most famous of all modern-day *shikaris* (hunters). His book, *Nine Man-eaters and One Rogue*, is a must for anyone remotely interested in hunting and a gripping read. Don kept us captivated with tales of the Indian jungle all through dinner and long into the night, every so often punctuating his stories with identification of the various animal sounds around us: the rooting of wild boar (less than 50 yards away), jackals calling incessantly and the occasional roar of a bull elephant. How we slept I'll never know.

Then in the early hours a steady, thunderous roar seemed to drown out everything else. Don said, 'Oh dear, they've opened the dam', which instantly put paid to any mahseer action for 10 days. The state of Tamil Nadu further downriver was like a dust bowl and the government had bent to pressure and was flooding the entire river valley in order to irrigate the farmers' paddy fields. Hence literally overnight, which just happened to be the first night of our trip to the river, the Cauvery rose fully 30 feet in just a few hours. Don said it was as high as we would ever see the river, second only to the full monsoon rains which raise it even higher throughout the summer months. We just had to be patient until it receded. At least this gave us time to explore the valley with Bola and Suban. We tracked elephant herds, located the marks of big crocodiles that basked on the mud slopes and hunted poisonous snakes. Sometimes we used a coracle which was kept at the camp to reach the other side, sometimes we swam across. Everything Bola did, Andy had to do, and so a 40 year old Wilson suddenly found himself attempting to do things that would have seemed downright dangerous back home, but when in Rome as they say... It was a wonderful chance to behave like a boy again and we both thoroughly enjoyed ourselves. So what, I hear you ask, has this odd, almost prehistoric carp-like fish got that all the others haven't? Well, to start with, mahseer specifically choose to live in the very fastest, most turbulent reaches of these big wild mountain-fed rivers. They select rivers up to 300 yards wide which every so often abruptly narrow down to just 30 yards, forcing their torrent through rocky gorges into unbelievably powerful rapids. In such a volatile environment you would quite reasonably think no fish could swim. But it does. In currents doing 10 to 15 knots which rip around great chunks of black rock from which the entire river bed is formed, in a lather of spray

and white water, the biggest mahseer are to be found. These massive river fish weigh anything between 40 and 100lbs or more, with scales and fins so large they seem disproportionate to their body size. The mouth is also enormous, coconut-size with thick-rimmed rubbery lips quite devoid of teeth. But back in the throat is the mahseer's secret weapon, its awesome pharyngeal teeth, capable of crushing to pulp both the fish and crabs which live amongst the rocks, plus the strongest of hooks should you be unfortunate and hook one in the throat. The mahseer has, in addition, seemingly endless stamina. Hour-long fights from fish in the 50-70lb class are commonplace, without the slightest indication of the creature tiring or that you might be getting the better of it. At any time during the fight the mahseer may suddenly rip off 50 to over 100 yards of 30-40lb test mono as though on its initial run. Often on that first frightening run, reels like the ABU 7000 or 9000 are stripped to the point where you either jump in and follow the fish down the rapids or hear the line crack like a pistol shot. Then quite suddenly, without any warning, after having given its very all, the fish bellies up with its great mouth wide open, ready to be hauled out, and even this is no easy job in water doing 10 knots or more.

With hands still shaking, a soft retaining cord is passed through its gill and out through the mouth to form a loop-like stringer and the fish is held steady in the flow with its head upstream until it regains its breath. Then and only then are trophy shots taken. With a strong sense of compassion for the great fish you wonder at its physical enormity as you cradle it lovingly in your arms before returning it from whence it came, to cheer the soul of another angler on another day. I ask you, how many freshwater fish can strip off 200 to 300 yards of line from a multiplier against the power of an 11 foot 3lb test curve rod and leave you feeling like a nervous fruit jelly within seconds?

When the river subsided, the kind of fights Andy and I enjoyed were simply unforgettable. Each day there was a fish to top the performance of the one before. Slowly we stepped up line strength from 20lb to 30lb and finally to 40lb test. The current speed, the rocks on which the line all too quickly became frayed, necessitated such tackle and it was none too light. Where the biggest fish resided was too fast for even a 4oz lead to hold bottom. So the method was to use just a little lead coil wound around the line, 12 inches above a 6/0 hook, and to encourage it, by casting across the stream and – giving a little slack, to catch around a rock. You then tightened up and waited, your nerve ends tingling in anticipation of the violent take of a big mahseer. Even moderate-size fish would have pulled the rod in, so it was held at all times. Whether using a huge ball of paste made from the staple millet grain flour of southern India called ragi, a river crab, or an eight inch live bait (any small rock fish will do), the 'take' when it comes can only be compared to the hook suddenly being transferred to a lorry doing 40 miles an hour.

Your thumb burns as the spool revolves at high speed and you frantically try to knock the reel into gear before setting the hook. Many big fish do in fact almost hook themselves; such is the force at which they belt off downstream. Very quickly your groin aches from the pain where the rod butt digs in. You change hands frequently throughout the fight to rest a tired arm and your buddy helps you gulp from the water bottle in between rattling off unforgettable shots on the camera. And afterwards if it is a big one, you are content not to cast again – lest you hook another! – such is the fight. Actually Andy and I made a pact from the start, agreeing that whenever one hooked into a good fish the other would instantly reel in and grab both cameras. This worked a treat. More than at any other time in our lives we learned to be unselfish.

Actually all species of fish grow large in the Cauvery River. It is so rich in all forms of life, from snails and aquatic insect larvae clinging to the underside of every rock, to the millions of tiny fry along the margins which peck at the bits of ragi paste as you rinse your hands after baiting up. Water temperature was an incredible 87 to 89 degrees Fahrenheit during our stay with the full Indian summer still to come!

In some of the steadier stretches of the four miles we covered, our guides would row us out by the coracle to a rocky outcrop in mid river where the current was fastest. We then got back into the coracle if a big fish set off downstream or upriver (most go down) and gave chase, finally clambering out on to the shore or a rock plateau during the closing stages of the fight. Without question seeking fish in the rapids provided the most thrilling, unforgettable – if not hairy and rather dangerous – sport.

After one week of crashing into unseen rocks without shoes and another of feeling sand and grit rubbing the skin away inside trainers, my feet were so sore I could hardly walk without wincing. Andy then suffered a badly infected left leg from ulcers which turned septic, a huge chunk of flesh and bone – yes, bone – having been gouged from his shin bone by the rocks. I made him take the bus with Suban from Sangham into Kanakapura (the nearest town) to see the doctor. Bandages and penicillin were handed out but a couple of days later, and fully two weeks before we were to be picked up by the Colonel at the end of our stay, Andy's leg was in a really bad way. His calf

BELOW

Despite a damsel fly finding my badly abused and painful feet attractive, I doubt there's any chance of a toe job here! This was the result of sand and gravel particles wearing away the skin within a pair of trainers: one reason why I now wear diving boots when mahseer fishing.

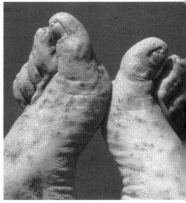

THE 1980s: TELEVISION CALLS   151

had swollen up larger than his thigh; even to touch his thigh brought gasps of pain. What to do? Then someone up there took charge. We were just about at our wits' end when suddenly we heard the comforting sound of a four-wheel-drive vehicle coming along the elephant tracks beside the river – the first westernised sound for almost three weeks. It was Susheel and Nanda Gyanchand, a husband and wife hunting and fishing team, with whom we had met and fished within the first few days of our arrival at the river.

Nanda was a practising doctor working at that time in Bangalore, whilst Susheel owned (and still does) one of the largest granite companies in south India. More importantly Susheel's father – and this was the miracle – was also a doctor and one of the top bone specialists in Bangalore. With a badly infected leg there was not a more welcome couple for Andy to have bumped into miles from anywhere in the Indian jungle. Although Susheel and Nanda had arrived for a three-day mahseer stint with mountains of fresh supplies including an icebox full of cold beers, they took one look at Andy's swollen leg, helped him into their Jonga and headed back to Bangalore. There Andy stayed for the following two weeks, leaving me to break camp two days before our flight home. Andy's condition could not in fact have been worse, despite his cavalier attitude. He had cellulitis of the bone, which apparently was only one step away from gangrene. Had our newly-made friends not arrived when they did I shudder to think what the consequences would have been. I guess with a whole host of nasties such as deadly poisonous snakes, scorpions and spiders – all regulars around our campsite – plus huge crocodiles in the river, you can understand why we had the entire river valley to ourselves for most of the time. The isolation was indeed wonderful for the soul but it was a bit inconvenient to be so far away from civilisation when medical help was required.

We built up a marvellous relationship with our two local guides, Bola and Suban, who swam out eagerly, regardless of currents, to disengage our lines from hidden rocks to stop a fish in its bid for freedom. We did have to suffer pretty basic Indian food for five weeks (during which time I actually lost two stone in weight!) but it was worth it. We counted no fewer than 12 different birds of prey along just four miles of river. Eagles, vultures and kites actually sat on nests high up in the tall mutti trees together with a family of monkeys right above our campsite, just a stone's throw from the river. In all we took exactly 60 mahseer from 5lbs upwards, including a dozen over 50lbs plus, the best two weighing 71lb and 87lb. Most came to ragi paste bait and perhaps a dozen or so came to live baits which the guides caught from the shallow pools in a cast net.

In addition to mahseer we caught, both on paste and worms dug from the river bank, numerous other, much smaller, exotic, peculiar-looking barbel-like tropical oddities, many with weird sucker-type mouths. These they used for sucking on to rocks in the fast water to eat the algae. Their shapes and bright colours were marvellous to behold. Catfish to about 5lbs were plentiful and these, when fried and curried, were very tasty. One morning it was my misfortune to hook on ragi paste a very large snapping turtle. It came up hissing loudly, its bright red neck seeming to extend for ever, so I cut the line to be on the safe side. I didn't like the look of it at all. Suban had never seen one before during a lifetime on the river.

Enjoying the spectacular scenery and battling with mahseer in the Cauvery River system was an experience and a privilege never to be forgotten, whether hearing a bull elephant bellowing from across the river at dawn whilst you kit up for another session, watching otters at play or listening to the repetitive rendering of the brain fever bird (the Indian cuckoo). Small wonder that Andy and I have returned to this wonderful valley time and time again. Needless to say Susheel and Nanda have remained firm friends ever since, and whenever Andy and I arrive in Bangalore there is a four-wheel-drive vehicle at our disposal.

Exactly one year later, in March 1989, Andy and I made our first return trip and, due to having Susheel's four-wheel-drive vehicle on loan, we were able to explore the Cauvery for several miles both up and downstream of our camp. One particular morning will remain in my memory for ever because I accounted for the best catch I have ever made in over 60 years of fishing. As usual we were woken long before dawn and quietly moved around the camp gathering everything we needed for an hour-long drive to a favourite hot spot. While Bola and Suban loaded the rods, cast net, cameras and a large bag of freshly boiled ragi into the back of Susheel's vehicle, Andy and I filled our water bottles from the filter unit, had a last look around the camp and told Raju the cook not to expect us back before dusk.

As usual, the dust from the narrow rock-strewn track following the river's path down the valley had covered everything by the time we arrived at the gorge, a wide flood plain, not of sand banks and marginal growth like higher upriver, but jagged, black bedrock – a spot known as Onti Goundu. Since time began the river had carved out its own identity through this primeval setting and was about 30 yards wide at our favourite spot, immediately above a succession of pools and foaming white rapids. With such strong, swirling currents and depths averaging between 20 and 30 feet most fishermen would never assume that this is where the largest mahseer of all prefer to live, in currents pulling as hard as a staggering 15

OVERLEAF
I doubt I'll ever beat this phenomenal catch, shared with guides Bola and Suban, and made in just a few hours from the Cauvery River: a magnificent brace of mahseer weighing 81lb and 92lb. My finest ever angling achievement.

knots – but they do. Humpbacked, fully-scaled monsters, seemingly part carp, part barbel (although the mahseer is in fact a barbel) and here attaining weights of more than 140lbs.

Andy and I had taken our fair share of whoppers from several spots along the valley – from the deep pools, from the rapids, amidst a mixture of boulders and white water. These were hard-earned fish indeed, all of which provided long, exhausting fights on our 11 foot, 3lb test rods and 40lb reel line. We fought battles that will be savoured and remembered for ever. But it was here in this hot desolate part of the valley, uninhabited except for monkeys, snakes and the odd wild boar, that both Bola and Suban felt our best chance of hitting a real monster existed.

It took the four of us more than 30 minutes to work carefully across the network of swift-flowing streams and rock pools on the outer flood plain, before reaching a mouth-watering spot where the river, running right to left, speeds around a double S bend with a long, deep straight between. Andy and Bola crept down to the bottom bend, while I settled quietly on top of a flat rock, above the upstream bend, with Suban at my side. A duck-egg-size ball of ragi paste was carefully moulded around the 6/0 hook and with 2ozs of lead strip squeezed on to the line 18 inches above the bait to catch on the rocks and hold bottom, I made a 20 yard cast downstream and across.

The bait was quickly gripped by the current and swept across the bottom of the pool towards an outcrop of rock at surface level where a defined crease suggested that a mahseer holding spot was immediately downstream. And it was! Quite suddenly the rod tip buckled over and the free spool beneath my right thumb became a blur as an unseen force rushed downstream at what seemed like 150 miles an hour. Disregarding the painful line burns, I slammed the 9000 into gear and watched helplessly as over 100 yards of the 40lb line disappeared in no time at all. Under full pressure the fish finally slowed down when it reached the end of the straight and circled around the wide bend where Andy and Bola sat, allowing me to screw the clutch down and regain some line.

What incredibly powerful creatures these big mahseer are! You would imagine that maximum pressure from a powerful rod and 40lb line would slow them down. But this stubborn fish managed to work up and down the long straight, almost at will, for close on three-quarters of an hour, characteristically ironing the line to the rock-strewn bottom as barbel do. Then quite suddenly it came to the surface, virtually beaten to a standstill, to reveal its enormous pig-like girth and cavernous open mouth. Suban climbed down to water level and gently cradled the great fish in his arms. It looked bigger than him and subsequently pulled the spring balance down to exactly 81lb. Gently, Suban sleeved a soft cord through its gills and out through the mouth tying a large loop, so that the fish could move about easily, and tethered it close into the bank around a stake. Big mahseer are always best left on such a stringer for half an hour or so to get their strength back before returning them to face the full force of the powerful current.

Andy and Bola had by now returned fishless from downstream to photograph the fight and so we all decided to retire to the shade provided by a large tamarind tree for a rest from the sun which now blazed overhead to a ferocious 100 degrees Fahrenheit. On our return to fishing Andy and Bola again went downstream to the lower bend and before returning my fish I decided to make just one last cast. This time I used an eight inch dead bait which Suban had caught in his cast net. As mahseer feed naturally upon small fish and freshwater crabs, a freshly killed dead bait bumping along the bottom from rock to rock is liable to be snuffed up immediately. And on this, Wilson's luckiest day ever, that's just what happened.

No sooner had I feathered the bait down to the bottom following a long-cast from halfway along the straight, where a huge slab of rock hung out over the river, than there came an arm-wrenching pull, which almost had me off balance and into the swirling water. Instinctively I knew immediately that this fish was big, very big. I had never before felt such awesome power and I immediately started to worry that it might zoom off downriver and over the rapids, a situation I would have been powerless to stop with such a large fresh fish. Fortunately, however, it reacted and fought totally differently from that first fish, spending the best part of the hour-long battle under my own bank, within a huge undercut, where current force over countless years had carved out a veritable underwater cavern. Try as I might, and I tried by heaving on the 40lb outfit until my arms ached, I could not prise the unseen monster from its lair and out into open water. I was at a complete loss, using up most of my own energy and powerless to stop the line shredding each time the mahseer lunged with its huge tail and bored further into the undercut. My arms were aching, my wrists were aching and my stomach was extremely painful where the rod butt dug in. I never believed that a close-range struggle could be so tiring, and every so often I had to ease off the pressure to relieve the pressure on my own spine – I obviously wasn't as fit as I had thought.

Eventually after more than an hour the fish did budge, and quite suddenly made a couple of rushes directly across the flow, before turning belly up completely exhausted only a few yards from where I sat. By now Andy and Bola were also crouched on the rocks with cameras rolling and it was Bola who offered to climb down to water level and heave the huge mahseer on to terra firma. It was something he did with unbelievable strength and agility. That was amazing because Bola couldn't possibly have weighed much more than the mahseer which scaled

an incredible 92lb. This was indeed my red letter day. Catching a brace of the world's finest freshwater game fish, weighing 81lb and 92lb, in just a few hours, remains – to the best of my knowledge – one of the most notable mahseer hauls in post-war times. It was certainly my greatest ever angling achievement.

A couple of days later it was Andy's turn to strike gold with a huge mahseer weighing 95lb from a spot only 200 yards downriver from where my brace came. And during the hour-long fight he had to swim across the river helped by Bola and Suban to avoid a series of rapids along our own bank. For most of the time I rattled off shots with a telephoto lens including the three of them returning with the huge fish slung across Bola's shoulders. Bola was actually running bare foot (as always) across hot rocks fully supporting a fish of around his own weight. The strength, courage and knowledge of natural history of our two guides, Bola and Suban, were quite phenomenal. My gratitude and respect for them are greater than for any other people I've ever met, sentiments that are shared equally by Andy.

In 1989 Andy returned the wonderful hospitality of Nanda and Susheel Gyanchand by taking them to Lake Turkana (formally Lake Rudolph) in Kenya to catch tiger fish and Nile perch. They hooked into dozens of perch in the 25-40lb range whilst trolling lures, as well as a most rare fish captured by Nanda. This was a golden Nile perch of around 60lb which, in colouration, is similar to our own golden tench, being banana-yellow all over, flecked irregularly with black markings, and with black eyes. In all other respects, the golden Nile perch is exactly the same creature as the common Nile perch *Lates niloticus* and, as far as I know, only in Lake Turkana is this stunningly-coloured variant to be found. I have certainly never heard of any being taken from either Lake Victoria or Lake Nasser, the world's two most prolific Nile perch habitats.

Immediately prior to our last memorable Indian trip I had been involved in a most interesting encounter back home fishing a series of three matches against the England team manager, Dick Clegg. These were organised throughout the 1989 winter by *Angling Times* (then edited by Neil Pope) as a modern re-run of the legendary match between the late Dick Walker and top Lincoln match man, Tom Sails. It seemed that after almost 35 years anglers still remembered the confrontation, and that even now few match men could swallow the fact that their hero had been beaten by a member of the 'floppy hat brigade', even if the victor was recognised as the finest angling brain of his time.

(A wonderful match-by-match account of this 1953/54 original epic incidentally was given in the 1960 *Angling Times* publication *Angling in the News* written by Ken Sutton. The matches took place on the River Witham, the River Bain and finally the Hampshire Avon. The series was won conclusively by Dick Walker, 2-1 with an aggregate of 27lb 4¼oz against 21lb 11½oz from Tom Sails).

Now it was all about to happen again due to a handful of *Angling Times* readers suggesting that John Wilson only caught fish on his *Go Fishing* television programmes because swims had been prebaited for weeks on end and that if he were to fish against an experienced match man he'd be crucified. So I had to take up the challenge! The stage had been set for the 'rematch of the century', as *Angling Times* called it, and they asked Dick Clegg to fish against me.

The showdown was to follow the original rules as closely as possible. Three matches would be fished with the venues chosen to re-create the atmosphere of the original encounter. Neither angler was allowed to use live baits or hempseed, and four hours only were allotted for each match. 'How much do you want me to win by?' said Dick Clegg when the challenge was issued? I was thinking that at least a comparison of our catches with those made on the same venues 35 years back should prove interesting. I was also secretly hoping that those club-and match-fishing days during my late teens and early 20's would stand me in good stead.

Round one took place on the River Witham at Tattershall, Lincolnshire, a typical fenland drain where you either built up a netful of roach or went for a 'bag of bits', as match anglers say. I arrived at the match stretch early when it was still dark and sat in the car watching dawn break, whilst looking for signs of roach rolling through binoculars. There weren't any. So right from the whistle I decided to go for gudgeon and ruffe (pope). Choice of pegs was decided by the toss of a coin and Dick won, selecting the downstream end peg of the stretch. And there we sat about 100 yards apart for four miserable hours in a chilly wind. Everyone had of course expected Wilson to use the big fish approach so there was no small element of surprise when I rigged up a 14 foot float rod, 2lb reel line with a terminal rig comprising a 22 hook to a pound bottom beneath a slim waggler. I was going to take Dick on at his own game and try to stay in touch. Fortunately for me I did rather better and produced what for Dick must have been a real shock result. Luckily I found I could catch more gudgeon by twitching my single pinkie maggot around, so as soon as it had fallen to the bottom of the swim I flicked the rod tip which often resulted in an immediate response. The roach Dick had hoped for were non-existent and by the time he switched over to pinkies to go for gudgeon I was too far ahead, weighing in 1lb 5oz of bits to his 11oz. I had upstaged the match man on his own patch and poor Dick must have taken no end of ribbing when the first match was given a centre-page spread the following week in *Angling Times*.

As with the Walker-Sails match, the tiny River Bain at Coningsby, Lincolnshire,

ABOVE

From Kenya's Lake Turkana, Nanda caught this extremely rare 60lb golden Nile perch on a small diving plug, during a trip organised by Andy for her and Susheel.

was our second venue. I won the toss and selected a long run overhung by trees along the opposite bank, a typical chub swim if ever I saw one. Dick however – we had the choice of two swims each – opted for a long straight from which both dace and roach seemed the most likely customers on his stick float set-up, Within an hour of the start however, neither of us had had so much as a bite as the rain lashed down accompanied by a chilly wind. Then Dick opened the score with a good dace, on trotted maggots. This prompted me to dispense with the mashed bread and quiver tipped bread flake approach intended for chub (which had produced just one missed bite) and to switch over to the centre pin and a light waggler rig. A wise move as it happened, because as the day progressed I managed to stay with Dick, fish for fish, and in the dying seconds of the match hooked my third eel of this round which clinched victory number two. My final score of three eels, a roach, a dace and a perch took the scales round to 1lb 11½oz, 5oz more than Dick. I had thus stretched my modest lead overall to 15oz, with one round left.

As everyone had expected from the start, everything rested (as indeed it had in the Walker-Sails match 35 years previously) on round three at the famous Royalty stretch of the Hampshire Avon in Christchurch. Everyone arrived at lunchtime the day before in order to recce the match length which was the tidal stretch of this mighty river immediately downstream of the motorway bridge. Graham Pepplar of Davis Tackle in Christchurch had provided us with an accurate low-down of this interesting beat which runs straight for around 200 yards immediately downstream of the bridge before dividing around an island. We even had time for an hour's fishing in the late afternoon in order to become familiar with the strong tidal currents. But apart from small chub and sea trout, we were none the wiser as to our prospects. The favourite swim looked to be a decidedly chubby overhang at the point where the river divided. But halfway down the straight there existed a deepish run in which lived a shoal of quality bream. I saw one roll as we trudged back to the cars and this, as it happened, influenced the result. In fact that evening back at the hotel before going down for dinner, I mixed up a huge tub of bread mash and crushed casters in the sink in my room. Wilson was going for bream and that strange straight swim if he won the toss.

Unfortunately, or fortunately as it turned out, Dick won the toss when we gathered at the river the following morning with Roger Mortimer from the *Angling Times* to adjudicate. Roger decided that the two swims to be fished were the straight and the overhang where the river divided and when Dick instantly chose the chub hole I was more than delighted. 'Put me down for a big weight of chub today' said Dick. 'Wilson's bubble is about to burst.' Within 15 minutes of the start Dick's prediction looked to be coming true. His carefully trotted stick float probed beneath the overhanging trees had produced a fine chub of 4lb followed shortly by a smaller fish. Dick had quickly forged ahead in aggregate weight while I remained without a bite. Actually for the first 30 minutes I trotted maggots, hoping for the odd dace or two, whilst every so often I introduced golf-ball-size helpings of mashed bread into the head of the long straight. For me it was really all or nothing, and depended entirely upon whether the bream would feed or not. Only with a bag of bream could I expect to beat Dick's chub.

As the tide started to drop noticeably I could see tiny vortexes going downstream in a straight line, about 15 yards out, indicating the existence of a long gravel bar with deep water on the inside shelf. If the bream were going to be anywhere they would be foraging up and down that shelf. It was time to switch from float to ledger. That first cast, presenting a large piece of bread flake covering a size 8 hook and the three swan shot fixed paternoster, decided the outcome. The swan shots bumped across the steep gravel bar and came to settle – just holding bottom. Within 10 seconds the quiver tip sprang back denoting a drop-back bite and I heaved the Avon rod back into my first bream which weighed upwards of 5lbs. In a stroke I had levelled our scores as Dick's swim had died following those two chub, though he did add another later.

For the remainder of the match those wonderful bream fed continually but they were decidedly finicky and I lost as many as I caught. By now depth had dropped to less than three feet – not your usual bream swim – and in such fast shallow water bream really use their deep flanks to good effect. It was so frustrating pulling out of what were bream going up to 7lbs or so and I truly think that, had I landed them all, 100lb catch would not have been unrealistic. When the final whistle blew, however, I had nine slabs plus a chub of around 4lbs to put on the scales for a total weight of 35lb 15oz. It was all over. The match man had been beaten 3-0 and the excuses had to end. What my hero, Dick Walker, had achieved 35 years before, I had now repeated, the final aggregate weights of our three matches being: John Wilson's 38lb 15½oz to Dick Clegg's 7lb 9½oz.

Dick was more than gracious in defeat, saying that 'John's mashed bread approach was perfect on the day and I can think of very few match men who would have had the nerve to try it. And if anglers remembered John Wilson beating me when we get to the year 2024 I'll be delighted.' My sentiments exactly. What a nice guy.

A New Beginning

Just as 1989 had ended that decade on a wonderfully high note, with those huge mahseer and my winning against Dick Clegg, so 1990 started in a very sad way. After 20 years of marriage Barbara and I agreed to separate for a two-year period prior to divorcing. The reasons for our split seem now to be academic and certainly not worth resurrecting, although at the time it was of course emotionally devastating for us both. As with all family break-ups it is the children who suffer most, and Lisa and Lee, now 17 and 19 years old, found the situation very hard to accept. Indeed, were I granted one retrospective wish, it would be for their father to have been more understanding of their needs. As it was I guess I was too wrapped up in the immediate problems of how I was going to continue living in the house, with a huge mortgage, and keep the shop to continue paying for it all when their mother left.

I made the decision to keep both house and shop, and promised to pay Barbara half the value of our estate within two years, to which she agreed. This was an enormous undertaking, on reflection, when I now think about the figures involved in the cold light of day. But I like to think I have never been afraid of life and I wasn't about to split in half everything I had worked so hard to build in the past 20 years. (However there is a rather funny postscript to Barbara's leaving – well, all my mates thought it was hilarious. She left her mother behind, who had lived with us for the past eight years! My mother-in-law stayed for six months more until I could persuade Barbara's sister to arrange alternative accommodation for her.)

Fortunately, *Go Fishing* was now enjoying its fifth series with the promise of more to come, so I literally put everything into my work. Boxtree wanted me to write a series of single species books endorsed by *Angling Times*, so I worked incredibly hard for the next two years, actually completing a total of nine books and 18 television programmes.

Obviously for both research and the actual filming I was away an awful lot which meant that, with Barbara gone, I had to find someone else to look after the shop. This was solved by my taking on good friend, Andy Jubb, as full-time manager, a position he had wanted for some time due to his loss of interest in the car-hire firm for which he worked as a mechanic. This was a good move for us both, as it happened, for the car-hire firm closed down the following year.

In 1991, series six of *Go Fishing* included what I thought were two extremely

LEFT
With the help of *Mirimba*'s captain, King, wielding the net here, I am about to land a giant vundu catfish from the Sanyati Gorge in Zimbabwe's Lake Kariba.

ABOVE
I took this shot of
the magnificent
Victoria Falls on
the Zambezi River,
which separates
Zambia from
Zimbabwe, from
a helicopter. Truly
one of the world's
seven wonders.

exciting programmes shot in Zimbabwe. We visited the Zambezi River at Imbabala, 50 miles above majestic Victoria Falls, to catch the legendary tiger fish. Then we boarded a 60 foot luxury cruiser, called *Mirimba*, on massive Lake Kariba. This is a location I had returned to during the past several years and one that was immensely popular with anglers enjoying guided holidays abroad, a service I teamed up with Tailor Made Holidays to provide. But more of this later.

The beauty of Kariba, apart from its wonderful sunsets, exotic bird life and unbelievable game viewing from on board a cruiser, is the diversity of its fishing. Whilst *Go Fishing* viewers will no doubt recall that huge 60lb vundu catfish which snapped my rod in three places following an epic two hour battle before it was finally hoisted into the boat, Kariba is in fact more highly regarded by both Zimbabwean and South African freshwater anglers as the tiger fish capital of Africa. In fact our filming on Lake Kariba coincided with the famous Tiger Tournament, then the largest freshwater game fishing tournament in the world, comprising over 1,000 competitors representing over 300 teams. Held over three days this competition boasted some mammoth prizes and attracted teams from as far away as Australia, Canada and the USA. There was even a Barclays Bank team from Biggleswade in Bedfordshire. All had to be ready for the six o'clock start each morning at Chiara Point where an assortment of over 300 competition boats lined up, ranging from outboard-powered dinghies to 50 foot cabin cruisers. Upon hearing the starter's gun each then raced for their favourite hot spots across the lake – a

RIGHT
Those who cruise
or fish on Lake
Kariba may wish to
take time off and
visit one of Africa's
largest crocodile
farms.

truly wonderful spectacle – which, at 170 miles long and up to 30 miles wide, is one of the largest man-made lakes in the world. I think it is also the most beautiful.

Huge numbers of large tiger fish were caught during this event, the heaviest in the 1991 competition of 20lb plus falling to the rod of a female competitor. Unfortunately all were killed in order to be weighed in and over the succeeding years anglers fear that just this one annual competition, together of course with heavy commercial fishing, has been responsible for considerably lowering the once high average size of the tiger fish on the lake. But don't get me wrong, Kariba still provides wonderful fishing. It's a hard lesson to learn but nowhere has an endless larder.

I witnessed a similar thing happening over a period of several years on another of Africa's huge lakes, Lake Victoria, the world's second-largest lake. It was featured in series five of *Go Fishing* in which buddy Andy Davison and I caught numerous Nile perch on trolled artificial lures to over 70lbs. Andy, incidentally, returned to Lake Victoria with his wife, Julie, on honeymoon in 1991, and landed, on a trolled Russelure, a mammoth perch of 191½lb. It held the International Game Fishing Association world record for eight years until it was beaten by a 213lb monster caught by Adrian Brayshaw from Lake Nasser in 1998. Sadly it was the policy at Rusinga Island on the Kenyan border, where we had both fished, to kill all perch caught. I remember asking the then manager, Antony Dodds, if he wasn't worried about the inevitable decline that would follow.

A couple of years later, in 1993, I accompanied two prize-winners of a competition in the *Daily Express*, Robert Duff and Geoff Neville, to Rusinga Island Lodge and although we caught plenty of perch to 125lb they were noticeably nowhere as thick on the ground. Almost every day our lures became snagged on sunken nets and

LEFT
In his Norfolk home my good friend, Andy Davison, lifts up son, William, beside his 191½lb Nile perch caught from Lake Victoria in Kenya, which held the IGFA world record for eight years.

long lines belonging to the commercial fishermen. The sight of refrigerated lorries loading up at lakeside villages was, I felt, the first nail in the coffin of the once wonderfully prolific Nile perch fishing available along the Kenyan border.

However, perhaps the fishing will survive. Lake Victoria, which has over a thousand islands, and is roughly the size of Ireland, is shared equally between Uganda and Tanzania, with just 15 percent of its massive shoreline owned by Kenya. So overall mass commercial fishing of the Nile perch within the Kenyan sector may not be significant after all. I certainly hope so.

Perch exist in all depths, all over the lake, and there are massive areas of 100 feet plus. But working the drop-offs along the shoreline and around many of the jungle-clad, steep-sided islands where the prey fish congregate most heavily, reduces the problem of the location. And even the largest of Nile perch will feed in just 10 feet of water.

Fortunately for me my two companions were both enthusiastic anglers and Buckley Hunt, who organised the package and with whom I had fished on a number of occasions, made up our party of four; a perfect number for fishing two to a boat. There was all the usual banter and friendly competition arising from two teams, and our discussions lasted long into the hot night over dinner. Even with sport somewhat reduced, in our opinion, most days at least one of the boats returned with perch over 50lbs, plus lesser fish in the 10-25lb bracket.

Following our five-day stay at Rusinga Island, we flew to the east African coast to Malindi for two days' big-game fishing before returning to the UK. Unfortunately, the three marlin we hooked (all stripies) each managed to jump off the huge kona head trolling lures. But we did enjoy a variety of smaller speedsters in the form of yellow fin tuna, sailfish, king mackerel, some giant trevally and several huge

wahoo. Robert landed the heaviest wahoo at a shade over 70lbs. What a superbly proportioned specimen it was, fully six feet long and unbelievably powerful.

During this same 1991 to 1993 period I also twice visited the Florida Keys to investigate the possibilities of filming there for *Go Fishing*. I was enjoying a wonderful time in my life because I had met Jo, who was later to become my wife. Actually we started off as badminton partners, though on opposing sides, but quickly became soul mates with so very much in common. Jo was already a keen and accomplished angler, loved animals and she had been brought up in the Suffolk countryside. We were, as they say, made for each other. Moreover, unlike my first wife, Barbara, who was unfortunately not keen on travel because she had a fear of flying, Jo was a seasoned traveller and relished the thought of exploring and fishing in the tropics. To this day she has shared my journeys whenever possible.

Anyway, a fan of *Go Fishing*, Peter Hazlewood, of Milton in Cambridgeshire made, completely out of the blue, an exceptionally generous offer, inviting me to make up a foursome on a shark fishing expedition to the Florida Keys. (Peter had on two previous occasions boated a tiger shark of 850lb measuring 12½ feet, from snout to tail, and a mako of 824lb whilst fishing out of Islamorada, and lost an even larger, unidentified monster – possibly a tiger shark – which he played for eight hours and 20 minutes before having to break off. The skipper on board *The Dawn*, Jimmy Taylor, estimated Peter's monster at something like 1,400 to 1,500lbs). Obviously I wasn't going to let such an offer pass me by, and I am glad I didn't because Pete and I have been firm friends ever since. In addition to sharing exotic trips abroad we also occasionally shoot together. But back to those trips to the Florida Keys.

On our first trip we split the week between deep water action on the Atlantic side of the 170 mile long Keys and back-country fishing by skiff on the quieter, very much shallower, gulf side. The waters around the Keys are unbelievably fertile. For all the tourism this angler's paradise is rather like old-time America and is geared totally to the pursuits of fishing and scuba diving. How I wish we had something like it within the British Isles!

We stayed in a small hotel in Islamorada and fished from Whale Harbour, some 11 miles out, drift fishing for big amberjack from *Afternoon Delight* – then skippered by Jimmy Taylor – over a huge plateau called the 'hump' which from 600 feet rises to within 300 feet of the surface. Using 50lb class stand-up outfits with a live mullet or blue runner presented on a size 6/0 hook and 100lb mono trace, taken down by 1½lb lead tied to a weak link, savage takes from amberjack often came within seconds of bumping the hump and winding up a few turns. There literally must have been thousands of jumbo-size amberjacks down there. Even with another 20 or so boats working the same mark, plus several commercial amberjack boats, which caught them on powered winches simply to be used, would you believe,

for fertiliser, we hooked up every drift through. Most were in the 40-60lb bracket with the occasional bruiser pushing 80lbs. Even on a 50lb outfit, the fight usually lasted 20 or 30 minutes unless, that is, a hammerhead came along and grabbed the amberjack – not an unusual occurrence over the hump.

The hammerhead led to us going specifically for sharks as well, and we enjoyed several wonderful scraps with these beasts up to 300lbs or so. Pete and I were more than a little surprised when, as each shark approached the transom and unhooking time had arrived, out from the wheelhouse would come Jimmy Taylor with a loaded 12-bore to guarantee its destiny. Somewhere along the line sharks must have featured rather nastily in his life! As exciting as sport proved to be on the deep Atlantic side of the Keys, which also included trolling for tuna, dorado and barracuda, Pete and I immediately fell in love with skiff fishing on the Gulf side.

Here amongst the tidal creeks and mangrove swamps, colonised by flamingos and pelicans, we caught an unbelievable number of different species using light tackle, including bonefish, sheepshead, spotted sea trout, barracuda, jacks and an assortment of small sharks. We also saw some huge tarpon and missed out on the chance of a big permit.

So impressed were we that on our next visit to the Keys in 1992, when I took my son Lee along, we made just a couple of charter-boat trips out of Whale Harbour to the hump and its amberjacks before spending the remainder of the week skiff fishing on the Gulf side with various guides working out from Bud and Mary's Marina at the southern end of Islamorada. On the very first morning Lee caught a huge bonefish that was approaching double figures on free lined shrimp. Then a few days later when I had teamed up with Peter, our guide Lonnie put us over an extremely aggressive pod of big tarpon, so we float fished live mullet and both

Peter and I had each taken 100lbs plus of tarpon before it was time to open our lunch boxes. Not since my time living on Barbados had I fished for tarpon and all the old memories came flooding back. It was great to experience again those epic boat-towing fights, which lasted for 45 minutes, during which these huge tarpon would fling themselves completely clear of the water every so often.

At the end of March 1993 I was asked by two friends, Simon Williams and Edward Rodbourne – who ran a sports fishing business at Foz do Iguaçu, called Dorado Sports Fishing – to visit Brazil, on behalf of Varig Airlines and Brazilian Tourism. So off I went to sample some of the finest freshwater fishing in South America. Think of Brazil, and the mighty River Amazon immediately springs to mind. Yet this vast country, which is larger than Australia, equivalent to all the European countries combined, and occupies nearly half the total land mass of South America, contains numerous mind-blowing rivers. These rivers are so awesomely wide, fast and deep and so incredibly powerful that even Ireland's Shannon, the longest we have in the British Isles at nearly 300 miles, seems a mere stream by comparison.

Many rivers run for thousands of miles, through tropical rainforests, beside which the 50 foot high canopy of palms, vines and bamboos, lining both banks, is so dense that you can see but a few yards into its mysterious darkness. Here beautifully painted butterflies flit from wild bananas to pineapples, and parrots squawk noisily overhead. The rivers are simply vibrating from the constant chatter of crickets and colourful finches, and the golden heron waits patiently among the

ABOVE
My son, Lee, proudly displays a near double-figure bonefish he caught on free lined shrimp using light tackle 'back-country style' in the Florida Keys.

LEFT
With guide, Lonnie, looking on I finally bring a 100lb-plus tarpon to the skiff following a spectacular half hour battle. The bait was a live mullet float fished.

dense marginal growth of sedges and rushes for a shoal of piranha to pass by. Birds such as egrets, cormorants, storks and cranes all earn an incredibly rich living from an abundance of the most unusual tropical freshwater fish you are ever likely to encounter. There are 186 different species to be precise, from freshwater stingrays to the strange Jau catfish, whose ultimate weight must surely double that of the 150-200 pounders which are regularly taken on long lines by local fishermen.

Brazil's seasons are exactly the opposite of Europe's, so it was high summer and extremely hot along the Paraná River, my final destination. The point at which this majestic watercourse converges with the Iguaçú River is the border of three countries, Brazil, Argentina and Paraguay. But even more dramatic, and in my opinion more breathtakingly beautiful than Zimbabwe's Victoria Falls, are the truly spectacular Iguaçú Falls, a vast column of white water, split into two main cascades. It attracts tourists to Foz from all over South America like bees to the proverbial honey pot.

Apart from emptying into the famous River Plate system, having flowed for a staggering 2,500 miles, the Paraná also boasts the largest hydroelectric power dam in the world at the southern end of Lake Itaipu. This immense structure took 95 million bags of cement and eight years to build, using a workforce of up to 40,000 men. It is five miles wide, 120 metres high, has 18 working turbines and provides nearly a third of Brazil's electricity. Phew! Yet these statistics alone cannot convey the sheer vastness of the Itaipu Dam where there is an experimental fish farm for species like paco, armado (an armoured catfish) and the famous dorado which are reared in floating cages for both food and restocking. So voracious are the young three tosix inch dorado's that they have to be fed six times a day, otherwise they chew each other up – rather like rainbow trout when retained in the confines of the stew.

It was to sample the fighting qualities of this magnificent sport fish, the – golden dorado, that had led me to the awesome Paraná River, immediately downstream of Iguaçú. The river varies between 300 and 700 yards wide, is never less than 100 feet deep through the centre channel and flows at an unbelievable six to eight knots. Huge vortexes of water churn the surface as a result of the current hitting the rock ledges and pinnacles some 40 to 50 feet below. It is not the easiest of fishing locations!

The everyday problems facing even the experienced angler are truly enormous, because the river regularly drops or rises drastically overnight. Within days it has been known to rise 40 feet or more due to a prolonged deluge occurring literally thousands of miles upstream. But what a fantastic challenge! Looking at the reading on the Hummingbird sonar screen never ceased to amaze me. Whitebait-size fish soup for a solid 20 feet below the boat, followed just above the rocky riverbed, sometimes over 100 feet down, by the big boys. These are the massive, beautifully marked tropical cats of the Suribi family, with wedge-shaped heads – designed to suit the strong flow – and incredibly long trailing whiskers sprouting from a strange, elongated expanding mouth.

Within hours of arrival I realised that in just a week's stay I was certainly not going to set the world on fire, so I followed the local technique for combating the depth and current by drifting with the boat side on to the flow (anchoring was simply out of the question) and exploring all the really productive, rocky runs or 'corridors' as my guides, Clemente and Jeorges, called them. The cast is made 20 to 40 yards upstream so that the bait then bumps back along the tops of the rocks, where the fish are, at current speed. What an enjoyable method this is. A small barrel lead, up to ¾oz, is sleeved on above a 12 inch wire trace to get the bait down. Reel line is 20lb test. Inevitably many end tackles are lost on the rocks which in some areas are bigger than cars. But that's where the larger dorado and monster cats are most densely concentrated and waiting to grab your live 'morenita' presented on a 6/0 hook. In Portuguese, morenita means 'little brown thing' and aptly describes the turiva, a lively scale less eel-like fish of six to 10 inches. It's not native to the Paraná but is sold locally in bait shops, imported from Paraguay. The golden dorado's simply love them.

A slamming take so typical of this aggressive sport fish can happen at virtually any time of the drift and, as most of the runs or corridors are half a mile long, you have to concentrate hard all the time. You must be ready to wind the bait up a little when the rocky bottom shallows off perhaps to just 30 feet deep, and then let out more line when it plummets down again even to 100 feet or more. It's not unlike working lures over wrecks and rough ground out at sea. If a particular run produces a few hits you simply motor upstream and try again; if not, the guides take you downriver to the next run and you drift over new ground. It's most exciting fishing for an extremely powerful adversary which jumps repeatedly high in the air between dogged runs and dives to the rocky bottom.

The dorado is a species not unlike Africa's tiger fish in the speed with which it moves and jumps, with the same horizontal lines of dark scales along its flanks. While the tiger fish sports red-orange fins, however, the dorado is bathed in golden-

RIGHT

A local angler
proudly displays
a 30lb plus
golden dorado,
an acrobatic
predatory species
that can attain
weights of over
60lb.

yellow; not just on the fins but along the lower flanks and belly too. Its huge tail is
marked horizontally all the way across with a distinctive thick black bar. Its jaws are
immensely powerful with the crunching power to easily flatten and straighten the
galvanised trebles on my favourite five inch Rapalas. The teeth are much smaller
than those of the tiger fish, without the overall 'Doberman' look. Even so the
dorado has to be unhooked very carefully indeed. One silly mistake and flesh will
certainly be ripped open. They are most common on the ground in the 7-12lbs
bracket and these are great fun on lures, with big double-figure fish always on the
cards. 20 to 30 pounders are fish of the week, whilst monsters up to 70lbs have
been taken by commercial fishermen. As an ultimate goal a 40 pounder is not out
of the question, and wouldn't I like to have caught one!

In all the slow, quiet bays and side streams off the main river shoals of piranha
wait to chomp your morenita in half, so a step down in hook and bait size is
imperative. There are even exotic, fruit-eating species like the paco, an amazingly
deep-sided, discus-shaped fish, which readily gobble up chunks of banana or orange.
The paco fights like stink and averages 4-8lbs with occasional specimens to 30lbs.
For mini-lure enthusiasts all kinds of weird and wonderful tropical toothy fish are
there for the taking. However most of all it was the massive catfish lurking there on
the bottom which captured my imagination. The pintado, which grows to 150lbs
plus but is more commonly caught in the 15-40lb bracket, also grabs your morenita
intended for dorado. Trouble is, before the warning bells sound and you have put
on full pressure, these crafty cats have taken your line through a minefield of rocks
and boulders from which extraction is more a matter of luck than judgement. I
have to be honest and say that in a week's fishing I hooked two big cats and failed
miserably, losing both in rocks literally within seconds of setting the hook. The

problems they pose are more than exciting, believe me!

Finally I must mention the fabulous nightlife in Brazil. There are numerous excellent restaurants serving international cuisine and charging very modest prices, all within easy reach of Foz. Better still there are numerous exotic, spectacular floor shows depicting local costumes, song and dance groups, with the emphasis on mulattos, those milk-chocolate coloured, scantily-dressed beauties, whose gyrating movements are enough to make any luncheon meat man turn to boilies!

However you do not always have to go to exotic locations in order to catch a species you have not previously seen. I love catching new species, so when my old pal, Dave Lewis, of Newport, South Wales, invited Jo and me at the end of May 1993 across country to sample twaite shad fishing in his nearby River Wye, I was like a kid in a toy shop. Timing exactly when to fish is of course critical because this rather special British migratory sea fish enters just a handful of our major river systems during the spring for the sole purpose of spawning in freshwater. Only during the months of May and June at locations such as Tewkesbury Weir on the River Severn and on the River Wye, where it joins forces with the River Monnow in South Wales, is the freshwater enthusiast ever likely to see – let alone actually catch – one of our rarest fishes.

Wherever shad congregate, often in their thousands, there is a chance of catching them using a super light spinning outfit and tiny vibratory spinners in the 00 size range. They can also be great fun to catch on the fly rod using attractor patterns, especially silver-bodied fish fry in imitations. We concentrated on our light spinning outfits however and for a good hour in mid morning, from a shallow run, we caught dozens of shad from around 1lb to almost 2lbs, all of which were returned. Shad all share the same characteristic of leaping repeatedly in a show of shimmering iridescence, not unlike a miniature tarpon. In fact they are not totally unlike tarpon in their physical characteristics too.

The current British record for the twaite shad is less than 3lbs so there is no chance of a monster but due to their acrobatics these lively fish more than compensate for their lack of size. What you immediately notice about this enigmatic species is the notch cut into the centre of its upper jaw, into which fits it's protruding lower jaw. This is a purpose-built strainer mechanism designed for plankton feeding. Its cavernous expanding mouth is however also quite capable of swallowing sand eels, sprats and immature herrings, hence its willingness to grab artificial lures. Colouration along the back is a mix of pewter and pale grey, sometimes with a distinct blueish tinge, and one of the shad's most recognisable features is a line of several dark, round blotches along the shoulder. These are often visible in the water but seem to disappear on dry land.

The twaite shad has deeply compressed flanks covered in silvery scales which easily become dislodged (just like those of its cousin, the herring) and a most defined keel along the belly. In fact from the small dorsal fin backwards it tapers rapidly towards the sharply forked tail. Confusion with another species is hardly likely, except with the now incredibly rare allis shad which, due to pollution and the construction of weirs and locks, no longer migrates up into British freshwater to breed. Allis shads grow to over 4lbs and are much deeper in the body than twaite shad.

Occasionally around the British Isles one is caught at sea, usually by someone feathering for mackerel, although I have regularly used allis shad for barracuda and shark baits when sea fishing in tropical waters. Incidentally the allis shad is now considered a threatened species and is protected under the provisions of the Wildlife and Countryside Act of 1981. It is therefore an offence to capture one intentionally. But let's be honest – you'd have a better chance of finding rocking-horse droppings!

In September 1993 Dave Lewis and I teamed up again to film one of my programmes in series seven of *Go Fishing*, our destination being the famous 'yellow reef' some 40 miles off Hansholm in northeast Jutland, Denmark. Our charter boat was the 55 foot *Thailand* which specialises in wrecking and boasts the largest ever rod-caught cod – a monster of 70lbs plus. I had researched the yellow reef the year before and lost a massive cod whilst on board *Thailand* but the two anglers working pirks on either side of me both managed to land theirs as we drifted over a particularly productive wreck. Both cod weighed over 40lbs. Boy, was I sick, but looked forward to returning to the yellow reef with video cameras. Actually the programme we subsequently made is probably one that most ardent sea fishermen will never forget. Whilst pirk fishing in water some 300 feet deep, Dave went and caught a massive 55lb ling. It provided simply marvellous action for our two cameramen, Paul Bennett and the late Ron Tufnell who, in addition to the big ling, also filmed Dave and me catching numerous cod up to 25lbs. The only downside was that as a foreigner Dave could not claim the huge fish as a new Danish record, which seems totally unfair. But so it goes.

On the same programme we also featured trolling for cod Danish-style fairly close in shore over rock and kelp beds in crystal clear saltwater up to 20 feet deep. For cod to chase our Rapala plugs being trolled at two to three knots, the water just had to be clear and while we were in fact after sea trout, cod on the troll proved quite some novelty to film.

In November 1993 Jo and I accepted an invitation from an old pal, Mark Longster, out in The Gambia, whom I had not seen for nearly four years. His totally unexpected fax simply read: 'John, the bottom fishing right now is fantastic – do you fancy a week's action?' Well, who would need asking more than once? The truth was freshwater anglers in the UK at that time (during October and November) were suffering the worst flooding for many years and my local Wensum valley in Norfolk was totally unfishable for weeks on end. So I really had no option but to accept Mark's offer!

Regular viewers of *Go Fishing* may recall that Mark and I had teamed up four years before in series five of *Go Fishing*, when a big lemon shark came along bang on cue for the cameras, providing some of the most exciting footage we've ever shown. The programme also included the usual assortment of weird and colourful critters you would expect to catch from the mangrove creeks. However due to lack of time plus the pressure of putting these sequences together, I felt I had rather missed out on the unbelievable choice of in shore boat fishing over reefs and sand bars that the Gambia River has to offer.

Incredibly, there are in fact over 30 different species within that meaty, arm-wrenching 30-50lb weight bracket that you could bump into, and half of these species can actually top three figures in weight.

Also in addition to at least seven species of shark there are several types of ray and guitar fish. There are several species of the jack family, African pompano, leer fish, cobia, dorado, several different types of snappers, kujeli, mackerel, tuna and even tarpon. In fact tarpon have been caught within Gambian waters to a staggering 380lb which is far in excess of the IGFA line class record.

Mark had specialised more and more on the range of in shore reef fishing options since my last visit, obtaining yet another boat with a particularly low-set cuddy, thus enabling him to pass easily beneath famous Denton Road Bridge (by the now defunct peanut factory) and straight out from the moorings into the Atlantic, literally within a few minutes' motoring distance of numerous productive reefs and sand bars. Those who have already fished in The Gambia will know full well that large craft can only get out through the river mouth and into the Atlantic by navigating a complex network of mangrove creeks which eventually lead to behind the harbour and around the coastline – all of which eats away at precious fishing time. So Mark's investment in *Black Warrior*, a beamy eight foot wide 22 footer pushed along speedily by a 75-horse Suzuki, had more than paid off, resulting in continuous bookings. There is of course nothing to stop you hiring a rowing dinghy to fish pieces of shrimp in the mangrove creeks or even, as some do (though it is exceedingly muddy), walk along the mangroves and bank fish. Standard carp-pike gear with a 10-15lb line will handle most likely customers, though you may have to go for the occasional long row or walk with a stingray.

You can stay anchored out in deep water right in the mouth of the river which is some two miles wide or motor inland where it is twice the width and fish the strong tide flow close to Dog Island and stake it out with big baits on the bottom for sharks. You can troll Rapala magnums around in shore reefs and even eventually find blue water and consequently add still more species to the list of those expected. For this, however, you need a large, fast boat and be prepared to

ABOVE

This 35lb cubera snapper is but one of numerous exotic hard-battling reef dwellers I contacted within the fertile waters of The Gambia, off shore from the capital of Banjul.

motor at least 20 or 30 miles to evade the colour spewed into the Atlantic by the Gambia River, which is some 400 miles in length with a tidal influence of over half that distance. (Giant catfish and tiger fish inhabit the freshwater high upper reaches incidentally).

We had already decided that our week was simply for enjoying sport with various battlers around the in shore reefs and sand bars. A trip to the local market close by the Sunwing Hotel quickly gave an excellent indication of what the local fishermen, who anchor over the in shore reefs, were taking on their hand lines. Big jacks, kujeli, snappers and even cobia were all for sale. I was surprised to see cobia (called black salmon locally) because I assumed they were really a blue water game species. But specimens to approaching 100lbs were there for the taking. Unfortunately a biggy never came my way although I did hook into one which characteristically rose up from the bottom (as opposed to most species which attempt to hang your line around the nearest rock) but slipped the hook after all too short a fight.

Known locally as cubera, the most common of the big snappers were successfully lured on whole belly fillets from a bonga. And it's interesting to note that these locally netted plankton eaters, the commonest fish seen in the markets, are to all intents and purposes an allis shad. Now a 30lb outfit to catch a 30lb snapper may perhaps seem slightly over the top but these unbelievably strong warm-water reef dwellers quickly shred through the rocks the lighter lines of anyone feeling more sporting. It is hit and hold arm-wrenching stuff at the very best. Holding the rod with the reel out of gear and the clutch preset quite firmly usually sees many more slamming takes converted into snappers in the ice box, due to the uncanny wariness of this fully scaled, you might even say carp-like fish. But there all resemblance ends because the cubera's teeth are strong dog-like canines and it's fighting capabilities, like all saltwater tropicals, put species like carp to shame.

Talking of fighting, one fish I hoped to get amongst during this Gambia break was the tarpon. Mark had taken them in the river mouth to 190lbs a few weeks previously but the surface was far too ruffled during our stay to be able to locate their characteristic rolling on the surface in large groups. (I did in fact experience this in the Florida Keys when fishing with Peter Hazlewood earlier on in the year). When tarpon are really on, anything can happen... But they will have to wait for my next trip to The Gambia.

What we did latch on to, however – and what a splendid acrobatic fish it is – was the tarpon's younger cousin, the ladyfish. Locally these silver streaks, looking for all the world like a stretched-out herring, are called nine bones and we boated them up to 10lbs on lures. A Rapala 'Slither' in lime green really did the business when trolled through shallow water no more than six feet deep between huge banks of sand which have built up around the outside entrance to Denton Bridge. Anchoring in these long rolling waves proved useful. We simply made long casts to the side presenting small mullet or herring live baits on size 2/0 hooks tied directly to 12lb test (with an ounce bomb attached via a link fixed two feet up the line using a four-turn water knot) and used the waves to bump the bait gently across the tide. This exciting technique also took those rather prehistoric-looking flat fish called bastard halibut (which also took Rapalas) and some jumbo-size kujeli (also nicknamed captain fish). These strange fish which have a built-in jelly-like transparent nose are actually threadfin salmon and whilst those we took went to 20lbs, Mark has seen them topping 100lbs.

After several days of fun fishing we anchored in the middle of the estuary mouth opposite Bangul with the hope of encountering some shark action. With over 60 feet of coloured water hiding the entanglement of rocks along the bottom and the tide ebbing strongly, expectations of something big happening along were very high. Before long something made off with a Spanish mackerel of fully 4lbs containing a double 10/0 hook rig. The reel started to squeal like a stuck pig with that uncanny suddenness only associated with shark fishing and when I slammed home the clutch to strike I was certainly not expecting a missile-minded barracuda. This metallic projectile veered across the tide going like a bat out of hell and performed multiple Polaris impersonations. This was despite the heavy shark trace and 50lb outfit which should have slowed it down but appeared to have little effect. Moreover the barracuda had completely swallowed the Spanish mackerel, but then it was close to five feet long and better than 30lbs. It was not a huge specimen by any means but a good one nevertheless, and typical of the quality in surprises you can expect when probing the deep-coloured and incredibly fertile water of the Gambia River.

During the winter of 1993/94 I spent an inordinate amount of time sifting through thousands of colour transparencies and hour upon hour of my taped *Go Fishing* programmes for clips of foreign fishing. The reason for this was that Pearson Publishing of Cambridge were going to produce the first angling CD Rom made in Britain, called *John Wilson's World of Fishing*. This mammoth work contains 17 exotic fresh and saltwater destinations around the globe with 600 photos and 150 video clips, plus over two hours of my narrative. It contains over 100 detailed destination fact sheets and a rundown of 68 individual species all of which can be printed out as required.

The project involved far more work than I had ever envisaged but turned out to be most rewarding. When first published in 1995 it was actually far ahead of its time, and it received rave reviews from several dedicated magazines including *CD*

Rom Today, *CD Rom User* and *Windows User*. If only they all knew that when it comes to computers I am very much a novice, and until five years ago when good friend Nick Beardmore set me up with a system and taught me how to use it, (this is now my fourth book typed by myself) I relied completely on my wife Jo, bless her, doing the typing. Actually in 1996 Eagle Moss Publications Ltd also produced a CD Rom called *John Wilson and Friends' Complete Guide to Coarse Fishing*. This was a 'how-to' spin-off from the weekly part work *The Art of Fishing*, with much additional material in the way of top-quality video footage in which well-known angling writers, Des Taylor, Bob Nudd, Matt Hayes and Keith Arthur, also featured. Personally I think books will always have the edge, although at this point in time, DVD's are becoming more popular.

On account of my having to rewrite my book, *Where to Fish in Norfolk and Suffolk*, for its fifth update, 1994 was another extremely busy year. My television series, *Go Fishing*, also demanded much of my time both in research and in the shooting throughout the summer months of six more half hour programmes.

During September I was to make one of my finest catches ever by landing no fewer than nine double-figure bream in one session from a 13 foot deep swim in a secluded 25 acre Norfolk still water I call the 'forgotten lake'. I marked an area in the middle of the lake with a buoy and heavily prebaited it for the two previous evenings with a mixture of stewed wheat, casters, maggots, chopped lobworms and brown breadcrumbs. I was confident of some action and arranged for the video cameras to be there. A thick mist hugged the lake from dawn until late morning which, although it restricted our

filming early on, encouraged the shoal of bream to continue feeding far longer than they would normally have done. This resulted in my enjoying unprecedented sport using a sliding float rig baited with a lob tail. Initially I had started with two 13 foot float rods but quickly put one away as bites were happening within a short time of the lob tail settling on the bottom. I had the choice of accumulating the largest catch of huge bream ever recorded, or taking the time whilst fishing to go through baits and explain in detail my sliding float arrangement with all the inevitable waiting around (when I could have been catching) that filming demands. Frankly I reckon I could have caught 20 or even 30 of those ravenous bream.

Filming is a really slow process, even with two cameras, and I have never regretted choosing the latter option, because not only did I finish with nine bream over 10lbs to 13lb 10oz (a fish which just seven years earlier would have broken the British record), a 4lb 1oz roach-bream hybrid, plus a 2lb perch, but we were able to put together a totally unique video. It was not only at that time one of the largest all-time hauls of double-figure bream ever captured but, more importantly, those bream were caught slider float fishing, and it was recorded on camera exactly as it happened.

Incidentally, together with a session after big carp on the River Test, this catch provided the basis for the first of five sell-through videos produced under my own label, Kazan River Productions.

I went on to take several more large bream from the forgotten lake during the following two seasons to 13lb 14oz, and a massive roach-rudd hybrid of 3lb 15oz. But never for me, nor anyone else, did that shoal ever feed so enthusiastically again. I did however account for a bag of five double-figure bream to 12lb 5oz in a single sitting on ledgered sweet corn a year later from a local gravel pit. This was on a morning shared with my brother, David, who took two superb doubles of 13lb 4oz and 13lb 8oz. Strangely, as I have mentioned earlier, during these past few years double-figure bream have become relatively attainable catches from estate lakes and mature gravel pit fisheries up and down the country.

A month after that fantastic bream season I was in a very different setting – the Seychelles. Bordered on three sides by the crystal clear turquoise of the Indian Ocean, the single runway of Mahé's international airport is not only situated in one of the most beautiful spots on this earth, it is the only terminal in the Seychelles which can handle jumbo jets. So to sample some of the world's most exotic blue water fishing you then island hop from

BELOW
Just a 20 minute northerly flight from the main island of the Seychelles, Mahé, lies Bird Island which, apart from being home to a world record number of sooty terns and everyone's idea of coral paradise, contains an infinite variety of exciting game fish in the deep blue water less than half a mile off shore.

RIGHT

Jo makes friends with the queen of Bird Island, 'Esmeralda', who at 150 years old and weighing over 700lb is reckoned to be the world's oldest and largest tortoise.

Mahé to a dozen or more paradise locations including Praslin, Silhouette, La Digue, Bird Island and Denis Island – none of which takes more than 30 minutes to reach via De Havilland Twin otter aircraft.

With *Go Fishing* in mind, I had researched part of this coral and granite atoll which rises from the depths of the Indian Ocean covering a staggering 250,000 square miles, two years earlier in the company of Buckley Hunt of Hunt Travel. We fished both Bird and Denis Islands plus further south at Desroches in the Amirantes Islands and experienced unbelievable sport throughout. But sadly I couldn't talk the television people into providing a budget for any such programmes at that time ... and still can't.

BELOW

Me hoisting a brace of large dorado caught on trolled lures.

The Seychelles was, however, the perfect place in October 1994 for Jo and I to get married, a facility organised by several travel companies and one I can thoroughly recommend. The wedding took place on Mahé, the main island of the Seychelles, and home to 90 percent of the 65,000 population of the 115 islands. We dragged a couple of fellow hotel guests from the beach for the afternoon ceremony as witnesses and, as though booked to order, a large stingray swam across the clearwater bay below the flower-covered terrace just as we made our vows. The champagne flowed, a small band played and we danced into the sunset as it formed a kaleidoscope of yellow, orange and crimson over the horizon.

The following morning we left Mahé to go island hopping and enjoy some fishing. Being the most northerly of all islands in the Seychelles and situated on the very edge of this shallow coral atoll, Bird Island and Denis Island offer unrivalled sport because very deep water is

just a few minutes' motoring away. Both islands maintain one fishing boat each, available to guests for bottom fishing or trolling. The accommodation comprises luxurious individual thatched chalets which are only yards from the ocean. Charges for the day are only half what you would expect to pay for blue water trolling off America's Florida Keys.

There is a never-ending choice of in shore and off shore banks in depths from 30 to 80 feet or you can troll along the tempting irregular line of drop-off separating the last visible reef from a deep blue, seemingly bottomless, void. Although occasional marlin are caught, sport with the spectacular and high-leaping sailfish is available virtually all year round. Sails in the 60-80lb class are everyday catches – often in multiples of two or three in just a few hours of trolling, so light 30lb outfits are ideal for maximum sporting enjoyment.

With just two anglers aboard plus a local skipper, the most workable routine is to fish four rods and two heavy cord hand lines – one off each corner of the transom. These pull teasers just 30 to 40 feet behind the boat, which motors at around six to eight knots and quickly provides enough bonito or tuna for strip baits. For sailfish Seychelles skippers prefer to add a 12 inch strip of tuna belly behind a plastic squid skirt. The bait is held in place with elasticated cotton wound around an 8/0 hook attached to a five foot 100lb wire trace – in case a barracuda or wahoo grabs hold! These are trolled around 30 or 40 yards behind and away from the boat on outriggers so they skip tantalisingly through the waves while the other two rods offer either Rapala Magnums (blue mackerel or red and white) or medium-size kona heads, or perhaps even one of each. Sometimes a big dorado or wahoo will gobble the tuna belly baits, or a sailfish will suddenly pop up close to the boat and make off with the kona head or diving plug. Yellow-fin tuna are particularly partial to big squid skirt lures or kona heads trolled just behind the hand line lures or single large feathers intended for bonito.

When a reel screams in the Seychelles you never know what's coming. It's the

THE 1990s: A NEW BEGINNING 181

most fabulous nail-biting blue water sport fishing I have yet sampled. Using my old glass Ryobi up tide rods and S320 reels crammed with 30lb line, Jo and I trolled for two days out from Denis Island bringing to the boat several sailfish and dropping an equal number. We were constantly on the look-out for birds working the surface – mostly terns or the odd frigate bird – which feed upon small shoal species pushed up to the surface by the much larger pelagic species. We enjoyed constant action from dorado to 30lbs, wahoo of the same calibre, some really large bonito, yellow-fin tuna and a lot more. We also dropped a couple of really heavy fish on the big Rapalas, which the skipper reckoned were dogtooth tuna.

On our final day at Denis Island, Sydney, our skipper, suggested that having caught two sails and dropped a third before lunch we might like to try a spot of hand line drifting for big red snapper. I never knew that hand lining in 50 fathoms could be such hard work. As we had no proper leads aboard we used 4lb scuba diving weights to take the huge chunks of fresh tuna hiding 8/0 hooks quickly to the bottom. Colourful reef battlers like brown spotted grouper and the outstandingly colourful moon sail sea bass and tomato hind were consistent biters within seconds of the makeshift rigs touching coral. Then I pulled into what Sydney assured me was a really big snapper – at least 10lbs. But I failed to notice a shark which grabbed the huge red snapper on the bottom hook of the hand line a split second before I could hoist it into the boat. The shark had probably followed it all the way up through 150 feet of water. My feeling of joy quickly turned to pain as the 10 yards of 300lb mono trace and the four-hook rig was ripped through my right hand, the large brass crimps joining cord to mono tearing out several chunks of finger flesh in a well of blood and gore. In just a few seconds my prize was gone.

Our last three days were spent on Bird Island which is not only home to the world's largest colony of sooty terns – over a million of them – but also the world's largest tortoise. Known as Esmeralda, this 700lb giant is said to be over 150 years old. Our Bird Island skipper, Clive, remembered me from a couple of years back and so Jo and I immediately felt at home. What's more the fishing hadn't changed one little bit. On our very first morning out Jo brought to the boat and released two large sailfish while I enjoyed some unrivalled sport on my ultra-light trolling outfit with huge garfish, green job fish, blue-finned trevally, rainbow runners and numerous barracudas.

With over 900 different species inhabiting those fertile blue waters we were totally spoilt for choice. Then all too quickly our honeymoon holiday was over. I was however sure that it would not be difficult to talk Jo into taking a second honeymoon to these bountiful islands in the future.

Life went on and then in March 1995 Jo and I were invited by our friends, Nanda and Susheel Gyanchand to visit South India for two weeks of mahseer fishing and wild boar shooting. We borrowed Susheel's four-wheel-drive vehicle for the first week which we spent in the Cauvery Valley with our guides, Bola and Suban. At that time there were absolutely no other anglers on the river; it was truly magical and felt just like coming home. Jo caught her first mahseer and then several others to over 40lbs plus but lost a real monster – certainly of 70lbs plus by the way it shot off downriver.

After a slow start using ragi (visiting anglers had now become more frequent with the result that mahseer had wised up to this bait), I switched over to a deep-bodied shoal fish, called a petagara, which is much loved by jumbo-size mahseer. On two consecutive mornings bumping these pound-size fish between the boulders in the rapids immediately below our Haira camp I hooked into two superb specimens

LEFT
Suban helps Jo to hoist up my 83lb mahseer for the camera.

of 83lb and 91lb. Each provided a fight to remember, not only for the unbelievable power of this phenomenal fish but also because Bola and Suban were at my side to assist and share in the excitement throughout.

Jo and I slept under the stars on a pair of old ex-army camp beds. We regularly watched otters play amongst the wide shallows opposite our camp and one evening were treated to the magnificent sight of a family of nine elephants plodding through the green, monsoon-fed jungle beside the river and stopping to drink not 50 yards away. Our week beside the Cauvery passed all too quickly and it was time to drive back to Susheel's farmhouse, south of Bangalore, to prepare for some local sightseeing and a couple of pig shoots.

Now whilst game shooting in India is technically illegal, Susheel is regularly called upon by local government people to deal with dangerous wild animals. Wherever a rogue elephant needs shooting or a man-eating panther – the leopard is called the panther in India – has to be destroyed within the state of Karnataka, Susheel gets called in. Several years back he built up a substantial reputation by tracking down a pack of wolves that was responsible for attacking babies whilst their mothers toiled in the fields. The wolves lived in a cave from which the bones of numerous babies were recovered and Susheel proved what many of the peasant farmers simply couldn't believe: that wolves were responsible for taking children. So Jo and I couldn't have been in better hands.

After spending a couple of days relaxing around the farm with parties in the evening for me to renew old friendships, Susheel arranged a driven shoot to the southwest of Bangalore near the ancient city of Mysore. (I had been there on several previous occasions. Once was to visit the world-famous taxidermists, the Van Ingens, two brothers of Dutch ancestry, who had been responsible over the last half a century for preserving many of Africa's and India's game fishes and animals. The world-record mahseer of 120lb caught from the Cubbiny River, a tributary of the Cauvery, was taken by the now late, Dewett Van Ingen back in 1920).

Without any form of government control to restrict the numbers of wild boar which regularly raid the paddy fields, and ragi and maize crops of poor farmers, the beasts are poisoned, mutilated in ancient traps and even hunted by spear. None of these is an effective method of culling them. Whenever Susheel arranges an organised shoot, with up to six guns, all the peasant farmers are only too pleased to act as beaters, because not only are the boar which ruin their crops culled but also everyone gets to eat pig meat. Meat is a luxury for these farmers who rarely have the money to enjoy more than a chicken every so often as a supplement to their otherwise vegetarian diet.

The huge hillside around which Susheel had arranged the beaters to work was unbelievably thick in thorn scrub, so rather than shoot from a low position which could easily become restricted, Susheel suggested a high rocky bluff at the very end of the beat from where we should be able to get off killing shots as the boar broke from one piece of thick cover to another. So we climbed carefully up the hillside and sat perfectly still amongst some huge boulders with a great view downwards to where Susheel said the pigs would break. Even before we settled

down and steadied ourselves in readiness to put our 3006 rifles into action the yells and screams of the beaters could be heard as they worked their way towards our position. Fire crackers were let off every so often and soon peacocks and jackals could be seen breaking cover from the dense thorn scrub across an open area about 100 yards wide where Susheel said I should expect to direct my aim.

There then came much unexpected screaming and shouting at what we later found out was the beaters climbing trees to avoid a female panther whose cubs appeared to be under threat. We actually thought the beat was over, completely ruined by the presence of the panther, when all of a sudden a large boar came running from the thorn scrub across the very spot predicted by Susheel around 150 yards away. How he does it I just don't know. It's as though he thinks like a wild boar, and I didn't let him down, giving it a good lead and dropping the boar with one well placed shot immediately above its shoulder on the run. Susheel

BELOW
Using Susheel's 3006 rifle I bagged this huge wild boar during a chase across terraced paddy fields in his 4x4 whilst lamping at night.

then thumped one into another smaller pig, which I just hadn't seen at all, and our shoot was over. Afterwards everyone sat beneath a large tamarind tree and sipped coconut milk in the midday sun while three beaters dismembered the two boars and shared out the meat. It had been a most successful hunt.

A couple of days later I accompanied Susheel and friend Sachi on a night-time lamping shoot. This consisted of chasing across paddy fields in the 4x4 trying to

pick out the forms of feeding boar with the aid of a million-candle-power lamp connected to the 12 volt battery. Talk about exciting! As usual Susheel and Sachi wanted me to get the first shot off and, after several unsuccessful hours of driving from one farm to another, I managed to oblige when a huge boar suddenly appeared in the searchlight. Trying to steady myself when the 4x4 lurched to a stop over the ruts of a paddy field, however, was not an easy task. I don't think I have ever been so hyped up before or since. It was so very different from shooting a pheasant or a rabbit.

Incidentally, killing for food certainly brings out the hunter in me and makes me realise how important it is that we constantly remind ourselves to be responsible for the food we eat which generally someone else kills for us. I have absolutely no qualms about shooting a live animal to eat. The necessities of man to enjoy hunting, shooting and fishing date back to our forefathers and it saddens me that a proportion of today's society wishes to suppress this heritage. So why Tony Blair's labour party spent such an unprecedented amount of parliamentary time in the 'unworkable' banning of hunting with dogs during 2004 still amazes me. While I do not go fox hunting for instance, I certainly don't wish to stop those who do. While those in the countryside do not preach to town folk, why is it that a townie might see fit to tell those in the countryside that hunting or fishing is wrong? Let's leave those living in suburbia to manage suburbia and those in the countryside to look after themselves.

Much of the summer in 1995 was spent filming series 10 of *Go Fishing* which included some fun carp fishing on the float at my local Catch 22 fishery at Lyng Easthaugh, tope fishing out from Brancaster Staithe in north Norfolk and trips for barbel and bream at the famous Throop Mill Fishery on the Dorset Stour near Christchurch in Hampshire. I also decided to include celebrity and lifelong angler,

RIGHT
During the filming of series 10 of *Go Fishing*, I teamed up with my old pal, Terry Houseago, for a real common carp bonanza at the prolific Catch 22 fishery in Lyng Easthaugh, Norfolk.

SIXTY YEARS A FISHERMAN

LEFT

The *Go Fishing* crew at Ringstead Grange Fishery in Northamptonshire in 1994. On my right: soundman, Dave Runciman, and cameraman, Paul Bennett. On my left: soundman, Steve Abson, and cameraman, the late Ron Tufnel.

BELOW

An aerial shot of Roger Daltrey's beautiful Lake down trout fishery in deepest Sussex.

Roger Daltrey. Actually, Roger and I had discussed teaming up for a *Go Fishing* programme a few years earlier and in order to provide viewers with an accurate image of Daltrey, the angler, trout fishery owner and trout farm mogul (he owned four trout farms at that time), we started filming in his trout farms in Dorset. Manager, Graham, was in fact an acquaintance from way back when he managed the Nythe Lake trout fishery in Arlesford in Hampshire, a location I often fished with my old mate, the late Trevor Housby, during the early 1980s.

Roger was nothing less than passionate about the quality of the brown, rainbow and brook trout he bred for stocking. These were destined for his own four-lake day-ticket fishery called Lake down in deepest Sussex, just 10 miles south of Tunbridge Wells, and for numerous other trout fisheries up and down the country. I think this aspect well and truly came across in our programme. For the vast majority of viewers who only ever thought of Roger as a rock singer and actor, our programme must have been quite an eye-opener, because his involvement in trout fishing then took up the greater part of his working life. Lake down Fishery, for example, conceived and built by him, was not only one of the most picturesque I've ever fished, it's incredibly well laid out and managed, with a comfortable lodge where guests can enjoy refreshments adjacent to the water. Whilst shooting the aerial introductions for the programme with cameraman, Paul Bennett, from a

helicopter, we both agreed that Roger's lakes were by far the most beautiful we had ever filmed.

Once we got down to catching some trout after all the preliminary filming, I forgot to tell Roger not to bash a trout on the head on camera. It's stupid, I know, because how on earth does a live trout finish up on your plate if it's not dispatched. But in television filming we have to work within certain rules and guidelines, whether we consider them stupid or not. But lo and behold when Roger caught his first trout of the day, he got his priest out, bashed the trout over the head and immediately gave an address on how, as hunters we should be responsible for dealing with the food we eat. No wonder the man's such a pro! Needless to say I left it all in and no one made the slightest comment. To top it all Roger then went and caught a superbly proportioned double-figure rainbow (the largest he had taken from his own fishery incidentally) to end what for me and my son, Lee, who had come along to help out, had been a most enjoyable shoot.

Later on in 1995 my hitherto partner in Kazan River Productions, Paul Martingel, decided to end our partnership to pursue a new direction in life. As Paul lived in Twickenham, south London, and I lived in Norfolk, it was indeed difficult to retain a close day-to-day working relationship, although it has to be said we had been exceptionally successful together producing six series of *Go Fishing* for Anglia Television.

Anyway, this enabled my wife Jo to become my partner, taking over all the bookwork and business side previously looked after by Paul, It was at around this time at the end of 1995 that East Midland Allied Press engaged our services to make a series of hour-long specialist angling videos to be sold through their eight angling magazines. So over the next few years – we produced tapes for *Sea Angler Magazine* with the titles *The Video*, *The Sequel*, *Mastercast*, *Cod* and *Bass*. In

RIGHT

Roger Daltrey was not only a wonderful host and enormous help in putting together our trout programme; he also went and caught the biggest rainbow!

addition we filmed a barbel and carp video for *Improve Your Coarse Fishing*, a fly fishing extravaganza for *Trout Fisherman*, and an epic for *Angling Times* entitled *The Lake Nasser Safari*, a production I shall elaborate upon later.

A large proportion of material shot for both the cod and the bass videos allowed me to team up again with good pal and Lymington skipper, Roger Bayzand, (now living happily in Australia) who single-handedly ran *Sundance II*. Roger had produced the goods for me on many occasions on both photo shoots for *Angling Times* and during the filming of series 11 of *Go Fishing*. He came up trumps again in the bass video which on paper had promised to be our most difficult challenge yet. There was Roger catching a splendid double-figure bass almost to order, just like the huge cod and pollack we subsequently enjoyed from pirking and jelly worming over one of his favourite south-coast wrecks. When you have only a day or two to film saltwater species there was no one better than Roger to find them.

Just before Christmas 1995 I received a fax from Dr Ian Fox of the Falklands Tourist Board, suggesting that these two islands might make a wonderful location for *Go Fishing*. I replied that I was sure they would but at present filming was restricted to the Anglia and Meridian viewing areas. Ian replied with a positive proposal nevertheless and invited Jo and me to the Falklands in March 1996.

This led to us boarding a Tristar at Brize Norton, Oxfordshire, and making the excruciatingly long flight to the Falklands: 17½ hours broken only by an hour's stop at Ascension Island. Legend has it that you can experience all four seasons in just one day on the Falklands. What they failed to mention is that you can get snow, rain, sleet, hail, and sun accompanied by near gale-force winds every damned day. Setting out each day well togged up and totally prepared for anything that comes your way is imperative.

Actually our flight seemed to pass comparatively quickly. I have certainly

LEFT
Jo and me in the office overlooking our Lakeland setting where the majority of my writing and scripting for video editing is done.

endured far shorter, yet considerably more uncomfortable journeys. When we finally arrived at Mount Pleasant Airport we were instantly whisked away to the capital, Stanley, surveying en route the barren scenery of rolling hills and grassy plains covered by rocky outcrops with tussock grasses, lichens and squat bushes covered in bright red berries. Immediately I drew a comparison with the Northwest Territories of Canada, where above the tree line there are no indigenous trees, although in the Falklands there is a handful of wind-breaking conifer varieties planted around most of the settlements. Against such a persistent wind they need them, believe me.

There are two main islands, east and west, divided by a narrow strip of sea which, together in land mass, easily equals that of Wales. With a resident population of fewer than 2,000 people (although there is a similar number of British military personnel stationed at MPA), you immediately realise that fishing in the Falklands is going to be both peaceful and unhurried. Some of the smaller outlying islands contain the greatest concentrations of penguins, seals and exotic birds. Sea Lion Island is an absolute must for visiting naturalists. We saw gentoo and rock-hopper penguins plus large numbers of seals, dolphins, giant petrels and black-browed albatross while staying at Blue Beach Lodge in the San Carlos estuary with William and Lynn Anderson on East Island.

The Falklands are indeed a stark, bleak, barren mixture of raw beauty and solitude that very quickly grows on you. The bird life is extremely varied, from the

flightless steamer ducks to turkey vultures, caracaras, and red-backed buzzards. Barn owls, short-eared owls and cassias falcons were present too, plus a galaxy of colourful smaller birds such as black-chinned siskins, long-tailed meadow larks and black-throated finches.

Several spate-fed rivers such as the Malo, Warrah, San Carlos, Chartres, Murrell and Pedro rise high up in the mountains from an amalgam of peaty ditches and streams. Throughout their length only rarely does the width exceed 30 yards so a single-handed 10 or 10½ foot fly rod is ideal for the superb annual run of sea trout which are a direct result from the stockings of brown trout from Chile and Britain between 1940 and 1952, further stockings being made between 1961 and 1964.

Our first taste of the fishing was with local guide, Nick Bonner, on the Murrell, a wide shallow estuary just half an hour's Land Rover journey from Stanley. Jo and I soon got into spinning Toby lures for sea trout and Falklands mullet; which is in fact an Antarctic rock cod. It looks more like a cross between a common carp and a bass, although it does have the characteristics of mullet, because it feeds high up into the river's freshwater reaches with the tide and it fights like stink. The food larder within Falkland estuaries is simply enormous, the two main items being the orange-red krill and smelt. Watching both sea trout and mullet smashing into the huge concentrations of young smelt (delicious when fried as white bait) in shallow water is a common sight.

Though I flogged away with my fly rod for the best part of our day along the Murrell I simply could not strip it fast enough to trick the sea trout into grabbing hold in the crystal clear water, regardless of pattern. So I borrowed Jo's spinning rod and promptly accounted for a dozen or more superbly marked sea trout in the two-to 5lb range, most of which only slammed into the three inch Toby at the very last moment. We then experienced similar sport on lures at our next destination on the San Carlos River estuary following an overland drive of some two hours. These islands demonstrate the need for which 4x4 vehicles were designed. Roads are so few and far between it would be simply impossible to be able to get around, let alone right down to the river bank, without one.

Though the record Falklands sea trout of 22lb was caught in 1992 by Alison Faulkner from a pool way up the San Carlos River, with autumn river levels being pathetically low (not a common occurrence apparently), we experienced only mediocre sport above the first tidal pool. But that's spate river fishing for you. Ever hungry wild brownies in the 4-12oz range grabbed both fly and spinner wherever we tried. From several locations in the tidal reaches, where the estuary is still relatively narrow, I took sea trout to close on 6lbs, the most successful pattern by far being a General Practitioner. The orange hue and shrimp-like appearance of the GP comes nearest to the trout's natural food in the salt, namely krill, which comes in shore in such dense concentrations that the sea turns red.

During the most productive part of the tide, the last two hours of the ebb and first of the flood, a 10 gram Toby quickly located groups of sea trout, whereupon I then usually switched over to the fly, depending on wind. Calm days in the Falklands are few and far between, so your approach to fly casting and presentation has to be altered accordingly. One useful option is to cast downwind with your back to the water (in a facer) and lay the fly down on the back cast. But this is simply not practical while exploring clear rain pools that are barely flowing, using the standard wet-fly technique of downstream and across when a howling wind is blowing directly upstream or straight into your face. The best answer is to start at the downstream end and stealthily work up, after first carefully wading over to the most approachable bank from which to get a line out. I also found that stepping up at least one line size helped combat the continual wind. As previously mentioned the GP, a size 8 double, proved an excellent pattern as did a size 8 or 6 Dunkeld. Black flies appeared to be the next best choice – patterns like Stoat's Tail and a black marabou-tailed mini lead head on a size 10 or 8 long shank. The weighted pattern helped enormously in straightening out the long cast, also providing me with a visible plop, thus giving its whereabouts.

From Blue Beach Lodge in the San Carlos estuary we flew by Islander over to the West Island to stay with guide, Robin Lee, at Port Howard Lodge on the banks of the River Warrah estuary. Again we were blighted by lack of rain, but fortunately most of the pools contained a handful of stale, yet catchable, fish in each, and I started with a 6lb cock fish again on a GP. I also saw the first double taken, an 11lb hen fish to the rod of Jim Jackson from New Jersey who was on a fishing holiday with his son, Darryl.

Incidentally together with my wife, Jo, we four were the only visiting anglers in the Falklands during the last two weeks of March. Now you can't beat that for solitude! The season for sea trout starts in October and ends in April. The lovely River Warrah really was a joy to explore and one afternoon a totally unexpected occurrence had us completely gob smacked. Well you don't expect several hundred pounds of sea lion to come zooming upriver pushing a wall of water in front like a torpedo while you are fly fishing, do you? But this dark brown monster, as thick as a wheelie bin, did exactly that.

I experienced another strange encounter one evening whilst spinning in the Warrah estuary. I looked down through the clear water beneath my feet to see a large octopus moving about – something which in cold water took me completely by surprise. I had of course speared numerous octopuses whilst living on Barbados but here in the Falklands its presence seemed bizarre. So I lowered down my Toby lure, yanked and there I was connected to a superb meal. In fact I severed the legs from its body before taking it back to the lodge and our host's cook prepared the octopus in chunks fried in breadcrumbs, exactly to our requirements. What an

RIGHT

Ex-pat, Paul Chapman, now settled in the Falklands, took me sea trout fishing in the tiny River Pedro near Stanley, and landed this magnificent 12¼lb sea trout on a small Toby.

unexpected starter!

Only a 90 minute drive overland from the Warrah is what I considered to be the most prolific sea trout fishing in the Falklands, namely the lovely Chartres River. It was certainly the clearest river by far, holding large numbers of both fresh run and dark fish in all the pools we visited for several

miles up from the estuary at Little Chartres. We stayed with sheep farmers Lyn and Tony Blake, and Tony acted as our guide. His understanding of the river was extraordinary. He seemed virtually to know what each and every pool contained and where the fish were lying. He had an uncanny knack of spotting fish movement even when the wind whipped the surface. My best of three days exploring the

Chartres resulted in no fewer than 51 sea trout from a total of 11 pools. The bulk averaged between 1-2lbs with the odd fish approaching 4lbs – and all on the fly. Tony was also a past master at preparing and frying up the milt and eggs from out-of-condition sea trout. He didn't care how 'black' a fish was, and I must admit to enjoying his fried goodies on several occasions.

Jo and I returned to Stanley by Islander for one last day's fishing on the renowned River Malo which is controlled by the local Stanley Angling Club. Being an early river, most of the sea trout had already gone upstream during spates in February, but I did manage a 7½lb hen fish on a Toby. What I also enjoyed was taking mullet from 2-6lbs one after another during that magical last two hours of the ebb from the estuary. All came to orange and red lead heads with marabou tails, fished down and across as the tide ripped out.

Due to our RAF Tristar running a day late, I was treated to an extra and totally unexpected day's fishing on the tiny River Pedro. Ex-pat Paul Chapman, from

Sheffield, invited me to join him on a rarely fished beat which meanders for mile upon mile from the estuary and through boggy marshlands – and it enjoys a really super-late run of big fish. Due to an overnight downpour Paul suggested that spinning would produce the best results, and he was absolutely right. Toby lures produced 13 sea trout totalling 96lb, the best three of 9lb, 11lb and 12¼lb falling to Paul's rod. My best went a shade over 8lbs and like all our fish went berserk on light tackle in the confines of small turbulent pools.

After spending over two weeks at various settlements comprising three or four dwellings each, Jo and I both felt not just a little sad on returning to the comparative civilisation of Stanley, which itself is little larger than an English village. Not only are the island people exceptionally hospitable and helpful, but the clear fresh air, remote farmhouse accommodation and total isolation all added up to a unique experience. I just hope we'll return one day in the not too distant future.

During the summer of 1996, having researched two large clear watered clay pits at Elstowe near Bedford during the close season for series 11 of *Go Fishing*, I finally achieved a life-long ambition and caught a rudd over 3lbs, and live on camera at that! It was all down to my nephew, Martin Bowler, really. He had previously not only caught numbers of huge carp from Elstowe to over 35lbs but had also been extremely successful in tracking down the small shoals of huge rudd for which the No.1 pit was renowned. Strangely most syndicate members only ever bothered with the carp.

My best of several beauties over the 2½lb mark weighed 3½lb and came on a simple waggler float rig baited with a couple of maggots, presented alongside a dense reed bed: classical rudd fishing no less. Martin also provided the location along the upper reaches of the Great Ouse controlled by the local Vauxhall Angling Club for a real barbel bonanza shown in the same series. I really warmed to fishing

the Upper Ouse again after, believe it or not, a 30 year lay-off and was surprised to find it flowing clear and fast over a gravel bottom. It is as fine a barbel river as you will find anywhere within the British Isles, and I was rather curious to know why.

Although barbel have been stocked by local clubs throughout much of the Upper Ouse during the past 20 years to supplement a small stock of resident fish, they really have taken off in leaps and bounds. This is due in all probability to the fact that all of the treated effluent from Milton Keynes is piped into the Ouse through a series of settling pits at Cotton Waterworks. This injection doubles the force of water and invigorates a river which otherwise, like many others, could now well be suffering from the effects of water abstraction. It's so nice to hear of a positive arising directly from sewage treatment.

Series 11 of *Go Fishing* was the last produced by my company, Kazan River Productions. The following six series reverting back to in-house Anglia Television productions. It was a move I actually welcomed because this kind of change injects new life, not only into the programme but also into the presenter. The changeover certainly had a great effect and after series 12 and 13 went out in January 1999, director Ron Trickett sent me some most satisfying statistics. In terms of percentage share (which is how shows are rated) *Go Fishing* was not only Anglia Television's top-rated programme but currently the longest running. It had taken me 90 half hour programmes, with all the associated problems of putting fish on the bank to order, to finally arrive. For me it has been perhaps a strange set of transitions from hairdresser to printer to tackle dealer to angling author and then to television presenter and producer. But it has been a fascinating learning curve that I wouldn't have swapped for anything.

Earlier on whilst recollecting filming experiences for series six of *Go Fishing* on Zimbabwe's Lake Kariba, I mentioned its immense value as both game reserve and

LEFT
Taken during a week's vacation on board *Mirimba*, friends, Andy Benham and Ed Pope, display the stamp of high-leaping tooth-laden tiger fish for which Zimbabwe's lake Kariba is justly famous.

exotic fishing location. It was certainly one of my favourites and I very much looked forward each year to escorting parties of up to eight anglers, organised by Christine Slater of Tailor Made Holidays, to renew my love affair each autumn with what is arguably Africa's most enchanting and diverse water wilderness. But it all changed in the late 1990s when Blair stopped subsidence payments to Zimbabwe (a deal brokered many years before when the country became independent) and Mugabe immediately went after the white farmers. The rest is now history.

Our base and home for the week was a 60 foot luxury cruiser/houseboat called *Mirimba*. It came complete with King, the captain, plus a cook, a crewman and four 14 foot tenders with outboards in which everyone set off game viewing and fishing into all those inaccessible spots.

Bordered on most of its northern shoreline by Zambia and by Zimbabwe along the southern bank, Kariba's charisma originates from the mighty Zambezi River. During the 1950s, to provide hydroelectricity for both Zimbabwe and Zambia, the river was dammed across the gorge in the township of Kariba, resulting in close on 200 miles of pristine nature reserve, where both game viewing and tropical sports fishing are truly spectacular, but may be enjoyed by boat only. It is an offence – and downright dangerous incidentally – to go ashore, because huge crocodiles bask on mud and sandbanks, craftily camouflaged by clumps of weed and flotsam on their backs. Otherwise it is in fact possible to get so close to the wildlife, elephants in particular, that a telephoto lens is an optional extra!

A good pair of binoculars is however essential for maximum enjoyment. Lunchtime is a wonderful time for game viewing, when you return to the houseboat from an early morning session in one of the tenders in search of vundu or tiger fish, just two of the exotic freshwater adversaries found in the Zambezi system, along with predatory bream, barbel, eels, electric catfish, tropical pike – over 100 species in all. Elephant, buffalo, baboons, hippo and water buck can all be comfortably viewed from mere yards away along the lush and thick marginal canopy of water hyacinth from the safety of your fishing tender.

To safari fishermen Kariba is arguably amongst the most exciting of all tropical freshwater sports fishing locations. Only in southern India, with its magnificent rocky, mountainous rivers and giant mahseer, and at Murchison Falls in Uganda have I experienced comparable challenges. But in truth Kariba has more overall appeal whether you choose to view the bird life or game animals through binoculars or tussle with Africa's largest and most powerful freshwater catfish, the vundu. This is prolific in the 25-50lb range, but grows to well in excess of the 100lb Zimbabwean rod and line record. And would you believe their favourite baits are luncheon meat and blue soap – yes, soap. The river gorges and entrances around the lake's southern perimeter seem to be the best vundu hot spots and the preferred method is to drift slowly with the wind gently bumping the bait along the bottom

LEFT

Hooked by my then 28 year old son Lee, from the deep waters of the Sanyati Gorge in Zimbabwe's massive Lake Kariba, Dad gives him a hand in displaying a 60lbs vundu catfish.

until a vundu picks up the scent and gobbles it up. Gear of 30lb test and a size 6/0 hook are none too strong for this extremely strong fighter, which is given a little slack line when it mouths the bait and is allowed to run for several yards before you bang the hook home. Vundu have no canine teeth as such, but are well equipped with crushing pads in both the top and bottom of their capacious jaws and in their throat, each pad being armed with thousands of tiny pin-like gripping teeth. A glove therefore is essential for unhooking vundu, to avoid painful scraping of the skin across your knuckles, back of the hand and wrists. Even my son, Lee, who has never really been a fanatical angler, was in absolute awe of the vundu's animal strength, landing specimens to close on 60lbs.

One of the best fights I have ever enjoyed was in fact a vundu shared with a lady guest, Ruth Taylor. I hooked what was obviously a big fish and handed the rod over to Ruth who hung on for spells of five and 10 minutes at a time, before handing it back to me again. This went on for the best part of an hour as we drifted fully half a mile from where the monster was first hooked. Finally its massive flat head and long whiskers broke surface. Then there were a couple of heavy swirls, where I just had to grab the rod back for fear of Ruth going over the side, and our prize finally rolled into the net. It was an incredibly long vundu that pulled the scales down to 95lb.

Once everyone had enjoyed their string being well and truly pulled by at least one big vundu, efforts are then concentrated close in around Kariba's irregular shoreline for the high-jumping, tooth-laden tiger fish. These acrobatic speedsters hunt tilapia and the lake's smallest fish, a sardine called kapenta, amongst the petrified tree tops of what were once large forests of hardwood trees, prior to the Zambezi valley being flooded. So-called 'fishing the sticks' is perhaps best compared to the unlikely situation of casting amongst tree tops from the platform of a hovering helicopter, except you are in a boat floating above them. Lines are of course always hanging over branches, which makes the extraction of each and every tiger fish a battle to remember. However, many are lost amongst the woodwork because tiger fish simply never know when to give up or when to fight fairly. Anyone who lands two from 10 hook-ups is not doing too badly! In addition to tigers, squeaker catfish and barbel; even the occasional vundu, are hooked on bunches of free lined kapenta, but few are ever extracted from the entanglement of skeleton bushes and tree stumps.

From a Harare taxi driver to the kapenta fishermen of Lake Kariba, that special Zimbabwean zest for life prevails in the friendliness of the people, in their humour and especially in their willingness to share such a beautiful and bountiful country with visitors. Immediately from the first blast of hot air against your cheeks whilst disembarking from the plane, the love-affair always resumes. It is an infectious, delicious and decidedly haunting experience based upon a love of exotic flora and fauna, combined with that exhilarating perfume which is Africa. It is a mixture of spices, dust, heat and pollen, as unique to the continent as the trumpeting, somewhat unnerving brass band sound of a bellowing hippo at dawn or the haunting cry of a fish eagle. It is what brought me back time and time again. Which makes the catastrophe caused by mad man Mugabe's greed all the more gauling.

(Of my three books written between 1992 and 1997, two contain snippets of Zimbabwe's magnetic fishing, *Go Fishing Techniques*, and *John Wilson's Coarse Fishing Method Manual*. Each, like many of my books, contains numerous diagrams drawn by my good friend and angling buddy, Dave Batten, who in my opinion has no equal in putting across technique in line drawing form).

In October 1996 the *Daily Express* contacted me and asked if I would consider writing a weekly angling slot for the sports section. I accepted and have since immensely enjoyed the exposure and platform which a column in a national newspaper provides for angling. But what with the then, never-ending workload of researching, filming and helping to edit six yearly *Go Fishing* programmes for Anglia, producing specialist angling videos for Emap through Kazan River Productions, writing monthly for two angling titles and periodically for others, not to mention all the work involved in our two carp syndicate lakes – now wonderfully mature and providing superlative fishing – trying to find time for John's Tackle Den became almost impossible. I think I was on the point of working myself into an early grave. Throughout the summer, following each hectic week's filming away from home, I then had to go into the shop on a busy Saturday in order for my manager, Andy, to have a day off. Quite simply, after 25 years of serving the anglers of Norfolk and Suffolk, the shop had to go. So I asked Andy if he was interested in buying me out and that is exactly what happened. For the first time in my working life I suddenly felt free and it took some time for me to adjust to my changed circumstances.

Having always worked on Saturdays for instance, both as a hairdresser and shop-keeper, for the best part of 40 years, it now seemed rather strange to have the day off. I felt as though I was cheating. However within a few months I soon warmed to the reality of more free time and not being constantly under the pressure of the retail trade. Besides, I felt that in latter years much of the fun had gone out of shop-keeping, due not only to the escalating crime of shoplifting but also because of the unsympathetic attitude of local government. For instance, when I fitted roller steel shutter blinds to my shop window the council sent someone round the next morning, ordering me to take them down. The shop was a listed building with some half-rotten squiggly woodwork at the top of one of the vertical window supports. The council were not happy that the box in which the roller blind retreated out of sight during shopping hours covered up part of this woodwork. They failed to take into account that during a 20 year period my shop windows had been broken on some 80 occasions. Yes, 80 times. I was a local joke when it came to broken windows! With a pub at both ends of Bridewell Alley in Norwich where my shop was situated, you can guess what happened when the drunks rolled out at closing time! On three separate occasions I had my windows broken twice in the same week.

Early break-ins were from louts stealing air rifles and pistols which I then sold. So I simply stopped selling air weapons. But even with two inch mesh grills solidly welded to heavy angle iron frames which each had to be lifted off and stored in the churchyard opposite every morning, come rain or shine the glass still took the impact and shattered. So while nothing was stolen, my insurance company finally reached the point of putting my excess up to what it cost to replace a glass window, so I had to fork out for every breakage. How I didn't give the shop up during that ghastly period I don't know.

Instead, I decided to fight the bureaucracy of the local council who took me to the local magistrate's court about my roller shutter. This was strange because numerous shops all over Norwich had (and still do have) roller steel shutters fitted, many of them to properties actually owned by the local council. Talk about hypocrisy. So one Sunday just before the court hearing a couple of days later, I walked through Norwich when all the shop blinds were down and used up two 36 exposure rolls of print film photographing each and every shop front – just like mine, hidden by shutter blinds. After the three magistrates had listened to the council's prosecutor and had then tried to find my shop on the four three foot by two foot boards I submitted, covered in photographs of all the shops in Norwich that had roller blinds, they chucked the case out!

I did, however, finally have to submit a year or so later when the council again tried to take me to court, this time on a technical point covering listed buildings – and a point of law from which I could apparently not escape. So I compromised and had to have six upright fibreglass 'wood-like' shutters made, to replace the roller shutter which still had to be removed every morning. What a waste of everyone's time and money... except the design company who charged me six grand for manufacturing and installing the shutters!

Much of this aggravation occurred way back in the late 1980s and early 1990s before Andy took over at John's Tackle Den, but I hope it illustrates part of the trials and tribulations of running a tackle business and why I was not sad at letting it go. Indeed far from it...

I could now accept offers of fishing in exotic places without having first to think of the shop. Indeed in March 1997 I relented because of the extreme pressure put upon me by brother Dave and good friends, the late Len Head and Jason Davies, and booked our flights to India for a fortnight's mahseer fishing. Each had heard all the stories of these great fish and could not wait to experience their exhilarating power first hand. Fortunately the Cauvery River was in fine form during our stay, running fairly clear and dropping steadily from the previous summer's monsoon rains, which gave everyone the chance of contacting big fish.

As luck would have it I managed to land a superb specimen of 91lb on only our second day on a dead bait bumped through a rocky glide immediately upstream of the Haira rapids. It led me a real song and dance for almost an hour. At one point it became stuck solid amongst several huge boulders in midstream, necessitating Suban to row me across to the other side in the coracle in order to apply pressure at a new angle on the hooked fish. Three days later I did it again with a mahseer of 78lb caught from my favourite swim called Centre Rock. Here a fast rip roars downstream around a large rock in the middle of the river upon which I sit (hence its name) and changes direction fully 150 yards downstream by going at right angles over a series of mini rapids. The exercise is to stop a hooked fish before it makes the

rapids. On this occasion I did, but in past years I have lost some real thumpers.

Meanwhile Dave, Len and Jason were slowly coming to terms with the very different problems and techniques of mahseer fishing. Len lost a huge fish one evening not far from camp as did Jason much lower downstream at a place we call Red Rocks. The look on his face when the hook inexplicably pulled out just when he was getting the better of what was obviously a big mahseer said it all – so near, yet so far. I then left the three of them on the river for a few days and joined my good friend Susheel and his wife, Nanda, for a few days' pig shooting up in the hills – bagged a boar too.

On my return to the river Dave was grinning from ear to ear, having landed a 68lb mahseer, while Len was equally happy with one of 57lb. Unfortunately only moderate-size mahseer came our way during the remainder of our stay and Jason had to settle for memories of his lost leviathan plus mahseer landed to 35lb, which is nevertheless still an incredibly worthwhile capture.

For my part it was most gratifying to share in my friends' success and sleep beneath the stars beside the majestic Cauvery River once again. It's a part of the world where little changes from year to year except river levels which, like the farming expectations of the local peasant farmers, are totally dependent upon the monsoon rains.

Earlier on whilst recalling the formation of my second lake back in 1985, I finished the chapter with the newly excavated fishery, landscaped, planted with trees and marginal shrubs and stocked with a variety of both fish and lilies. There was now, together with the small lake, around two and a half acres of water which needed time to mature. And over the years that have elapsed since I am proud to say my dream has grown and blossomed beyond all my expectations. It's required not just a little help along the way of course, and pruning back both trees and lilies which can grow all too rampantly within the confines of what is, after all, a relatively small fishery is an on-going job. Beauty does in fact come at a price and each summer my diving wet suit comes in very handy for the work of cutting back lilies and submerged tree branches plus replacing the front support logs of each swim as nature rots them away. But it's a real labour of love, and there is invariably someone available to help who owns a similar fishery and requires a selection of lily roots or young saplings.

Initially just about all the carp could be landed successfully using just a 6lb reel line. But as both lily beds and the size of carp have grown, an 8lb outfit using a heavy Avon-style rod is now required, with the exception of catfish that is. For extracting these and the larger carp from beneath submerged trees (mainly in the old, smaller lake) beefier tackle is imperative. But overall a fun 8lb line outfit will suffice in the majority of swims. To date incidentally, in case you are wondering how the fish have matured, the lakes have produced eels to 6lb 4oz, chub to 6lb

ABOVE

Nestled amongst the woods adjacent to the house, it seems as if the new (now 24 year old) lake has always been there.

2oz, wels catfish to 20lb, golden orfe to 6lb 6oz, grass carp to 21lb 5oz, crucian carp to 2lb 14oz, plus mirror carp to 24lb 1oz, common carp to 20lb 8oz and metallic carp to 18lb 12oz. In fact the lakes contain such a prolific stock of various carp with most fish into double figures, plus the odd 20, that there is no need to bivvy up for days on end to enjoy catching carp. Most of the syndicate members prefer to spend just a few hours or so at the waterside, which was my original intention. The bank sides consequently never look bashed or even well trodden. After all it is our front garden in addition to being a fishery around which we walk our dogs several times each day.

For the first 12 years of the new lake's life I owned and took a long time in training a wonderful German Shepherd called Buzzy, a large black and tan, big-boned dog with such a friendly nature, yet incredibly strong and instantly aggressive and protective if he thought those he loved were in danger. It is a trait born into most German Shepherds which I guess is responsible for the breed being used almost exclusively by the police and security firms. With Buzzy sadly gone, however, we then had two more German Shepherds, one white and one black and tan, a West Highland Terrier and a huge Rhodesian Ridgeback-Bull Mastiff cross who had the habit of returning to the house every so often with someone's tin of half-used luncheon meat or a bag of floating carp pellets. Funnily enough no one ever seemed to complain, although that could have something to do with the fact that Max weighed in at close on 13 stone! Today as I write this in 2008, sadly, of the previously

mentioned four dogs only our little West Highland Terrier Bola remains, together with four year old Alfie, a French Mastiff of some 11 stones. This unusual breed *Dogue de Bordeaux* was featured in that comical motion picture *Turner and Hooch*. And our hooch 'Alfie' is just as slobbery. Much to Jo's dismay.

I think one of the greatest successes of the fishery is the way in which the metallic carp have flourished and added that hint of mystery and beauty to everyone's catches. With such a high stocking density I never expected them to all become 30 pounders. From the outset it was my wish for most of the carp to grow into double figures and thus provide exciting sport on relatively light tackle. There are enough under-stocked big carp fisheries around as it is, where everyone knows the name of the fish they are after. This is not my idea of carp fishing. It is perhaps interesting to note that I kept many of the (now large) metallic carp in my garden ponds prior to moving to Lake House so these are all well over 20 years old. Whether I shall live long enough to see them all reach their optimum age is doubtful – carp can live for up to 50 years. Come to think of it my African Grey parrot, Cheeko, who is nearly 30 years old, will in all probability outlive me too.

Keeping a record book of how the lake has progressed these past 24 years has also highlighted how weather patterns are changing. Today it seems everything is in extremes: the coldest this, the hottest that and so on. For instance, November

ABOVE
Jo with Max, Bola, Toby and Sam, at our lake's southeastern end.

BELOW
Grass carp like this 21 pounder have fared particularly well in the new lake, together with the stock of golden orfe, Wels catfish, chub, big eels and numerous king carp.

1994 was the mildest ever since records began. The 1988/89 winter was the mildest for 300 years and the driest in the southeast of England for 100 years. We had fresh lily pads up on the surface during February and flowers actually out during March. Conversely, the October 1987 gales were the worst in living memory, though fortunately only a few elderly alders and birch fell around our lakes. And February 1986 was one of the coldest in living memory with an average temperature of just -9 degrees centigrade. The lakes were frozen over for the whole of February that year which necessitated my having to keep an area (by the bridge) clear of ice each morning to allow the rising gases from rotting vegetation to escape. Unfortunately many owners of small, overgrown, shallow and well-stocked fisheries that winter who failed to appreciate possible deoxygenisation lost their entire stocks. Paradoxically, January of 2008 was the warmest in living memory.

The earliest that carp have ever spawned in the lakes was on 1 May 1993 and they kept at it for three days. This was followed by later spawnings during June and once more in July. In my experience, carp never get their reproductive cycle over in one go. They usually spawn from the early hours of the morning until the sun is well up, and many anglers never get to appreciate that there are several spawnings each summer. Also breeding successfully in the small, now wild, pond is a colony of the rare and protected great crested newt which spends much of its life in the water. These were actually featured in one of my *Go Fishing* programmes filmed around the two lakes and they share their sub-surface home with smooth newts, frogs and toads, all of which reproduce annually in profusion.

The number of different species of birds which now annually use our Lakeland setting for breeding is simply staggering. Four or five pairs of greylag geese fly in to start sorting out their nesting sites during March and once their goslings are but a day or two old they walk them across our drive and down through the woods to someone else's eight acre lake which is at the bottom of our lawn on the opposite side of the house. It's as though they know our lakes are simply too small for so many geese but that the islands are perfect sites for nesting. In recent years the odd pair of both Egyptian and Canada geese have spent a day inspecting the islands for nesting but the greylags are too intimidating. There are of course resident moorhens, mallards and at least one pair of tufted ducks that reproduce each spring.

The poplars and conifers have grown to more than 30 feet high and the hundreds of willows and alders provide numerous nesting sites as do the self seeded gorse bushes. Fortunately all around our property is dense, mixed woodland so together with what I have planted around the lakes; there is now a superb habitat. Resident birds include wrens, tree creepers, robins, whitethroats, chiffchaffs, blackbirds, song and mistle thrushes, wood pigeons, collared doves, tree sparrows, kingfishers, nuthatches, chaffinches, greenfinches, gold crests, reed warblers, herons, great tits, blue tits, coal tits and long-tailed tits. There are also green woodpeckers, great spotted woodpeckers plus the occasional visit from kestrels and sparrow hawks. It is indeed vastly different from when I purchased the property back in 1982, when the majority of it was silver birch scrub providing little in the way of suitable nesting sites.

I had, (stopped making wine due to cholesterol problems a few years back) however, found one very good use for mature birch trees, say from eight to nine inches across and larger: birch sap wine. This delightful tangy wine, which clears quickly and is similar to fruity vodka, is quite drinkable within three to four months of being taken off the yeast. After a year or so it will blow your head off. In fact in Russia entire birch woods are destroyed by the over-zealous tapping of mature birch trees. To obtain enough sap for a gallon or two you do in fact need to drill into the bark of a tree. This must be done – indeed it can only be accomplished – during late March or early April when the birch sap is rising. Choose your tree and use a brace and one inch diameter bit to drill through the bark. Make the hole around two and a half feet off the ground, angling the bit slightly upwards, and stop when the sap starts pouring out. Sap rises up the tree on the outside of the wood, immediately beneath the bark, so be careful not to go right into the tree.

Now fit half a drilled demijohn cork (cut in half crossways) into the bark and gently push in around two feet of quarter inch clear tubing. This goes straight into a clean demijohn and, hey presto, within 24 hours you can obtain up to a gallon of the clear sap from just one tree. If not, simply drill another, remembering to plug each hole afterwards with a solid cork bung. The next step is to boil the sap together with the pared peel from three oranges and three lemons for around 25 minutes. You then add 3lb of sugar and stir until it is dissolved. Then set aside to cool. Once it's cooled add the yeast and the juice from the oranges and lemons, and leave for three days (covered by a muslin cloth) stirring twice daily. Then strain off the liquid and funnel straight into a demijohn. Fit with an air lock to ferment off. For those who have never made their own wine, it might be worth investing in a basic book on the subject and then follow these simple steps. You won't regret it!

I have also made elderberry and blackberry wine from our own fruits and have acquired a taste for wild mushrooms. Those which commonly appear are the parasol mushroom, *(Lepiota procera)*, which has a lovely nutty smell and is deliciously rich to eat, and the shaggy inkcap, *(Coprinus cornatus)*, also excellent eating when no more than a day (or two) old. We also eat the St George's mushroom, *(Trichorna gambosum)* when it appears at the end of April.

Incidentally, Jo makes a delicious spicy mushroom pâté from the large parasols. She starts by melting 4oz of butter in a saucepan to which three chopped shallots (or one medium onion) are added and cooked for four minutes until soft. Then 12oz of chopped mushrooms plus two teaspoonfuls of Worcestershire sauce and half a teaspoon of cayenne pepper are added and cooked gently for half an hour

with the lid on after stirring well. Then put into a blender, whiz until smooth and return to the saucepan and add a beaten egg. Cook gently (on a low heat) until thickened. Then put into a small dish, so it almost reaches the top, and chill in the fridge. When cold, pour 1oz of melted butter on top and pop into the fridge again. It's absolutely delicious!

Watching the lakes grow up has also increased my interest in and love of lilies, surely one of nature's most beautiful aquatic plants. I have been surprised at the durability of most ornamentals within an angling environment. Those most breathtaking of all, the reds, suffer no less when a hooked carp goes charging through their stems than the common yellow, *Nuphar lutea*. In preference I would choose William Falconer and Attraction, with the deep red of James Brydon as the most beautiful of all the red lilies. I have also been extremely impressed by Commanche, which is a coppery-orange, and two pinks, Rose Arey and Helen Fowler, the latter having large beautiful flowers held well above the surface. Of the 20 plus varieties of ornamentals in the lake I also like *Marliacea chromatella* which has distinctly variegated pads and creamy flowers. Many water gardening books list this particular lily as a yellow. But having had it now in both pond and lake for over 20 years, the flowers have never been what I could call yellow. Obviously planting such an array of ornamentals in addition to the common yellow lily means annual cutbacks and clear outs, as I have already mentioned, to keep them all in check. Nevertheless the entire project has proved such an enjoyable and rewarding part of my life, I wouldn't change anything for the world.

In fact, in May 1997, Jo and I were invited to the Café Royal in London for the Sand and Gravel Association's annual restoration awards presented by Richard Simmonds CBE, Chairman of the Countryside Commission. There were six winners, each recognised by SAGA for the quality of restoration work turning ex-gravel workings into nature reserves and fisheries. I am exceptionally proud to say that on behalf of Atlas Aggregates, who shared the honours, I accepted an award

LEFT

Much of what
I have written
during a period
covering 30 years
of water gardening
has appeared
in specialist
magazines such
as *Coarse Fishing
Handbook*,
*Practical Fish
keeping*, *Water
Gardener* and *Koi
Carp* Magazine.

for our own lake in Great Witchingham. The award report described our lake, and I quote, as 'an idyllic tranquil masterpiece' and 'a jewel in the landscape'. The SAGA award plaque is now proudly displayed in the cedar wood summerhouse which provides a panoramic view across the lake.

What I find even more exciting is that, through these awards, gravel companies are at last not just rewarding landowners for restoration work; there is an awareness in planning habitat-rich waters which will provide a future for freshwater fishing in this country. As our rivers sadly decline through water abstraction and damage from farming chemicals, what I have been saying for many years is now coming true: that we shall be relying more and more on gravel pits to provide quality freshwater fishing in the future. So if, in some small way, the creation of the lake can act as a blueprint for small still water fisheries of the future I will be a very happy man indeed.

August 1997 was the beginning of what was to be a hectic few months of foreign reconnaissance fishing trips, with a destination that can only be described as desolate. Thank goodness Jo is such an understanding partner. She understands my needs, through writing commitments, to be for ever zooming off here and there to places far and wide – often leaving her at home. Following a long haul from Heathrow to Halifax in Canada, plus an internal prop jet flight from Halifax to Deer Lake and from Deer Lake to Goose Bay, my journey into the province of Newfoundland was almost at an end. But not quite. Canada's far north is one hell of a country. I was met at Goose Bay by Englishman, Jon Cumming, of Friends of the Innu UK, and following a quick tour of the native Innu settlement we met Canadian photographer, Ted Ostrowski, and loaded all our gear into a De Havilland Beaver float plane – our final destination being Mastastin Lake. Called Kamastastin by the Innu Native Americans who for over 8,000 years have laid claim to this land, the lake is situated due west of Davis Inlet and south of the 56th parallel. Measuring some 14 by eight miles it is a massive sheet of cold, unbelievably clear

OVERLEAF

My favourite
view and piece
of natural history
that I had both
the opportunity
and privilege of
creating.

water. But more importantly it is home to huge lake trout and the most exquisitely coloured arctic char. The climate of the area is in fact sub-arctic, where the ice and snow which covers everything all winter doesn't melt until June and then it starts freezing over again come the end of September. We had but a few weeks left until the harsh annual cycle started repeating itself.

Until being encouraged into living within government-run settlements, the Innu had led a completely nomadic life for thousands of years, hunting porcupines, bear, goose and caribou, in addition to catching and smoking fish. Labrador is a large peninsula and does in fact boast the biggest concentration of caribou in the world, estimated at in excess of half a million animals. But few Innu hunt them now. Suckered into an easy, predictable but boring life in the settlements, the nomadic self-supporting ways of these gentle people are fast eroding, with the result that alcoholism and suicide are very real problems. Like so many situations the world over, from the Australian Aborigines to the Native Americans, their unique culture has been repressed by the greed of the white man. And being white there are times when I genuinely feel ashamed in that it was my forefathers who started slavery and the decline of such peoples.

The Innu, however, are fighting back and hoping to set up country wilderness camps for hunting and fishing to attract tourists, which is more or less where I came in. I had been invited by the Innu to help research fishing potential of the Kamastastin lake and river system from which summer camps could possibly be managed. During the two hour flight from Goose Bay to Kamastastin where our guides, John Pierre Ashini and ex-pat, Tony Jenkinson, had gone ahead to set up camp, my eyes were continually drawn to the wilderness through the clouds several thousand feet below. I contemplated the immortal words used by the famous explorer, Jacques Cartier, who described Labrador as 'the land God gave to Cain'. It certainly did look cold, harsh and forbidding.

The roads ended only a few miles north of Goose Bay leaving a true wilderness landmass best described as being similar to a mixture of both the Falkland Islands and British Columbia, where I fished several years back. And though in mid summer areas of snow could still be seen, water in the form of lake and river systems was everywhere, interspersed with tundra, bog and forests of black spruce, birch and red willow. I just wanted to put the plane down everywhere so I could sample it all: thousands of square miles of virgin game fishing. There was however time enough, for we were soon skipping over waves at the eastern end of Kamastastin Lake where three white tents and a pile of cut logs were the only sign of civilisation I had seen during our 250 mile flight. Talk about being isolated!

We were greeted warmly by John Pierre and Tony and their families, who much preferred the isolation of Kamastastin to the inherent problems of government settlement life, and shown to our trapper-style tent where the traditional carpet of spruce tips had been arranged to cover the ground. With a basic iron stove for both warmth (at night) and cooking, it took us no time at all to fall into the Innu way of life and our very first meal consisted of smoked arctic char.

During the following week we grid-searched the marginal contours along the lake's shoreline with my portable Hummingbird fish finder unit and found that in places the lake floor actually ran off the 120 foot depth limit, less than the equivalent distance out from overhanging cliff faces. But although quite awesome to contemplate, the lake's depth did fluctuate enormously and by far the best hotspots for char and lake trout were where rivers entered in relative shallows of between five and 20 feet. Here we caught on both wet fly and spoons superbly coloured char to 8lbs and lakers to over 15lbs.

But in truth during a week on Lake Kamastastin you can only scratch the surface. My favourite location was at the lake's outlet where it becomes the Kamastastin River which cuts through a steep-sided pine-stacked gorge. Here the arctic char provided unbelievable fights on a wet fly or on lures in the countless pools. The most effective lure by far was an 18g Toby.

However, I must warn anyone planning such a trip during August that, in addition to mosquitoes, you have the fierce biting black fly to contend with. Frankly it is not everyone's cup of tea, but I loved it. I'm sad to report that there is no happy postscript to this adventure because, due to the discovery of an incredibly rich nickel deposit at Voseys Bay, there is a Canadian government plan to dam Lake Kamastastin across its outlet to provide power in the form of hydroelectricity. Now far be it from me to stop progress, but what is more important – the native Innu re-establishing their culture in the land they have roamed for thousands of years or the 'get rich quick' attitude of the Canadian government? I'll leave you to decide.

Now we swing from one extreme to the other because in September 1997 I had the opportunity to come to grips with the most exciting battler of them all. For less than a mile off shore from the second tallest cliff face in Europe – an awesome granite feature separating landscaped terraces of fruit trees, vineyards and flowers on either side – the sea bed continues to shelve steeply downwards to over 2,000 feet. Here the warm sea is a majestic purple-blue, and flying fish and dolphins skip the waves. Go a mile further out, to where small groups of commercial tuna boats chum live mackerel on the drift in search of big eyes, and the depth more than doubles. Such is the incredibly deep and fertile habitat along the south coast

of Madeira, which lies some 360 miles off the west coast of Africa, just north of the Canaries. It is a truly magical island, perhaps most loved by tourists for its winding roads and panoramic views, exotic flowers and wines, yet revered throughout the 1990s by big-game fishermen everywhere as the blue marlin capital of the world.

To do battle in the fighting chair against these mammoth creatures which average between 600-700lbs, blue water fishermen come from Cairns in Australia, Fort Lauderdale in America and most places in between. There were more 'granders' (marlin topping a 1000lbs) off Madeira's southern coastline at that time than anywhere else on this planet. This is a phenomenal statistic indeed when you also consider that most were taken trolling within just two to seven miles of the picturesque shoreline, which is dotted with white-painted houses with terracotta roofs as far into the hills as the eye can see.

So after just 10 minutes from leaving the marina in Funchal, the capital of the Madeira Islands, giant kona head lures were run out behind the boat and the chance of a jumbo-size marlin begins. But, as my boat partner and I were to experience, such gladiators do not happen along willy-nilly, and towards the end of our fourth day nothing had so much as even poked its bill out above the waves to inspect the carefully arranged formation of six marlin lures being trolled at around nine knots.

Fellow angling journalist, Dave Steuart (lead writer for *Angling* magazine during the 1970s) and I had been invited along by angling fanatic, Frank Perry, who was a British karate champion for several years and then ran Madeira Sports fishing with two superbly equipped big-game fishing boats out of Funchal marina: *Margarita*, a 35 foot Maine Coaster, and *Lara Jade*, a 33 foot Cyfish which actually held the world record for catching more granders than any other boat. Frank's business was previously owned by my old mate, Roddy Hays, who was responsible for putting Madeira slap bang on the marlin map several years ago with outstanding catches of huge blues all caught and released during the season (which runs from May through to November), many exceeding that magical 1000lb barrier.

Regular viewers of *Go Fishing* may remember that Roddy and I initially teamed up for a wreck fishing programme when he lived in Alderney in the Channel Islands, accounting for numerous 20lb-plus cod and big double-figure pollack on pirks from a deep water wreck some 11 miles off shore. Then several years later we got together for some big eyed tuna action in Madeira from his old boat *Anguilla*. But the vision of sports fishing in Madeira waters goes back further still to the pioneering exploits of another very dear friend, the late Trevor Housby, whose catches over 30 years ago indicated the island's untapped potential. By sheer coincidence Ilda Housby (Madeiran by birth) and Trevor's 17 year old son, Russell, were holidaying on the island during our stay and it was like going back full circle for me, having Russ actually crewing on our boat. But Russ couldn't make those marlin move any more than Frank could.

To change our fortunes we even tried a day's shark fishing on *Lara Jade*, skippered by Anibal Fernandez and Richard Howell, with four big mackerel bails set at different depths beneath partly inflated balloons, drifting along away from the boat in a superb slick of mackerel rubby dubby. But nothing! Then we had a go at drifting for broadbill swordfish at night using large, whole squid presented deep down beneath clear plastic bottle floats, each illuminated from within by a different coloured light source. It was great fun and I especially enjoyed catching the squid for bait using mackerel tail and jigging lures. But nothing again and I could sense Frank's frustration at those big blues not wanting to play ball. He was certainly up for Dave and me sampling some 'Madeira magic'.

On the positive side even during our short stay (while fishing from *Lara Jade*) – and four days is not nearly enough time for marlin – a monster blue of 950lb was taken on *Margarita*, skippered by Mark Ryder Haggard and Mark Ryan. So when I fished from *Margarita* and finally that 80lb line class reel screamed into action like a scalded cat, with just two hours remaining on my last afternoon, for an instant I thought the miracle just might have happened. As we were trolling around the commercial tuna boats however, pulling a mixture of both marlin and tuna lures in the hope of last call action, commonsense suggested that a big-eyed tuna had grabbed hold and immediately sounded deep. But I was far from complaining and was into the fighting chair like a shot, quickly clicking the bucket seat straps on to the reel lugs. The fish was by now a fair way behind the boat still ripping line down into the blue depths, so I slowly increased the lever drag to slow it down before pumping the rod quickly up and down to gain line. Lovely stuff! Suddenly the world was a better place. As the converted know only too well, tuna really do wrench your arms out of their sockets and for 10 or 15 minutes I really had my 80lb string well and truly pulled, savouring a great scrap and tug of war with what materialised into my largest big-eye ever, a corker of 220lb.

No sooner had I arrived back from Madeira than an invitation arrived through the letter box from Linda Patterson of CSS International Ltd in London. She was asking me to compete in the first world invitational Bone fishing Championship (fly only) as the UK entrant alongside anglers from Japan, Italy, the United States and the Bahamas. How on earth could I refuse? The Bahamas have in fact the largest bonefish habitat anywhere in the world. Situated in the southwestern corner of the Atlantic, due east of Miami, this coral archipelago wonderland comprises 100,000 square miles of shallow ocean plateaux from which sprout over 700 exotic islands which, incidentally, were under British rule until independence in 1973. Add sumptuous seafood, exotic colourful cocktails, the friendliest people in the world and you are only just starting to appreciate this group called the Bahamas.

The highest point is just 200 feet above sea level and the average all-year-round temperature is in the mid 80s. It is indeed a tropical paradise with unrivalled hospitality and friendliness. It sports over 20 dedicated world-class bone fishing resorts separated by coral reefs, caves and mile upon mile of sparkling white sandy beaches and mud flats. When illuminated by sunlight, the crystal clear sea takes on all manner of breathtaking colours from shimmering jade green to cobalt blue, from aquamarine to turquoise or emerald green.

Following the flights from Heathrow to Miami to Nassau and to Exuma, it was difficult to believe that over 30 years had flown by since I had last fished in the Bahamas. My mind instantly returned to those carefree early years in the Merchant Navy when on board P & O cruise ship *SS Oronsay* I enjoyed some fabulous battles with sharks in the warm blue waters off Nassau. Now I had returned for this, the first championship of its kind. It was held in the middle of the Bahamas on Exuma, a 90 mile long chain of islands of James Bond fame (both *Thunderball* and *Never Say Never Again* were filmed on location here) which has 365 separate cays (pronounced keys) offering a wide diversity of bonefish habitats from the classical wide sandy flats to dense mangrove inlets, swamps and lagoons where goliath herons, sand pipers, egrets and even ospreys are sighted daily.

The local Bahamian guides have unbelievably sharp eyesight plus a vast knowledge of their particular patch and whilst wading, drifting or poling you along, they are continually pointing out barracuda, tarpon, permit and any one of several species of sharks which also hunt bonefish along the same shallow flats. However, unlike the fly fisherman, these predators do not practise catch and release. Huge stingrays are also regularly encountered, sometimes in mere inches of water, and, on one occasion, I was treated to the exceptionally rare sight of a huge sawfish, fully 12 feet in length, digging aggressively into the bottom mud's for crabs using its tooth-laden saw.

The competition was exceptionally well organised and run over four consecutive days from the club Peace and Plenty by the most enthusiastic Ministry for Tourism team. Every entrant was allocated a different guide and a different observer (to see fair play) each morning which ensured that the same ground was never covered

twice. Only specimen bonefish measuring more than 22 inches from nose to tail fork counted for points in the competition (we are talking of bonefish weighing 6lbs and upwards here), so the guides were continually searching for schools or pods which contained the odd sizeable fish or they were on the lookout for those single, lone bonefish which generally averaged a larger size. This necessitated continually zapping across the flats and reefs at speeds approaching 30 knots from one favourite hot spot to another, and covering anything up to 40 or 50 miles during a day which started with lines in at 7.15 am and lines out at 3.15pm.

The reason bonefish are held in such esteem by international fly fishermen is that they not only accelerate faster from a standing start than any other light-tackle sport fish but scream your entire 30 yard fly line out in a matter of seconds followed instantly by anything up to and over 150 yards of braided backing. Their power is truly phenomenal, and, combined with the fact that in these crystal clear shallow waters you must track, stalk and then systematically sight cast individual fish often over distances of 25 yards plus in a stiff breeze, they are indeed a most challenging adversary.

To combat the prevailing exceptionally windy conditions I used a 10 foot Masterline, Avantage Venom rod and a WF9 floating line joined to 300 yards of Pro micron backing. Competition rules dictated a tippet strength not exceeding 8lb and my choice of adding around eight foot of fluoro carbon to the upper half of a big butt leader helped turn over enormously. I tried all the favourite local fly patterns, and the acclaimed Gotcha special – tied with a pearl glitter tail and body, long pink throat hair and chain eyes, to imitate a shrimp – really did the business. Whether being stripped in using slow even pulls or allowing it time to sink, those bonefish inhaled it like the last shrimp in the sea. Hook-ups were no problem; it was landing them all that proved difficult. Trying to stop a bonefish, for instance, from winding your line through an entanglement of mangrove roots when it's doing 20 miles an hour is not easy, believe me.

The classic time for hunting these wily speedsters is at low tide on the mud flats in water mere inches deep where their tails and dorsal fins stick out above the surface, as they search nose down for crabs. As the tide floods you then swap location and drift along the edge of the mangroves into which the bonefish eventually move for the rich pickings and to avoid capture by sharks. It's all simply wonderful fun. How did I do? Well the list of lost fish and hard luck stories would, I am sure, bore you sick. It included losing a real monster literally, on my very last cast on the final day, which is one reason why I just can't wait to get out on those flats again. But everyone experienced the same problems and I did in fact manage to get amongst the prize money by finishing in third place behind Buck Buchenroth of Jackson, Wyoming and Henry Roberts of the Bahamas (both bone fishing guides incidentally) which for a self-confessed bream basher is better than I had ever hoped.

Exactly one year later in November 1998, Jo and I accepted an invitation to go on a media trip as guests of the Bahamas Ministry for Tourism and were shown exactly what these fabulous islands have to offer the international fly fisherman. I can tell you honestly there are not enough days left in my life to be able to experience it all.

Following flights from Heathrow to Miami and on to Grand Bahama, we stayed at the Port Lacaya, a resort near Freeport, with our first destination along at the island's eastern end at the renowned deep water Cay Club which provides excellent accommodation and facilities, managed by husband and wife team, Paul and Alison Adams. By coincidence our guide was Henry Roberts who pipped me into second place in the tournament the previous year and he poled the skiff for hour upon hour over some of the most beautiful and challenging flats I have ever fished. They had some enormous bonefish too: specimens in the 7-9lb bracket were common, though I also saw several whoppers well into double figures and only wished we had had time to do them justice. Alas the weather stayed overcast and windy throughout the day with only modest-size fish landed, the big fish seeing us first and spooking before an effective cast could be made. Then again, as a bonefish of just 3-4lbs will strip off your entire floating line plus 100 yards of backing in just a few long surges, every fight gets the adrenaline flowing.

The following day fishing was provided at the North Riding Point Club situated on Grand Bahama's southern shore and managed by Ben and Judy Rose. Here boats are trailered to a galaxy of flats, inlets and mangrove cays covering several hundred square miles along the island's northern shore. In just a three hour afternoon session with the help of the experienced eyes of Ken, our guide, I hooked and released eight bonefish to around 6lbs, having pricked or lost even more. Again also sighted were some jumbo-size bones plus the occasional tarpon.

After enjoying the Las Vegas show at the Princess Casino that evening we left Grand Bahama and island hopped to Abaco the following morning, our host being a larger-than-life woman in the form of Nettie Symonette who runs a unique ecotourism resort called 'Different of Abaco' where, in addition to enjoying her menagerie of animals which include wild boar and iguanas, guests live in superb accommodation along a powdery white beach and get to explore an outstanding assortment of marls along the west side of the island. I teamed up with good friend, Terrie Yamagishi, Japanese editor of the *American Fly Fisherman* magazine, and we hooked into a whole bunch of hard-battling bones which came most aggressively to our 'Crazy Charlies' virtually all day long. The following morning our entire group of 11 anglers travelled south to Sandy Point to the Bone fishing Paradise guest house managed by Stanley White, and again the fishing was superb. Despite only two hours of actual fishing time, my guide Kendall put me over so many pods of quality bonefish that I was happy to hand my rod over to organiser Nalini Bethel of the Tourism Office in Nassau, so she could experience the exhilarating power and speed of a hooked bonefish.

There is a story behind the legendary 'Crazy Charlie' flies that is well worth mentioning here. In 1974 on the Island of Andros, a Bahamian bone fishing guide by the name of Charlie Smith invented a devastatingly effective fly that was to revolutionise the sport of bone fishing. In fact just about every pattern of bonefish fly that has been created since follows the 'Crazy Charlie' theme with a pair of bead brass or lead eyes tied on top of the shank (so it fishes upside down and doesn't foul bottom weed) to resemble the shrimp upon which bonefish feed. So to actually meet Charlie Smith on this particular trip and watch him tie some bonefish flies was indeed a privilege. In fact Charlie tied two shrimp imitations for me, but I know I will never take them out of my fly box in case I lose them.

After Charlie we visited the famous Andros Island Bone fishing Club managed by Donna Reeny and I teamed up with Cordell Thompson from the ministry to fish a fabulous flat interspersed with mangrove cays at Behring Point on the east side. Our guide, Nick, predicted that bones in plenty would leave the mangroves where they feed on blue crabs and head in our direction once the tide started dropping away – and he was spot on. For an hour I literally had trouble in choosing which fish to single out for sight casting. What a whirlwind week!

There was, however, more to come that autumn, as I had been invited with friend and fellow angling journalist, Dave Lewis, to Tanzania on Africa's east coast, by Annie Ayton of Safari Plus. We were to make a reconnaissance trip, incorporating game viewing and tropical freshwater fishing at the famous Selous which lays a

LEFT
My good pal, Terrie Yamagishi, editor of the Japanese edition of *American Fly Fisherman*, casting to bonefish on the flats in front of Andros Island Bone fishing Club. Florida sports fishing writer, Walt Jennings, looks on.

little southwest of Dar es Salaam. Following our long haul from Heathrow, to reach our final destination at the panoramic Sand Rivers Lodge, which overlooks the coloured waters of the fast-flowing Rufiji River, required an hour's flight in a light aircraft from Dar es Salaam to Kiba airstrip. In fact, the mighty Rufiji River actually borders the Selous after gathering stature from an amalgam of wild, sandy rivers like the Kilombero, Great Ruaha and Luwegu, thus creating the largest river basin in Africa. Opened by the Germans in 1905, and said to be a birthday gift from the Kaiser to his wife (some present!), this 30,000 square mile nature reserve is the largest protected wildlife sanctuary in Africa, possibly in the world, yet it is inhabited by fewer than 200 people – a fact I found quite staggering.

Dave and I had but a week to explore the exotic freshwater fishing of what was pristine wilderness comprising woodland, grassy plains, swamps and marshes interlaced with natural lakes. There was also the muddy, shallow, and the exceptionally fast flowing Rufiji in which there were more hippos and large crocodiles than I had ever seen in my life before. The comfortable lodge was managed by an English couple, Alex and Harriet Edwards. Alex was extremely knowledgeable about the local natural history and the perfect guide for game viewing sorties into the bush where elephant, buffalo, giraffe and a galaxy of the most breathtakingly coloured birds were daily sightings. On one occasion we had the good fortune to study the feeding habits of an entire family of the now quite rare African hunting dog's only minutes after they had brought down an impala. All manner of fish were on offer here including several species of catfish plus the legendary tiger fish. At some of the more remote locations, using a variety of baits

from luncheon meat cubes to small freshly killed fishes, we caught several weird and wonderful species of tropical catfish. The bottom of this unusual river is simply paved with pussies from the spined and heavily armoured catfish called squeakers (similar to those I have encountered in the Zambezi incidentally) to monsters of five feet long, though what the species is called I am not sure.

Tiger fish strike everywhere and I would have dearly loved to have stayed attached to two huge fish in particular which, like so many, stayed on the hook for just a few seconds before jumping off. Presenting huge chunks of buffalo meat on strong wire traces in the hope of really big quarry certainly produced some screaming runs on my 30lb class multiplier outfit but in every case fish were not responsible for these runs. It seemed bizarre to be standing beside the river on a sandbank playing crocodiles which simply sat on the bottom after grabbing the bait! Fortunately they either bit through the wire trace or we pulled for a break lest they walked up the sandbank towards us.

We also enjoyed some exciting sport in one of the many adjacent lakes. In addition to numerous tiger fish in the 4-6lb range and similar-size sharp-tooth catfish caught using free lined dead baits and artificial lures I also, for the second time in my life (the first was in India), landed a snapping turtle. This one had an exaggeratedly deep shell and must have weighed the best part of 20lbs. Fortunately the hooks came out cleanly and it plodded off into the depths of the lake seemingly none the worse for its experience.

The Rufiji is certainly one of the most exciting rivers I have ever fished. Simply travelling upstream with a guide winding the aluminium punt through pods of decidedly hostile hippos would for some prove excitement enough. These particular

THE 1990s: A NEW BEGINNING

hippos openly disliked the whine from the outboard engine to such a degree they were for ever charging across the shallow flat in mock attack (we hoped). Should the punt have been overturned however the chances of making it to the shore with so many large crocodiles about, basking on the sandbanks, let alone those not visible, were, I would think, very slim indeed.

Naturally, before, in between and after this string of exotic locations I was still fishing locally. In fact during the 1997/98 winter I teamed up with my two nephews, Richard and Martin Bowler, for a concentrated assault on the big perch inhabiting the upper reaches of the Great Ouse above Bedford. Both had caught perch from the meandering overgrown reaches of this habitat-rich river during the autumn to over 3½lbs on lobworms. But once low winter temperatures set in sport died away to very few bites. My first two trips in fact resulted in complete blanks but at least I had the opportunity of both walking and, more importantly, plumbing depths along a most interesting two mile winding beat enticingly overhung by gnarled old willows and large blackthorn bushes.

Then at the beginning of February whilst sharing a wandering day with Richard with the Ouse running slow and quite clear, I managed to catch a nice brace of stripies on trotted worm from a deep hole on an acute bend, weighing 2¼lb and 3¾lb. Just a week later I again fished the same swim with Richard who on quiver tipped lobworm managed to induce a perch bite from amongst the hoards of signal crayfish which along this part of the Ouse almost pave the bottom. They are in fact a horrible nuisance but obviously responsible for the phenomenal growth rates of the adult perch. Richard's prize perch fought strongly in the now heavily pulling river and was in absolute spanking condition. It pulled the scales down to 4lb 5oz.

A week later during a particularly promising mild spell I was back on the banks of the Upper Ouse though rather disappointed to find it bank-high and coffee coloured. Three days of incessant rain had turned every ditch and side stream into raging torrents, but at least for February the weather was surprisingly mild, despite a continual downpour which started when Martin and I arrived at the fishery at half past seven, and was still coming down when we finished at five o'clock. Never before in fact can I remember actually sheltering beneath the brolly for the entire day. Strangely however it did not deter the big perch from biting, although our initial decision of concentrating upon the same deep bend where Richard and I had scored only weeks before proved a total failure, due I am certain to a farm drainage dyke immediately above the bend spewing its filthy water into the river. A complete lack of bites, save for the attention of bait-robbing signal crayfish, which are continually active (except when perch are on the prowl), meant that the perch had been sickened by the filthy orange water which no doubt included a proportion of silage.

So at around midday I walked to the top of the meadow well above the farm dyke and catapulted a couple of dozen broken lobworms into an acute deepish bend. Here a huge mat of brown rotting bullrushes lining the inside bank would have provided a superb hide-out habitat earlier on in the season throughout the summer and autumn months. My intention was to move in just above the bend for the remaining few hours of the day. It was the best bit of forward planning I have ever done. On arrival back at the deep bend Martin was about to lift out a crayfish firmly attached to his lobworm. That did it for me. 10 minutes later I was nicely settled in at the upstream end of the bend with my 13 foot rod presenting a stret-pegged worm close beside the bed of decaying bullrushes in a depth of seven feet. Once the float had settled at a half-cocked position indicating that the bait was static on the river bed, I cast out a second rod presenting a three swan shot ledger into the middle of the bend pointing it directly at the huge lobworm and clipped on a bobbin indicator between butt ring and reel.

When I looked up again I found the float had disappeared and my instinctive strike resulted in a lovely throbbing, head-shaking resistance deep down, so characteristic of a big perch. With just a 2½lb test reel line on the centre pin I was afraid to bully it and so enjoyed a spirited fight until it was up on the surface and ready for the net, all 2lb 2oz of it. A fine start, that. As soon as I had popped it into a pre-soaked sack at my feet the ledger bobbin jerked twice and slowly climbed to the butt ring in that classical, confident way big perch inhale a lobworm. And what a big perch it felt too. Taking line against the clutch, it powered upstream for a few yards before turning back downriver across the swim, boring deep all the time, and it stayed close to the bottom while I pumped it cautiously upstream to where I sat beneath an old willow tree watching the rod tip didn't catch in the branches above. It seemed an age, but finally my perch came up through the coloured water into view and thrashed the surface displaying its massively deep flanks and fat belly. Perhaps with more pressure than I should have used I quickly bullied it straight into the waiting net and heaved it ashore. On the scales it weighed exactly 3lb 10oz which made it my second-largest perch ever. What a day – and it was far from over.

After introducing some more broken lobworms into the middle of the bend I eased· another worm on to the size 4 hook and plopped it out to exactly where the big perch had come from. Within less than a minute the bobbin shot up and I struck into yet another biggy which after just four or five seconds unfortunately slipped the hook. I automatically feared that this would unsettle the shoal which it certainly did for a good hour or so. Then almost simultaneously bites came on both rods as the shoal again moved over the carpet of broken worm pieces. The float was first away and I struck into what felt like another whopper which bored away downstream taking several yards of line before I managed to turn it level with the end of the rush bed. Unfortunately it veered inwards towards the near bank and became stuck fast in the bed of decaying bullrushes. When I pulled steadily

the hook came free. Was I gutted, though I had little time for self pity because from the corner of my eye I witnessed the ledger bobbin jerking slowly upwards to the butt ring. This time the hook set firmly as the fish belted off downstream against a firmly set clutch, obviously another whopping great stripey by its head-shaking antics and dogged resistance. My Avon quiver tip rod and 6lb reel line were stretched to the full with this fish which led me a merry song and dance by screaming off upriver past where I sat, just missing a sunken willow branch, before I could get it back again under control and beneath the rod tip ready for netting. It was by far the largest perch I had ever seen on the end of my line in over 50 years of angling. It was a monstrously hump-backed specimen sporting wide, dark brown stripes, beautiful crimson fins, an incredibly fat belly (full of crayfish no doubt) and a huge mouth. It pulled my dial scales down to 4lb 1oz exactly, and boy, was I over the moon.

By now Martin had moved into the sedges bordering the next bend downstream but his ledgered lobs could attract small perch only. I experienced yet another lull for over an hour before the float suddenly shot away again resulting in my last perch of the day, another superbly fat specimen of 2lb 3oz. It too was stuffed full of broken worms, coughing up the remains of at least 20 into my hand after removing the hook. So I'd got four perch weighing together exactly 12lb. It was difficult to believe that I would ever better such a catch. At least those were my thoughts as Martin and I trudged wearily yet happily back to the cars across muddy meadows with the rain still falling heavily. Little did I know then that the following winter would produce totally staggering results!

At the start of 1998 I was asked by Polish publisher, Jerzy Markiewicz, if I would visit Warsaw to be the guest of honour at their annual angling exhibition in mid February. As Warszawski Dom Wydawniczy had already translated several of my Boxtree books to be published in Poland, and taken four of my Kazan River Production fishing videos also for translation into Polish (I'm called Johna Wilsona out there – honestly!), I was indeed very proud to attend.

I flew out to Warsaw with Jerzy's son, Bartek (then studying over here at Warwick University), who acted as my interpreter and was totally gob smacked by my popularity amongst Polish fishermen. Following television interviews and book signings I was escorted around the exhibition by Jerzy and his manager, Janusz Dobrzelecki, who speaks good English, and was most surprised to see posters from my books and articles all over the place. Manufacturers were continually giving me samples of their floats and excellent plugs and spinners, and when I stopped to look at a Polish copy of a British reclining carp chair, little did I know that very item would be wrapped up and waiting at my hotel the following morning. Their generosity and hospitality were second to none and it was a good job I didn't look at any boats. But when it came to eating out on boiled mirror carp and jellied grass carp, would you believe I tried my best to assure them that although an angler I didn't like eating fish. Which is perfectly true? But I nevertheless did down a few mouthfuls of each (ugh) just to be polite. Apparently at Christmas in Poland the national dish is not roast turkey but – yes, boiled carp!

I was later presented with a large polished box full of wonderfully hand-crafted artificial lures at yet another dinner where I met the editor of *Wiadomosci Wedkarskie*, Poland's most successful angling magazine, which has a staggering monthly readership of 140,000, (for whom I later was to write articles for several years) and fellow author in the form of Tadeusz Andrejczyk (translated to Ted Andrews) who, like me, also wrote about scuba diving in freshwater for *Angling* magazine back in the 1970s. So there was much to talk about.

What with a quick sightseeing trip around old Warsaw to witness how superbly some of the old buildings had been restored and even totally rebuilt to their original specifications following Hitler's madness during the last war, followed by lunch at a Mexican restaurant (my choice) only to find they served up chocolate chilli con carne – yes, it really did taste of chocolate – my all too brief visit to Poland was over. It was fascinating to say the least.

When viewers sit back to watch *Go Fishing* I am certain they never fully appreciate the frustration and trauma that go into bringing fishing into their homes on the small screen. Naturally they only ever see the sun, sand and specimen fish. So even now after over 20 years of presenting, directing and producing through Kazan River Productions the fishing videos and Anglia-Meridian, and Discovery programmes for British television, I often ask myself why I still enjoy the hassle of something which is tantamount to knocking your head against a brick wall. Because it is only great when you wrap and go home with sufficient 'in the can' as they say. Due to weather and water conditions, plus that old luck factor, our favourite subject has no equal in unpredictability. Sports such as football and boxing, in fact most organised events, are by comparison an absolute doddle to film. At least you know at what time the action is going to start and in most cases even when it will end. But can anyone ever predict when a fish is going to bite? I reckon it is this unpredictable factor which gives me such a buzz and keeps me for ever looking for new challenges.

I was therefore really looking forward, at the end of March 1998, to our planned trip to Lake Nasser in Egypt in the company of Emap's then fishing publishing

editor, Andy Benham, to make a 90 minute safari-style video about this 300 mile long water wilderness, home to the world's largest freshwater gladiator *Lates niloticus*, the Nile perch. Just as easily however, being the producer, it could have also turned into my personal nightmare. Had we taken the right generator along for charging camera batteries? Had we sufficient tape stock? What if our camera went down out on massive Lake Nasser, hundreds of miles from nowhere? Would our delicate filming equipment and precious rod tubes all even arrive in Aswan via Cairo in working order? I once had my fishing rods sent to Japan instead of back to Heathrow from Canada where I had been filming *Go Fishing*. Fortunately this was on the way back. But should it ever happen to the flight out, what a disaster!

I had first fished Lake Nasser back in April 1996 with my wife Jo, plus Christine Slater and her daughter, Emma, on a reconnaissance trip for Tailor Made Holidays. We were guests of Kenyan-born Tim Baily who, as The African Angler, operated six specialised fishing boats on the lake plus two supply vessels. We had a fabulous time, starting our safari at Abu Simbel where the huge statues of the Pharaohs built by Rameses II to impose fear upon the Nubians preside over the water, and slowly motored in a northerly direction up the lake towards Aswan, catching dozens of perch to 70lbs trolling around the islands and rocky shorelines. This trip led to my accompanying guests on further safaris, right up to the present day in fact.

There is indeed something rather enigmatic and mystical about Lake Nasser which is of course the valley of the River Nile flooded all the way from the Sudan to Aswan, where the high dam protects the city from the waters of this enormous man-made reservoir. Of course the Nile itself is an amalgam of the Blue Nile which originates in Ethiopia and the White Nile whose source is none other than Lake Victoria. But enough of the geography. Let's return to our meeting Tim Baily in Aswan airport at the start of our Lake Nasser Safari video shoot.

I had chosen the end of March because usually at around this time of the year the weather is wonderful. I was expecting clear blue skies, daytime temperatures in the

SIXTY YEARS A FISHERMAN

90s and warm, sultry humid nights that barely necessitate a sleeping bag while you drift comfortably into oblivion admiring the stars, sleeping on the open deck of your 25 foot fishing boat which is literally your home for the week. So when Tim gave us the news of some most inconsistent fishing due to completely unprecedented cold, windy weather and sand storms, it was hardly a promising start.

Unfortunately I had told cameraman, Dave Allen, and sound recordist, Dave Runciman, that all they need bring along were a pair of shorts and a few T-shirts. They were not happy bunnies. El Niño had a lot to answer for.

Worse still, once out on the lake with the camera starting to roll, one of Tim's front teeth suddenly dropped out! Never mind, I thought, a quick drop of Super-glue should do the job. Within minutes, despite almost sticking his lips together, I had fixed it back in place as good as new. Fortunately we were tied up to the shore well away from the white horses out on the lake in a quiet cove at the time, shooting an intro to the video in which Tim obviously did not fancy looking like Goofy. But halfway through the second take his tooth flies out again and plops overboard straight into the lake several feet from the boat. Immediately a plastic bottle marker float and lead line (used for buoying underwater pinnacles) was thrown over the spot. Mohammed, our ace diver, who thinks nothing of recovering expensive lures caught up in submerged tree tops in 20 feet of water, was quickly over the side after the elusive tooth. Alas, an hour later, Mohammed was completely knackered and had reluctantly to allow Tim's tooth to rest in peace. So minus his front tooth Tim and I eventually started the video's introduction. It was now 48 hours from checking in at Heathrow with not an inch of action in the can.

Fortunately, Lake Nasser is blessed with a truly fantastic head of Nile perch which breed most prolifically and enjoy a diet of tilapia, small perch and tiger fish.

They exist all around Nasser's countless islands and irregular contoured shoreline, so Andy and I were into some exciting action once the wind finally started to drop on the following morning. By trolling CD Rapalas and Buchertail depth raider plugs at between two and three knots close around rocky headlands in depths of between 15 and 30 feet, where clusters of boulders the size of a family car provide the perch with a variety of ambush points from which to dart out and grab their prey, we were soon providing cameraman, Dave Allen, with some spectacular footage. The great thing about Nile perch is that each and every one of them including the 'buffalos' (100lb plus fish) treats you to a head-shaking, gill-flaring exhibition of tail walking at the end of the fight once they finally hit surface, following a powerful, deep and dogged battle. They are certainly one of the most obliging sports fish it has ever been my privilege to film.

We literally lost count of the specimens between 30 and 50lbs taken on the troll and so decided to dedicate part of the video to shore fishing which to the ardent lure angler represents truly amazing prospects. Where else, for instance, can you stand on the shore from amongst the rocks, or cast from a position high above sheer-sided rock faces and hook into freshwater gladiators possibly of over 100lbs? Even, would you believe it, 200lbs! Several monsters approaching 200lbs have in fact been landed from the shore on Lake Nasser, using little more than stepped-up pike tackle.

We also caught a few perch fly fishing, and whilst working dead baits sink-and-draw style. A supply of freshly gill-netted herring-like fish (alestes) and some

SIXTY YEARS A FISHERMAN

LEFT

What a whopper!
My 120lb Nile
perch was quite
some lump for
me and guide,
Mohammed, to
hold up for the
camera.

small tiger fish were swapped for a bottle of Coke and a few hooks with the local fishermen, and once rigged on a pennel set-up incorporating two size 7/0 single hooks tied direct to a 100lb mono trace (wire is not necessary for perch) these naturals really scored when retrieved slowly. They glinted most attractively through the dear, blue depths (where visibility often reaches 10 feet) and suddenly to observe the dark shape of a big perch following the bait was nerve-racking to say the least. Takes were extraordinarily savage and nearly ripped the rod from my grasp. So after a while I knocked the ABU 10,000 multiplier into free spool when drawing the dead bait upwards, which was often when the perch made a grab, engulfing the fresh fish in its huge jaws. Several yards of line could then be given without the perch feeling resistance before lowering the rod tip, engaging the clutch and slamming into the perch when all was tight. Great stuff!

Using lures we also hooked into numerous tiger fish averaging between 3-6lbs, accidentally hooked the strange-looking freshwater puffer fish every so often and lost a couple of huge vundu catfish. There are some enormous vundu in the lake but few are ever landed because they dive to the bottom having grabbed a lure on the troll or being worked from the shore and immediately wind your line around and even under the rocks. Tim has however taken them to over 70lbs. There are also some bagrus (sementundu) catfish which reach close on 100lbs and the horrible electric catfish which is capable of generating electrical pulses and discharging over 300 volts. Fortunately being coloured in pale grey with large black spots, this particular species is easily identified and not to be messed with. The two I have caught of around 3lbs and 6lbs respectively both fortunately worked themselves off the lure without my having to consider a way of unhooking them.

During the making of this video I also finally fulfilled a personal ambition of catching a freshwater fish exceeding that magical 100lb barrier (though strangely

I've lost count of 100lbs plus fish since including arapaima and catfish in addition to Nile perch). Following goodness knows how many mahseer and vundu catfish to over 90lbs and dozens of perch to close on the same weight from both Lake Victoria and Lake Nasser during the previous decade, plus a couple of lost monsters that were far in excess of 100lbs, I became soundly attached to a whopper on the troll, which really made the 35lb reel line sing in the wind while it did its best to reach the sanctuary of the rocks on the bottom of a 50 foot deep gulley. My powerful voyager rod was dragged over into an alarming bend for a good 20 minutes but eventually the pressure told and the great fish finally hit the surface in a shower of spray close alongside the boat, wallowed a couple of times and lay there totally exhausted. It was an immense creature, so incredibly deep in the body, which measured five feet long and weighed exactly 120lb. Was lover the moon or what!

The bird life on Lake Nasser is wonderfully diverse which is not what most visitors expect from, what is after all, a flooded desert. Daily sightings might include egrets, Goliath herons, vultures, kites, Egyptian geese, pelicans, owls and terns, even flamingos plus numerous colourful, land-based finches which congregate around the shrub-like bushes along the shoreline. There are of course no trees as such but it's certainly not difficult to fall in love with such a seemingly barren environment. For those who look there is a truly fascinating ecosystem. Sightings along the shoreline and on the larger islands include camels, goats, donkeys, desert fox, jackals, giant spiders, scorpions, snakes and lizards. Some of the monitor lizards, which are woken from having a snooze upon a flat rock as your boat trolls close by, are up to six feet in length and quickly crash dive into the lake like mini dinosaurs.

Being part of what was once the River Nile, Nasser also contains huge crocodiles which, unlike those I have encountered in other African rivers, such as the Rufiji and Zambezi, are not to be feared. In fact it is most difficult to approach them close enough to obtain a photograph. This is because they feed mainly on fish and, due to the total lack of game around the shoreline, are not used to gorging on herd animals such as wildebeest and zebra in shallow water. So for the most part, a dip in the lake to cool off every so often is not only safe (fingers crossed here) but extremely pleasant.

Though we had shot an enormous amount of footage during our week's stay on Nasser in March we were still short of some general views such as sunrises and sunsets, plus various aspects of natural history. So as I was returning with guests on escorted trips in April and again in May, on behalf of Tailor Made Holidays, I took up Dave Allen's offer of purchasing his compact digital video camera, a Panasonic AG-EZ1E, complete with standard and wide angle lenses. I also bought an underwater housing for the camera plus a super wide angle lens, to enable me to take a few sub-surface shots when we returned. Until now I had always stayed away from getting

involved with the filming side of my videos, preferring to produce good stills rather than mediocre video footage. But I was pleasantly surprised by the results which were no doubt helped by the fact that as I was both directing and paper editing the video, I knew exactly what clips were required.

An unusual and rare opportunity presented itself one particular evening when on seeing some jackals not far from where our boats were tied up, Tim walked ashore in the pitch black helped by a torch beam and deposited the leftovers from dinner on top of a mound not 40 feet away to see if these normally inquisitive but naturally timid animals would come closer. Having taken my Samalight HD lighting unit along (what a superb piece of kit) should such a situation occur, I positioned the powerful main beam of light on top of the dinner scraps and set up the camera on a tripod on the sandy beach just a few feet from the supply boat, to see if the jackals would play ball. I am glad to say they did. At one time no fewer than five were captured in the light beam and by using maximum gain on the digital camera I recorded this truly memorable occasion of wild animals feeding, seemingly oblivious to more than a dozen humans staring in wonderment. You could have heard a pin drop.

Jackals and the desert fox are in fact regular campsite visitors around Lake Nasser during the quiet hours of darkness once everyone has turned in, as their pawprints seen in the sand on the following morning testify. But rarely do you get the chance of actually seeing them at such close quarters, let alone recording the occasion. It was a privilege indeed. Our encounter with a noisy frog however was entirely different. Once all the tit bits had been cleared and the jackals moved on it was time for everyone to resume drinking before thinking about getting their heads down. But not three feet from the bows of the boat on which I slept there was a large frog squatting in the mud, puffing its cheeks out every few seconds and creating the loudest, most irritating 'RIVET' you have ever heard. He didn't seem to mind me picking him up and depositing him in the reedy margins fully 50 yards away and I walked back to the boat, making sure there were no snakes in the torch beam, to continue some serious drinking. It was a sultry, warm intoxicating evening, the kind where your mind is truly at peace. 10 minutes later, in exactly the same spot to the inch, I swear, sat exactly the same frog which of course brought a hail of disbelieving laughter from everyone who thought I was batty anyway moving the frog in the first place.

Up I got again, and this time I walked fully 100 yards before dropping him into a dense bed of marginal reeds and again returned to the boat. Yes – you've guessed correctly. 20 minutes later (a determined frog this one) a loud indignant 'RIVET' told everyone that he was back again. I suffered in silence while everyone laughed themselves silly. Not long afterwards however the riveting was finally halted by someone who got up, walked along the bows of the boat to just above the serenading frog and urinated all over him. And I'm not saying who that person was.

Even before I got around to editing our *Lake Nasser Safari* video, which had become easily the most exciting television I have been involved with, in June 1998 I was off abroad again. I was making a long-awaited return trip across the Atlantic to see my old mate, Stu Makay, at Lockport Bridge Dam, near Winnipeg in Canada on the fabulous Red River. This is a fishery simply stuffed full of common carp, most of which have yet to see a baited hook, and the unbelievably hard-battling channel catfish. Both species incidentally average high into double figures in this part of the Red River, a phenomenon I first encountered around 10 years ago whilst travelling back from researching the lake trout fishing on Lake Nuletin in northern Manitoba with Martin Founds of Anglers World Holidays. I can remember then saying to Stu, who runs the fishing and accommodation at Lockport, that he was sitting on a gold mine. In complete contrast to how we British anglers put tremendous value on the carp as the supreme freshwater adversary, with species like zander at the bottom of the list, North American anglers put walleye (their zander) at the top and, for the most part, are not the slightest bit interested in catching carp regardless of their size and how they fight. Odd, isn't it?

In fact most Americans and Canadians would really rather catch a bundle of 2-3lb walleyes, which merely flap around like a bream of similar size, than have their string pulled by long, lean and unbelievably hard-battling common carp which are so plentiful in the 10-25lb range, their sheer density in numbers takes some believing. I thought I had experienced prolific river fishing for carp when I first sampled the Rio Ebro in eastern Spain for my *Go Fishing* programmes. Its coloured

ABOVE

These common carp and channel catfish from the swirling waters of the Red River at Lockport Bridge Dam near Winnipeg in Canada are everyday catches. On my right is Stan Povey and on my left, guide, Stu Makay, and Christine Slater of Tailor Made Holidays.

water then (prior to the catfish explosion) was simply stuffed full of common carp and barbel, but most were on the small side and double-figure carp were not regular catches, whereas on the Red, doubles are the norm. My old mate, Fred J Taylor, likens the river to a fish factory, and he's right.

Lockport Bridge Dam with its churning maelstrom of white water offers quite staggering boat and bank fishing. Channel catfish and common carp to over 30lb exist here plus the exciting freshwater drum, a predatory bream-like fish that is always willing to have a go at your fish strip, worm or fly. Add shiners, goldeye (a roach-like silver shoal fish and channel catfish bait par excellence), walleye, saugers, sturgeon, white bass, bullheads, pike and other oddities, and you can understand why parties of British anglers visit the Red River during the summer months, June until September being prime time. From October until early May it is completely iced over, such is the severity of Canadian winters.

Our party of eight, including Christine Slater of Tailor Made Holidays who organised the trip, stayed in Stu Makay's anglers' accommodation which commands a wonderful panoramic view across the river, with the custom-built boats less than a stone's throwaway.

But before getting afloat everyone had a whiff of Stu's stinking corn, the carp bait supreme. What is stinking corn, do I hear you ask? Well you tip 50lb of hard maize into a large plastic bin which has a lid. Several bags of sugar are then added – you don't have to be accurate, say 10-20lb – and the whole lot is covered by a few inches with boiling water and stirred thoroughly to dissolve the sugar. You then put the lid on and leave it for several weeks, or a few months if you like, for a ripe fermentation to take place. Those who make their own wine will understand the process here which benefits from a thoroughly good stir once a week. It is wise to put your bin full of stinking corn at the end of the garden well away from the house because when ready, and you will know, the smell is next to unbearable. You then scoop out a bucketful, a lid is also imperative here during transportation, and go carping. Loose feeding and styles of fishing are then the same as for baiting with sweet corn, maize being the hard variation of corn on the cob anyway and ridiculously cheap to purchase from the local corn merchant.

Strangely your 'Stinkers' will not have softened to any great degree and the best presentation is to use two to four grains on a hair rig whether ledgering or float fishing. Alternatively it is possible to side hook one or two grains. Either way, don't forget an old piece of towelling for wiping your hands on. Now stinking corn works anywhere, believe me, and on the Red River those carp simply queue up once they've got a sniff. Incidentally a large ladle-type spoon lashed to a stiff two foot cane serves as an ideal throwing stick for loose feeding.

On our first carping session Stu ran the 18 foot aluminium boat hard up on to a shallow gravel bar, where a wide drainage dyke joins the Red River not 200 yards from our accommodation, and scattered several scoopfuls of maize just 30 feet out. Within minutes there were so many tails sticking out of the surface knocking our peacock quill 'lift' floats, it was sometimes difficult to distinguish between line bites and the real thing. True, Stu had prebaited the evening before, but what followed was quite staggering. Having seen it all before Stu sat back, with a grin on his face, to see how his three guests would enjoy Canada's carping hospitality. To cut a long story short, although we fished for but only four or five hours, it was the most hectic sport with double-figure carp and cats (they take maize too though prefer fresh fish cutlets) that it has ever been my good fortune to experience. What a wonderful change from the over-fished carp waters of our British Isles.

Incidentally, tell a Canadian that you love catching carp and he will give you a quizzical look for sure. But mention that you actually catch the same fish twice back home and even give them names, and he will drop his beer from laughing in disbelief. It is simply beyond his comprehension, because most Canadian carp have yet to see an angler's bait. This probably explains why in just a few hours and from little more than two rod lengths out from the boat, my two guests, Roberto Ferrario (who had travelled from Italy) and Richard Ward from Southampton and myself accounted for exactly 50 superbly conditioned common carp between 11lb and 24lb, nine channel catfish to 23lb and eight drum to 7½lb. All came to stinking corn and bread flake baits and on several occasions two rods were bending simultaneously. At one stage all three were fully bent! We only stopped when we did in mid afternoon because Stu said, 'Hey guys, let's call it a day at 50, eh!' He was right, of course. The fishing is so prolific there is no point whatsoever in trying to fill your boots on every session.

Throughout the week we sampled carp in other locations off the Red River system including creeks, vast swamps, and wide channels, all with similar results.

Beautifully proportioned common carp simply knock the spots off a pot-bellied mirror of twice or even three times the size. Their strength and stamina were quite phenomenal.

We all enjoyed equal success with channel catfish and it was fun at the start of each session to waggler float fish pieces of worm to catch goldeye for bait close alongside the boat jetty. Each goldeye is then sliced into five or six cutlets and just one gently nicked on to a size 4/0 barb less hook. By the way, barb less hooks are compulsory in Canada as is the use of one rod only at all times. Mind you, the fishing is so fast and furious how anyone could look after two rods simultaneously (let alone three or four) is beyond my comprehension. Holding the rod and feeling for bites is imperative or the pussy lets go of your bait. A foot or two of line is given the second that a cat mouths the ledgered bait, followed immediately by a quick wind down and firm strike. Pound for pound the carp fights faster, but channel catfish (and I used 14lb mono and an 11 foot 2lb test curve rod for both) will pull harder and for longer. Incidentally, regular viewers of *Go Fishing* will perhaps remember that I featured the channel catfish of the Red River with Stu Makay several years back in series six and, unlike sport in our British waters, I am pleased to say that it hasn't changed since – not one little bit.

Due to heat wave temperatures, anchoring the boat amongst the deep swirling waters of the dam weir produced the most consistently hectic action with channel cats during the daytime. You can night fish of course but this was supposed to be a leisurely holiday and as two anglers sharing a boat often accounted for four or five cats apiece between 10-20lbs in just a few hours, there was little point in losing valuable drinking time during the evenings. Best pussy of the week was a 27½ pounder to the rod of Richard Ward who boated another of 25lb.

An additional treat was in store for our guests that week because my old mate, Fred J Taylor, who used to spend several weeks with Stu each summer, just happened to be at hand to organise some of his legendary riverside cook-outs. So most evenings saw us watching the sun go down in wonderful company, having a good old guitar-backed singsong around the camp fire. There was yet another surprise for me personally in the form of jolly Keith Sharp from Ferguson Lake Lodge in the Northwest Territories, who was now noticeably slimmer than his former 23 stone when we were last filming *Go Fishing* together eight years previously and he fell through the ice – a story I mentioned earlier. Keith was staying at nearby Winnipeg recovering from a triple bypass operation and had popped along to Stu Makay's place completely unannounced. How wonderful it was to be in the company of such great friends. There most certainly followed a night to remember, although in the morning I couldn't remember much about it. Christine said if she hadn't caught him from falling forwards off his seat, Fred J would have toppled over into the fire. Fred said I wouldn't stop singing even though he couldn't remember the

Spotted gully sharks, like the beauty held here by Italian angling journalist Robert Ferrario (left) and our guide the late Ottmar Leipert, are regular catches from the beach along Namibia's Skeleton Coast, together with several other species of sharks including Bronze whalers between 100-300lbs and big stingrays.

chords to the Grand Coolie Dam, and apparently Stu sat there totally out of his tree but contentedly happy all evening.

Upon returning from Canada in time for the start of the river coarse fishing season I got well and truly stuck into filming series 13 of *Go Fishing* visiting some wonderful locations. I fly fished for mullet and bass at Kimmeridge Bay in Dorset with fellow journalist, Dr Mike Ladle, battled with conger eels inhabiting a south-coast wreck with skipper, Brian Joslin, out from Rye in Sussex, took some fine chub over 4lbs and pike to 20lbs from the Hampshire Avon near Ringwood and actually managed to catch on cue from the Upper Ouse a big perch for the cameras which weighed 3lb 12oz. But the most beautiful fish filmed in the series that summer was undoubtedly the near 20lb golden coloured ghost carp I caught on float tackle from Heacham Park Lake in north Norfolk.

In the middle of the filming, at the end of July to be precise, Christine Slater of Tailor Made Holidays asked Emap's publishing director, Andy Benham and me if we fancied making up a foursome together with Roberto Ferrario (who came to Canada) on a research trip. This was to be to Africa's southwest coast in Namibia to catch sharks from the beach and then head inland for some tiger fishing along the upper reaches of the Zambezi in Zambia. Obviously we jumped at the opportunity, and what an exciting whirlwind trip it turned out to be. I can never recall cramming so much travelling and fishing into such a short period of time. In fact we travelled 21,000 miles in just five days.

Our first destination was to Windhoek (pronounced Vintook), the capital of Namibia. We then chartered a six-seater Cessna 210, piloted by JC, for a one hour flight heading due west to Swakopmund on the Skeleton Coast. Here we were introduced to Ottmar of Levo Sports Fishing, a short, most enthusiastic and rather eccentric German guide, who for several years had been taking visitors shore fishing by Land Rover and off shore ground fishing on board an 18 foot ski boat powered by twin Honda 90s. The sea was extremely rough with huge rollers crashing up the sandy beach which stretched for mile upon mile in both directions for as far as the eye could see. Namibia's famous 'Skeleton Coast' no less.

Ottmar decided to drive our party of five, which now included Peter Sawyer of Namibia Travel Connections, 20 miles north to where a huge reef broke the force of the waves 400 yards out leaving a large area of fishable water between it and the beach. He provided all the tackle and soon had us all rigged up with one-piece, 14 foot South African-style surf rods, multipliers loaded with 40lb test and a simple swivelled paternoster rig combining a 6oz lead with a fresh mullet head on a size 6/0 hook: his standard shark terminal rig, until the big boys put in an appearance. When they do the mono trace is replaced with 150lb wire and 8/0 hook. In case you are wondering, the 'big boys' are bronze whaler sharks weighing anything from 100 to 300lbs plus. Cow sharks of between 80 and 150lbs also feature in everyday catches here. Trouble was, our visit being in July (the African Winter) conditions were not really conducive to these particular sharks coming close in shore. Anytime between January and April, we were told, would virtually guarantee action with bronzes, as Ottmar affectionately called them. I had no reason to doubt his words because we caught everything else he said we would, including three black spotted gully sharks of between 50 and 70lbs plus a couple of 40lb plus hound sharks which are in fact our 'smooth hounds. Add three more lost of similar size and it was pretty impressive action for just an afternoon's sport at the wrong time of year.

When the water warms, big kob, steenbrass and three species of ray are also regular captures from the shore along the prolific Skeleton Coast. My old mate, Dave Lewis, from Newport, together with fellow angling journalist, Clive Gammon, who regularly wrote for *Angling* magazine during the 1970s, had been after the sharks only a few months before our trip. They travelled further up the coast and got stuck into several 150lb plus bronze whalers, the best weighing 250lb. What marvellous and unique beach fishing.

Exactly one year later in February 1999, Dave accompanied a party of 10 British shore anglers to the Skeleton Coast and in six days they landed a staggering total of 15,000lb of sharks. This included no fewer than 88 bronze whalers between 145lb and 280lb plus smaller sharks and nine other species. That is certainly the best haul from the beach I can ever recall being taken anywhere. But back to our whirlwind tour.

Following a night in the superb Swakopmund Hotel, where we enjoyed a magnificent meal including wine for around £8 a head, we were collected by Ottmar at seven o'clock to go out fishing on his boat. We were back in again by 10 o'clock having caught 50 or so catfish and kob to around 4lbs on cut sardine bait at anchor. Honestly, it was amazing light-tackle sport. Then we boarded the Cessna for our next leg of the journey. Well I did say it was a whirlwind tour and I meant it!

Heading in a northeasterly direction over desert and the savannah, JC brought the plane down four hours later at Mpacha airport in Katima. Here our Land Rover transfer was waiting to take us over the border into Zambia where we followed the course of the mighty Zambezi River upstream for 80 miles along a dust track to the lodge at Mazeba Bay. This bumpy route should have taken around three hours but was nearly doubled on account of two punctures, the second within just five miles of our destination which left us without a spare. So Shaun the driver had to thumb a lift and returned an hour later with another wheel. By this time it was pitch black and quite chilly, so we lit a fire in the middle of the track and huddled around it. After a warm welcome from our hosts Andre and Janine Van der Merwe and a much-needed evening meal, everyone crashed out only to rise the next day at six for an early morning session by inflatable boat up the fast-flowing Zambezi.

Now whilst I have enjoyed catching the tooth-laden tiger fish in Zimbabwe from the Zambezi River immediately above Victoria Falls and way below in massive Lake Kariba, and from the lower reaches 100 miles below Kariba, until now I had neither seen nor fished the Upper Zambezi. Tales of its remoteness as it cuts through the Zambian jungle and of narrow but deep swirling pools and eddies where monster tiger fish lurk, had always captured my imagination. It sounded so very different from the wide, reed-lined expanse of the lower reaches where hippos wallow on the sandbanks and muddy pools, and where animals of the savannah come down to drink.

Accommodating just 12 visitors at any one time in unique A-frame thatched lodges set high off the ground, with breathtaking, picture-book views across the Zambezi, Mazeba Bay offered anglers unparalleled sport with specimen tiger fish to 20lbs, barbel (sharp tooth catfish) of 30, plus several species of colourful predatory bream. Much of the river here runs through a rocky gorge and so is never netted by the locals. Consequently it is simply full of fish and there were some mouth-watering pools screaming out to be fly fished. Most of the rocky runs however were best fished by trolling from the lodge boats or shore casting using big single hook spoons or Rapala shad raps and CD 14 magnum plugs, the rear treble of which is replaced by a strong size 4/0 single hook to improve the ratio of fish hooked and lost to fish landed. When you do hook a tiger fish in these fast currents the ensuing battle, can only be described as spectacular. Their initial run, always followed by an explosion of spray as they catapult themselves high into the air in order to throw the hooks, is like no other freshwater sport fish. My outfit consisting of a small multiplier loaded with 17lb test and 30lb wire trace, and an eight foot fast tip spinning rod, was certainly none too heavy for these tigers. From a couple of dozen hits on our first session we boated and released just six deep-bodied specimens to around 6lbs. But don't run away with the idea that Mazeba Bay is all fishing. You can take a flight up the valley to view the falls from above in Andre's micro light, go game viewing by Land Rover in a nearby national park, tackle white-water rafting, or simply take it easy and enjoy the exotic bird life through binoculars.

By nine, the sun's brightness terminated any further action from toothy predators, so we beached the boat and walked way upstream through the bush to marvel at the magnificent Ngonye Falls (a mini Victoria Falls), one of the major attractions at Mazeba Bay Lodge, although I am sure some guests would give me an argument in favour of Lilundu, a four year old orphan elephant. She was raised by the Van der Merwes from just a few months old, and visitors get to share their afternoon back at the lodge with her which is a fascinating experience, to say the least. Sightings of fish eagles, hornbills, pied kingfishers, crocodiles and breathtaking views across the Zambezi valley, accompanied by two further tiger sessions with fish to 7lbs in the boat and a lost beauty of double the size saying goodbye in a kaleidoscope of spray, terminated our stay.

Following a long hectic summer continuing the making of my *Go Fishing* programmes, I decided to devote time to catching those jumbo-size perch of the upper reaches of the Great Ouse above Bedford once autumn settled in. It's a 250 mile round trip from my Norfolk home necessitating an early start. This is a long haul for a day's sport but as I had caught a four pounder there the previous February and was optimistic of the chances of more to come, I felt the loss of sleep was well justified. My first session in mid October proved the point. As I have already said, the reason for the Ouse producing these huge perch in such numbers is due to the proliferance of the dreaded signal crayfish.

Unfortunately neither of my nephews, Martin and Richard (whose company I had enjoyed along the river here last winter), could spare time to join me for the

LEFT
Everyone loved playing with the baby elephant at Mazeba Bay Lodge on the upper Zambezi River.

THE 1990s: A NEW BEGINNING 237

These six big perch from the Upper Great Ouse weighed an ounce under 24lb and contained four over the 4lb mark. A catch considered by the National Perch Fishers Group quite unprecedented, and the most remarkable haul of four pounders ever reported to them. Lucky me!

day, which simply cried out big perch due to a strong, warm wind from the southwest accompanied by a cloudy sky through which the sun occasionally shone. Changing light values are so important in my opinion for keeping predatory fish willing to feed throughout the day. I settled into a favourite swim half an hour after dawn.

Flowing left to right the river here is about five feet deep through the centre run with an old willow lapping the surface on the opposite bank about 40 yards downstream. All along my own bank are thick beds of yellow lilies whose sub-surface lettuce-like leaves provide sanctuary to dense fry shoals. That is one very good reason I am sure why big perch patrol along the cabbages, as they are called. As is my usual preference when fishing for perch along the Upper Ouse, I fished with two rods. With eyes glued to the sensitive tip of my Avon quiver-tip rod, one of the lobworms (on fixed paternoster rigs holding three swan shots) was placed halfway down the run, with the second worm cast into a clearing amongst the cabbages, and a bobbin indicator clipped on the line between butt ring and reel on the Heritage quiver-tip rod which has a softish tip. In both set-ups line strength was 6lb test with size 2 hooks tied direct.

Fishing two outfits in this way, both in different parts of the swim, I find I can locate perch far more effectively than by using just one rod. Moreover because I am continually twitching one worm, whilst allowing the other to remain completely static for up to half an hour before recasting, the perch are given a choice depending upon their mood on the day. This is most important. On so many occasions, having remained bite less for 20 minutes or so, has an immediate response resulted from lifting the rod or pulling the bobbin line down to move the worm a few inches. It is as though the perch is lying there daring the worm to get away before pouncing in exactly the way a cat behaves with a mouse or small bird it has caught.

I missed the first bite, but the second resulted in that satisfying, head-shaking feeling of a big perch doing its best to rid itself of the hook. They are able to do this with surprising ease if the slightest slack is given. But this one stayed on and after a begrudging dogged fight, so typical of big perch, it was safely in the landing net – all 3lb 14oz of it. What a start! There then followed one of the most extraordinarily productive catches of specimen fish it has ever been my fortune to experience, a catch I rate amongst my top six in over 60 years of fishing.

Strangely those fish never really went mad, and I invariably had to wait 15, even 20 minutes for a bite. But the swim remained active literally all day long as various

SIXTY YEARS A FISHERMAN

groups of perch and pike moved through attracted by my continually catapulting out broken lobworms. And do you know, not once did I experience that continual twitching on the quiver tip which denotes that crayfish are on to the worm – such was the predatory aggression within the swim. The next bite produced a magnificent perch weighing 4lb 2oz and shortly afterwards a pike of around 5lbs grabbed my ledgered lobworm. I then pulled out of a good fish on the strike (which could have been perch or pike) but fortunately the next stayed on and in came a perch of 4lb 1oz. Two four pounders in one session! I just couldn't believe my good fortune. But there was more to come in a glut of pike, with fish of around six, 10 and 14lbs (I didn't bother to weigh the pike) roaring off with the ledgered lobs. For a minute or so I actually thought the largest must have been a barbel, such were its speed and power.

It's funny how you can thoroughly enjoy the fight of a big fish on light tackle for several minutes until it rolls on the surface and reveals itself to be a pike, whereupon its stature suddenly becomes somewhat diminished. In fact I thought the next bite was from another pike and so bullied it upstream through the swim towards me in cavalier fashion only to have a huge perch slide into the net. Another four pounder no less, weighing a massive 4lb 7oz – then my biggest ever by far.

I was by now wondering whether this was all really happening but there was still more to come in the shape first of another fish lost halfway up the swim which I thought would put the kybosh on any further bites. But it didn't. The next perch weighted 3lb 5½oz and at around half past two my last, another four pounder, pulling the dial scales round to 4lb 1½oz. Three of the six perch had come to static worms and three within seconds of twitching the lobworm, of which I used well over 100. Was I in a dream or what? Four perch over 4lbs in a single session plus the two three pounders which collectively made the catch amount to 23lb 15oz. It was quite a remarkable catch to say the least.

It was no good, I just couldn't fish on. At 3 o'clock I decided to set up the camera on the tripod to photograph the catch, always a frustratingly lengthy operation when fishing alone, before the sun started to drop too low. And I'm glad I did. In retrospect I am sure a few more bites were left in the swim but there comes a time, though I must admit it has arisen on only a handful of occasions with this angler, when your soul has been so well and truly satisfied that continuing is impossible. My two huge mahseer from the Cauvery River in India mentioned earlier weighing together over 170lb and a catch of nine double-figure bream to 13lb 10oz in a single session from a Norfolk lake immediately spring to mind. They were times when I simply had no interest whatsoever in fishing on. Another similar and memorable catch happened back in the mid 1980s whilst stret pegging at night with a beta light float on a favourite stretch of my local River Wensum at Drayton. Using bread flake I took a mirror carp of 10½lb followed by a barbel of 12¾lb, then a roach of 2lb 7oz; followed by a chub of 4lb 6oz on four successive casts. After this I just couldn't cast out again.

Following this unique catch of huge perch I was asked by the national Perch Fishers' Group to write about my exploits for their magazine, which I was only too pleased to do. Having compiled record lists of all the big perch caught within the British Isles since the turn of the century, it was most gratifying to know that the Perch Fishers considered my catch of whoppers quite unprecedented and at that time, the most remarkable haul of 4lb plus perch ever reported to them. What with my 120lb Nile perch caught from Nasser whilst making the Safari video there for Emap back in March and then in October to catch four perch over 4lbs in one sitting, you might say 1998 was one hell of a big perch year for me.

It is indeed most satisfying every so often to improve on your personal best, if like me you have a leaning towards the pursuit of larger and larger specimens. Being on a bit of a roller at the end of 1998 it actually came as no great surprise to experience similar good fortune whilst grayling fishing. Although I had caught three pounders (and that's a big grayling) from Canada's far north, plus numerous 2lb plus specimens over the years from the Tay, the Test, the Kennet, the Dever and from the Frome, I had never caught a British grayling over the 3lb mark – my best weighing 2lb 14½oz from Dorset's tiny River Frome. So when in December my good friend, Trevor Stroud, invited Bruce Vaughan and me along for a day on the

RIGHT

Long-time fishing pal, Bruce Vaughan, and I, display some of the monster grayling we caught long trotting the upper reaches of the River Frome in Dorset.

Frome, which is his local river and noted for biggies, I was all keyed up and ready to go as usual.

To break the long drive down to Dorset from Norwich I motored across country to Oxford in order to collect Bruce and then on to Dorchester where we stayed overnight. Now being both a chalk stream and a spate river, I have always been puzzled why the Frome throws up so many huge grayling. In looks and sheer breeding power Hampshire's River Test would seem to possess all the credentials for record-breaking grayling, dace – even roach – potential. But this isn't so. Instead lesser-known fast-flowing rivers, due to unidentified factors, can have the ability to produce specimens of truly huge proportions which is strange in this case because Frome trout are nothing out of the ordinary.

When my old mate and one of the greatest British all-round anglers who ever long trotted, the late Trevor Housby, first took me grayling fishing on the River Test I was like a boy in a sweet shop. I photographed everything we caught and I even took two large grayling home with me (they were unwanted on the exclusive trout beat of the Test we fished) for preserving. They weighed 1lb 10oz and 1lb 14oz and they stare down at me from their bow-fronted glass case high on my office wall as I write this. I feel proud of them because not only did I catch them, I also stuffed them. I later preserved a 2½lb grayling that Trevor caught which still hangs on the wall in the house where his wife, Ilda, and son Russ live. That grayling encompasses all our feelings not only of the angler we loved, but of this enigmatic species.

Inevitably these and many more memories ran through my mind as I belted a bait pouch around my waist and filled the two pockets, one with red worms, the other with maggots. Sadly the light values never climbed above a thirtieth at 2.8 (keen, old-time film photographers will identify with such problems) throughout the entire day, so any kind of action photography was out. It was a case of fill-in flash trophy shots or nothing which was a pity because the river is so attractive and with the flow extremely fast and the water clear, some quality grayling were certainly on the cards.

Despite our casual start following a prolonged evening meal at a local Indian restaurant and a late night, we systematically wandered the river trying numerous swims for perhaps 30 minutes at each run or so before either scoring or moving on. This of course is the way to treat grayling fishing. If they are having it, a fish usually comes on your very first or second trot through – 13 foot trotting rods, centre pin reels loaded with 3lb test, and Avon and chubber type floats carrying a heavy shotting load being order of the day.

On one particular acute bend where the flow angles sharply across to the far bank, leaving a defined crease on the inside line along which I steadily guided the double maggot bait, an instant bite produced a superb grayling of 2lb 11oz. I expected nothing more but on the second trot through, gently holding back on the

7AA Avon float, the tip dipped positively again and when I struck the rod arched over to the vibrating pulse of what was obviously not a trout or grilse, but a big grayling. It is the way they hang in the flow and twist whilst you try and force them upstream, which makes you realise that on the end of your line attached to just a 16 hook, is a specimen 'lady of the stream'. So your heart is in your mouth throughout the entire fight, right up until it glides over the net. Weighing in at 3lb ½oz this particular grayling, a male complete with splendid sail-like dorsal fin edged in crimson, was just one of four biggies I caught that day. A specimen of 2lb 10oz and a brace of 2lb 11oz completed what for me was the best quartet I have ever landed in a day's fishing. I told you I was on a roller, didn't I! Indeed, that three pounder was for me the pinnacle of half a lifetime of long trotting in swift, clean-flowing rivers for this, one of my favourite freshwater species.

Not far into January 1999 I was back on the upper reaches of the Great Ouse once again in search of big perch. I had made one more trip in the meantime following that memorable quartet of four pounders, taking one three pounder whilst fishing with Martin Bowler who caught a surprise 5lb chub just before we packed up and headed for home. Martin was also on a roller during this period due to his exploits with the monster Ouse barbel inhabiting the famous stretch immediately below Adams Mill, which were regularly making the angling press. After several huge doubles Martin finally broke the British record with a 16lb 13oz beauty caught on a paste-covered bailie, ledgered on the bottom of a slack in appalling conditions with the Ouse in full flood and all over the fields.(Little did we know then that barbel over 20lbs were to be caught from the same stretch several years later.) Unfortunately the very same fish was caught just two weeks later by another angler (now weighing a staggering 17lb 3oz) before Martin's record claim could be endorsed. Nevertheless, albeit for a short period, Martin was the captor of Britain's largest ever barbel. The very same barbel became the then record when it was caught for a third time by Ray Walton at 17lb 6oz a few weeks later, just prior to the end of the river season on 14 March. But back to those Upper Ouse perch.

Now with an entire day to myself again and the river nicely up and heavily coloured, I tried the productive cabbages swim and in the first two hours caught perch of 2lb 12oz and 4lb 4½oz, both on static lobworms. The thought that I might be in for another bumper haul did, I admit, cross my mind. But by early afternoon I had not had another bite. So I carried on moving back upstream towards the car trying several favourite swims en route, all to no avail. With an hour or so to go before calling it a day my final choice of swim was a large slack that had formed behind a huge sunken willow on the opposite bank – a veritable floodwater haven to any perch living close by and a swim I had not before fished. Within minutes, quite literally, the quiver tip buckled over as something big (I suspected a chub) grabbed the worm and screeched line from the reel as it made off downriver. After several heavy runs and much head shaking I drew yet another huge perch over the landing net. It weighed 4lb 4½oz, exactly the same as the four pounder I had caught earlier over a mile away. There was then barely time for me to set up the tripod and take a few trophy shots using the self timer and fill-in flash before darkness loomed over the Ouse valley.

Martin's brother, Richard, visited the river a few weeks later and accounted for a fabulous catch of specimens, both on ledgered lobworms. They were a perch of 3lb 13oz and a chub of 6lb 10oz. What a brace!

A few weeks after this in mid February Richard and I teamed up for a day which though mild enough and seemingly pregnant in big perch potential, due to a strong southwesterly wind, produced little until later afternoon when light values started to stop. We put this down to a now low and quite clear river which had a visibility of at least two to three feet following several weeks of extremely cold weather. Fishing several yards apart in a deep bend of the river amongst sunken branches along the opposite bank, Richard had three bites in quick succession, connecting with two, both of which were perch of around 1lb. I then struck and pulled out of what felt like a good perch but hooked into a small pike on the very next cast from the same spot. I then lifted into what I thought was a crayfish bite in order to shake it off and the crayfish materialised into a chub of exactly 4½lb.

With an hour or so to go before we called it a day and rain now starting to spit, the bobbin on my near rod jerked up to the butt ring positively and I struck into another whopping great perch which fought as hard as I have encountered from any 4lb fish in British freshwater, making several unstoppable runs against the clutch until the Avon rod eventually got the better of it. I lifted the monster out and we quickly recorded its weight on Richard's scales – 4lb 7oz – exactly matching that of the largest I had caught last October and bringing my total of 4lb plus perch caught in less than a year to eight. Some kind of record in itself then. Having read over and over again the legendary perch captures of the late Dick Walker from Arlesey Lake back in the 1950s, little did I ever believe then as a teenager even in my wildest dreams that I should be emulating his remarkable achievements 40 years later.

Just for the record concerning famous Arlesey Lake in Bedfordshire, Dick did, in fact, share with Bob Rutland during the 1950/54 period dozens and dozens of 3lb plus perch on long-range ledgered worms, with a total of seven over 4lbs. Dick's largest was 4lb 13oz and Bob's was 4lb 10oz.

At the beginning of February Jo and I flew off for a week in The Gambia quite literally on a whim. I had just completed a retrospective piece about fishing in The Gambia for my page in the

BELOW

Martin Bowler's huge barbel of 16lb 13oz from the Upper Great Ouse which broke the British record in 1999, albeit for just a few weeks, until the very same fish was caught again at a heavier weight. Little did I know then, that I was to equal this monster with a fish from my local River Wensum several years later.

Express when Jo said, 'Hey, why don't we have a week there?' And away we went, meeting up again at Banjul airport with good friends, Tracey Day and her partner, Mark Longster, with whom I made two *Go Fishing* programmes several years back, as I described earlier.

It was great to be back in The Gambia again, where Mark ran his fishing charters from the river at Denton Road Bridge, and the beach hut at the Sunwing Hotel where we stayed. With exotic seafood's readily available, it was indeed tempting simply to lie by the pool or on the beach and stuff on grilled lobster and the biggest jumbo shrimps you've ever seen in your life, whilst knocking back the piña coladas. But I'm no Del Boy (although Jo would give you an argument) and so we split the week between relaxing and fishing. As I'd had my fill of fantastic reef fishing on past trips with kujeli, cassarva, barracuda and cubera snappers, we decided to go for broke by attempting to track down those monster tarpon for which the Gambia River is justly famous. In recent years monsters weighing up to a massive 385lb had been caught here but not ratified by the International Game Fishing Association. In just three days' fishing, however, anchoring in the river at its widest point, some four miles across at a location known as Dog Island, I was over the moon just to experience, on one of those days, a truly unforgettable occasion with literally hundreds and hundreds of 100lb plus tarpon rolling all around the boat. I have never seen so many huge fish in one area before. They could be seen wallowing and crashing through the glass-like surface and stretched for at least 200 yards in all four directions around the boat. But could we get a run? Could we hell. One of our bottom-fished live mullet had been grabbed by a 40lb flat-headed catfish prior to the tarpon moving in an hour before the top of the tide, but though we put live baits out on floats way behind the boat, wobbled baits using an erratic retrieve and even presented baits at mid-water, those tarpon were frustratingly not interested. Then Mark decided to put a general outfit over the side as our 50lb class rods were doing nought. Within just a few minutes of him lowering jumbo shrimp down to the bottom on 20lb gear, it was grabbed by; yes you've guessed it, a huge tarpon.

Immediately Jo helped wind in all the rods while I rushed up front to buoy the anchor as Mark's tarpon did a 100 yard sprint followed by two high, acrobatic jumps when it completely cleared the surface in a kaleidoscope of shimmering spray. It was an immense fish which we both put at 200lb plus. But on 20lb line?

Getting on for three-quarters of an hour later, the great fish, having been slowly and skilfully played by Mark, was now on a short line and literally walking him around the boat with me in close pursuit trying to record a jump on camera. It really looked as though the impossible was going to happen. It was now slack water and we were inwardly thinking about all sorts of line class records. Then the inevitable suddenly happened with the line cracking off like a pistol shot. Swearing loudly as we both did achieved nothing, for the 20lb monofilament was heavily frayed for several feet and I suppose the outcome was inevitable from the beginning. But full praise to Mark who really hung in there. So my big Gambia tarpon will have to wait and by big I do mean record fish and hundreds of them to boot. The memory of fish upon fish rolling within yards of the boat permitting appreciation of their enormous bulk while we drifted slowly in pursuit of Mark's tarpon will stay with me for ever. Like a drug, The Gambia – not forgetting the company of Mark and Tracey – will have Jo and me returning again real soon.

Back home again and it's 1 March with just two weeks of the river fishing season remaining. I rose at 4am and headed for Bedfordshire once again. My passion and quest during the past two winters for the big perch of the Upper Great Ouse had not waned an iota despite the long drive. The day however did not start particularly well when I saw in the rear mirror that irritating flash of a speed camera recording my number plate as I obviously exceeded the speed limit going through a sleepy village. The rain was lashing down heavily but it was due to clear later and, most important of all, the estate's outside temperature gauge read a warm 11 degrees celcius. I just felt it was going to be a good day for perch.

Martin Bowler had visited the stretch a week previously and taken a marvellous brace of perch weighing 4lb 5oz and 4lb 14oz, so the chance of a five pounder was not such an impossibility. He was in fact due down at the river to join me for the afternoon session through until dark, so from dawn until around two o'clock I decided to have a lone roaming stint fishing numerous swims for short periods of time to evaluate how the perch were reacting to such mild temperatures once again. Would they be holed up in the deep feature swims or starting to group up and moving about?

By the time Martin arrived I had caught several small perch, plus a good fish of 2¼lb and as many jack pike on the statutory ledgered lobworms from no fewer than seven different swims, and had blanks in a further two. So few conclusions could be drawn, except that if we were going to get amongst some whoppers, with the river being so clear (a two to three foot visibility and so different from when we fished together here last March when it was in heavy flood), it would happen during the last two hours before dusk. And that's exactly how it turned out.

On arrival Martin moved into the long straight where he recently caught the big fish while I decided to spend the rest of the day in a swim that I had always fancied for some really big perch, due to its immense promise provided by a depth of six feet running close beside a thick bed of sedges, which ran right to left downstream along my own bank for over 40 yards. Several past sessions however had produced just one 3lb perch and little else in the way of bites. Nevertheless something made me feel extremely confident as I settled in presenting the quiver tip rod worm dose beside the sedges on a long cast, and the second in midstream just 10 yards away. After clipping the ledger bobbin indicator between reel and butt ring on the second rod, my Heritage Avon quiver tip, I catapulted out a dozen or so broken lobworms (which I obtained through the post from the aptly named 'Wiggly Wigglers' on a next-day service) and sat back to wait events, every so often adding the extra broken worm or two. At around 3pm up went the ledger bobbin and the soft tip of the Heritage Avon curved over into that satisfying throbbing, head-shaking power arc produced only by big perch. This particular rod has been instrumental I'm certain in my landing an exceptionally high percentage of big perch hooked, due to the soft tip, allowing me both to enjoy a powerful fight and then draw safely over the net perch in which the hook is barely set or is held in by a mere sliver of skin.

The first fish weighed 3lb 2oz, shortly followed by a massive stripy of 3lb 15oz, only an ounce below that magical 4lb barrier. This was quite unreal perch fishing but there was more to come. In the space of an amazing 45 minute spell prior to dusk falling, the big boys went on a real feeding rampage for my continual supply of broken lobs. I feared that Martin would become cheesed off leaving his swim to help weigh my catches but he was equally as excited as I put monsters of 4lb 3oz, 4lb 4½oz and 4lb 8oz (my personal best at the time) into the weigh net. Surely that was it for the day? But no, on the very next cast I did the unthinkable and bumped off the hook another whopper. After this, sport died for a while followed by several small fish in the 8oz area which had moved in over the carpet of worms once the big boys had vacated the swim. One more bite immediately before darkness set in produced a perch of 2¼lb, and then all action in the swim ceased.

Martin had anticipated that a serious photography session was in order with such a catch while we could still see the fish without a torch and had walked up to my swim. He duly obliged using my new camera, a Nikon F100, coupled to a 2.8, 2035mm CPU autofocus lens and SB28 speedlight flash gun, and ran off a couple of rolls of Fuji 100 Provia film. I splashed out on such an outfit specifically to overcome the inconsistency problems with fill-in flash that I had experienced over the years with my old Nikon 301 cameras. And I must say that due to the speedlight firing a series of imperceptible preflashes which are detected by the F100 camera's five-segment TTL multi sensor and then analysed for brightness and contrast, exposure problems with flash instantly became a thing of the past, even out in the field when tingling with excitement and it's getting darker by the second.

I really did assume that my catch of six perch for 23lb 15oz (that contained four over 4lbs) and which I detailed back in October 1998 was a one-off but here,

just a few months later, the Upper Ouse had provided me with yet another haul destined to rewrite the record books: five perch for 20lb ½oz – and what magical beauties they were too. Massively deep bodied and in fair bristling condition, they were absolutely scale and fin perfect. I was even happy about making the long drive home and content about managing to achieve some unprecedented hauls of monster perch. I hadn't spent much time on the domestic scene due to commitments with foreign fishing. For instance during those two perch-rich winters I visited the upper reaches of the Great Ouse specifically to catch perch on a total of just 17 days, which was hardly blanket fishing.

ABOVE
Five huge Upper Ouse perch totalling 20lb ½oz, which included specimens of 4lb 3oz, 4lb 4½oz, and 4lb 8oz, my largest ever.

Having now caught no fewer than 11 4lb plus perch during that time, with Martin on a score of six, and Richard Bowler with two, I could only ponder what the future held for the river now that we had taken the perch record list apart. Will all those monsters grow on to be five pounders or were we (which is why I fished so hard for them) at the very peak of this remarkable era? After all it's got to stop somewhere. Adult specimens do eventually stop growing, prior to their imminent death. Nothing lasts for ever as all experienced anglers know full well and I'm just thankful that I have been around to experience this truly amazing and unprecedented fishing not only for river perch but for perch from any type of water.

That exceptional perch catch was in fact the last I recorded as the 1998/99 river season came to an end. I fished in the company of Martin and Richard for the last two days but the Ouse had risen almost to flood level again and was thickly coloured. However while Richard and I could attract only small perch and the occasional pike to our lobworms, Martin really finished on a wonderful high note by taking from the same swim, which produced a 4lb 7oz perch for me a few weeks before, a magnificent brace weighing 4lb 3oz and 4lb 11oz. What an unbelievable year's perching we three had enjoyed, accounting between us for no fewer than 21 perch over that magical 4lb mark.

Immediately after the end of the river season I switched species and countries

dramatically, and my old mate, Andy Davison, with whom I had first experienced the mighty mahseer of the Cauvery River 11 years before, had now left the oil industry, was to accompany me to southern India during the last two weeks of March.

We were met in Bangalore by our old friend, Susheel Gyanchand, and driven to his farm to chill out for a day prior to a couple of early morning wild boar shoots before we borrowed his four-wheel-drive, Mahindra – a cook and handyman – and headed for the river. Now Susheel knows full well we both love pig shooting and had organised a dawn start in a beautiful valley a three hour drive north of Bangalore which meant two already knackered travellers rising at 3.30am.

Alas it was all to no avail because at the climax of three different beats the boar always broke too far away from the guns. However, towards the end of the final beat I was treated to a wonderful sight as a small herd of black buck, which are around the same size as our roe deer, came jumping through the thorn scrub directly to where I stood stock still in the shade of a large bush, not daring to move so much as an eyelid. Shooting boar is not just about helping farmers to cull wild animals that do so much damage to their crops, with the added bonus of a delicious meal thrown in. It is also about appreciating all the other animals and birds you see during the course of a beat. I feel exactly the same when on a driven pheasant shoot at home, incidentally, and I felt privileged to study the dozen or so black buck that came literally to within 20 yards of where I stood. For perhaps 30 seconds they all looked directly at me with a mixture of curiosity and fear, before suddenly bounding off through the scrub as quickly as they had appeared. I felt compassion for the 30 or so villagers and peasant farmers who turned out and literally ran their legs off along a steep-sided valley over a mile wide and two miles long, thickly covered in thorn scrub and eucalyptus trees, in the hope they would be eating meat. That rare treat however, was withheld from them this time.

For us however it didn't matter, because from his freezer Susheel stacked onto the barbecue the largest boar chops which turned out to be the most delicious I've ever eaten in my life. They were equal in size to the biggest T-bone steaks you can possibly buy. For the first time in three nights we slept like babies.

The following morning, however, it was another early call and a long drive in order to get the guns into position at various points along a wide valley before dawn broke. Susheel insisted that Andy and I be put in prime positions where the boar usually broke early well ahead of the beaters, which resulted in our bagging three each. There was thus more than enough meat to go around between the farmers and villagers who were so unashamedly grateful for our presence. It's perhaps difficult for us to understand that a single rampant elephant or a herd of wild boar can in a single night completely destroy a peasant farmer's work for an entire year.

On day three we finally made the 60 mile journey south to the river in good time to meet up with old friends Bola, Chick Ragu and Boss Ragu, and that first sight of the Cauvery River valley as we descended around hairpin bends towards Sangham village was as magical then as when I first clapped my eyes on it over 11 years previously.

Tall parched brown hills bordered along the floor of the wide flood plain with the bright green of trees nourished by monsoon rains contrasting starkly with the blue of the river itself. With black eagles, ospreys, fish eagle and kites working the thermals high overhead, and dusky terns noisily protecting the turbulent shallows, it was as though the valley had not changed at all. Immediately I felt as I always have in this hot, harsh and beautiful land. I felt I had returned home.

The river itself, however, was not in the best order for mahseer. Due to the next state downstream of Tamil Nadu requiring extra water for their paddy fields, a dam way upstream near Mysore had released a large quantity of water, (ironically,we suffered this on our very first trip to the Cauvery) thus lowering the temperature of the river and adding around two feet to the height of what we expected for the end of March – and it was still rising. Worse still, it was to rise throughout our entire week's stay. Nevertheless we were of good heart and made camp at Haira, our favourite location, from the equipment Susheel had provided and quickly had a pot of boiling water going to make a batch of ragi bait.

Earlier on I mentioned that to be successful when fishing the Upper Ouse for big perch or chub you need to be always alert and concentrate as though you have just missed a bite and are expecting another. Mahseer fishing is no different; only the circumstances and location are changed. With buttocks perched uncomfortably around jagged rocks and one knee raised to support the rod against the unbelievable force of the current, you patiently wait with a ledgered duck-egg-size ball of ragi paste or a 6oz dead bait cast downstream and across, conveniently caught with a small spiral of lead, amongst the rocks in the middle of the river. You wait for those thick rubbery lips of the mahseer's cavernous mouth to vacuum the bait up and belt off downstream, thus almost hooking itself in a similar fashion to how our European barbel bites. In the meantime your mind greedily drinks in all the wonders of the river valley.

You hear the distinct, did-de-do-it, did-de-do-it of the red wattled lapwing as it mobs an eagle or crow venturing above its nest. You watch the inquisitive Indian otter at play or an elderly woman cow herder scold her buffalos as they graze on coarse grasses provided by the life blood of India – the monsoon rains. On one memorable evening we were treated to the kind of experience that still may not

ABOVE

Andy and I
with Susheel
and Phutana
behind (and with
Susheel's young
son, Sharan,
sandwiched
between us), get
together with
the farmers and
beaters at the
end of the shoot.
There's enough
roast boar for
everyone.

happen were you to spend a month of Sunday's bird spotting in Scotland. Fishing just above our camp down a long turbulent pool for over 20 minutes we watched an osprey (seemingly oblivious to our existence) searching the shallows along the opposite bank. Every now and then it would hover in that strange wing-flapping leant-back stance with talons outstretched, not unlike a goose coming in to land, before plummeting down to grab its prey, which turned out to be a mahseer of around 1½lb. What a truly majestic sight! It then flew upstream almost opposite us as if to say, 'I've done it' before slowly flying with its meal back down the valley to its nest.

Every lunchtime, we had a swim to cool off following each morning's session, and in almost a week we connected with just one 30 pounder each plus a couple of babies – much more meagre results than we had expected. Our camp cook, Purusho, served up some great food, such as dahl and pallya with several deep-fried purees to scoop it all up, washed down with slugs of Hercules brand XXX rum and litchi juice to which the same quantity of water is added. Wonderful stuff, then we both enjoyed a snooze until the evening session.

Just beyond the folding camp table the shoreline sloped down to the water's edge, thickly carpeted in clumps of tussock grass to which our coracle was tied. In its shade were hundreds of large water skaters and whenever my eyes looked up and across the 300 yard wide expanse of the Cauvery at our campsite my mind suddenly pondered that top surfcasters in the UK, like my old mate, Neil Mackellow, actually put a 5oz lead out the same distance, yet sitting there it seemed impossible. I wondered how Jo was managing at home. Being two o'clock Indian

time and with the UK being five hours behind, she would no doubt be walking the dogs around the lakes after breakfast. As the coarse fishing season was now closed, we would shortly be feeding up the carp in our two lakes so they'll be in tip-top condition when spawning time comes around. And some of those same carp that were caught by syndicate members just a few weeks before would soon be accepting bread scraps from our hands from the bridge connecting the two lakes.

Bola our faithful friend and guide (sadly Suban was now guiding much further downstream at a Muslim fishing camp) was doing everything in his power to ensure Andy and I hit into the stamp of mahseer we enjoyed on all past visits. But due to river conditions I feared he was trying in vain. We had concentrated on all the favourite pools and rapids that had produced countless hour-long battles with 50 and 60 pounders throughout the previous decade, plus the 70s and 80s, and even 90lb monsters. But all to no avail.

Then lo and behold on the very last morning (of course it had to happen on our last morning) the river actually started to drop with a noticeable increase in air temperature, though water clarity seemed the same. And from one of our favourite pools at Kangal I banged into a 35 pounder first cast and missed only the fourth bite of the week, while Andy really hit the jackpot with a superb golden mahseer of exactly 70lb which led him and Bola a merry song and dance in the coracle for a full 45 minutes. What a wonderful ending to our week, which highlighted the fact that no one can ever succeed and enjoy success without the help of others. That is for certain

During May through to October of 1999 I spent much of my available time on

RIGHT

Andy and Bola
gently cradle
mahseer of 70
and 35lbs. The
river gave up its
fruits on our last
days fishing.

the domestic scene both researching and filming series 14 of *Go Fishing*, (screened the following year) which as I explained previously could only be filmed in the Anglia and Meridian television area's as a co-production between those two companies. So I selected a variety of disciplines and locations from catching zander (not too successfully I might add with just small fish turning up) at Bury Hill Fisheries in Dorking, and modest-sized chub from the diminutive River Rother in West Sussex, to successfully catching double figure rainbows from Norfolk's Narborough Trout Fishery, and drifting for bass 20 miles off shore from Orford in Suffolk with my old mate Stewart Smalley. Stewart even winkled out a magnificent 12lb specimen for the camera's on our first run through, (thank you lord) and we finished the session with a dozen fish ranging between 3 and 8lbs. Although we nearly had a catastrophe in the form of our sound man going overboard when he and the cameraman swapped boats in a worsening swell late in the afternoon to shoot the 'reverse' angles. Yes, those wide shots of Stewart and I fishing away, alone in the boat, which really give any fishing programme product quality, had to be filmed at some stage. Fortunately, he was grabbed before sliding in between the two rocking boats when his foot slipped, and immediately hauled in.

Another interesting programme at sea in this series arose when I talked my wife Jo (who's a good sailor incidentally) into a day's deep water 'bull huss' fishing off shore from sunny Weymouth on board jovial Chris Caines boat 36 foot *Tiger Lily*. Well, it was certainly nice and sunny in Dorset when we arrived the evening before, and so I suggested Jo and I look all summery by each wearing shorts and colourful shirts.Wrong move. Because when out to sea the following morning, the day immediately turned grey and heavily overcast, accompanied by spitting rain and a bitingly cold wind (although you can never see this on the screen) and Jo was not a happy bunny at all. In fact whenever anyone mentions the programme, off she goes about how inconsiderate I was by making her wear shorts. But she did have the last laugh (or grimace) by boating the largest fish of the day, a 30lb conger. Bless her.

Actually, this series was certainly not without its problems. The beautiful, secluded, lily-clad

ABOVE
Suffolk skipper Stewart Smalley always produces bass to order, like this 12lbs beauty, caught during the making of series 14 of my long running Anglia TV series *Go Fishing*.

estate lake in Sussex that I had chosen to float fish from a punt for tench looked on our arrival, nothing like when I had researched it in late June exactly one year previously. A large proportion of the common yellow lily tubers were floating on the surface and a ghastly brown colour, due to a beetle infestation. It looked so bad that I was almost on the point of re-locating (though I didn't know where) when we found one particularly 'tenchy' looking corner where we could shoot using two cameras and where strangely, few of the tubers were floating and subsequently came up with enough early morning tench for the programme, plus some evocative footage of grebes and their young. Phew! It gets close sometimes, believe me. Like the carp programme I'd arranged on my good friend Andy Davison's picturesque, shallow estate lake in North Norfolk.

I'd planned to boat fish using float tackle for Andy's carp which ran to well over 20lbs, and were nicely baited up in a willow-clad, deepish corner close to the house, enabling the second cameraman to capture some high zoom shots through the upstairs windows, but still cutting off the main wide camera on the bank, situated close to and immediately opposite my little Samalite 'foldaway' dinghy anchored just 30 feet out. Yes, I know it all seems a bit of rigmarole, but for the most part this is how watchable fishing programmes are put together. Simply wandering around with a camcorder won't do. Trouble was, no one had contemplated (least of all me) that Andy's carp would decide to spawn on that very day. And while there were fish in the swim responding to loose feed in the early morning while we were painstakingly setting up, suddenly, there I was like a bride at the alter without a groom, while all the carp moved up the lake to a shallow area where amongst an

ABOVE

Long time buddy
Andy Davison
gets a lift from
top Lake Nasser
guide Mohammed
to display one of
his four 100lbs
plus Nile perch
taken during
our memorable
week's safari.

entanglement of fibrous willow roots they were audibly shuddering and crashing about procreating their kind for the remainder of the day, while I did my best to salvage a programme by switching from carp to pike.

I had in fact brought a nine foot wobbling rod and several packets of smelt along, just in case the carp slowed up and I needed to add a pike to complete the action. And was I glad, taking several incredibly scrappy pike into double figure plus a sizeable bonus perch, to save the day. Job done, as they say.

In three episodes however everything did go according to plan when I landed a superbly-scaled 20lbs plus mirror on the fly rod and glued-on mixer biscuit, plus others to 24lbs using a floater rig from friend Chris Newell's lovely lake in West Norfolk. Followed by several double figure, wonderfully spotted, tail-walking pike to 18lbs on static dead baits from beautiful Stradsett Lake near Kings Lynn, again whilst fishing from my little Samalite foldaway dinghy. Which was easily pulled round by the sheer power of these early winter pike?

Chub stalking is a favourite pastime of mine, and with the River Wensum just a few minutes drive away, I wanted something 'special' in the can for this particular series. (Incidentally, as the crow flies, it flows not 150 yards from where I sit typing this.) So I chose a favourite stretch near Ringland controlled by the Wensum Valley Hotel Golf and Country Club, owned by a good friend of mine one Basil Todd. And just a day before our planned shoot I walked the 1½ mile stretch wearing Polaroid glasses armed with a bag of various baits.

There were chub everywhere, and amongst the general run of 3-4lb fish I spotted several in the 5-6lb category. Through the crystal clear water illuminated by the sun I plopped in large baits such as lobworms and pieces of bread flake to individual whoppers, and watched their reactions, and even managed to induce them up into the surface film for mixer biscuits. But when I arrived the following morning with the film crew, gone was the hot, sticky air stream of the day before, replaced by low cloud and a chill wind. There was absolutely no chance of visibly selecting individual whoppers as planned. So I was forced to fish blind, free lining both lobworms and bread flake, upon which I took several lovely chub to close on 6lbs, plus another of 4lbs on the fly using a brook rod and slow falling nymph. It was indeed a satisfying conclusion.

In December Andy Davison and I joined Tim Baily on Lake Nasser in Egypt for what turned out to be one of the most bountiful weeks Nile perch fishing ever experienced on this huge, enigmatic water. I documented this particular trip, because it was quite unique, exhaustively in my book *Greatest Fishing Adventures*, and so not wishing to repeat myself, I will simply give you a potted account here.

With the lake's level way up and with my good friend and favourite guide Mohammed steering the 25 foot trolling boat, within just a few hours of arriving we four were heading south through the centre channel of this 300 mile long lake to where a series of sunken islands and huge boulders provided a myriad of ambush points in depths of between 15 and 30 feet. 'Buffalo Bay' this area has subsequently been named, because during our week's safari, Tim, Andy and I accounted for no less than 10 Nile perch over that magical 100lb barrier, with a total combined weight exceeding 2,500lbs, comprising no less of 35 perch averaging 75lbs apiece.

Andy took four 'Buffalo's' as we call fish over 100lbs, due to their striking 'hump' back, the largest at 139lbs. I caught four too, the best at 141lbs, while Tim had one of 129lbs, and Mohammed a monster of 162lbs. Ironically, this particular fish which took an orange Rapala CD 18, actually came on Tim's rod when he handed it over to Mohammed whilst he steered the boat over a particular sunken island. Isn't it ironic? For so many years I had wanted to catch a Nile perch over that magical 100lbs barrier, finally succeeding just a few years back with that 120 pounder whilst shooting my *Lake Nasser Safari* video. Now seemingly with ease, I had caught four in just a few days. I lost a really huge vundu catfish too having played it for quite some while, only to lose it in a commercial long line.

Large plugs both sinking and floating divers including Rapala's CD 18, Russelures, Reef diggers, Nilsmasters, and Buchertail Depth raiders, were the killing patterns, as indeed they usually are on the lake. But we figured that so many adult fish were gathered over this particular area, possibly as an early grouping process prior to their eventual spawning throughout January and February. I can still picture those great fish now, lunging and tail walking with gills flared, in that sort of 'slow motion' way that only huge Nile perch do.

A New Millennium

For me the year 2000 started slowly on the domestic scene with thick ice covering our two lakes for week upon week, so I relied upon chub in my local River Wensum for sport, plus sorties down south to Hampshire's marvellous River Test to catch her 'ladyship the grayling'. At the end of January however came an opportunity to join fellow angling journalist and one of my best mates, Dave Lewis, on a trip out to East Africa and the Sesse Islands on massive Lake Victoria (the world's second largest sheet of still water) to troll for Nile perch, followed by a long, (six hour) overland drive from Entebbe, to what I now rate as the most evocative, inspirational, and exciting river fishing on this planet. Murchison Falls in Uganda, where the entire might of the enigmatic River Nile, (over 200 yards wide above the falls) drops over 100 feet below into a huge churning pool, where a maelstrom of white water would seem to preclude any kind of fishing. Within its depths and fierce currents however, live Nile perch to over 200lbs, both vundu and sementendu catfish to over 100lbs, plus tiger fish, alestes, owaka's, squeeker catfish, eels, and a myriad of strange and colourful species, plus monstrous 'snapping' turtles the size of dustbin lids. When we had dustbins.

Having teamed up with guides Jonathan Wright of Semliki Safaris, and Paul Goldring of G & C tours, we started our fishing on Massive Lake Victoria and around the Sesse Islands of which there are 84. The entire freshwater archipelago being just a 20 mile boat trip away from Entebbe. Nile perch to an unratified, 250lbs have in fact been caught from around the Sesse Islands (I have seen the photographs) and during our short stay amongst a plethora of 30-50lbs fish (Dave's first ever Nile perch) all caught trolling in depths from 10 to 15 feet, one pushing 90lbs came to the rod of yours truly on a small green Russelure. I just loved fishing around the tropical- jungle habitat of these islands, where we were trolling so close to land following a 12 foot depth band on the sonar screen, that every so often we had to duck in order to avoid overhanging branches and vines. Many of the bank side boulders playing host to huge monitor lizards, which simply gazed in our direction as the boat passed them by. With exotic bird life continually chattering away in the greenery and with kites and fish eagles high overhead looking for an easy meal, these Islands would rate as a 'twitchers' paradise.

Then it was time for our long overland drive to Murchison Falls, the splendour of which first captivated my young imagination way back in the 1950's when living

LEFT
The awesome spectacle of one of the world's most evocative fishing locations. Murchison Falls in Uganda, where the full force of the river Nile is channelled between a narrow gap in the rocks to drop over 100 feet into a huge foaming pool below. The most dangerous freshwater spot I have ever fished from.

in a flat in North London, and I watched that (still) fascinating motion picture King Solomon's Mines, starring Stewart Granger and Deborah Kerr, with Murchison Falls, (named in 1864 by explorer Samuel Baker after the president of the Royal Geographical Society Sir Roderick Murchison) filmed as a stunning backdrop.

Although you can walk down from the top of the falls to fish from the rocky promontories at the Devils Cauldren and from the famous 'jackpot' swim, where currents surge along at up to 20 miles per hour, something I shall elaborate upon further on in this book, on this first safari we stayed a few miles down river at the Nile Safari Camp below the ferry at Paraa, and each morning motored upstream (passing numbers of huge crocodiles and hippos on the way) to the bottom of the falls gorge, in the Murchison National Park 25 foot boat, Mamba.

We then sometimes fished from the boat tied up to the shore, or went ashore and took the narrow, rocky pathway all the way up to the bottom of the falls. To say this is the lure fisherman's paradise is perhaps even understating the amount of tantalising eddies and pools to be explored. It would take a month of Sunday's even to make just one cast into each and every one of them. And most contain Nile perch in the 10-60lbs bracket, with numbers of sementendu catfish on the bottom. Dave Lewis accounted for a chunky sementendu catfish of over 40lbs (heavily scarred, as many of them are from croc attacks) whilst ledgering a dead bait, and we both banged into 30lbs plus perch on lures. What a place. We also met local expert Marco Magyar who took a mammoth perch here of 237lbs on a free lined live bait just a few years previously.

What a truly mesmerising and inspirational place Murchison Falls is. And were I granted just one day's last fishing on this earth. That is where I would choose.

Having barely recovered from our long safari in the tropics, at the end of February I was off with a party of six to Africa again, on behalf of Tailor Made Holidays, only this time to South West Africa and Namibia, who's famous 1000 mile long 'Skeleton Coast' is sandwiched between south Africa and Angola. Namibia is in fact the third most under populated country on the planet, and boasts some of the most exciting shore fishing for sharks, mostly bronze whalers in the 100-250lbs category, in the world. Amongst the six man party were my son Lee and two nephews Martin and Richard Bowler. All bent on catching a shark from the shore, and our guide Ottmar Leipert of Levo Sports Fishing who I met when researching this location two years previously, did not let us down, helped by another local guide Neill Van Rooyen.

From our accommodation in Swakopmund, Ottmar collected us after breakfast each morning in his land rover complete with a box full of fresh bait in the way of mullet heads (top shark bait) and one piece 14 foot surf rods already made up. He provided everything unless you wish to use your own tackle, which I do whenever possible. Terry Carrol of ZZiplex having kindly made me up a 14 ½ foot 'sharking' special comprising of a 6½ foot butt and 8 foot tip, which I am glad to say was given a real workout and more than stood the test. And has on several occasions since.

Terminal rigs were uncomplicated. A 20 foot 100lbs test rubbing leader, knotted to the 30lbs reel line was joined to a strong swivel to which both 20 inch 150lbs wire trace and 9/0 hook and a 20 inch 40lbs test mono lead trace were also tied. Simple, but most effective as we were to find out. In fact our six days fishing went by so quickly because one or another of us was always into sharks. Rarely did a location not produce at least two or three 'bronzies' as Ottmar affectionately called them, or numbers of sand sharks (guitar fish) spotted gulley sharks or hound sharks (our smooth hound no less) some of which were slit from gills to vent and staked out on the beach to allow the tide to wash out the blood in order to attract bronzies.Which it did on most occasions with frightening speed.

During the week we accounted for over 50 bronze whalers, with numbers of them exceeding 200lbs. Which is one hell of a fight from the shore on just 30lbs test line, believe me. My best was estimated by Ottmar at around 240lbs and took over an hour and a half to bring to the shore, during which time the line remaining on my ABU 10,000 reel was reduced to just a few coils on several occasions. Each time however, by clamping both thumbs around the spool to totally lock it up, swearing loudly to force yet more adrenalin into my system and crabbing myself slowly back up the beach, I managed to make the shark kite either to the right or left and subsequently get some line back on the reel by running back into the surf as I wound frantically.

Without question, these epic encounters with bronze whalers from the shore were the most gut busting, arm wrenching battles with big fish I have ever experienced from terra firma. Sure, a 200lbs shark fought from the comparative comfort of a boat, even if you choose not to use the fighting chair, is hardly going to be a drawn out affair, because the skipper simply moves the boat closer to the fish when his customer starts getting red around the gills and looks like he's going to have a heart attack. But from the beach with over 300 yards of line out, stretched so tightly it's singing in the wind, and little left on the reel, you are on your own.

Upon returning home following our awesome Namibia experience, there was but a couple of weeks of the river season left, with so much to fit in now that conditions had turned mild. I fished the Wensum for chub with good friend Bruce Vaughan accounting for a shared bag of no less than 20 fine chub, all over 4½lbs, with the best weighing close on 6lbs. And the Tidal Waveney at Beccles for pike with long time friend Jinx Davey, who boated a 17 pounder amongst a string of lesser fish, all of which fought incredibly hard in the strong flow. Jinx really did the business however a week later when we teamed up on the upper reaches of the great Ouse near Buckingham with Martin and Richard Bowler (both now recovered from their Namibia sharking) by catching on ledgered lobworm the biggest perch not only of the day but of his entire angling career, weighing just 1½ozs short of 4lbs. While Martin, Richard and I accounted for several between 1-2½lbs. It was a most satisfying end to yet another river season.

After that wonderful trip back in January to magical Murchison Falls and the Sesse Islands on Lake Victoria in Uganda, I never imagined that I would be returning so soon. But an invitation from good friend Christine Slater of Tailor Made Holidays came along to join her and a couple of guests on a research trip. Well. Like I'm always saying, someone's got to do it haven't they? So following an eight hour Air Alliance flight, we were met in Entebbe by guide Paul Goldring and whisked 20 miles across the fertile waters of adjacent Lake Victoria to the Sesse Islands. Our base being the 'Islands' club on Kalangala, which is just one of the Lake's 1000 tropical, forested islands, where daily sightings include giant kingfishers to paradise flycatchers.

SIXTY YEARS A FISHERMAN

Our deep diving Russelures and Rapala's trolled at around two knots on 30lbs class outfits soon attracted sizeable perch. Christine boated a high jumping beauty of nearly 70lbs, while guest Brian Garnet from Barnet (would you believe) landed a monster of 143lbs. By far his largest fish ever. After three days of exciting action, interspersed by feeding dead fish to the African Fish Eagles, which would obligingly zoom down from their perch high up in the tall hard wood trees, upon hearing our whistling and waving the fish about, (I required camera shutter speeds of a 1000th of a second to capture the action) we boarded a light plane back in Entebbe and an hour later arrived at Murchison Falls air strip on the northern bank of the River Nile.

The river was running on the low side which allowed us to bank fish in some of the tempting pools around the Devil's Cauldron, not usually accessible. And using a large, free lined live bait I shortly found myself connected to a real monster deep down in a huge back eddy, which promptly removed over 100 yards of 35lbs line from my ABU 10,000 before lunging out across the surface over on the other side of the wide pool in order to shake the hook out. A fish looking well in excess of 100lbs, which I then managed to pump back over to my side of the gorge, back to more or less where I had first hooked it. Then quite suddenly and inexplicably the single size 8/0 hook came out. I experienced virtually a repeat performance an hour or so later, only this fish wasn't having any from the get go and ripped the line to shreds through the rocky bottom within a minute or two of hooking it. Murchison Falls is truly an awesome location.

Strangely, I managed to land perch to around 30lbs plus a 60lbs vundu catfish from the very same pool, on a Depth-raider plug would you believe, (my largest vundu ever on a lure) and several sementendu catfish up to 30lbs, also on free lined live baits (although they gobble up fresh dead baits just as greedily) when we boarded 25 foot Mamba, the National Parks boat, to search the deep wide reaches way below the falls at the end of the gorge where the Nile widens out to fully half a mile across. Here elephants, kudu and buffalo are just some of the game which can be seen leaving the dense jungle on both banks in order to drink from the Nile. Hippos and monstrous crocs are of course always in sight wherever you cast.

Upon arriving back in the UK, trout fishing was in full swing and I managed to bag a beautiful big 11¾lb brown trout from famous Dever Springs in Hampshire, which fought like stink and because it was so remarkably spotted, I asked my taxidermy pal Dick Brigham (I gave up stuffing fish several years back because I never seemed to have the time) to set it up together in the same case with a 15lbs 10oz rainbow, that I was to catch (also from Dever) later that year. Dick made a splendid job of them and the huge case which looks down from the wall in the hall by the front door is the first thing anyone sees when entering our house.

Series 15 of *Go Fishing* for Anglia and Meridian Television was now in the pipeline and so all my thoughts were geared to the filming of 12 segments (six in Anglia and six in Meridian) to produce another six half hour programmes, starting with fly fishing for trout in Norfolk at Whinburgh Trout Lakes near East Dereham. Now a private concern, unfortunately. We also filmed catching both salmon and sea trout on leaded nymphs and a brook rod from the Test wood Fishery near Southampton, tiny brown trout (plus a big carp lost in an adjacent lake) from the Upper reaches of the diminutive River Bure in North Norfolk, and brownies from the lovely little River Rother in Sussex with good mate Chris Sandford, whose stretch of the Rother contains the largest gudgeon I ever seen, and it was great fun to catch them. I managed to take some medium-sized pike and perch on lures from massive Graffham reservoir,(lost a monster pike on a spoon too) before the weather really blew up, tail-walking pike into double figures on wobbled dead baits from Whitehouse Lake, and was joined by Martin Bowler to catch some beautifully coloured Koi carp from Wintons Fishery in Sussex, although we were really hoping for catfish. I did however lose a big one that refused to be hauled out of a sunken tree. It felt so awesome, that even now I wonder how big it was?

Friend Alan Pearce joined me at Ardleigh Reservoir in Suffolk on what was to have been purely a bream programme, but I fluked out a big carp, and enjoyed a wonderful session on the River Kennet at Padstow weir with Dougle Gray, where the barbel were most obliging. I chose a lovely estate lake in Norfolk to portray the subtlety of ledgering for tench, but hooked another big carp, even before the radio mike was clipped onto my waistcoat. I should never have cast out till ready really. From Roger Bayzand's boat *Sundance 11* out from Lymington my son Lee and I shared a wonderful haul of big cod and Pollack, then, whilst tope fishing off Alderney in the Channel Islands, fishing was so fast and furious that all the crew had a go, and at one time there were five or six fish on simultaneously. With all the resulting tangles to follow. That's what happened when Roger and I switched out of professional mode to let the crew have a go. Mind, we did have more than enough footage in the can first. We were not that daft.

In between filming for *Go Fishing* during spring and summer I also made a couple of foreign trips on behalf of Tailor Made Holidays. One was to Lake Nasser, where friend big Marc Pickering from Birmingham, whose previous best fish was a 20lbs pike, took huge Nile perch on consecutive days, weighing 165 and 175lbs respectively. Who says dreams don't come true? The second trip with an eight man party being to the Florida Keys at Islamorada, where long time pal and Essex skipper big John Rawle put no less than 27, high-leaping tarpon between 65 and 160lbs our way during early morning sessions between a 3am start and 8am finish, when everyone came back for a cooked breakfast. What fantastic, hour-long battles everyone enjoyed with these high-leaping crazy fish called tarpon which literally averaged over 100lbs. It was like returning to those early days on the west coast of

Barbados when I hooked my first big tarpon from the beach at night. Each encounter makes the hair stand up on the back of your neck as the reel screams into life and you knock the multiplier into gear, waiting for that explosive, acrobatic jump high into the air accompanied by a kaleidoscope of spray. Following a long siesta, everyone then got back into the 17 foot skiffs for fun sharking in the afternoons on the shallow flats for lemons and nurse sharks up to 200lbs.

More foreign trips on behalf of Tailor Made Holidays were made in the autumn and early winter of 2000, firstly to Impalila Island in Namibia to the fabulous Zambezi, where colourful, predatory bream to 5lbs (three different species) and tiger fish to 13lbs were the target fish. Then, to where I now honestly consider the most 'blue-chip' freshwater location anywhere in the world for catching big fish. Because if you can't catch fish here, you won't catch them anywhere. Namely the fantastic salmon and giant white sturgeon of the mighty Fraser River system in Canada's British Columbia. And I can honestly say that were I a young man again, I would be clutching a one way ticket to the vast, open and 'nanny-free' life of Canada. Yes, like many Britons of my age group I think Blair has an awful lot of negatives to answer for in how our British laws, values and lives have been devalued during his Labour reign in that 'black'decade from the mid 1990's to 2007, when the British public, amongst numerous other blunders from pensions, 24 hour drinking, to immigration, were then not allowed a referendum on the EU that they were indeed promised when Labour came to power. Beware of the smarmy smiles of politicians. British democracy? Sadly, it has started to smell.

Christine Slater of Tailor Made Holidays and I, accompanied by a few friends had seen photographs of the 1000 mile long Fraser River where it joins the Harrison Lake and river complex at Chilliwack, which lies about 70 miles east of Vancouver, and countless trophy shots of the five species of Pacific salmon that run the Fraser system, (pink, Coho, sockeye, chum and Chinook) plus those awesome sturgeon, including photographs of monsters in excess of 1000lbs. And following a long haul flight to Vancouver, with just a short road transfer to Chilliwack, we were ready to get our 'strings pulled' as they say. And we were not disappointed.

What kind of freshwater fish requires a pack of mules harnessed to it to pull it out of the river? Yet such stories are indeed part of the folklore surrounding this enigmatic species, which is by far the largest fish to be caught in freshwater on this planet. And unlike many other huge fish living in freshwater such as the giant Mekong catfish of Thailand and the Arapaima of South America's Amazon system, which are both sadly in decline through commercial fishing in their indigenous regions (though as you will read later on, it is ironically, now easier to catch an arapaima in Thailand) giant white sturgeon are unbelievably common throughout over 100 miles of the lower Fraser, all the way into the ocean off Vancouver.

And while 1000lb monsters of the past still exist and are even hooked on modern sports fishing tackle (though few are landed) fish in the 100-250lbs bracket are actually, believe it or not, everyday catches. With real numbers of monsters in the 300-700lbs range there for the taking.

Much of the present quality in sturgeon fishing is due to the Fraser River sturgeon Society, made up mostly from local guides, such as our host in Chilliwack Fred Helmer and Tony Nootebos of Harrison Bay Guiding Services whom have both become firm friends since, and who together with several others, being government sanctioned, realised that to protect their sport they needed to really understand this prehistoric-looking creature, by measuring and electronically tagging it to evaluate age, growth rates and length, plus the fish's movement patterns up and down the river. And what an enviable fishery they have subsequently created.

Our party of six anglers quickly realised why the white sturgeon is such an incredible 'angling' fish. It bites most readily on small fish baits (a lamprey head is magic) and on golf ball-sized salmon 'egg balls' (made from wrapping fresh salmon eggs, upon which it is constantly feeding naturally, up in a piece of ladies stocking or tights) ledgered from an anchored boat. A strong size 6/0 short shank hook is gently nicked through the stockinet, and the 4-16oz lead (depending upon flow) cast directly downstream. The rods being powerful seven foot models, with an all-through action and 130lbs braided line on smooth-lever-drag multipliers. The braided hook length itself is just two to four feet. Then the fun begins when you smoothly remove the rod from its rest (less the fish feels the movement and drops the bait) and lift into a gentle but determined nodding of the rod tip as a sturgeon 'probes' with its four long sensory barbules situated just in front of its mouth and sucks in your egg ball with its strange, fully protrusible, Hoover-like mouth, which on adult fish is designed for sucking up whole, small salmon carcasses from the gravel river bed in addition to eggs. Because, instantly, the sturgeon goes charging off down river and you increase drag pressure, it suddenly comes shooting up from the bottom through 12-60 feet of water to catapult itself high into the air, shaking its pointed, armoured head vigorously, amongst a kaleidoscope of spray, before crashing back into the river and charging off again.

Strangely, there are days when each and every sturgeon whether its 30 or over 300lbs will jump (what an incredible sight as an eight foot creature becomes airborne) within a short while of being hooked, and even continue jumping several times throughout the battle. But then you'll hook consecutively into several fish, none of which fancy jumping. It's all great, unbelievably exciting arm-wrenching, back breaking stuff. I can remember when Christine Slater with whom I shared a boat and took it in turns to hit bites, hooked into her first sturgeon, a fish of around 150lbs that went like a bat out of hell, afterwards she said, 'you can hit the next few runs John'. She was that shattered.

We also enjoyed truly incredible sport with salmon, particularly in the crystal

clear water of the Harrison River (where you can clearly see huge concentrations of fish at close quarters and watch them actually hit your fly) fed by 40 mile long Harrison Lake with over 50 million salmon running the Fraser system annually, it is in fact rightfully classed as the worlds last remaining, great 'un-dammed' salmon river. The smallest of the five Pacific salmon is the pink (averaging 4-8lbs) which run every other year, and as our trip was not during a pink year, we didn't see any. But there were plenty of sockeye about (averaging 8-14lbs) and strong shoals of brightly coloured Coho (of between 6-12lbs) which were great fun on light spinning tackle.

For sheer numbers and high average size during our weeks stay (there are of course huge concentrations of varying salmon constantly making their way up river through both the Fraser and Harrison Rivers at this time of the year) big chum salmon averaging between 12-25lbs proved prolific and truly phenomenal action on both spinner and fly rod. Of the Chinook, by far the largest of the worlds salmon which are caught in the Fraser to over 70lbs but which are said to top 100lbs, we saw very little, although I did take a silver, fresh-run baby of around 10lbs on a lure.

Sadly, though it is natures way of feeding her own, and unlike our Atlantic salmon, many of which recover after the act of spawning and run to sea again, Pacific salmon all die, and literally 'litter' the spawning reds amongst their eggs. Consequently, bald eagles by the thousand, crows, gulls, black bears and of course adult sturgeon all enjoy an absolute feast. Only the steelhead (a sea running rainbow) returns to the Pacific after spawning. But I return annually each October to the marvellous Fraser system taking Brits on a 'blue chip' holiday of a life time, where during the past eight years I can count on the fingers of just one hand guests who failed to catch at least one sturgeon over 100lbs during their weeks stay. What a place.

Upon arriving home I enjoyed a trip out to The Gambia on behalf of Masterline

International to help run the West African Shore Fishing Festival where it was great to meet up again with Mark and Tracey. Had Dave Lewis and his lovely wife Alison over from south Wales to Norfolk for a spot of zander fishing, successfully I'm glad to say. And just before Christmas, spent a couple of day's grayling fishing with my old mate Jinx Davey down south on the River Test near Stockbridge, who took amongst many others, his first ever grayling on long trotted maggots. And suddenly, another year was over.

January 2001 started cold and frosty with chub only on the cards, although I did manage to fluke out a mirror carp of 22½lbs from the Wensum whilst chubbing. Lost another too, during the same session. Like most rivers in the country, due to winter flooding my local River Wensum regularly receives complimentary stockings of gravel pit carp that escape into flowing water over flooded marshlands.

Then things warmed up, first with a holiday my wife Jo and I made to East Africa to stay with Stewart and Ellen Smalley at Hemmingway's who were catching numbers of chunky yellow fin tuna, giant trevally and king mackerel on light tackle, followed by a visit to the famous Masi Mara game reserve. And secondly, a weeks fishing in Spain with good friends Simon Clarke and Keith Lambert of the Cat Fish Conservation Group at what must surely rate as Europe's premier big fish destination, the junction of the Rio Ebro and Rio Segre at Mequinenza. Which is just a two hour drive from Barcelona, following a two hour flight from Luton airport.

We stayed as guests of the Bavarian Guiding Service, the first organised fishing camp in this area, and soon made friends with guide Gary Allen who originated from St Albans in Hertfordshire. Though to hear him speaking the local lingo you'd have though he had been in the area all his life.

Gary gave us a great week's fishing with numbers of zander into double figures working lures and mounted bleak using the versatile *Drachkovitch* rig which comprises a lightweight, V-shaped sprung wire stem inserted down the throat of the dead bait, to which at the top is attached a ball weight of between 4-12 grams. Also attached to the clip is around six inches of stiff copper wire which is threaded through the bleak's shoulder and then wound around the body. So the bait does not come loose whilst being worked. Lastly, two single trebles joined to wire, one short and one long, are pushed into the baits flank and tail root on opposing sides to ensure a good hook-up from whatever angle a zander grabs hold. Small synthetic rubber artificials can also be presented most effectively on the same rig, as indeed we were to experience, when fresh bleak became difficult to catch.

Talking of bleak, which like the zander, and wels catfish were not present in the Ebro system prior to the 1970's, they were in fact introduced by German anglers along with the zander (as a zander food source) around the same time that catfish were stocked. All illegal of course, but thoughtful eh?

During our weeks stay we took several pussies over 100lbs (my first ever ton-up) using small carp live baits, and what fabulous scraps they put up, the best falling to Keith's rod and weighing 136lbs, plus numbers of back-up fish in the 60-90lbs range.

What a place. It was somewhere I was destined to return to regularly over the following years.

Apart from a plaice fishing weekend down south with pal Stewart Smalley over the 'shambles' out from Weymouth on Chris Caines boat *Tiger Lily*,(bagged some beauties to over 4lbs too) followed by still water trouting sorties to two of my favourite Hampshire fisheries, namely Rookesbury Mill and Dever Springs during March and April, I once again needed to get my head around spending the next few months researching and filming series 16 of my *Go Fishing* programmes for Anglia Television. With each of the six, half hour programmes comprising of footage filmed both down south in the Meridian TV area and in East Anglia.

You'd think no doubt that after 16 consecutive years of filming fishing for TV, that running out of ideas would be par for the course. But no, it made me all the more determined to feature lovely locations and some big fish, plus involving a few of my friends at the same time. For the Anglia sea fishing strand I engaged Southwold skipper Nigel Hayter and his boat *Mistress* to enable my old mate Jinx Davey and I to haul up mountains of double figure cod on pirks over war time wrecks, whilst south coast skipper Spike Spears, took *Bessie Vee* 12 miles off Selsey Bill to provide my wheelchair bound mate Ritchie Powell with some unforgettable action with tope and numerous big smooth hounds. Ritchie catching his biggest fish ever in the form of a 35lbs tope.

Skipper Spike, who as I write this in 2008 is bravely fighting cancer, actually broke the British starry smooth hound record that day with a beauty of 29½lbs, 1½lbs over the current record. But in no way was he going to claim it, as records are not accepted if weighed on a boat. So back it went. Spinning for grey mullet in the confines of Christchurch Harbour with friend (stainless-steel) Steve Batchelor, added a more intimate angle to catching sea fish. For there is no more difficult species to fool than the thin-lipped grey mullet.

Also in Hampshire I teamed up with barbel guru Pete Reading who provided some mouth watering swims on the Avon, crammed with big fish, but we could account only for single figure specimens, though the chub averaged high and gave great fights on trotting tackle. I have to admit, due to the fantastic river fishing on The Avon, The Test, The Dever, The Anton etc, there are times when I wished I lived in Hampshire. And of course the chalk stream river trouting and still waters fed by chalk streams are indeed the envy of fly fishermen all over the world.

Small wonder I chose the pretty John O'Gaunts Two-Lake, day ticket Trout Fishery located near King's Somborne, two miles south of Stockbridge, to fish for its prolific stock of hard battling rainbows, which provided marvellous action for our two cameras, as did the two 20lbs plus carp I caught respectively on worm and floating baits at beautiful Sway Lakes, just eight miles northeast of Christchurch.

Also coming within the Meridian area, we visited beautiful Aldermaston Mill on the River Kennet near Reading for chub and barbel to 6lbs on both feeder and trotting tactics, where anyone can fish for the price of a day ticket. And here lies a peculiar phenomenon, which from the feed back I get from a proportion of people who come up to speak to me at angling shows, would indicate that I only ever fish private, pre-baited waters. Which simply couldn't be further from the truth? Aldermaston Mill being a prime example. It looks secluded and private but is in fact a day ticket fishery.

Incidentally, on the way home to Norfolk from a successful shoot at Aldermaston Mill, whilst driving on the M25, came the horrendous 9-11 report on radio's talk sport with the voice of Mike Parry, describing live, what was happening over on the other side of the pond in New York to the Twin Towers. They do say you never forget where you were at such times, and 'they' whoever they are, are so right. It was truly unforgettable.

In the Anglia region I chose a mixed bag of freshwater locations, from the Grove

Water Trout Fishery near Norwich, then managed by an old friend, experienced gamekeeper Tony Smith, (with rainbows to 8lbs) to a three acre lake in Weybread, Suffolk, where the late owner Denis Gartell assured me we would film bream in the 2-5lbs bracket, readily coming up to the surface for mixer-biscuit floaters amongst the fisheries stock of big roach and carp. And he was so right. And still, though I've fished around some, I cannot think of another fishery where I would guarantee catching bream off the top. Could you? It's an intriguing phenomenon.

I rather think the highlight of this particular series was the camera finding me 20 foot up in the boughs of a large Alder, loose feeding sweet corn to a group of large carp feeding in the shallows beneath. And when I hooked into a huge mirror of over 30lbs, live on camera having simply free lined sweet corn, it not only made my day, but provided unforgettable viewing. And the truth was it was supposed to be a 'tench' programme. Only they were not feeding, so I left the film crew to enjoy a coffee break while I wandered around only to find a group of big carp in a feeding mood, not 50 yards from where we had parked the cars. Opportunism at it's very best.

Having already joined me for a pike programme in series 10, (he caught fish to 23lbs too) I asked brother Dave (who presently lives in Thailand) if he fancied facing the cameras again to help me catch the big, double figure bream of the famous Breakaway Pit at Wilford Bridge near Melton in Suffolk. To which he agreed and even chose to 'Bivvi-up'whilst the rest of us (the film crew) returned to our hotel overnight. And I said to Brother Dave, whatever you do don't fish off camera. If we can't film it, it's a wasted catch. Just keep the bait going in, so that 'on camera' over two days we stand a good chance of succeeding.

Needless to stay Dave didn't listen and actually took a bream of 12½lbs while we slept. He admitted this to me a few days after the shoot incidentally. But we did scrape through with a fish just topping 10lbs to save the day, (poetically to my rod) amongst a few nice tench and modest-sized carp. The last Anglia location of series 16 was an 18 acre pike lake, situated (so army clearance was imperative) within Bassingbourn Barracks in Cambridgeshire, and was I glad, after watching the groups of spotted-faced, 'squaddies' marching round, that I'd never contemplated joining the Army. The lake did however produce some exquisitely marked pike into double figures on static dead baits. So it was 'job done'.

In the autumn once filming for *Go Fishing* was finished, my wife Jo and I joined Christine Slater of Tailor Made Holidays on a research trip to the lower reaches of the famous Zambezi River which throughout much of its length separates Zimbabwe and Zambia, at the Royal Zambezi Lodge way, way below Lake Kariba. And here, guided by Steve Maartens in a truly unspoilt, pristine, wilderness environment, due to the 'national park' status, hippos, and the most monstrous crocodiles were always within sight while we drift fished strip bait on size 6/0 hooks on 30lbs test

wire traces (filleted chessa and nkupe) for tiger fish and anchored up in the deep holes, using ledgered luncheon meat or chessa heads to tempt vundu catfish to around 60lbs. Jo incidentally, catching the biggest tiger fish of the week at 13½lbs. What a fascinating stretch of the river, over ¾ of a mile wide in some parts, averaging between six to 12 feet deep with a strong flow, and with elephant and buffalo nearly always visible along the margins, and yellow billed kites working overhead. There was certainly no need to go on a game drive to appreciate the animals of Africa. Although we did one evening, adding lion, hyenas, warthogs and various antelopes to our sightings.

Upon our return to the UK it was straight across country to Bewdley on the River Severn to attend a charity event that had me shaving mate Des Taylor's beard off. Trouble was, we had a few drinks first with Margaret Des's wife round at the house before being driven to the local commercial fishery where the event was going to be held, and the look on his face when I took out a cut throat razor with shaking hands (hamming it up of course) was pure magic. Actually I did deliberately nick him a few times to get a little blood trickling for *Angling Times* cameraman Mick Rouse and the gathering crowd, most of whom were unaware that I used to be a hairdresser. But it was all good fun and made a great feature in addition to raising money for charity. We ended the weekend by Des and I visiting a little pool he leases a few miles away where on waggler-fished maggots we enjoyed a great session with specimen-sized roach and chub. My best

chub surprisingly, weighing a shade over 6lbs. What a lovely weekend.

In November it was out to The Gambia again for the third Masterline International Shore Fishing Festival, where numbers of large cassavas and Kujeli were taken. Alan Yates of *Sea Angler* magazine catching the best at a shade over 24lbs. As usual the long distance casters took all the top positions including a first prize for Alan's son Richard Yates. The 75 competitors sharing more than £7000 in prize money, plus £20000 in tackle prizes compliments of Masterline International.

Though sipping jugs of chilled sangria and munching on giant grilled prawns in the tropics was all very nice, (well someone's got to do it) I was itching to get back home however and take

delivery of my new 14 foot aluminium boat on its own trailer and christen it with some pike fishing on the Broads.

Fineways Leisure of Wroxham (tel 01603 782309) specialise in and are agents for custom-finished 'Sea Strike', unbelievably beamy and stable, aluminium boats from 10-18 feet in length, to which customers may add their own modifications. A wonderful opportunity for someone like myself who after four decades of boat fishing the Broads, to finally own and fish from a boat that is both highly functionable and comfortable. So I did away with the middle, of their standard, three, 14 inch square box-type seats, for instance, each packed with high density foam that makes the boat unsinkable, to allow for maximum room in the middle of the boat (where you need it) for unhooking big fish. But used the same amount of foam beneath a three foot long top covering the bows to provide a water proof compartment for cameras and spare gear etc. This allows me to leave things like the trailers spare wheel, drogue, fire extinguisher, tool kit, unhooking mat, and a couple of life vests etc permanently on the boat, which remains completely dry beneath a strong, waterproof cover.

On top of each of the two box seats I had three-sided 'saddles' made of aluminium, (22 inches wide) with foam rubber beneath to fit snugly, to accommodate American-style, swivel, padded, folding seats. This allows me to sit much higher with a comfortable back rest, as opposed to sitting with my knees round my neck, which has been the case over the years with all other dinghies. The saddles can be lifted in a jiffy to position the folding seat anywhere along the length of each box seat to balance the boat out when two anglers are fishing. What a boon these have proved to be. On each side of the boat at midships I screwed on 'vertical' 'three rod' holders to take up to six rods whilst travelling along or whilst moving position, and had Fineways fit a built-in bilge pump into the transom. Automatic, rope holding cleats were screwed on each side at the transom with a single cleat at the bows. The bow anchor being a 56lbs steel mud weight (as fitted on Broadland cruisers) that lowers and is retrieved around a pulley system, so that bottom mud never comes into the boat. The stern mud weight, also steel is 40lbs. And they have simply been the best of investments. There is nothing more annoying than being pulled out of position and drifting helplessly away from a prolific area due to strong winds because your mud weights fail to hold. A thing of the past for me, I am glad to say.

The actual hull is of the semi-flat planning design which combines stability with easy steering, and the raised floor (by three inches) I covered in non slip ribbed rubber sheeting for easy cleaning. It was a wise move to spend extra on having the sides of the boat painted in British racing green. Not only does it eliminate the 'flash'

ABOVE
Small wonder Alan Yates is smiling. This 24lbs Kujeli (threadfin salmon) took specimen fish honours in the third Masterline International Shore Fishing Festival held in The Gambia along the lovely sandy beaches around the capital of Banjul.

LEFT
Old pal and fellow angling writer Des Taylor didn't fancy (I'd had a few mind) having his beard shaved off with my cut throat razor. But it was all for charity after all.

of unpainted aluminium hulls that could easily scare fish in clear, shallow water, it looks pretty cool too. And as I write this after seven years of truly wonderful, comfortable boat fishing, I'm pleased to say that I would not change a thing. Except that I'd love a larger outboard engine than my old Johnson 4½ horse twin to see what the boat can do, but with a five mile an hour speed limit throughout the Broads, what's the point?

January 2002 started great on the local scene, with a 24lbs pike from the lower Waveney for my long time pal Jinx, which really christened the new boat (named *Kaveri* incidentally, which is Indian for the wonderful Cauvery River) and a fat chub of 6lbs 6oz from the Upper Ouse. My only bite during a day after ledgering lobworms for those big perch. They don't always bite. Then I really had to get my head down by updating my 190 page book *Where to Fish in Norfolk and Suffolk*, for local publishers, Barnwell Publishing. Its seventh update no less since I put the first edition to bed back in 1973. What an awesome job this is from the outset, of week upon week checking up on phone numbers and addresses of all the stretches of rivers and pieces of still water within the counties of Norfolk and Suffolk, plus of course the entire Broadland system with its interconnecting network of tidal waterways, plus the entire coastline from Hunstanton to Felixstowe. But within a few days I always seem to get really into it, and it doesn't appear nearly so daunting. You ought to see our phone bills however.

I enjoyed a short break from it all at the end of March when accompanying mates Keith Lambert and Simon Clarke to Mequinenza in Spain to team up with guide Gary Allen for some great carp and cat fishing. Followed a few weeks later by a stint in the Florida Keys with Graphic Display boss Pete Hazelwood from Ely and four friends, where skipper John Rawle, as he always does connected us with many a high leaping tarpon to 150lbs, and a whole string of shallow water sharks. The largest, a nurse shark of fully 300lb falling to Pete's rod. What a trip. I still wonder however about the weight of a particular tarpon that I could still do nothing with after the best part of an hours battle. We had seen the fish airborne on a couple of occasions and it looked closer to 200lbs than anything we had ever hooked. Then, just when I felt confident of eventually seeing it beside the boat it made yet another long run, ripping a good 60-70 yards of 30lbs test from the multiplier, followed by a horrible 'grating' sound from the reel. We looked down in horror to see a bird's nest that had obviously been simply 'wound over' by the previous guest, whereupon seconds later the line parted at the Bimini knot just below the float. Boy was I sick. And I cannot repeat what John Rawle said. It was his tackle.

After what has become an annual trip to Lake Nasser in May for Nile perch on behalf of Tailor Made Holidays, (we took some beauties too in the 70-80lbs bracket) in between updating the where to fish book I also researched and filmed from May through to October series 17 of *Go Fishing* for Anglia Television. This was filmed entirely (due to the politics of both Granada and Carlton TV) within the Anglia Region and was in fact, sadly to be my last series for Anglia Television. But what a run I had enjoyed, though more of this later. The format of having two different disciplines and locations in each half hour programme was continued and I presented the usual mix of coarse sea and game fishing. We visited Rutland Reservoir for double figure pike on artificial lures with *Angling Times* photographer and long time mate Mick Rouse, and Ravensthorpe Reservoir for rainbow trout with the then head warden Nathan Clayton. I even got to feature the fun of 'float-tubing', and the film crew and I had a real laugh putting this section together. Another trout session was filmed at Coston Fisheries in Norfolk where amongst several lively rainbows, I was able to relate back to when the three lake, 'gravel-pit' fishery was first excavated and the fossils of Bison, Reindeer, woolly mammoth and woolly rhino's were found. Creatures that roamed these lands in East Anglia amongst a carpet of spruce and pine forest during a warm period in the last ice age, 60,000 years ago. These fossils incidentally are exhibited and on show in local museums.

With tope in mind I engaged the services of good mate and top skipper John Rawle out of Bradwell in Essex (back from his tarpon exploits in the Florida Keys) who as always did the business with a lovely big 44lbs male tope plus several smooth hounds for the cameras, as indeed did jovial Brian Riches out of Thornham in North Norfolk. We had expected a slow session, (Brian had actually rung the night before to report nothing from his previous three trips and suggested calling it off) but I suggested we went anyway, and would you believe, all three of my rods produced tope runs within half an hour of anchoring up. Moreover, we finished the day having boated a dozen good fish to over 30lbs, and we lost count of the number of runs we had up-tiding fresh mackerel cones and flappers.

I targeted pike in my new boat from the lower reaches of the River Waveney where several nicely marked doubles provided the action, and took a huge tench approaching 9lbs from a gravel pit complex close to home where only hours before a big double figure bream (my intended target species) had promptly fell off the hook mere feet from the net. From another local fishery, the day ticket lakes on

Two of the big, beautiful tench of between 6-7lbs that came my way from the day ticket Common Lakes Fishery in Lenwade Norfolk, during filming series 17 of *Go Fishing*. The last series I made for Anglia Television before the accountants moved in and crucified local broadcasting budgets.

Lenwade Common I enjoyed a fabulous morning after tench with several specimens between 6-7lbs coming to ledgered corn and casters. But I needed to scale down to a 3lbs hook link in order to induce bites.

Brothers Richard and Martin Bowler featured in two of the programmes. Richard in a barbel and chub session on the middle reaches of the Ouse at Harrold, and Martin shared a day with me after crucian carp at a lovely little, weedy pit. We accounted for specimens to 3lbs too plus some wonderful close-up sequences of a robin sitting on our rods. And Martin later went on to break the British crucian record with a monster of 4lbs 8oz from an adjacent fishery whilst filming for his TV series *Catching the Impossible*.

But I think the episode I enjoyed most was finally drawing a 20lbs carp over the net at a beautiful yet snaggy, local mere (sunken trees and the like) following an exciting scrap having hooked it float fishing at close range on a 1¾lbs test curve rod and small multiplier reel. My own 'Six Shooter' reel in fact marketed by Masterline International. The programme really highlighted what I have been preaching for years. That the super-smooth clutch of a small multiplier, around whose spool the line is wound 'without' going at right angles around a bale arm roller, (just like a centre pin reel) is far superior in playing fish to within a 'gnats' of the lines breaking strain, than fixed spool reels. For pike, for carp, for barbel (my largest ever barbel of 16lbs 13oz came on a multiplier) and yes, even for tench, small multipliers are unbelievably effective. Try it and see.

I also carp fished at a lovely little lake, just off the A10 in Hertfordshire, (Manor House Farm) taking some super commons to 20lbs amongst a patch of red lilies on floaters. Though I failed miserably with my chosen target species of Wels catfish with which the lake is well stocked.

I finished the session with a double figure mirror carp on free lined worm cast into the flow of where a small waterfall enters the lake. But on the sixth attempt? For each of the previous five casts I literally watched my lobworm disappear into

ABOVE

This eight foot long
300lbs giant white
sturgeon came in
Canada's British
Columbia from
the famous Fraser
River, to the rod of
David Chesterman.
(Second left). No
wonder its ear to
ear grins all round.

the carp's mouth, but when I struck, it was into thin air. The worm coming out free each time. I just couldn't understand it. Even the camera crew were getting impatient. Then when the worm and hook came out in the landing net prior to displaying the fish, the penny finally dropped. The carp in fact had a broken lower jaw and could not actually close its mouth. At one time I thought I was going mad. But as always there is usually a rational answer to most mysteries.

This last series for Anglia, though shot in 2002 was of course not screened until 2003, and as it kind of drew a line beneath my angling and filming exploits all over southern England, East Anglia, Ireland and in no less than 11 other countries in two decades of presenting angling on TV (Morocco, Zimbabwe, Austria, Madeira, India, Denmark, Kenya, Gambia, Spain, Canada, and Sweden) let me for once put the demographic record straight. Because even to this day I still here that, 'no wonder John Wilson always caught fish on TV, he only fishes private waters,' or, 'he always has his swims baited up for a week before hand'. Quite how you arrange for a wreck lying 200 feet deep in the English Channel, or a fly-only trout reservoir both to be pre-baited I'm not exactly sure. But people do love to imagine.

Truth is, and here is a demographic breakdown, of the 160 locations used in the 108 half hour programmes made for Anglia TV (16, six part and one 12 part) with series nine to 17 filmed in both the Meridian and Anglia regions creating two locations each per episode, over the period from 1985 to 2002, only 26 were in fact filmed at private fisheries. 32 were filmed at club waters or syndicates open to anyone. 57 were filmed at day ticket fisheries and no less than 45 were filmed at locations where the fishing is entirely free. Stats that even I found interesting when I sat down to work them all out.

Following the end of filming for *Go Fishing* in the autumn of 2002, I first whizzed over to Winnipeg in Canada with a party of Brits to the marvellous Fraser River System for Tailor Made Holidays where David Chesterman boated a 300lbs giant white sturgeon. What a fish. Then it was out to the Gambia again for Masterline

ABOVE

Martin Bowler eases the net below a big River Segre common carp for Adam Penning during a short winter break along the famous Rio Ebro system. Spain's foremost carp and catfish location.

International's fourth West African Shore Festival. Whilst all this was going on two computer – whiz kid, fishing mates, Nick Beardmore and Simon Lawford did their best to bring me out of the dark ages by setting me up with a computer system so I could type all my own articles and books. So after over 40 years of scribbling out long hand I just had to bite the bullet and put up with a mountain of teething problems that they assured me were inevitable.

At first I doubted that I could type (and still can't) at anywhere near the speed of longhand, and I was concerned that my thought process would slow down to the detriment of what I was trying to put across. But I was worrying for nothing and after week upon week of frustration of hitting the wrong key and instantly loosing hours of what I'd written, when had I a house brick close to hand, I'd have gladly smashed it into the monitor, I was slowly won over. And of course now I can't imagine how I ever managed writing longhand, with all the associated 'waiting' involved for my ever patient wife Jo to type an article, or my then typist Jan Carver to type book chapters. And once sending digital photos became imperative as it is today as I type this in April 2008, downloading images onto a CD or DVD for sending to publishers is so quick and easy. But more about digital photography later.

January 2003 started with all kinds of problems, both personal and work-wise, in that after getting nowhere with Anglia TV (owned by Granada) following a year of talk s about filming a 12 part fishing 'Safari Series' that I had been researching for the previous two years, Discovery Home and Leisure Television became interested and put me touch with Tony Baines who was head of sport at Granada Television at Meridian in Southampton, to produce it. And a filming schedule was set up with Granada Sports as the production company, with me presenting and directing. Now I can well understand the confusion of anyone who asks, if Granada owned Anglia TV, why couldn't I simply stay at Anglia and make the new series there? But that's the politics of TV for you. I've long since stopped trying to understand it all.

Before any filming of the new series started however, I made best of a few spare days in January to pop over to The River Ebro in Spain with Martin Bowler and Adam Penning for a spot of winter carp fishing on the advice of guide Gary Allen who was catching some whoppers from the River Segre in Mequinenza, with the intention of writing a feature for *Angling Times*. And on the very first afternoon I jammed out a superbly proportioned common of 35¼lbs fishing bolt-rigged boilies. But then the weather suddenly changed to the coldest experienced in Spain that winter, with minus four and five temperatures overnight, and little above freezing during the following two days, which miraculously saw us catching a few more fish to 28lbs, with the ground still carpeted in harsh frost in mid afternoon. I can remember running on the spot every so often to keep the blood circulating through my frozen feet. Hadn't considered the possibility of subzero weather out in Spain of course. So had left the thermal gear behind. It was actually much warmer back in the UK. But a lovely break none the less.

Our first *Fishing Safari* shoot had been organised with my son Lee after the Bronze Whaler sharks of Namibia's famous Skeleton Coast towards the end of February. But after returning from BUPA following a 'well man' health check up insisted upon and arranged by my wife Jo (I felt a bit off but couldn't put my finger on the problem) it transpired that my PSA. level was particularly high; 29 to be exact. So my doctor referred me to a specialist at the Norfolk and Norwich Hospital who after taking a dozen snips of my prostrate, confirmed that the biopsy revealed a cancerous growth. The level was apparently too high to operate on, and apart from leaving it, which was not an option, several weeks of vigorous radiotherapy were recommended to quarterise the growth. But this could not happen for at least three months till a slug injected into my stomach had released enough female hormones to stop me from producing testosterone and thus shrink the prostrate gland. Then I could have radiotherapy, and a series of dates over a six week period were arranged for June- July. Not exactly what I wanted to hear only weeks after securing an international TV series that I had set my heart on filming. But by carefully arranging the shooting before and after radiotherapy, all seemed attainable. The only cancellation I had to make, being my annual casting demonstrations at the Game Fair in July. Something the specialist said that I would be in no condition to enjoy. And he was so right.

Being the world's third most under populated country, whether you target catfish or tiger fish in the Zambezi River up in the northeast of Namibia, or battle sharks along it's famous 1000 mile long Skeleton Coast, over crowding is never a problem. In fact there are more cape fur seals along it's coastline than there are people, in a country four times the size of the UK, with a population amounting to just over one million. The Skeleton Coast faces the Atlantic Ocean stretching from Angola in the north, all the way down to South Africa, and is so named due to the amount of ships that run aground on its dangerous in shore reefs. And this is partly why the shore fishing is so unbelievably prolific. Whilst back from the sandy beaches stretching far into the distance is the Namib Desert, from which this fascinating country derives its name.

I was so enthralled with the desert, that I fancied shooting a 'tongue in cheek' intro sequence to camera with 33 year old son Lee and I perched on camels. Fortunately we located a lovely lady just north of our Swakopmund base, originally

a German settlement town, who was only too pleased for yours truly to feature her camels on telly (she operates short camel rides for tourists) and even provided our Yassa Arafat style 'tea-cloth' headgear. Lee was not impressed at all. But I managed to worm half a smile out of him during filming which took far longer than it should have done due to a sand storm blowing up.

Here lies much of the time difficulty in filming fishing for television. All the little fun pieces and especially the picturesque views etc take such a disproportionate slice out of the allocated filming schedule, which on this particular shoot was just seven days to make two, half hour programmes. And while this may seem time in plenty, we did not in fact catch a shark from the usually shark infested beaches both north and south of Swakopmund, for the first three days. During which time my hair probably turned an even lighter shade of grey. It was so uncharacteristically slow, due to unprecedented warm winds coming down from Angola, which sent our main target species, the bronze whaler, which is a temperate water shark, well off shore.

But having researched these beaches extensively over the previous couple of years I was not worried. I was simply terrified. Our very first shoot of a brand new series- and nothing to film. Naturally I panicked and tried to book later flights home (to hell with the budget) but all were full. So in the hope that all would come together during the last few days (which is fortunately exactly what happened – phew!) I concentrated upon filming the camel intro plus another at the local Swakopmund aquarium, together with some wildlife strands including pelicans, flamingos and cape fur seals, by visiting the largest local colony at pelican point just south of Walvis Bay, which itself is a little south of Swakopmund.

Here, and if you think we have cormorant problems read on, live nearly half a million black death's, most of which roost nightly on a specially constructed platform well out into Walvis Bay. Why! Because the platform produces 900 tons of cormorant guano (fertiliser) annually. But to be fair, these seas are not virtually fished-out commercially like our own around the British Isles. Stocks of mullet, pilchards and kabeljou, a bass-like species growing to 100lbs plus, are simply phenomenal. Add stingrays, guitarfish, catfish, Steen bras, black tail, and several species of sharks including our own smooth hound (appropriately called 'hound shark) and black spotted gulley sharks, a hard fighting , beautifully coloured species growing to over 70lbs, and you'll appreciate how the Skeleton Coast can support such a plethora of cormorants and cape fur seals.

Our guide and good friend Ottmar Leipert of Levo Sports fishing based in

Walvis Bay, with whom I first fished here back in 1998, and who helped pioneer shark fishing for bronze whalers along the Skeleton Coast, was rather philosophical about our predicament and suggested that in addition to catching some spotted gulley sharks (always on the cards) to start our programmes, we should film one of his dolphin and seal-tourist boat trips out of Walvis Bay, whilst waiting for the bronze whalers to come back in shore. Which worked an absolute treat? In fact I would love to have included much more of our dolphin and fur seal footage in the two finished programmes. Ottmar had been painstakingly training a handful of known (by name) previously wild fur seals, for many years, to the extent that when his 20 foot boat appeared in Walvis Bay, they not only swim towards it, they actually jump on board. I was totally dumbstruck when from nowhere 'Bushman', Ottmars pet name for a 500lbs male

fur seal, suddenly jumped up onto the port gunnels, mere inches from where I sat. After a minute or so of cuddles, Bushman quickly became my friend, so long as I continued to slip fresh pilchards down his throat. All of which was simply marvellous footage for cameraman Paul Bennett, who incidentally I have worked with for the past 18 years since the very first series of *Go Fishing*.

Who the hell needed sharks? We did of course, after all we were making fishing programmes, and while I have always maintained that a strong natural history element be part of my approach, bronze whaler sharks were badly needed. And though late, they came. I used my ZZiplex 14 ½ foot sharking special, together with an A B U 10,000 reel loaded with 30lbs mono to which a 20 foot rubbing leader of 100lbs mono was joined using a 'Bimini' knot. On the business end was a 20 inch, 150lbs nylon-covered wire trace and 9/0 hook. With a 20 inch link of 40lbs test mono carrying the 5oz lead, the mullet or mackerel head bait was easily cast around 80 yards out. Not exactly hi-tec, but very effective. And soon both Lee and I started connecting with our expected quarry; bronze whaler sharks,

BELOW
The final result following a long, exhausting battle from the beach. Lee puts a nice bronze whaler shark on the sand. A fish we badly needed on camera.

though nothing matched my previous years encounters with bronzies as Ottmar affectionately calls them, when specimens to 240lbs came my way.

For the camera however, and this is what it was after all, all about, we did beach a succession of bronzies to around 170lbs, plus a much rarer cow shark which Lee caught. All providing wonderfully long stand up fights lasting up to 45 minutes from the

sandy surf beaches. Believe me; for those who relish the pain and long, gut-busting, arm-wrenching battles with fish that often make you wish you hadn't hooked them in the first place, Namibia's Skeleton Coast has it all.

There is I am afraid an exceptionally sad post script to this particular shoot. Several months later when Ottmar travelled to South Africa for what should have been a simple shoulder operation, he never came out of the anaesthetic, and died.

So I never got to fish with this lovely person again. His enthusiasm was the most infectious I had ever known.

Upon returning to the UK there was little time for local fishing, though I did enjoy an impromptu session along my local River Wensum with *Angling Times* photographer Mick Rouse, and we both took chub over 6lbs on quiver tipped bread flake, amongst a bakers dozen, from a lovely, winding stretch of the river in Ringland. It was particularly rewarding because I knew Mick had always wanted to catch a chub over the 6lbs mark. So I put him in a swim where he had a good chance of a whopper, and mere minutes later his ear to ear grin said it all as he lifted out a beauty of 6lbs 2oz that had inhaled his quiver-tipped bread flake. Then it was back out to Africa again.

Were I to choose the most awesome, most dangerous, yet beautiful, game-packed and photogenic angling location from all the 60 plus countries I have fished during the past 40 years, then spectacular Murchison Falls in Uganda, would win hands down. Even surpassing the legendary Cauvery River in Southern India, where for some 15 years my love affair in search of those massive 'mahseer' literally became insatiable. Yet quite simply there is in my mind, no where to match the inspirational spectacle of Mother 'Nile', at Murchison Falls. They are even more breathtaking however in the flesh, with one small and one monumental cataract. In the dense equatorial canopy of hardwood trees overhanging the main pool, aptly called the 'devils cauldron' where rocking water hurtles downstream through a long gorge, between banks over 300 yards apart, live some of the most brilliantly coloured birds I've ever seen, from carmine bee eaters and weaver birds to the majestic African fish eagle. After half a mile of seemingly unfishable water (to the uninitiated) though these, the most productive spots of all, I find by far the most exciting, comprising of fierce currents and swirling eddies, some an acre or more in volume and over 30 feet deep, the Nile slowly starts to widen and reduce in speed to a fast walking pace.

Now it is half a mile wide between tall sedge and reed-lined banks where Cape buffalo and elephants are likely to venture out from the jungle to drink. So boat fishing here whether on the drift or at anchor is far safer than bank fishing. Whereas up at the falls, casting from the rocky promontories into the swirling pools below, is order of the day. Though should you fall in? Well! It's a case of 'goodnight nurse'. Subsequently, I divided these two entirely different styles of approach into two separate programmes. One at the falls presenting lures and free lined dead baits, and one in the slower water below, where drifting whist bumping dead baits 30 yards behind the boat, proved as successful as anchoring up. Logistically however, neither was easy to organise, and I shall be forever grateful to my guide and fishing partner Paul Goldring of 'Wild Frontiers' in Entebbe for his organised Safari-style approach which included a mornings trolling on Lake Victoria (the source of the Nile) around Ngamba, better known as 'chimp island' where we filmed the chimps and caught perch to over 30lbs before heading up country in Pauls 4x4 to Murchison.

What I've failed to mention about fishing at the falls is that it is a long and extremely steep walk down to reach a fishable level, in the most intense heat, and with the added problem of tetse fly bites. Tetse's are similar to our horse fly in that you can't feel them land, only the bite when they fly off. And some peoples legs and arms puff up to unmoveable proportions. Then at the end of the days fishing you must start the long, unbelievably steep and strength-sapping climb back up again. Whereas to boat fish below the falls in the slower water, a suitable craft is hired at Paraa Ferry, some four miles downstream from Murchison. And here occurred our second catastrophe whilst filming. The first being our second cameraman pulling out just a few days before flying out to Entebbe, due to both the UK Foreign Office and the Ugandan Tourist Office warning tourists not to travel to Uganda because of guerrilla attacks in the north of the country. Fortunately an instant replacement was found, Robin Broomfield, who worked for Granada and was all up to date inoculation and visa wise. And so we went anyway.

Upon arrival at Paraa Ferry however we found that *Mamba* the 25 foot, beamy boat I'd reserved for filming (six months earlier) was out of commission. No one had bothered to order spare parts for its engines (Africa remember) and so we either went home or made do with the only boat available, a wobbly 20 foot long fibreglass canoe, barely four feet at its widest. Which in a river full of hippos and crocs, most of them as wide if not actually wider than the canoe, was not exactly good news. But it was all we had so we made do by lashing a larger 'tourist' canoe to ours for the three man film crew.

On day two however, our fishing canoe was missing upon our dawn arrival. Apparantly, someone had fallen off the back of the ferry the previous evening and drowned, so they used our canoe to look for the body. It came back by 11am however

BELOW

Whilst waiting for our filming canoe to return (it was appropriated to search for a dead body down river) I used the time to scan through footage already in the can at Paraa Ferry on the River Nile below Murchison Falls.

(you don't want the gory details) and so that's when we started filming again. But despite even more set backs, Wild Frontiers guide Paul Goldring and I captured a whole string of both Nile perch and catfish to over 60lbs. I did manage to lose an absolute monster perch that inhaled an 8lbs catfish I was reeling in, ripping over 100 yards of 35lbs test line from my 10,000 multiplier, despite our up anchoring and following in its pursuit. Unfortunately, the flying hook (of a pennel rig) had reversed into the catfish and once we came up close to the perch it simply spat the catfish out. How big? Well I've lost count of the huge perch that I've taken from Lake Nasser weighing between 100-150lbs. This felt larger by far and I would have loved to see it jump for our two cameras. But it wasn't to be.

If only viewers knew what a frustrating business putting fishing on the box can be. For instance. Our seven day filming shoot in Spain during April on the marvellous River's Ebro and Segre which converge beside the sleepy town of Mequinenza in northeastern Spain, just a two and a half hour drive from Barcelona airport, (where I caught that 35¼lbs common back in January) started in the worst possible way. British Airways lost an important piece of our baggage, a huge aluminium box full of batteries, chargers and a play back monitor. Not during the two hour flight from Heathrow to Barcelona, which is usually what happens to my rod tube? No, this particular box without which we could not start filming didn't even make it onto the plane after check-in. Apparently some bright spark thought it might be a bomb which meant it had to be passed through a pressurised machine. This took several hours, while we waited at Barcelona airport expecting it to turn up on one of the next two or three flights. It was not however couriered to our hotel in Mequinenza by B A until the following morning, resulting in an entire days loss of filming. And one day out of seven means everything when you are endeavouring to produce two half hour programmes from just a weeks fishing. Wilson was 'not' a happy bunny.

What saved our bacon, because two of the remaining six days turned out deeply overcast and very windy (hopeless for filming whilst boat filming) is the unique and quite unbelievable proliferation of both big carp and catfish in the River Ebro system. And this has all happened in little over 30 years, since the early 1970's when German anglers first introduced Wels catfish. The rest as they say, is history, resulting today in every third catfish caught from the Ebro- Segre system in the Mequinenza area weighing over 100lbs, and every other carp (they are all beautifully shaped big commons) topping 25lbs. Honestly!

The only river in the world that I've fished and filmed to come anywhere near this phenomenal ecosystem is the Red River which flows through Winnipeg in the province of Manitoba, Canada. But the indigenous stock of 'pussies' in the 'Red' are channel catfish which top out at between just 30-40lbs, while the equally prolific stock of common carp average into double figures, with the occasional specimen over 20lbs. So the two systems do not compare.

The Ebro system is at this point in time quite remarkable, and with catfish preying upon the smaller sizes of carp, which obviously results in their monstrous average size, it won't be long before someone lands a 70lb common. The best I have heard of so far weighed 67lbs. And the heaviest catfish, over 230lbs; 300lbs being not an unrealistic top-out weight for these monstrous, extremely well fed pussies, which now benefit from mountains of free feed in the form of halibut pellets. Pre-baited by the sack full.

While I've old friends Keith Lambert and Simon Clarke of the Catfish Conservation Group to thank for putting me onto the fabulous fishing at Mequinenza, I did in fact film one of my international *Go Fishing* programmes on the Ebro in conjunction with old friend Martin Founds of Anglers World Holidays back in the early 1990's. But that was much further downstream and before the enormous, indigenous shoals of barbel and carp started to be thinned out by Wels catfish.

Fishing at Mequinenza is all made possible by The Bavarian Guiding Service which provides boats, tackle, experienced guides, and accommodation at its purpose built camp with an excellent restaurant on site, situated just a short cast away from the River Segre. In addition to this self-catering camp which is open all year round, the Guiding Service also has alternative villa-apartment accommodation on the opposite side of the river, where visitors enjoy their own boat docks.

Source of the Segre is close to the French border, with tributaries Rio Cinca and Rio Noguera Ribagor Cana, adding to its volume before it merges with the mighty Ebro at Mequinenza. And it was in the wide reaches of the Segre, close to the camp that top guide Gary Allen and I fished together for carp whilst filming the first of our two programmes.

Following a few days pre-baiting with a mixture of maize, hempseed and chopped boilies, Gary virtually had those big commons feeding out of his hand. And I cannot ever remember enjoying such a hectic session after big carp. What's big? Well how about my best five commons for the morning averaging 29½lbs. And we wrapped, as they say at noon. Need I say more? All came to 20mm boilies

hair-rigged to a size 6 hook, and 2½oz semi-fixed bolt rig cast just 50 yards out. And what incredible scraps they provided on 15lbs reel lines for our two cameramen, Steve Thorpe and Ray Warner.

For making the catfish programme we were joined by co-owner of The Bavarian Guiding Service Jurgen Stegherr who kindly ran the second (camera) boat when we visited the wide and deep reaches of the Ebro way above the hydroelectric dam at Mequinenza. In this, the beautiful 'upper lake' as these flooded reaches are often called, (it looks more like a lake) where ospreys, vultures, kites and buzzards fly overhead, we enjoyed some exciting sport with catfish of all sizes from 20lbs kittens, to six foot long lunkers well in excess of 100lbs. The potential here is simply mind blowing, with over 50 miles to go at between the top weir and Mequinenza. At the town of Caspe, 25 foot cruiser-houseboats can be hired from The Bavarian Guiding Service, enabling visitors to fully explore this fascinating section of the Ebro, with 16 foot skiffs included to fish from.

The zander fishing, including a good sprinkling of 'doubles' can at times prove hectic in the 'upper lake' both to lures and dead bleak mounted sink and draw style. American black bass have also been introduced here, and provide the occasional surprise. But 'the' two species are carp and catfish.

During our filming sessions Gary suggested that eels set a couple of feet above bottom beneath a pike float, and trotted down with the flow, would produce our best results. And he was spot on. Working big rubber shads, float-fished carp live baits and dead baits etc all work effectively, as does the technique of 'bouy' fishing.

For this bouys on ropes with heavy mud weights are rowed out to desirable areas. Then each live bait in turn (1lb plus carp) set beneath a large pike bung, is rowed out to the bouys, with 10 foot of 15lbs mono break line connected to a bouy and to a swivel immediately above the pike bung. This of course permits baits to

be positioned accurately over choice 'feature' hotspots, without fear of them roaming all over the river and tangling with the other lines.

Once attached, you then row or motor back to shore whilst thumbing out the 130lbs braided reel line from the multiplier (big pussies remember) and rest the powerful 10 foot rod in an upright (beach-style) holder. The line is then wound up tight. It is then a waiting game, and catfish hits are registered

LEFT

Gary Allen lends a hand to help me display the full length of a 100lbs plus Wels catfish. A fish I caught on trotted eel live bait from the upper reaches of the Rio Ebro, following a spectacular battle amongst the turbulent waters of a huge weir pool, during the making of my *Safari* fishing series for Discovery TV.

in two ways. Either the rod lurches over and you wind down tightly before striking extra hard to sever the break line, hence it name, or the catfish does it for you, whereby the rod bends over alarmingly before springing back violently. Either way it's best to set those hooks immediately. There then commences one of if not the most powerful, arm wrenching encounters you are ever likely to experience in European freshwater. Believe me.

The best I caught on camera was around 120lbs, an immaculately marked fish, its smooth body a mosaic of pewter, sage green and cream, with a very much larger specimen lost. The hook popping out when I perhaps put on rather more pressure than I should have, to stop it from heading way down river in a fierce current. But so it goes. We never the less returned to the UK with some wonderful footage, despite losing that days filming due to British Airways incompetence.

For our fourth *Fishing Safari* shoot I'd asked mate Chris Tarrant, who ironically is a patron of The Prostrate Cancer Charity, if he would accompany me to The Florida Keys to make two programmes at the beginning of May. One on catching big tarpon at night, and the other catching big amberjacks from 300 feet down out in The Atlantic. Being a fan of my *Go Fishing* programmes for many years, Chris had always said that if I asked he would oblige by appearing in a couple of episodes, and he stuck to his word, without asking a fee I might add.

While I shall be forever grateful to Discovery for providing the necessary budget to make an international series, at the same time, I felt saddened that TV licence payers who had faithfully followed my exploits for the best part of 20 years, and who cannot afford satellite TV, would not be able to watch the series I was in the middle of making. Frankly it's scandalous.

So what is it that stops you the viewer from being able to watch fishing on terrestrial television having duly paid your licence fee? After all, aren't BBC2, Channel 4 and Channel 5 supposed to be providing 'niche' and 'fringe' programmes? But when do you ever see table tennis, karate, shooting, judo, archery, kick boxing, weight lifting, water sports etc, (I could go on) and of course angling on these channels? Is it because most programming commissioners are female and leftist,

anti-field sports, anti-life, vegetarians or vegans?

The only exception has been my long running Anglia-produced *Go Fishing* series which for 17 years was the only 'regular' angling series on terrestrial TV. All be it, for the last few years of its run, available to Anglia and Meridian TV viewers only. It's all very sad when you consider that one in every 20 people in the UK go fishing. Even worse is the constant diet of football, reality shows. Football, makeover shows, football and even more football, that television continues to spoon-feed us with. Do they want us all to become zombies? There, I've had my say, now onto fishing in The Florida Keys with good friend and fellow TV presenter Chris Tarrant.

For anyone who has never experienced the gut-busting and arm-wrenching pain of fighting a 50lbs plus amberjack up from 300 feet down on stand –up 50lbs class gear, it is to say the least, quite devastating, and by the tortured expression covering Chris Tarrant's usually jovial face, I could only assume he must have been enjoying the occasion. Where were we? On board 47 foot *Blue Chip two* skippered by Skip Bradeen, some 11 miles off Islamorada (our base in The Florida Keys) out in the deep-blue Atlantic where the sea bed rises from 600 feet to a plateau just 300 feet deep. And it would be difficult to find a more fish-filled hot spot for amberjacks anywhere else on this planet. The top of the plateau always appears to be 'paved' with lunkers in the 40-70lbs bracket, plus the inevitable horde of hammerhead sharks averaging 200-300lbs. And guess what their favourite snack is? Fortunately as I recall, sharks were not a problem during our session, but I have on past occasions when on holiday here with mate Pete Hazelwood, lost as many as four or five big amberjacks in a single sitting. And there's nothing funny about reeling in a beautifully conditioned 10lbs amberjacks head, having risked initiating a hernia whilst playing its owner for 20 minutes. Believe me.

This fantastic, if somewhat frenzied sport happens on the drift, and is based on who can get a speedo (a mackerel species caught over in shore reefs) using 1lb of lead above the long, 100lbs mono trace, down to the bottom, fast enough. The savage hit from an amberjack often occurring within seconds of the baits arrival. I rather think Chris slept well that night after hauling up five whoppers to around 60lbs. One particular fish we actually shared the honours with as viewers got to witness, when for a good 20 minutes we were both playing the same amberjack.

SIXTY YEARS A FISHERMAN

Both our 7/0 circle hooks being in the corner of its mouth. Have you and your fishing buddy ever hooked up simultaneously with the same fish having gobbled up both of your baits? I have on several occasions in fact.

An even more unlikely double hook-up I shared with mate Dave Watson several years ago, drifting along Africa's mighty Zambezi River in the rich, wide waters of the Lower Zambezi National Park. And again, which makes the occurrence totally bizarre, we were casting free lined fish strip on opposite sides of the boat for tiger fish, which can at the best of times prove finicky feeders, and will eject the bait when feeling resistance. So how we both hooked up, literally within seconds of each other, to the same 11lbs tiger fish beggars belief. But both our hooks were in its tooth-laden jaws. I'm sure it grabbed the second bait, on the run, when already 'struck'.

My very first double hook-up experience happened getting on for 50 years ago however, when my brother Dave and I, both in our teens, were free lining for brown trout in Hertfordshire's diminutive River Mimram, casting lobworms beneath a huge overhanging willow. I was casting downstream from above the tree, and Dave flicking his worm upriver into the same area from below the tree. As it was dark at the time we were not exactly sure where the worms were landing anyway, but we both exclaimed 'I'm in' simultaneously. And then for the next few minutes each trying to figure out why, a brownie of around 2lbs was fighting like a 10lbs salmon. Then the penny suddenly dropped. We were both hauling away at the same fish from opposite directions, which of course had both our hooks down its throat.

But I rate the strangest double hook-up of all, and I can recount no less than nine separate, shared catches including pike, sharks and even giant white sturgeon, was when Tim Baily of the *African Angler* adventures on Egypt's massive Lake Nasser, and I, found ourselves 'both' playing the very same 75lbs Nile perch. Miraculously it had grabbed both our large diving plugs, and must have taken the second when already hooked. So much for fish feeling pain eh?

Hauling heavyweight jacks from the depths of the Atlantic however, was far from Chris Tarrant's most memorable battle however. I had arranged a tarpon fishing trip out with my old mate and skipper John Rawle with whom I made several *Go Fishing* episodes out from Bradwell in Essex. From March through to the end of May however John is based in

BELOW

It's that man Tarrant again. Now with a 130lbs tarpon (hooked on free-lined blue crab) all but beaten. Great action for our camera team (in the second boat) and all down to the knowledge of another good friend, top skipper John Rawle (far right) who really laid it on for us out in the Keys.

RIGHT

You certainly need help in hoisting up a 150lbs fish for the cameras. And my heaviest Nile perch ever, which grabbed a deep diving, 'reef digger' plug on the troll, is in the safe hands of old friend and experienced guide Mohammed. Boy did it fight.

Islamorada where from his 17 foot Maverick skiff guests can target shallow water sharks, bonefish, barracuda's, redfish, snook, jacks etc, and in our case, monstrous-great tarpon topping 100lbs. And mostly all from the warm, shallow waters of Florida Bay.

In 20 years of making angling TV programmes and videos I had never tried filming during the hours of darkness. But John said our best chance of monster tarpon was from 3am till dawn, which I knew to be true from past trips, so after showing Chris what big tarpon looked like along at famous 'Robbies' bar and boat dock (hundreds of huge tarpon gather there to be fed by hand would you believe) we set off the following morning to film by torchlight. And very well it came out too, I'm surprised to report. Though I doubt cameraman Paul Bennett would want to film in the pitch black on every shoot. I managed my largest tarpon ever estimated by John at around 160lbs, while after much sweating and cursing Chris finally brought to the skiff his best (and first) tarpon of 130lbs. Both incidentally were caught on just 20lbs test line and came to float-fished blue crabs really making our weeks filming in the Keys a most memorable occasion.

Mind you as Chris said, everything he hooked turned out to be a personal best, including would you believe no less than five permit in a single session when we motored over 70 miles out (yes 70) into the Gulf of Mexico to the famous 'blue hole' on board skipper Randy Towes 35 foot contender. And every one topped 20lbs. That's comparable almost to a golfer downing five holes in-one during the same session. Mind he nearly lost one of them because a monstrous jewfish estimated by Randy at 500lbs, came up from the depths to grab hold. Fortunately it missed. All great stuff for our programmes, all of which was captured in close up on video. As were our exploits with sharks, both lemons and nurse sharks, plus my losing that same monster jewfish and boating a 70lbs baby, which also happened to be a PB. What a trip.

Upon arriving back in the UK I had but a few days to spare before taking yet another party of Brits out to Egypt's massive Lake Nasser. Safaris that I always look forward to and during this particular trip I had good reason, for it produced my personal best Nile perch. A monster of exactly 150lbs, which grabbed a 10 inch 'reef-digger' plug, trolled 20 feet down in a gully between two islands near Madig midway down the lake. In no time at all we had drifted over 200 yards to where the bottom started to shelve up steeply and I feared the 35lbs mono would scrape over the rocks. So guide Mohammed kept shouting out depth readings while I piled on the pressure to lever the big fish up to the surface. And suddenly, following a powerful battle its immense bulk was on the

surface, connected by the prong of one treble only. But I needn't have worried. Mohammed stretched his long arms over the gunnels to get a firm grip around its lower jaw with a gloved hand, and it was all over. What an end to a great week's safari, in which our eight British guests caught nearly 100 sizeable Nile perch, three of them topping 100lbs.

With no more overseas filming till October I settled down to local fishing only throughout June and July whilst having radiotherapy on my prostrate. And thank goodness I had cancelled the Game Fair. With the tubes of both my bladder and bowel rendered totally unpredictable and uncontrollable by having 10.000 volts aimed at my prostrate gland (accuracy is not what you imagine here) I just couldn't risk wearing a pair of light coloured shorts and demonstrating the finer points of casting a fly for bone fish, which was what I'd planned. Or any other technique for that matter. After just two weeks of radiotherapy I felt completely drained and could never have made the nearest toilet quick enough.

So I concentrated upon making short, impromptu stalking sessions for barbel along my local River Wensum at Lyng (which was all my strength would allow) and

ABOVE

Jo and I take time off during the CLA Game Fair held at Romsey in Hampshire.

BELOW

A lovely barbel pushing 14lbs, taken from beneath a 'snag' swim where a sunken willow reaches almost across the river, during a short, impromptu session at a local stretch of the Wensum at Lyng, at a time when despite the 'Wilson smile' I was not at all well.

actually accounted for several doubles to 13lbs-10oz from a couple of favourite 'snag' swims beneath over hanging willows where barbel were sheltering during the heat of the day, and not once out of eight or nine sessions did I fish longer than an hour or so. Most rewarding fishing indeed and great, short but hectic and truly exciting battles at close range with powerful fish. Exactly the kind of fishing I adore.

By October I felt strong enough to start filming again, which was just as

well because we were off across the Atlantic to Canada. Now I've said it before, but I'll say it again. Were I a young man I would emigrate immediately to Canada and the province of British Columbia. I certainly had my chance back in the swinging late 1960's whilst working on P & O cruise ship *SS Oronsay*. Every three months on those fabulous around the world trips we berthed in Vancouver harbour, and the first thing I did was get into a taxi to Horseshoe Bay opposite Vancouver Island and rent out a fishing boat. I immediately loved about Canada, as indeed I still do, its pristine wilderness aspect and ridiculously low ratio of population to landmass. But hindsight is a wonderful thing and I couldn't foresee back then how small Britain would become and to what extent our rivers would deteriorate. Otherwise I might well have stayed.

I have been so impressed with the Fraser system in recent years, which is undammed throughout it's 1000 miles and one of the worlds last remaining great salmon and sturgeon producing rivers, that I chose to target sturgeon in the Fraser with guide Fred Helmer of Freds Fishing Adventures in Chilliwack, who pioneered sturgeon fishing here. And salmon with ace fly fishing guide Tony Nootebos of Harrison Bay Guided Services. Although both rivers are rich in both species, especially salmon. It is indeed difficult until you have witnessed these phenomenal concentrations of salmon (50 million ran the Fraser in 2003) to appreciate the demise of our British salmon industry.

As the Fraser and Harrison rivers converge near Chilliwack just 70 miles east of Vancouver, visitors can either base in Chilliwack or be collected from their hotel by their guide each morning who then slips his 20 foot jet boat in 10 minutes away at Island 22 on the Fraser. Or, meet their guide at Harrison Hot Springs Resort boat dock at picturesque Harrison Lake (where we stayed) which leads into the Harrison River, and is also within minutes of the wide junction with the Fraser. How? These aluminium jet boats motor at between 40 and 50 miles an hour. That's how.

Having both been around a while, Fred and I naturally gelled instantly, and so did our quarry the sturgeon. Fishing just a few miles downstream from Island 22

SIXTY YEARS A FISHERMAN

and ledgering golf ball-sized bags of fresh salmon eggs (the sturgeon bait) wrapped up in sections of nylon tights, nicked onto a 7/0 hook, Fred and I hit into a dozen or so high-jumping, fast running sturgeon in the 40-80lbs class. Teeth cutting fish as he calls them, and great action for our two cameramen Paul Bennett and Robin Broomfield, who in addition to the jumps, captured the scanning and electronic tagging of each fish for the Fraser River Sturgeon Conservation Society formed in the late 1990's, with which Fred is very much involved. His immediate group of guides having tagged and released some 14,000 sturgeon during the three years prior to 2003.

Our powerful stand-up rods and 130lbs test braided reel lines on sturdy multipliers might to some anglers have seemed a trifle over gunned. But when you consider that sturgeon in excess of 1000lbs live in the Fraser, which is up to 500 yards wide and anywhere between 10 and over 50 feet deep and running like the clappers, the correct tackle selection is imperative. On our first move downriver I immediately connected with something very much larger, which treated us to a couple of classical 'polaris' style leaps. Some will perform up to several more leaps at various stages of the fight, whilst others you just do not see till the end. After a wonderful battle lasting around 15 minutes my sturgeon came alongside the boat and was ready to be photographed, all six and a half feet, and 160lbs of it. And the safest way to record the capture for both angler and fish (lines of sharp 'skutes' evenly spaced along its back and sides can inflict nasty flesh wounds) is to slowly tow it to shore. Whereupon the guide dishes out chest waders enabling everyone to kneel on the bottom of the shallow margins to hoist the sturgeon up for a trophy shot. Easier said than done, believe you me.

Fred and I then accounted for another biggy, perhaps 20lbs larger, once we were anchored back in the deep channel again, but viewers didn't see this particular fish, because quite frankly we caught too many sturgeon to feature them all. And because later on that afternoon, I finally banged into a real whopper. Fred had commented earlier that you can go on doubling the weight of your biggest sturgeon all the way up to over a 1000lbs, from 100 to 200, to 400, to 800 etc and so I was more than content with my next fish which put up an incredible scrap for over half an hour and which measured eight foot two inches long. Fred estimated it at least 300lbs, and being my largest freshwater fish ever I was ecstatic. Whatsmore, we had the entire sturgeon programme wrapped up in just two days filming, which left us time in plenty for the salmon.

I was looking forward to getting stuck in again to hard fighting chum and Chinook salmon which are common in the 20-25lbs bracket, like I'd caught on fly during almost the same calendar week a year earlier. But two things I had not taken into account. Firstly, the Fraser River system was two feet down on normal level, and most of the larger salmon were still in the estuary mouth awaiting rain. Secondly, every two years sees phenomenal runs of pink salmon. And this was one of those years, with over 20 million pinks in the system, making it virtually impossible to get through them down to the small numbers of chum and big Chinooks that had made an early migration. How I wish we had the very same problem of 'too many salmon' in Britain. Eh?

Needless to say, Tony Nootebos and I enjoyed some simply magical sport using 8 weight trout fly rods, completely losing count of the pinks we caught between five and 10lbs. And to vary the filming we blasted along 40 mile long Harrison Lake one morning to the other end where the beautiful yet diminutive, glacial fed Lilluet River flows in, catching dolly varden, wild rainbow trout, (my first ever totally wild rainbow trout incidentally, all those we catck in the UK being 'reared' fish) even more pinks, and sockeye salmon. I even hooked into a fair sized chum salmon, but unfortunately it slipped the barb less hook (mandatory in British Columbia) in the fast, shallow water, where overhead turkey buzzards, ospreys and bald eagles were daily sightings.

The crew and I hardly had time to get our breath back in the UK after such a busy time in Canada, before we were off again, back to Africa for the last shoot of my *Fishing Safari* series. In famous Victoria Falls, one of the seven natural wonders of our world, and Lake Kariba, one of the planets largest and most beautiful dammed watersheds, the Zambezi River is certainly rich in both scenery and fishing potential. But there's much, much more. This majestic river, Africa's fourth longest (behind the Nile, Congo, and Niger) at 1700 miles from source to where it finally pours into the Indian Ocean in Mozambique, also contains two monumental predatory, freshwater

adversaries. The high-leaping, tooth-laden tiger fish which grows to over 30lbs and who's dentistry leaves even great whites at the end of the queue. And Africa's largest catfish (capable of topping 100lbs) the awesome vundu, one of the worlds finest freshwater battlers. Add to all this another 70 or so colourful, powerful, and curious species, plus, some of the most spectacular game viewing in Africa, (much of it on show while you are fishing) and you'll perhaps understand why I chose the wide, jungle-clad lower river reaches, adjacent to the Lower Zambezi National Park, for my two 'Zambezi' programmes. The river here is in fact the borderline between Zambia and Zimbabwe. And to reach the river from Zambia's capital Lusaka, following a long haul flight from Heathrow, we chartered a Piper Chieftain from Pro-Flight Services which in just 25 minutes took us over the mountains to the dirt air strip of our final destination, The Royal Zambezi Lodge. Set in pristine, riverine forest on the banks of the river, the comfortable meru-style tented and thatched accommodation is literally a stones throw from the Zambezi.

My guide for both of the two programmes was good friend Steve Maartens who is also the valley manager for both the Royal Zambezi Lodge and Mwambashi River Lodge, which is actually situated within the Lower Zambezi National Park several miles downriver. And while the fishing is of a similar nature at both locations, Steve and I decided to first feature the fabulous tiger fishing from the Royal Zambezi Lodge in Steve's 20 foot aluminium boat. By tying up close into the bank against a huge bed of sedges covering a sunken hardwood tree, where the currents are noticeably slower, we caught fresh bait in the form of silver-sided bream-like species called chessa. These came readily up to around 1½lbs on ledgered worms. It was just like quiver-tipping for chub back home, except that these warm water species size for size, fight twice as strongly.

Any number of different fish are likely to turn up from small tiger fish, nkupe, sharp toothed catfish, tilapia's etc, and a strange fish (capable of emitting an electric shock) called bottlenose, of which Steve caught two, both into double figures.

With kites and fish eagles searching the river overhead, and a myriad of colourful birds chattering away in the jungle from carmine bee eaters to hornbills, plus inquisitive

ABOVE

There are few places on this earth to match the sunrises of the Zambezi River. I took this photo from the Royal Zambezi Lodge close to Zambia's Lower Zambezi National Park.

BELOW

Elephants constantly crossing from one side to the other are daily sights whilst fishing the Zambezi River. It is arguably the most animal-rich fishing location on this planet.

monkeys studying our every move, simply being afloat on the Zambezi is a magical experience. An elephant or two can usually be seen from where ever you're fishing, along with herds of Cape buffalo and countless pods of hippos. Fishing is simply the icing on the cake. You do however have to be particularly watchful of hippos when approaching a family, and never force them against shallow water. Otherwise they are likely to run at their aggressor and turn the boat over the river is of course full of extremely large crocodiles, so its best never to antagonise the hippo's which weigh around two tons apiece. These vegetarians are obviously not interested in eating you, simply retaliating against those who invade their space. Henry however is different. This decidedly friendly hippo (who allows anyone to get up close for a photo) has been around for at least the four years that I have now been visiting the Royal Zambezi Lodge. He munches water hyacinth and reed stalks all day directly opposite the veranda bar, and after dark he comes ashore to graze upon the grass between your accommodation and the river.

To catch tiger fish you can either anchor up and ledger a fillet or cutlet of fresh chessa. Or, and this is by far the most exciting technique (next to fly fishing) you simply drift with the flow which runs at around walking pace, casting fish strip on a size 6/0, wide gape hook twisted onto 30lbs wire, upstream into deep drop-off's, or alongside structure swims where fallen trees provide cover for bait fish. And thus great tiger ambush points. In deep runs a swan shot or two is pinched onto the trace to help get the bait down near the bottom. But generally speaking, these lower reaches are wide (up to a mile across in places) but quite shallow, between four and eight feet deep, with a hard sandy bottom. So only very occasionally does the bait foul bottom whilst drifting, which is the perfect method for searching the river. I prefer to keep my 6501c4 multiplier (filled with 30lbs test braid) in free spool whilst feeling for bites, because occasionally a fish will gobble up fish strip and run towards the boat. Otherwise, bites are unbelievably fast and aggressive, and you need to wind the reel into gear quickly and to set the hook before they eject the bait. There then follows an exhilarating battle which usually includes several high leaps (only tarpon can compete) and numerous changes of direction. Only the larger tigers of say 12 or 13lbs upwards are likely to jump just once or not at all. And those triangular, interlocking teeth are something else. 10 in the upper jaw and eight in the lower, all razor sharp and so disproportionately large for the size of the fish. The best we managed to land (so many defy hook penetration) was one of my largest ever, a superbly coloured and proportioned specimen of 14lbs plus, which had teeth fully ¾ of an inch long.

For our vundu programme Steve accompanied our film crew, Paul Bennett-main camera, Robin Broomfield – second camera, Dave Runciman-sound, and yours truly several miles downriver to fabulous Mwambashi River Lodge, which is actually a collection of meru-tented, thatched lodges built on the banks of the Zambezi within the National Park, with elephants walking through and around in camp, par for the course. An option here is also to explore the park inland in the lodge's 4x4, should you fancy a break from the fishing. Lion, leopard, buffalo, kudu, waterbuck, impala, warthogs, monkeys etc and a myriad of exquisite birds are everyday sightings. And in the river, big vundu catfish in the 40-60lbs category are potentially every day catches. Best baits being cubes of ledgered luncheon meat and chessa heads (the heads hold more blood) on 30lbs test outfits. On Steve's advice I tied up 7/0 hook traces using 40lbs nylon-covered wire, because with fresh fish, big tigers are also liable to grab hold. As indeed several doubles did during our shoot which produced several nice vundu to over 50lbs. And what marvellous fights they gave in the strong current.

Back in the UK I more or less went straight down to Southampton to Granada's editing suites for several weeks, after providing editor Phil Witcher with some fairly accurate (but over-length) paper edits as I had been doing throughout the filming since returning from our first shoot back in February. These I do, (which is my preferred way of paper editing) by having all the master tapes duplicated onto VHS tapes with burnt in time codes, (so the masters do not have to be ran backwards and forwards through a play back machine) before subsequently working out a story line for each programme and writing it down in a succession of time codes. Phil then tweaked each programme and added the music, into an off-line version for showing to Discovery, in case there was anything they didn't like, after which they

BELOW
Big tilapia (called 'bream' locally) like this beauty held by guide Steve Maartens, are not only the staple food diet of many Africans, they fight hard on light tackle too. So this one went back.

were fine tuned and finished off in the sound dubbing studio. Remember, there are so many sound effects that have to be added during editing. There is never a microphone close up to a jumping sturgeon when 70-100 yards away it leaps out and then crashes back into the river. But you the viewers expect to hear that noise nonetheless. Otherwise you would not enjoy the programme so much. Think about it. So that sound has to be re-created.

I hasten to add here that I am probably the only angling presenter in the UK who insists on being involved to the extent of creating his own paper edits in addition to researching,

presenting and directing. And yes, it is much, much more work than anyone out of television would ever imagine. But I think the result is well worth it, and I consider *Fishing Safaris* one of the most colourful, exciting and nature-packed, series that I have made and co- produced. It is something of which I am extremely proud.

In early December Discovery's publicity department wanted a photo shoot to help publicise the new series, due for screening early in the New Year, and so I suggested we take the party of seven selected journalists to one of the locations featured in the series, namely where the Rivers Ebro and Segre converge at Mequinenza in Spain. It was close to home without the need for arranging long haul flights, and guide Gary Allen offered his experienced services for our three day stint. Good old British Airways did it again however (you'll remember they left a case full of our filming equipment on the tarmac at Heathrow, thinking it was a bomb when we filmed in Spain back in April) by losing the tube containing my carp rods. And delivering it to our hotel in Mequinenza, an hour before we set off to fly home. But Gary lent me a pair of his rods, and though the weather was miserable, five of our seven man party put 30lbs plus commons on the bank to help advertise the series. Not bad at all for December.

A week later I flew out to Egypt's Lake Nasser with mates Andy Davison and east coast skipper Stewart Smalley for a week's trolling for big Nile perch. And though one 100lbs buffalo did come our way (fortunately to my rod trolling a red and white Nilsmaster) the general run of fish was on the modest side.

Upon returning to the UK I was extremely proud to find out that *Angling Times*, Britain's largest angling publication in their 50 years of fishing 1953-2003 birthday special collectors' issue voted me number one of the top 50, greatest anglers of all time. Phew! What an accolade. And what a lovely surprise to come during a year of very mixed emotions, starting with being told I'd got prostrate cancer back in January. And now being told that the radiotherapy had apparently worked and that my PSA level (following a recent blood test) was back down to

SIXTY YEARS A FISHERMAN

normal again. Proof to quote a favourite saying of mine, that there is always light at the end of the tunnel. But I shall need to have blood tests every six months from here on incase the cancer returns.

Naturally, I started 2004 on a real high, indeed who wouldn't, but with more and more carp being killed in our two-lake fishery, and left in the margins with their throats or bellies eaten out, for foxes to run off with, (which is why it takes so long for the penny to drop with fishery owners not actually living beside their lakes) I finally really had to do something about the otters that do-gooders had introduced along stretches of my local River Wensum which is but 150 yards from where I sit typing this. And once the otters, which are totally indiscriminate killers, as well as being furry and cuddly, who think nothing of maiming one large fish before dropping it and grabbing another, realised there also were plenty of double figure catfish in my lakes, well, for a couple of weeks they actually targeted catfish because compared to carp, they are so easy to eat.

Commons and mirror carp to over 20lbs, cats to over 20lbs and a 21lbs grass carp,(three feet long no less) over 40 fish in all, (as far as I know) were killed within a space of four months, with just as many injured. From December through to March, when I guess the food cupboard of the River Wensum was at its most bare. Of course during the summer when frogs, toads, newts, slow worms, lizards, snakes, water voles, dabchicks, moorhens, and the young of mallards etc are all added to the otters food list (and yes they do eat waterbirds) they leave my lakes alone. But not wanting to endure another winter of discontent, I decided to have a 235 yard long, six foot high chain-link fence erected, completely along the 'Wensum side' of my two lakes (where they were obviously coming in) with two foot buried in the ground, so they could not burrow beneath, and an 18 inch crank top to stop them from climbing over.

I hired a local contractor to erect the fence, (before the summer growth made work more difficult) which my wife Jo said 'looks a bit of an eyesore' at a cost of slightly more than what my first bungalow set me back in the early 1970's. I know that is not a fair comparison, and I truly wonder whether these so called 'do-gooders' realise that you cannot have any environment over run with predators. Gamekeepers who once used to preside over our countryside estates knew how to keep everything in order. But talk now of shooting predatory birds like jays, crows and magpies etc and every old dear in the village shakes her RSPB membership badge at you. Welcome to the 'nanny state'.

BELOW

Was I made up or what? When in their 50 year birthday special collector's edition, *Angling Times* voted yours truly number one of the top 50 greatest anglers of all time.

Having been gradually stripped of its wonderful silver fish heritage by cormorants during the past couple of decades, the Wensum now also has both mink and otters to contend with, to the extent that the latter are of course now targeting large specimen fish in the river itself. And a double figure barbel is nothing to an adult otter.

I truly feel sorry for fishery owners who like myself have spent half their lives creating their own fisheries only to have their largest specimens (which provide the easiest targets) duly killed. Because even if the cost of erecting a fence can be met, due to the undulating ground of most gravel pits where the roots of mature trees create enormous erection problems, (Viagra wont help either) it is not in many cases possible to fence in a lake entirely around its perimeter.

Incidentally, the aftermath of a substantial otter kill at your fishery is discovering a few weeks later, 'stinkers', or carp that were badly mauled and got away from the clutches of the otter, only to eventually die on the bottom where they subsequently gas-up and rise to the surface in a most grotesquely bloated state a few weeks later. Fox's smell these 'bloaters' out from a long way away. And those carp that were simply 'played' with, having had their fins partly chewed (usually the tail) and managed to get away, will in time regenerate their fin tissue. It grows thinner and usually of a noticeably lighter colour. There are in my fishery at least a couple of dozen (incredibly lucky) carp that have all noticeably regenerated their fin tissue from otter attacks.

Throughout January I targeted the chub and bream in a local weir pool on the Wensum (thankfully as yet not ruined by otters although there are not so many chub around as there were a few years back) and popped down to Hampshire with mate Val Tomin from Harrold in Bedfordshire, who had been pestering me to take him grayling fishing for years. We had some great long trotting in the River Test above Stockbridge too, with fish to over 2lbs, (those interested in winter grayling along Hampshire's chalk streams should ring the Orvis Tackle Shop in Stockbridge on 01264 81001) and I was most interested in Val's compact digital camera. It seemed the answer to my lugging an entire SLR system around all day when roaming, when all I required was a trophy shot pic for my weekly *Sunday Express* column. So I went out and bought a pocket-sized Casio Exilim, 4 mega pixel (the highest available at that time) digital camera, with a 3X optical zoom (which I never bother with) and a large display screen. And I'm pleased to say I've never been without it since. I particularly loved the ease of downloading and storing images on my computers hard drive, and the camera's self timer function that takes 3x frames at 10 second intervals. So I always carry a camera -bank stick thread adaptor for self photography. But more of digital photography later.

When my brother Dave moved home permanently to Thailand in 2002, I knew it wouldn't be long before yet another door to the fascinating world of international fishing became open to me. And so at the end of March my old friend John (Jinx) Davey and I made the long haul flight from Heathrow to Bangkok, to meet up with brother Dave and his lovely wife Boon, for a week of arm wrenching encounters with a phenomenally powerful species called 'Pla Buk', the legendary Mekong catfish.

I had expected to be fishing one of Thailand's wide, jungle-type river systems for Mekong, but Dave was quick to point out that due to commercial netting, the chances of catching them in flowing water were rather slim. Apparently even the Mekong River itself, once famous for producing the worlds largest freshwater catfish, monsters in the 400-600lbs bracket had suffered badly, and that now such leviathans were so thin on the ground, angling for them was actually prohibited.

Close to where Dave and Boon live however along the Gulf of Thailand coastline in the town of Hua Hin, (130 miles south of Bangkok) one of the many lakes in the area had been stocked with Mekong. Which is how Jinx and I came to fish the Cha am Fish Park with Dave. A tree lined heavily coloured lake of around five acres which slopes away from five feet deep in the margins to around 16 feet in the middle. And it's simply stuffed with Mekong catfish to close on 100lbs, plus several other exotic species from giant piranha's to Siamese giant carp. But Mekong catfish were our target species, and we soon experienced why this particular fish has a reputation (well deserved in my opinion) of being the strongest battler in freshwater on this planet. To be fair to India's 'mahseer' however, which I have yet to catch in a lake, a true comparison cannot be made, but these Mekong pussies don't half have some stamina. Even a baby of 5lbs hooked close in on a substantial 2¾lbs carp outfit with 15lbs reel line, will pull so hard and for so long, you'll expect to see at least a fish of 10-15lbs when ready for the net. And those larger specimens of 40lbs upwards, 'well' even using a 30lbs outfit, the very same gear I use for Africa's 'legendary vundu', the Mekong is simply in a different league. And while the vundu can run much faster under pressure, it has nowhere near the overall stamina of the Mekong which derives enormous thrust from a huge forked tail and an unusually long anal fin. And phenomenal 'suction' with the bottom, from which it hates to be separated, due to its wide head. Its pectorals are also large, as is the eye, strangely, set slightly below a line with the jaw hinge, and if anything angled downwards providing it with poor peripheral vision. But tailor made for inspecting bottom algae upon which it feeds naturally. Though in Thailand's sport fisheries

ABOVE

My life-long pal
John 'Jinx' Davey
from Bungay in
Suffolk, cradles
a weird-looking
50lbs Mekong
catfish. Note the
wide mouth, low
set eye and huge
fins. A species I
personally rate
as the hardest
fighting fish
in fresh water
anywhere in the
world. Just one of
the many exotic
species we caught
with brother Dave,
from the Chaam
Fish Park near Hua
Hin in Thailand.

such as Cha am, everything stocked has been weaned onto bread.

The technique used by most Thais to catch these enigmatic catfish, and the several species of carp also present in Cha am, is so unusual it deserves explanation. But I would have to be feeling particularly courageous to use it in the UK for carp. Though I guess on small, highly stocked commercial waters no doubt it would work. It starts with a sliding float rig, (a large bulbous-pike size float) set with stop knot and bead to present the bait somewhere between two feet and 10 feet below the surface using a 30lbs reel line. The end tackle consists of a wire, coil-type method feeder tied direct to the reel line, with a hook length tied below (same as reel line) varying between just three and 20 inches long. The size 2 extra strong hook (it needs to be) is baited with bread flake, with the point and barb protruding, and gently nicked into an orange-sized ball of slightly dampened bread crumb ground bait, firmly squeezed around the feeder with both hands.

Upon casting out, somewhere between 20-40 yards, the rod tip is dunked well beneath the surface and line freely given so the ground bait ball quickly sinks to the desired depth and the float settles. Then the reel is put into free spool with the ratchet on. Personally I much preferred the directness of my 10,000 multiplier, although casting needs to be smooth or the ground bait flies off. Dave used a bait runner fixed spool and is prepared to suffer the inevitable 'line twist' that results. Though in latter years he has switched over to braid and suffers not. I just cannot wean him onto the benefits of multipliers.

Almost immediately after casting (Cha am is ridiculously well stocked) the huge float started bobbing away as carp and catfish attacked the ground bait. And when one sucked in the hook bait, bouancy from the huge float acted like a bolt rig, with the fish on most occasions hooking itself and tearing off across the lake, providing a screaming run. Mekong catfish due to the aggressive manner in which they compete for food seem particularly susceptible to this ingenious set up, and every so often either a silver, or red or giant Siamese black carp, known locally as 'Kahore' would grab hold. In fact these particular carp have been caught on rod and line from the renowned Bung San Ran fishery situated on the outskirts of Bangkok to close on 300lbs. The largest from Cha am topped 100lbs which is still one hell of a carp. Unfortunately, nothing over 30lbs was caught during our stay. But Dave winkled out a 25lbs beauty on float fished (using the 'lift' method) bread flake from the margins. What a breath taking creature. It was almost blue-black in colour all over with a huge head and bright red flash on its anal fin and a large mouth. Typical of cyprinid mouth filterers.

Humming in the strong wind like a taut guitar string, my 30lbs reel line scythed upwards at an acute angle, as over 80 yards out from where I was precariously perched on a huge slab of rock 20 feet above the lakes surface at the entrance to a wide khor at Sabora, the great fish shot upwards like a Polaris missile from 50 feet down where it had grabbed my artificial lure, a 110g Toothy Critter 'hot tail' shad. Yes, I was back out on massive Lake Nasser again for my annual safari on behalf of Tailor Made Holidays, with a party of Brits. Leaving Gatwick less than a week after returning from Thailand. No wonder my wife Jo reckons I get away with murder. Hope she doesn't read this.

Seconds later the surface erupted in an enormous kaleidoscope of spray as getting on for 200lbs of Nile perch (it could even have been bigger) attempted to tail walk in a shuddering, head shaking, gill flaring display, almost in slow motion, before diving deep down again. And fortunately, the single hook held.

Save for a 300lbs white sturgeon landed on much heavier tackle from Canada's Fraser River, this leviathan was by far the largest freshwater fish I had ever connected with. And though I've personally lost count of the perch exceeding that magical 100lbs which have come my way from the lake, the monster to which I was now connected, was in a different league to any of them, even my best, a 150 pounder.

After a further 10 minutes of arm-wrenching battle during which time it stayed deep down, I slowly and patiently (I wasn't going to risk hurrying this baby) managed to pump it to within a couple of feet from the surface immediately below the rock face. At something like six feet in length and two feet deep with enormously wide shoulders, it's sheer bulk viewed through the clear water was simply awesome and I was I admit starting to count my chickens though shaking with adrenalin. It then decided to dive down deep yet again, not liking the bright world above the surface, and once it reached a happy level the single hook of my rubber lure simply fell out inexplicably . I didn't know whether to throw the rattle out of the pram or scream. Few lost fish have ever affected me so. But that's life aint it!

The nice thing about this bountiful lake is that when you loose a biggie, another could be just around the corner, and I did in fact finish the safari with a beauty of 120lbs caught trolling a 'reef digger' lure close to the bottom on the edge of a deep drop off. Two other guests, Keith Potter and Steve Rutherford also accounted for 100lbs perch, while Dave Harding and Peter Plant both boated 10lbs tiger fish. Fabulous, fabulous fishing. But I still cannot erase the memory of that lost monster.

During May I was able to make up for my lack of sea fishing over the past months, 'big time', by visiting the tropical and beautiful coastline of Mozambique in southeast Africa during a research trip with Christine Slater of 'Tailor Made Holidays' and two friends, Dave Nevatt and Ken Sheath. Following flights from Gatwick to Johannesburg and from Jo'burg to Maputo, then finally onto Zongoene Lodge which nestles beside The Limpopo River where it empties into the Indian Ocean, our adventure began. Enthusiastic Zongoene guide Craig Harburan said that due to heavy rains upriver which had coloured the normally clear sea water, our best chances of experiencing what Mozambique had to offer lay with boat fishing a few miles off shore. And although we accounted for one decent leopard ray and several giant gar fish during a short beach session, he was so right. Incidently, angling guests at Zongoene have full use of Kawasaki quad bikes to explore literally mile upon mile of virgin shoreline. But due to the prevailing conditions, our destiny lay off shore. The lodge operates two excellent boats. A 30 footer sporting twin 225 HP Mariner engines and a 25 footer pushed along by twin Yamaha 115's. We fished from the latter, and took several small grey reef and black tipped sharks, plus bluefish, javelin grunters and a chunky 30lbs Limpopo grouper.

Big king mackerel, sailfish, ragged tooth sharks, bull sharks plus several species of trevally including the ledgendary 'giant trevally' are all commonly taken from Zongoene's boats, but with only a day to sample such a wealth of exotic sports fishing we had to move on. If somewhat frustrated by freak river conditions.

Our next port of call, Inhaca Island, lay due east of Maputo and produced some fabulous sport on both surface lures and the fly rod from an off shore reef within 30 minutes of our base at Inhaca Lodge. Ken Sheath boated a superb 15lbs yellow spot trevally which grabbed a Rapala 'Skitter pop', while I took on fly another yellow spot, plus a small 'GT', and lost two biggies that severed my 15lbs leader over the coral following lengthy battles on my 10 weight outfit.

We then travelled north to one of the largest archipelagos in the Indian Ocean next to the Seychelles, situated over 400 miles north of the Mozambican capital of Maputo to paradise itself. The Bazaruto Archipelago, which comprises five remote islands, offering truly spectacular scuba diving and sports fishing over pristine coral reefs.

Benguerra Island instantly became my favourite location when we teamed up with Benguerra Lodge guide Andrew Parsons who specialises in fly fishing for big GT's, king mackerel and would you believe 'sharks' over deep water reefs. Using Hi-D lines and large saltwater flies, we enjoyed unbelievable action with big trevallys, king mackerel and the largest shark I've ever beaten on fly.

For the umpteenth time during the hour long

BELOW

Beach fishing by 'buggy' is very much part of the fabulous set up in Mozambique where the Limpopo River joins the prolific waters of the Indian Ocean.

battle the unseen force dived deep again in an effort to reach the reef, ripping the entire fast sinking fly line plus 50 yards of backing from the reel against a heavy drag setting. And I was powerless to stop it. The eight foot, 15 weight rod, hooped over, as it had been from the hook-up, in a truly alarming curvature. Yes! I even started to ask myself why I'd hooked what was obviously a big shark, on a fly rod in the first place. But these

situations do sometimes happen in warm, tropical seas. And there are few spots around the globe to match the quality and diversity of tropical saltwater sports fishing that I was experiencing here in the Bazaruto Archipelago. Andrew Parsons had taken Christine and me out some five miles in a fairly choppy sea in his 17 foot boat to fly fish on the drift over a particular deep water reef. And first run through I hooked and played to the boat a sizeable green job fish. There then followed, using a 6/0 clouser minnow fly on a short wire trace of 60lbs test, a succession of big fish including giant trevallys and king mackerel in the 20-40lbs, each grabbed by sharks on the way up. Just when I was becoming confident of seeing them in the boat following fabulous scraps. Then the inevitable happened. A hefty shark actually inhaled my clouser minnow before anything else could grab it, which for a while felt extremely strange. It just didn't know it was hooked I guess. But guide Andrew had of course seen it all before, and reckoned I was in for a rough time.

He was right of course, but as Christine and I had landed no less than nine big green and yellow spot trevallys to around 20lbs earlier on in the day using small sardine live baits along an in shore reef, I decided to see if I could eventually beat what was obviously my largest shark ever hooked on a fly. My largest anything hooked on the fly, come to think of it.

Fortunately the 60lbs mono leader was not severed by the fishes rough skin, and so following an epic and knackering encounter I was able to play the shark, a black tip of around 120lbs, up to the boat where Andrew quickly touched the leader (to verify the catch) before it snapped the line itself while Andrew held tight, with a somersaulting dive, soaking us in a shower of spray.

The following day we enjoyed some great trolling for yellow fin tuna, big bonitos and king mackerel out from Marlin Lodge, also on Benguerra Island,

before sampling what Bazaruto Island had to offer at fabulous Indigo Bay island resort. And again, the trolling off shore for a variety of hard battling speedsters was fabulous. Dave Nevatt landing a superbly coloured Dorado that lit up like a neon sign. We shall all certainly be back again.

The Brits Vs Yanks second annual Shark Fishing Competition was held over a three day period from 22 – 24 June in New York state out of Montauk Yacht Club on Long Island, (a most prestigious and exciting tournament) which found buddy Pete Hazelwood and I with a free day before everything got under way. So we decided to find out what the general sea fishing was like off Montauk Point, by chartering *My Mate*, a 41 foot Hatteras Captained by Joe McBride with Pete Casale as mate. And am I glad we did, because from May right through until December the in shore fishing for striped bass and bluefish is quite phenomenal.

Later on in the year striped bass, which reach weights in excess of 70lbs but are common in the 15-25lbs range, can be taken on live baits using light tackle. But in June, apart from fly fishing the shallow water of the many inlets around Montauk, the deep, turbulent rips off Montauk Lighthouse, demand a stainless steel wire trolling line to get the lure down close to the sea bed where the larger bass congregate in depths of between 30 and 45 feet.

Two trolling techniques are practiced in these coloured seas. 'Jigging' and fishing the 'umbrella rig'. We started with jigging which revolves around trolling at around two knots, a green 7/0 buck tail parachute lure, to imitate the swimming action of the squid, by letting out somewhere between 80-150 yards of wire line behind the boat. Red, white and blue markers on the line at 50 foot intervals helped in depth selection, and once the skipper was happy the lures were fishing close to the rocky, kelp-covered bottom, we commenced jigging, which proved to be quite the most tiring and strength-sapping technique I have ever experienced. You simply hold the seven foot boat rod pointed at the lure with the 6/0 metal spooled (and heavy) multiplier reel beneath the rod, and 'jig' the tip smartly downwards towards the boats stern every three or four seconds until a bass grabs hold. The strain on wrists and forearms literally becomes intolerable after an hour or so, but it's a method that really produces.

Pete hooked up first, and following a scrap of several minutes our first 'stripey' was netted out by the mate. A superbly proportioned specimen of 20lbs plus, which in shape and fin structure was not unlike our British sea bass except that true to its name the striped bass has lines of prominent black 'mullet-like' stripes along its deep flanks. A most striking fish indeed and apparently exceedingly good eating.

Several more weighing between 25-26lbs came our way before the skipper decided to give us a break and change our single lures for 'umbrella rigs' which consist of no less than four attractor rubber lures and four rigged with hooks, (to imitate a shoal of small fish) with the rods held at an angle for the tip to show when

LEFT

Pal Pete Hazelwood and I experienced great action with numbers of big striped bass in the 20-30lbs size range, like these beauties, whilst trolling off Montauk, Long Island, as a prelim to the Brits V Yanks sharking tournament hosted by Montauk Yacht Club.

something had grabbed hold. A totally 'bizarre' rig to any British sea angler, but we did take several more 'stripies' (including two 20 pounders on the same rig-would you believe) plus some bluefish (up to three at a time) in the 7-9lbs bracket. What a mornings fishing. But it was nothing compared to the sharking tournament itself which is the brainchild of my good friend Christine Slater who operates Tailor Made Holidays in the UK. Held over three days out of Montauk Yacht Club, this catch, tag and release event, attracted a total of 48 competitors fishing from 24 big game boats, with one Yank and one Brit in each.

The boats set off each morning at 6 o'clock, venturing as far as 40 miles off shore to locate the most prolific sharking grounds, with lines in at 8 o'clock and lines out at half past three. This was all drift fishing using a rubby dubby trail of minced fish and oils to attract mako, thresher and blue's, which are by far the most common shark in these prolific, clear, blue waters, with a scoring system of 250 points for a blue, 350 for a mako, and 450 for a thresher, if beaten on a 50lbs line class outfit. Each angler using one 50lbs and one 30lbs outfit. But if the fish was beaten on the lighter (30lbs) outfit, each shark was worth a further 100 points. It was then a case of back to the Yacht Club bar to see who had obtained the most points, at the end of each day.

While most of us took the competition seriously, there was great camaraderie and many new friendships were made. Last year (when due to prior engagements I couldn't attend) the Yanks one by a narrow 450 points, so having been given the job of team captain I was rather hoping us Brits could reverse the honours, which I'm pleased to say we well and truly did by no less than 7550 points. Around 27-30 sharks. In all a staggering 839 sharks (817 blues, 17 mako and five threshers) were caught and released. Truly astounding fishing, (though this proved an exceptional year for sharks) even on a world wide scale. In fact I cannot think of any other destination to match such hectic shark fishing. I even clocked up my personal best mako ever with a 200lbs plus specimen and lost an even larger fish when the hook pulled following a lengthy fight during which the mako completely left the water in an explosion of a jump. But 'the' most desirable and outstanding specimen of the entire tournament was the massive 400lbs plus thresher caught by a Brit, Stan Povey. Another Brit Lance Briggs caught a 300lbs blue, and Yank Steve Veerkind took the biggest mako at over 400lbs.

Our British team won the coveted Sloan Shark Cup designed by copper sculptor Hanes Hoffman, donated by the Yanks team captain and event co-organiser Stephen Sloan, with prizes awarded to the top anglers and boats, and funds from the event donated to support skin cancer research. Top Yank was Mike O'Reilly and top Brit was none other than Christine Slater who also came third overall. What a great tournament, and well done Chris on behalf of all the British team.

I wouldn't want to be a charter boat skipper for all the tea in China. It's such an awfully unpredictable occupation, due entirely to our British weather. Take a trip I made for instance, only a week or so from getting back from Montauk, when I was due to be down at Lymington Quay in Hampshire on the Saturday morning for a much looked forward to six day trip over to the Channel Islands on board my good friend, Roger Bayzands boat *Sundance*. I'd been invited along by members of the Red Deer Angling Club in Totton, who were all bent on getting their string well and truly 'pulled' by the tope, bass, turbot, pollack, cod, and brill out from the Island of Alderney, our base, with accommodation and some sumptuous lobsters suppers organised at the Harbour Lights Hotel. But 25 mile an hour winds in the English Channel delayed our departure till the Sunday morning. Already one day's earnings lost.

We stopped to drift for mackerel in order to fill the cool box with fresh bait on the way over to Alderney, followed by one of the most hectic sessions of catching tope I've ever experienced, accompanied strangely, by lashing rain. Within just a few minutes of Roger putting the anchor down in 90 feet of water over a rocky bottom around two miles off the Island at 'Burhou', at least half of our 11 man group were connected to hard battling tope in the 25-35lbs range. The successful tactics being a fresh mackerel on a size 8/0 hook and 1lb of lead to take it down to the bottom. It was simply 'manic' fishing throughout the early part of the ebb, and I was kept busy on the camera with something like 20 or so good fish coming over the gunnels before the feeding frenzy started to slow down. All I might add were returned.

Needless to say everyone slept well that first night, and in the morning after feathering up some fresh 'launce' (greater sand eel) to compliment our stock of mackerel bait, we drifted for turbot and brill over a series of sandbanks only a few miles off shore where depths varied between 20 and 100 feet. Wilson accounting

for a 10lbs turbot on the very first drift. My largest ever. Several others to over 11lbs were taken plus some sizeable brill, and for the afternoon session Roger switched over to a deeper series of banks in order for everyone to drift for bass using live sand eels. And numerous fish in the 3-6lbs bracket were caught. What a great day out. But our euphoria was to be short lived. That evening the met office forecast gale force winds and heavy rain for both the Wednesday and Thursday. So we had to hightail it out of Alderney on the Tuesday evening having enjoyed just two and a bit days of our proposed six day jaunt, (a further two days earnings lost for the skipper) stopping en route back to Lymington over a deep water wreck to load up with some cod and pollack on pirks. Like I said, no way would I like to try and earn a living by being a charter boat skipper. And I certainly take my hat off to those who do.

Those who attended the 2004 C L A Game Fair held in July in the 'Capability Brown' landscaped gardens at beautiful Blenheim Palace in Woodstock, Oxfordshire (I felt back up to scratch again to demonstrate casting each day, following my tangle with prostrate cancer the previous year) will already know of the huge, tree-lined lake. But perhaps what isn't common knowledge is that anyone can in fact book, through Blenheim's estate office, a days fishing on this magnificent 30 acre plus water where great oaks and beech along with tall fir trees like the Cedar of Lebanon adorn the sloping banks from the palace all the way down to the boathouse. Great rambling bushes of purple-flowered rhododendron then take over adding a superb splash of colour to the jungle-like margins, interspersed here and there with thick beds of sedge and the dark green bulrush.

Incidentally, Lancelot 'Capability' Brown, as he was better known, and still is to this day, designed no less than 170 of the finest country houses, estates and gardens during the mid 1700's. From his first employment at famous Stowe in 1742, (I was fortunate to shoot one of my *Go Fishing* TV programmes at the innovative lake land setting, overlooked by those famous follies, several years back) this man with extraordinary vision eventually became Master Gardner at Hampton Court in 1764. He was of course responsible for many of the beautifully matured estate lakes we anglers fish today, where by the damming of a river or stream at the foot of the valley a lake or series of lakes were created that were easily visible from the great Halls owned by the gentry of that period.

Yes we anglers have much to thank Capability Brown for, because estate lakes are amongst some of our finest and certainly the most enchanting and beautifully matured of all still water coarse fisheries. And because most were formed by the damming of a river or stream with shallows at the streams entrance and the deepest area always in front of the dam, winter pike fishing for instance, can even become quite predictable, because the main concentrations of silver shoal species, especially young roach and rudd, will all pack into the relative sanctuary of deeper water beside the dam once the water turns crystal clear and temperatures drop drastically. In fact, in many of the 20 or so estate lakes in my home county of Norfolk and in Suffolk that it has been my good fortune to fish, many of which were designed by the great man himself, three quarters of each lake contains little in the way of sizeable fish once the severity of winter has set in. But I shall digress no further, so its back to Blenheim.

You can fish by boat only at Blenheim, (there is no bank fishing) and very good punts are provided for the traditional pursuit of tench and bream fishing on the float, from June 16 onwards, as I experienced when Masterline International Ltd representative and an old friend, Dave Barnes from Royston in Hertfordshire treated me to a day on the lake. And am I glad that he did, because right from our six o'clock start, those lovely slab-sided, olive-flanked tench decided to feed most aggressively, despite some bouts of heavy rain during the morning.

Dave and I first met over 30 years ago when I opened my tackle shop in Norwich back in 1971 (now no more) and he was the very first rep to walk through the door. But over all those years we had in fact never been fishing together. So the occasion definitely deserved a nice bottle of red which I'm sad to say went all too quickly while we set about sorting out Blenheim's wonderful stock of prime tench.

Our tactics were simple. Presenting baits like maggots, sweet corn, red worm and cubes of luncheon meat, just 30 feet out from the punt, hard down on the bottom beneath 3BB waggler float rigs, with a single no 4 'tell-tale shot' fixed just eight inches from the size 12 hook. And strangely, most of our fish which ran between 4 and 6lbs and which fought like tigers in the 10 foot deep swim, repeatedly making, long, unstoppable runs (fabulous 'centre pin' sport) showed a distinct preference on the day for luncheon meat. In particular small quarter inch cubes. Anything bigger and bites were a long time coming.

In total we finished with no less than 27 prime fish, several of which were slab-sided bream in the 5-6lbs range, and these showed a preference for a single kernel of sweet corn. What a fabulous day of continual sport. I do hope Dave invites me back.

P'ssst. Want to know the best kept trout fishing secret in East Anglia? It's a fabulous, four acre, unbelievably clear water lake by the name of 'Bean

Mere', situated on the Chigborough road near Heybridge in deepest Essex. (Tel 07702 244440 for bookings.) And it is extremely well stocked with monster, beautifully proportioned brown and rainbow trout (quite the nicest I've caught anywhere with huge, fins) ranging from around 5-6lbs up into double figures. Fish which are fascinating to stalk and 'sight cast' to in the clearest water I have ever fished and which when hooked, scream the entire fly line from your reel, right down to the backing.

Old friend Brian Furzer invited me down from my Norfolk home to sample the delights of Bean Mere, and literally within minutes of quietly stalking the banks using a 10 foot, six weight outfit with floating line and a 'long' 6lbs test leader, I was into my first fish, which I saw inhale the black Fritz lead head on the drop. And what a memorable scrap it put up, making run after run into the middle of the lake. Brian came along to do the netting, and as my prize came up through the crystal clear depths a rainbow that I had mistakenly guestimated at between 8-9lbs turned on its side to reveal massively deep flanks, and subsequently pulled the scales down to 12 ½lbs. Boy was I over the moon, but perplexed at my inability to put an accurate weight on the fish in the water. I guess it's all to do (as I have experienced before) with such clear water. Depths at Bean Mere for instance shelve down to between 12 and 16 feet in many of the gullies, yet you would swear the lake was no deeper than nine to 10 feet.

Though we hooked, lost and landed several more beauties of between 6-8lbs (Brian found an olive gold head the most successful pattern while I naturally stuck with the black 'fritz') my monster turned out the largest of our morning session. After which we enjoyed a bottle of red and a light lunch back at the Fisheries lodge which nestles beside 16 acre 'Home water, another of Chigborough's four trout lakes (I filmed one of my *Go Fishing* programmes there several years ago) where over 100 different birds have been recorded, including bittern and ospreys. There is also a smokehouse on site, and four adjacent coarse fishing lakes (three on day ticket and one 'members' lake) containing carp to over 30lbs, bream to 12lbs, tench to over 9lbs, catfish to over 60lbs and monster eels averaging between 4-6lbs, which are nothing to the 11lbs leviathan which is the lake's record. The lakes are open all year through and open at half past seven and close half an hour after sunset. Yes, I really wish I lived closer.

I never cease to be amazed at how frustratingly difficult the art of catching big fish can be one moment and the very next, surprisingly easy. Take a weekend in early August for instance when my wife Jo and I were invited over to famous Homersfield Lake, where the River Waveney is the county borderline between Norfolk and Suffolk, by owner and dear friend Norman Symonds for a fishing-come barbeque afternoon. Norman's son Martin was already fishing upon our arrival and together with his two young daughters had in fact been taking some nice carp using long range boilie and bolt-rig tactics, from a gulley running parallel with the first island in the 36 acre lake.

Being in the middle of a heat wave sport on the lake bed had naturally slowed down by our late morning arrival although there were odd groups of big carp bow waving through the surface film which looked as though they might be receptive to 'floaters'. And this was just as well really because Norman introduced me to 15 year old Ollie Burgess, whose parents had also arrived for the barbeque, hoping that I might show him one or two of the finer points of carp fishing. Something incidentally that I was looking forward to, on account of not actually fishing at Homersfield for the best part of 10 years (my how they fly – don't they) when I filmed one of my *Go Fishing* TV programmes, catching several 20lbs plus mirror and leather carp on a 9 weight fly rod outfit, using floating mixer biscuits instead of a fly.

I wasn't sure that Ollie would be up to the demanding technique of 'fly rodding' for Normans big carp however, most of which have grown on considerably over the years, so I made up an 11 foot, soft action rod with an 8lbs reel line and floating 'tenpin' controller rig, stopped three feet from the size 10 hook by a tiny rubber bead and five turn stop knot. And simply super-glued a 12mm floater biscuit onto the hook shank, having first showed Ollie how to cut a shallow grove with a piece of fine-tooth hacksaw blade.

It was time for a spot of serious stalking over on the other side of the lake where a nice 'chop' ruffled the surface and we catapulted out well upwind, enough floaters

BELOW

Young Ollie Burgess landed this superb 30lbs common carp following a long, exciting scrap using light tackle whilst floater fishing with me at friend Norman Symonds wonderful 36 acre lake at Homersfield on the Norfolk and Suffolk border.

to both attract carp and pacify the hungry attentions from a dozen or more mallards. We soon managed to 'feed off' the ducks from where our floaters had drifted beside a line of tall willows, leaving several big carp slurping the remnants down, in glorious swirls.

I suggested Ollie cast way beyond the feeding fish and slowly wind his bait back so as not to scare them, and this worked a treat when a monstrous, thick-backed common carp confidently sucked in his floater after two near misses, and went charging off across the lake. Ollie's face was a picture. He would happily have settled for a 15 pounder as his biggest carp ever, but here he was connected to a monster of twice the size. And that's exactly what the great fish weighed (exactly 30lbs) when Norman appeared with the scales and hoisted it up in the weigh sling, following a simply fantastic battle lasting for several, long, minutes. I don't know who was more pleased; Norman, Ollie or me.

Appreciating a raucous dawn chorus including the

SIXTY YEARS A FISHERMAN

bellowing sound of hippo's not a 100 yards from my meru-tented lodge situated on the banks of the Zambezi River, is what fishing in Africa is all about. And it draws me back year after year. Though elephants wander casually through camp, with cape buffaloes, waterbuck, wart hogs and huge crocs etc, all visible from the boat dock, I had in fact returned to the Lower Zambezi National Park, situated south of Zambia's capital, Lusaka, not for game viewing, but to do battle again with the legendary tiger fish and vundu catfish.

It's my luck that good friend Steve Maartens is not only the general manager of both The Royal Zambezi and The Mwambashi River Lodges, he is also top guide in these mile-wide lower reaches of the Zambezi National Park on the northern, Zambian side of the river. The southern bank belonging to Zimbabwe.

Tiger fish which average between three and 15lbs along this section of the Zambezi, not only jump completely clear of the water several times during the fight, they also have the largest teeth of all the species I have ever encountered in both fresh and saltwater anywhere in the world. They almost 'surgically' cut smaller prey fish in half, so a 30lbs braided wire trace is imperative whether fly fishing or presenting fish strip mounted on a 5/0 wide gape hook. Flies are best tied on size 4/0 wide gape hooks and need to be 'flashy' in order to score. Mwambashi guide Garth Hovel ties some great patterns with crinkle-flash wings in blue and white. A great colour combination. In one afternoon for instance casting from a long island to structure runs behind fallen trees, He, Steve and I accounted for no less than 42 tiger fish to 7lbs, all on the fly, in just a few hours, with as many missed hits. Honestly; what a memorable, arm wrenching session.

We caught far fewer on fish strip of course, but for a higher average size. My best pulling the spring balance down to 14lbs plus. A truly awesome fight from an equally awesome adversary. Drift fishing by boat is the most successful way of covering long sections of the river which generally flows at around walking pace, but in some sections is noticeably faster. The best tiger hot spots. My outfit being a nine foot heavy spinning rod and 6501 multiplier loaded with 30lbs test braid, plus 20 inch wire trace and three by one inch strip of fresh fish fillet. The cast is made 30-40 yards across and upriver so that the bait trundles back along the sandy bottom at current speed. And very effective it is too, the savage hit and run or a tiger fish bite coming at any moment. So it's best to keep the reel in free spool, allowing a couple of yards to be taken, before putting it into gear and tightening up firmly. Incidentally, no less than 39 double figure tiger fish were taken by our eight man party in six days fishing. Quite phenomenal fishing.

There are in fact some 360 different species in the Zambezi, with possibly only two other African river systems as rich. The Congo River with over 600 species and the Nile, which has around the same number as the Zambezi. The largest catfish being the hard fighting vundu.

In years past particularly when fishing on Lake Kariba , although baits like ox heart, worms, luncheon meat, liver, trout pellet paste and fish fillet etc all caught vundu, by far the most effective was a chicken egg-sized lump of the bog-standard African blue soap (made from animal fats) which slowly released an oozy cloud. And because nothing else gobbled it up, save for the very occasional sharp toothed catfish, it was the most selective vundu bait

by far, which could be presented on a 50lbs test monofilament hook trace without fear of it being bitten through by toothy predators.

Nowadays however African soaps come heavily perfumed and my favourite vundu bait seems to be obtainable no more. Such was the dilemma during our 'Zambian' trip whilst seeking vundu from the fast waters of the Zambezi at Mwambashi. Some of our 10 man party stuck to big cubes of luncheon meat (half a tin on a 6/0 hook), which only rarely attracts unwanted species, while the rest including myself took the advice of experienced guide Garth Hovell, and fished 'stinky' (two or three day old) fish heads. These were mostly from the favourite bream-like 'chessa', which are caught daily for use as tiger fish strip bait. And of course a nylon covered wire trace of 50lbs test was imperative to alleviate bite-offs from the occasional tiger fish and other species which ran off with them. I've actually known big tiger fish pick up a whole pork sausage (when luncheon meat was scarce) honestly.

All this naturally spawned a light hearted luncheon meat against chessa heads competition amongst the lads which, following several sessions of serious fishing, resulted in nine vundu and several double figure tiger fish plus, for Paul Dawson, a 19lbs Cornish jack, all to chessa heads, with only 3 vundu falling to luncheon meat. The biggest caught by Trevor Peverall. It was indeed a most interesting comparison. Most of the vundu incidentally were in the region of 40-60lbs and provided some long, memorable battles in the fast currents on our up tide rod and multiplier outfits and 30lbs reel lines.

For those contemplating trips after these fascinating catfish, it's worth remembering that areas around pods of hippo are often the best hotspots, because their excrement and muddying of the water attracts all kinds of small fishes and thus vundu. But beware of pushing hippo's into shallow water when positioning the boat. When cornered they could feel threatened and charge. So allow them to reposition in deep water before getting the rods out.

SIXTY YEARS A FISHERMAN

In November I returned to Lake Nasser with a party of eight Brits, where the best fish of the week was Dougie Davison's from Surrey, 92lbs Nile perch, which grabbed a depth raider, plug on the troll. I then popped over to the majestic River Wye in Herefordshire at picturesque Symonds Yat with Martin Bowler and Terry Thoebald for a spot of pike fishing and research. 'Theo', as he is better known, put us onto some simply mouth-watering barbel and chub swims that I hoped to feature if another TV series was (as it eventually did) to come my way. And we caught a few pike to around 17lbs in the fast currents on wobbled dead baits. A great weekend, but I was to really finish the year in style at the beginning of December when taking Martin Bowler and wildlife cameraman Hugh Miles out in my boat on the lower reaches of the River Waveney and on Oulton Broad. Because I went and fluked out a huge pike weighing 27½lbs which hoovered up a well-punctured lamprey head (there's more blood in the head end anyway) and gave a great account of itself, ripping line off and making some crashing dives close to the boat which was exactly what Martin and Hugh were after for their TV series *Catching the Impossible*. Hugh filming the entire sequence from line evaporating from the multiplier when the pike went off with my lamprey, to striking, playing and finally presenting to camera. It could not have worked out better if we had written the script ourselves. And when things actually happen to order, everyone immediately gets on a high. Incidentally. We caught a few more mid doubles on the Broad, all on static dead baits, but just one tiny jack from the Waveney itself during our three day stint. I felt so happy in having the guys on my boat and actually producing the goods.

Whilst pike fishing with good mate Nick Beardmore, also on Oulton Broad back in November, he told me something extremely interesting. That a colleague of his had just bid on eBay over £150 to secure a copy (long out of print) of my first ever hard back book entitled *A Specimen Fishing Year* which retailed at just £4.75, published by Adam and Charles Black in the heat wave year of 1976. It was a time

just before fishing exploded really, of pre-boilies, pre carbon rods, pre designer bivvies, when children started fishing by float for roach dace and goggle-eyed perch, and were happy doing so, and not double figure carp on bolt rigs, or some hole in the ground on the pole. The record for tench was just 9lbs 1oz, bream 12lbs 14oz, and barbel 13lbs 12oz. Most captors of such specimens nowadays would not even send their report in, let alone claim a British record. My how things have changed, and in my humble opinion not always for the good. And this really got me thinking.

Indeed, I'll wager few other angling writers ever have the chance of penning a sequel, to a book they wrote 30 years ago, and my mind was racing ahead with the unique opportunity of making comparisons about my own fishing, life style etc, and how attitudes have so drastically changed, that another, up to date year book could achieve. Which in a nutshell, is how my entire fishing year for 2005 came to be documented in a new title, *Another Fishing Year*, published by Green Umbrella and retailing at £16.99. A book which like the first, recalled in detail each and every trip I made between January 1 and December 31 2005, blanks and all. For I am of the firm belief that we all learn something from each and every trip whether we actually get to see our rod bend or not. But dear reader, my 2005 *Another Fishing Year* book, leaves me in no small dilemma within the pages of this autobiography. I'm sure those who already have a copy will not wish me to duplicate what they have already read about 2005. Then again, those who have not, will I am sure wish to know at least a few of the most important happenings. So here goes. A précis or very 'potted' account of 2005.

During the first half of the year on the local scene I enjoyed some great pike fishing by boat out on local lakes and the Norfolk Broads, with grayling to over 2lbs when trotting Hampshire's chalk streams, and chub to over 6lbs from my local River Wensum, with good mates Terry Houseago, Nick Beardmore and Jinx Davey. But I guess the best catch of all was my accounting for nine perch in a single

LEFT
I'm glad my guide 'Jim' was holding this strange-looking aruana. Just one of the many weird and wonderful species inhabiting Brazil's Rio Negro.

BELOW
Pal Gary Allen and top guide on Spain's Rio Ebro System, hauls out a nice pussy. Taken whilst trotting baits downriver from the confines of a small dinghy.

session from Buckinghamshire's Upper Great Ouse, all on ledgered lobs, which included five over 3lbs and three over 4lbs, the best (my largest ever incidentally) at 4lbs-10oz. Foreign adventures produced from The Rio Negro in Brazil, peacock bass to 13lbs and red tail catfish to over 70lbs, with several monster ton-up pussies lost amongst the plethora of sunken hardwood trees. 100lbs plus Nile perch from Egypt's massive Lake Nasser also came my way, as did 100lbs catfish and beautifully proportioned common carp to over 30lbs from Spain's Rivers Segre, Cinca and Ebro, with friends Simon Clarke and top guide Gary Allen.

From Jersey in the Channel Islands, whilst researching for TV on board skipper Dave Nuth's boat *Theseus 11*, I had congers and tope to nearly 50lbs, bass almost into double figures plus rays, turbot, brill and jumbo-sized black bream to over 4lbs. From the bountiful seas off Montauk in New York State during the Brits Vs Yanks annual shark tournament with Pete Hazelwood and Christine Slater, came bluefish into double figures and striped bass to 25lbs, plus numerous 100lbs plus blue sharks, with some great fly fishing action for stripers and blues with ex-pat guide Matt Miller out of Sag Harbour. A sharking trip I shared with my daughter Lisa incidentally, who caught far more sharks in the competition than her dad. Also had some sizeable blues back home whilst out with Dave Lewis on board Andrew Alsop's boat *White Water 11*, over 30 miles off Milford Haven in Wales. Again researching for TV.

On the local freshwater scene I accounted for some lovely big tench at close range on the float (using the lift method) from a local gravel pit, the best 9lbs-5oz (a personal best, and a fish that would have broken the

British record back in 1976) and enjoyed as always, amongst local carp and bream fishing sorties, the countries two largest angling events, the *Go Fishing* show at the NEC in Birmingham and the CLA Game Fair held in the grounds of Belvoir Castle in Leistershire. Enjoyed some autumnal barbel fishing with Des Taylor and Martin Bowler on the Wye and on the Lower Severn where it joins the Teme in Worcester, and then the tiger fish and vundu, not forgetting the spectacular wild life, of the Lower Zambezi River in Zambia.

Also during the autumn I caught numbers of salmon to 20lbs and sturgeon to 250lbs from the Fraser River system at Chilliwack in Canada's British Columbia, followed by another safari to Lake Nasser with perch to close on 100lbs. Then it was out to see brother   Dave in Thailand for some unusual and most exciting fishing which included finally landing a massive arapaima of somewhere between 130-140lbs after an hour long struggle all over the five acre lake, which included a hilarious (well it was afterwards) if somewhat frustrating 10 minutes, when it decided to swim into an aeration unit and out the other side. It was a fish I never in a minute deserved to land but miraculously did. From the same lake we also caught (South American) red tail catfish to over 70lbs, and numbers of swai catfish (a Mekong look-alike) to over 30lbs.

From Cha am Fish Park near Hua Hin where Dave lives, we had Mekong's to over 50lbs and a Kahore of 45lbs, while from Thailand's most famous big-fish lake, 40 acre Bung Sam Ran situated northeast of Bangkok we took Chao Phray catfish to 80lbs, Mekong's to 70lbs, swai catfish to nearly 40lbs and I lost another large arapaima on a live bait. In fact I have never lost or pulled out of so many huge fish either before or since. This was easily the most heavily stocked big fish water I have ever seen let alone fished (with continually rolling monsters crashing out all day and all night long) and also the most heavily populated; with anglers. You can imagine the noise, commotion and crossed lines that arise from over 200 people all crammed around its perimeter. At any one time, dozens of bent rods can be seen,

their owners playing Mekong's of anywhere between 20 and 200lbs. Fortunately however, Dave had the sense to book one of the 30 or so bungalows (wooden garden sheds on stilts) in advance, which are spread out one entire length and along one complete side of the fishery, which is an old clay pit with depths to around 20 feet. So at least we had somewhere to get our heads down during our all night and all day experience. One feature I really warmed to was delivery ladies on grocery bikes who took your order for cold beers and spicy Thai food, and promptly delivered it to where you sat. What an experience, is fishing at Bung Sam Ran.

SIXTY YEARS A FISHERMAN

The year ended with a pike session on a local lake with Masterline rep Dave Barnes, with fish to 18lbs and then a three day stint down south with old pal Bruce Vaughan to trot the Rivers Anton, Dever and Test for grayling. This included an over night stay and lovely day at an old friend's place in Romsey where Dave Stueart and his wife Kay (the most successful husband and wife team ever in the history of British angling incidentally) maintain a pristine length of this magical river. We had numbers of fine grayling, big dace, chub to 4lbs and Bruce had a roach over 2lbs.The sad post script to this however was that Kay sadly past away after bravely fighting illness for some time, a year and a half later.

Obviously I haven't included every session during this potted account of 2005, but what a year and so very different from 1976 and that *Specimen Fishing Year* diary. I now actually seem to fish more, and regularly travel abroad to exotic destinations (I never want for my enthusiasm to wane, though I guess old age will eventually creep up) with an equal love of coarse, game and sea fishing. Whereas 1976 was all domestic and mostly coarse fishing, plus a few scuba diving sessions into the depths of local gravel pits and weir pools. My aluminium compressed air bottle and demand valve are still in the garage incidentally, where they have lain unused for over a decade. Think I'm getting too old for all this physical stuff.

January 2006 started in traditional form with grayling down in Hampshire and pike from the Norfolk Broads. One, an 11 pounder from Heigham Sounds, had a flounder down its gullet in addition to my lamprey head. But local fishing was again going to take a back seat as Discovery Television came back to producer Tony Baines (now of Big Easy Productions) and I with a firm commission for us to film a new 15 part series that I had entitled *Dream Fishing*. All the research I'd done (which I guess most people never even think about) during the past two years had come good. Trouble was, I had already mentioned to Christine Slater of Tailor Made Holidays (way back in September last year) that as Discovery hadn't been in touch, (we had been waiting for several months after a meeting for a new commission) I would have more time for her escorted foreign fishing safaris in 2006. So with Discovery's commission contract suggesting a first screening date for the end of October 2006, (with TV it is very much a case of 'be there when they want you') I was about to be chasing my tail again and swanning off to fish and film in no fewer than 10 different countries in 2006, including Madeira, India, Egypt, Wales, Scotland, USA, Norway, Namibia, Canada and Thailand. But not before Jo and I took a long awaited break together in Cancun, Mexico.

Swimming with the dolphins and snorkelling in the warm water of Mexico certainly recharged our batteries, and at the beginning of February, cameraman Paul Bennett, sound recordist Dave Runciman and I flew off to Madeira to team up with skipper, the late Ron Cowling, hopefully to catch some big sting rays and groupers for programme one. But the fish knew better and after four days at sea with little to show for our efforts except a few moray eels to around 12lbs (hardly programme material, well not my programmes anyway) having already shot some stunning general views around the Island and an introduction at the colourful, fish market in Funchal, we had to cut our losses and return to the UK. Contrary to popular belief, TV doesn't wait too long for results.

Sadly, jovial Ron Cowling who did everything in his power to connect me with a whopper, passed away just a few months later. And that trip to Madeira was the only shoot in over 20 years of capturing fishing through the lens of a video camera, that I have returned WITHOUT a programme, or EVEN PART of one 'in the can' as they say. It was not a good omen I thought, for the very first shoot of a new series.

Ironically, our second shoot didn't start any better. Upon invitation from Rhys Llywelyn of the Wales Tourist Board who put me onto experienced guide Andrew Cartwright, on a lovely beat of the upper River Severn, I decided to film a grayling programme there. Wrong move unfortunately, because due to permafrost (10 foot high banks of snow lay beside the narrow roads) and the fact that nothing in the picturesque river was feeding, (not a bite from salmon par, trout or grayling on trotted maggots so something was wrong) I'd had enough of freezing my 'whatsits' off, wading waist deep in the river for an entire day in order to capture some stunning scenic elements on camera. So upon arrival back at our hotel, not wishing to risk the three days we had left, I made a few phone calls to the right people, allowing us to drive down to the comparative warmth of Hampshire, less the shoot develop into another 'Madeira', and filmed some lovely footage on the River Test, accounting for grayling to around 2lbs in glorious sunshine, with snow drops out everywhere and new born lambs in the meadows. We even had a buzzard fly, on cue, directly overhead whilst I was playing a grayling.

With giant Griffin vultures and Palisters fish eagles soaring high above the steep-sided gorge, making full use of the 'thermals' to spot their next meal, and a Barking deer calling from amongst the boulders and thorn scrub along the opposite (Nepalese) bank just below the thundering rapids, I moved a yard along the bank and made yet another long cast downstream and across, into the smooth, blue-green, snow melt-fed water in the hope that a mahseer would grab my Rapala fire tiger, floating magnum plug as it came around wiggling and diving enticingly over the smooth stones at the end of the glide. Had I died and gone to heaven or what? No, I was simply on a research trip in March with Christine Slater and a party of friends to Northern India after Mahseer.

That's how mahseer fishing has truly always affected me since I first explored the famous Cauvery River in South India in the state of Karnataka back in the 1980's over 20 years ago, with my old mate Andy Davison. Simply being there as part of the flood plain in a pristine wilderness, amongst the intense heat of 100

SIXTY YEARS A FISHERMAN

LEFT

In order to reach remote pools on the Maha Kali River in Northern India, we used inflatable's on our way downstream to negotiate several sets of rapids. Exciting mahseer fishing.

BELOW

The men don't have it too bad along the River Ganges. It's the women who make daily visits down the mountainsides from their villages to collect building sand from the river. British WAGS, please note.

degrees plus, with exotic wildlife in full view, is, and has always been enough. A mahseer, whatever its size is merely icing on top of an exceptionally beautiful cake. Not that I was ever going to taste this particular fish. The rod suddenly buckled over alarmingly for perhaps three or four seconds as 50lbs braid hissed from the multiplier at ridiculous speed, before springing straight back. Again, and something of a regular occurrence when lure fishing for mahseer, as opposed to bait fishing, the hooks had unfortunately not set.

At least here along the upper reaches of the Maha Kali River which for much of its length is the borderline between India and Nepal (yes we were that far north, in the foothills of the Himalayas) we were hitting into some fish. Rewards for the previous three days having been scant indeed, after our hopes were brought to bursting point by the sight of huge shoals of mahseer and several huge goonch gathering to be fed by visitors beneath the suspension bridge across the mighty Ganges in the holy town of Rishikesh. It had given us false hope however. For not only is fishing forbidden in this holy town, only vegetarian food is served and

alcohol is strictly forbidden. Worse still, upon arrival much higher up the Ganges at famous Byas Ghat, water temperature was below 50 degrees and our efforts could produce only the occasional baby mahseer. Their larger brethren were obviously in a state of comatose. Mind, temperatures didn't stop the women living in the village overlooking Byas Gat, dressed in pretty saris, carrying building sand back up from the river on their heads, several times a day. While the men rest in the village. How very strange our cultures are.

So we travelled on in an easterly direction and then further north in our Indian-made Bolero and Scorpio 4x4's for an entire day through the most beautiful of forest gorges in the state of Uttaranchal, to the temple at Pansheskar where the crystal clear spring-fed Sayru River joins the aquamarine, glacial-fed Kali, forming a succession of simply mouth watering pools. And here our fortunes changed immediately. Basingstoke dentist Simon Channing, who I last, fished lures with on Lake Nasser in Egypt only a year previously, really went and hit the jackpot by accounting for a superb brace of mahseer weighing 32 and 51lbs respectively. And didn't he deserve them, choosing to plug away throughout the entire night in a gin clear pool, (while most of us caught up on our badly needed sleep) where mahseer could clearly be seen during daylight, but which could be tempted to take neither fly, plug nor spoon. Although I did experience an abortive but 'clouting' take at dusk on a green and white clouser minnow. An excellent pattern for the river incidentally.

Simon's perseverance paid off again on our second night camped close to the pool, with a beauty of 40lbs, which immediately belted off downstream through a set of long, shallow rapids, and into the mainstream itself. A distance of fully 200 yards, where he eventually beached the great fish following an hour's running battle across large boulders along the shoreline. I am afraid I followed on a very poor second with a single five pounder that gobbled up a Rapala J13 jointed floater, at the very tail of the pool. But then it was a mahseer after all, and each and every fish here is well earnt, believe me. These northern Indian rivers are certainly not suited to the inexperienced.

Our trip was indeed an out and out 'boy's own' adventure, packing all the kit away and into dry bags every other day as we rafted downstream through stunning

RIGHT
The rewards are rich indeed when everything goes according to plan. British dentist Simon Channing with a 50lbs mahseer taken on a floating/diving plug from the Maha Kali River, following an epic, half hour battle.

SIXTY YEARS A FISHERMAN

rapids up to grade three, to explore virgin pools and glides of simply breath-taking splendour, and to camp out under the stars. With languor monkeys watching our every move en route, peacocks continually calling to each other, and at dawn, finding the pug marks of leopards in the sand close to camp, I cannot think of anywhere I have fished more inspirational, beautiful, or so remote. At the end of our week on the river, we were given the choice of going further down river to the waiting 4x4's, with the possibility of turning over whilst negotiating a series of grade five rapids, or walking up a hill to the transfer vehicles. Well, what would you do? Half way up the 'so called hill' I asked our tour leader how high it was. 'Oh around 4300 feet', was the reply. As the highest mountain in the UK, Scotland's Ben Nevis, is around 6000 feet, you can imagine why it took us over five hours to reach the top. Even the mules carrying our bags over took us all. Honestly!

During this trip incidentally I used my new Nikon D200, 10-2 MP digital camera. Shooting in JPG format rather than RAW, the three Sandisk, Extreme 3, One x GB cards I took along, providing me with at least 168 shots a card, even using large pixels and the finest resolution. Over 500 shots being at my disposal. The equivalent (in old money) of some 15 rolls of 36 frame rolls of transparency films, which amounts to quite some bulk to carry around. And that's of course only part of the benefit provided by digital photography. I did in fact return with less than 300 good shots after deleting the dross each day, although this tends to drain battery life significantly, going backwards and forwards through material. And I was glad I'd taken along a second, fully charged EN-EL3e battery. No electricity in the Indian jungle remember. Another wonderful benefit of digital photography, perhaps the most important of all to those who wish to capture 'action' shots such as big fish crashing and jumping out of the water, is the instant ability of raising the ISO number, which allows you to have both a high aperture for maximum depth of field combined with a high shutter speed to freeze the action. As I did when taking the

shot below of a jumping Lake Nasser Nile perch. Something that was only possible during the days of film, by putting a 'fast' roll of film into your camera. Something rated at 400 ASA or higher. Unfortunately, this made your shots rather grainy with a much reduced density of colour? This is why most experienced photographer's preferred to shoot on relatively slow films with a rating of 100 ASA. But with digital photography, increasing the ISO number merely creates what is called 'noise', a slight peppering of the shot. But only when you drastically increase the ISO.

When exploring truly wild, open expanses of inland water, the lure enthusiast has above all, to keep an open mind and be prepared to try various techniques. Because someone always keeps moving the goal posts. Lures that worked on one safari, and the areas where fish were concentrated, may very well not produce mere months or even weeks later. For instance, last November when I escorted a safari of Brits on behalf of Tailor Made Holidays to Egypt's massive 300 mile long, by 25 mile wide Lake Nasser, which stretches all the way from Aswan to the Sudan, the level had dropped fully 10 feet since my visit of the previous April. And now in April again, it had dropped a further eight feet since the November trip. Now that's an awful lot of lake gone missing (don't worry, it's still 200 feet deep in the middle) due I presume partly to reduced rainfall higher up the Nile, but mostly because of the new Toshka Canal and lake-land complex situated on the west bank 40 miles north of Abu Simbel, which constantly has water pumped into it from Lake Nasser. After all, Lake Nasser was constructed for the purpose of irrigating Egypt's desert landscape, in addition to providing hydro electricity from the High Dam in Aswan. So anglers have no say whatsoever and never will.

Trouble is, so far as the visitor is concerned, trying to locate Nile perch hot spots within an ever shrinking environment is far from easy, as favourite, boulder-strewn mountain tops that once produced a plethora of perch ambush spots and home to groups of big, resident fish, have now been left 'high and dry'. And this provided little opportunity for shore fishing along the western bank and throughout the middle section where our safari based itself. We concentrated or efforts therefore on trolling around sunken islands which were now thrusting out of the once un-fished depths, and around shallow, weedy bays where the tilapia were spawning-with perch in attendance. It certainly made our boat guides re-think their strategy in that we explored far shallower, weedy areas within the 10-18 foot depth band, than at any other time during the 10 years I have been enjoying predatory sport on Lake Nasser. And for these shallow plateaux which often are festooned with natural snags in the form of trees and bushes littering the bottom (these were never cut down of course while the lake was being flooded) one lure stood out in it's effectiveness above all others. Rapala's floating/diving Super Shad Rap, which on a 30lbs test monofilament trolling line, runs at about eight feet deep.

The relatively new 'jointed' Shad Rap incidentally, works a couple of feet shallower and was particularly useful when working over exceptionally weedy shallow bays. On low diameter braid incidentally, Super Shad Raps work a foot or so deeper, as does the CD (count down) 'sinking' Shad Rap. Which, because it can be counted down (at around one foot per second) before starting the retrieve, is also a most handy lure for working along shoreline ledges and casting to steep-sided rocky outcrops from a drifting boat? That dying (come and get me) wounded fish action of the entire Shad Rap family can prove devastatingly effective with Nile perch. In fact, if I were restricted to just one lure for fishing on Lake Nasser, both trolling and casting, it would be a countdown Shad Rap.

LEFT
The lake was exceptionately low during our safari. Something immediately obvious from the algae-encrusted rocks in the foreground (recently under the water) in this quiet bay where our boats were tied up for the night.

Every guide has his favourite colour. Some swear by fire tigers, while others go straight for a red head. From the dozen or more colour patterns available, I also like the shad and gold fish variations. And of course the perch colourations come extremely close to the natural markings of the tilapia, which are the staple food source of Nile perch. Although they also feed upon their smaller brethren, puffer fish, tiger fish and even baby crocodiles and monitor lizards, plus dozens of other weird and wonderfully coloured species inhabiting the mysterious River Nile. Anything that can be inhaled and swallowed whole by those huge, expanding jaws. They are certainly not fussy. And a buffalo (the name given to perch over 100lbs, due to their distinct humped back) is equipped with a mouth capable of swallowing a rugby ball.

For exploring deeper areas, particularly within the 25-50 foot depth band, we found the Magnum X sinking diver quite lethal. This relatively new addition to Rapala's extensive trolling range of plugs, is available in a dozen colour patterns and strongly constructed (so important when targeting Nile perch) with excellent split rings and trebles. Best of all, it has a huge lip which zooms it straight down to 20 feet plus when trolling at around 3-4 knots. On a braided reel line it reaches 25 feet. The thinner reel line really does make that much difference, where depth bands are critical. Although wherever rocks are encountered, as many have found to their cost, bog-standard 30-35lbs mono is far more durable and abrasion resistant and refuses to fracture across rocks as easily as braid.

Reef Diggers, Depth Raiders, Mann's 25 plus, and my old favourite, the aluminium Russlelure, also produced fish from the deeper bays and gullies. And for the rare occasions we were able to go ashore to work drop-offs close in, Bull Dawgs, and especially Storm Shads which have a large single hook in the top (so they don't hang up in the rocks as easily as sinking plugs) proved invaluable. And really, this is what working lures is all about. Horses for courses. It is imperative therefore, and nowhere is this more important than in wild, open waters like Lake Nasser, to know exactly to what depth each artificial is capable of reaching on the troll, and whether it will sink quickly if being counted down from the shore etc, long before you ever start worrying about its colour. Invariably I find myself thinking (about the differences in actual colour) did I catch the fish because of (its colour) or in spite of?

Due to the amount of times Nile perch must surely hear the approaching engines of trolling boats, a particularly effective ploy we have used in recent trips, once a fish has been caught on the move from a particular area, is to cut the engine and drift silently whilst casting. As a result, I'm sure many more perch have been caught by casting lures (or mounted dead baits) all around the boat, than by continuing to troll. You certainly become aware that temperatures soar to well in excess of 100 degrees, once the boat has stopped, and the 'silence' is most welcome.

For these tactics I very much like sinking 'Depth Raiders', CD Shad Raps and CD 14's and 18's. Each cast like bullets and will quickly descend to a take able depth whilst the boat drifts slowly along. And if the wind is too strong, we simply anchor up over different areas for around 15-20 minutes a time till perch are located. I would certainly advise anyone visiting Lake Nasser for the first time to persevere with these tactics, and for both maximum casting range and the subsequent enjoyment of playing big fish, to step down a notch from trolling gear. For instance, to accommodate the rigors of trolling an up tide rod (my nine and a half feet Masterline 'Voyager' rod was custom designed for the job) coupled to an ABU 10,000 or Shimano Calcutta 700 etc, is required. Whereas for casting from both boat and the shoreline, a 10-11 foot powerful carp or pike rod (so long as the handle is not over-long) or salmon spinner, coupled to an ABU 6500 or 7000, or Shimano 400 Cardiff, fits the bill admirably. My favourite being a BG, fast retrieve 7000c. Yes, I much prefer a left hand wind when I am shore or boat casting.

Incidentally, if like myself, you prefer to use braid for casting, as an insurance policy against chaffing and possible fracture from subsurface rocks, use a long (20 foot) 80lbs test monofilament rubbing leader. Easily joined to the braid using the unbelievably neat Albright knot.

On this trip the perch really were as fit as butcher's dogs, having fed up on breeding tilapia, and packed on firm body tissue since their own spawning back in February. In this silver condition they fight like tigers and really thrash the surface when tail-walking. That's what I most love about the species. Following a dogged, deep-down battle (possibly with a jump upon being hooked) they invariably treat their captor to some exciting acrobatics close to the boat. But as we all know, that's when even treble hooks unfortunately come out, and monsters descend back into the depths leaving their would-be captor shaking like a nervous fruit jelly and wondering for the rest of his angling life, could he have done anything differently to have changed the out come.

At this point, some say dropping the rod tip alleviates a break-off, which I guess is true for any fish which might fall heavily on the line. But with a slack line the actual weight of the artificial (big plugs in particular) tends to act like a disgorger. And perch have no trouble in shaking them out. So personally, I like to keep a fairly tight reign throughout the battle, progressively slackening off on the clutch as a big fish nears the boat or shoreline, anticipating one of those spectacular, last ditch dives on a short line (at which perch are past masters) when stretch is at a bare minimum. With braid it is non existent remember.

For the first trip ever on the lake, I actually witnessed the police catching black market fishermen. We were trolling around a headland at the time, and first noticed two 40 foot police launches lying in wait. Within minutes three police inflatables zoomed towards an island we had just passed, where fishermen in at least four black market rowing boats were about to lay their tilapia nets. During the tilapia breeding season all the licensed commercial boats leave the lake for one month, and anyone caught still gill-netting has their nets confiscated, their boats trashed and a year's jail sentence.

Half an hour later the same police inflatables passed us carrying several black-market fishermen to be taken back to Aswan. Though I felt a tinge of compassion, I also felt that if we in the UK were as a nation perhaps less forgiving to criminals in our now politically correct, nanny state (thanks to a decade of 'Blairism') trespassers against us might not be so keen to offend. But enough of my political feelings. Back to those lovely big perch of Lake Nasser, where despite low water levels, my back to back weekly safaris of Brits did manage to catch enough specimens in the 20-75lbs bracket, for a memorable experience, all on lures.

The big multiplier on my 50lbs stand-up outfit suddenly broke the eerie silence by clicking a couple of times (*Jaws* style) and then shrieked steadily as over 500 feet down on the bottom (yes, that's no misprint) the wings of a giant common skate were propelling its huge, flat body powerfully over the muddy sea bed. It had inhaled a 3lbs spur dog tipped with a couple of squid, presented on a 12/0 hook, and I quickly slotted the rod's gimble into my butt pad before winding like a madman till the 50lbs mono became guitar-string, singing in the wind-tight, and I could actually feel the awesome weight of the monster down in the deeps. Which literally felt like the bottom?

There is of course absolutely no point whatsoever striking with over 500 yards of monofilament out. The stretch factor alone is phenomenal. And phenomenal, best describes the arm-wrenching, strength-sapping fight ahead for anyone connected to these prehistoric-looking beasts of the deeps. Big men even, have been known to cave in and hand their rod over. For such is the gut-busting battle that follows. You cannot horse or power-haul these whoppers in. They simply beat you up. So a long, patient battle consisting of steadily pumping and regaining line whenever the fish allows, is imperative if you wish to see your trophy coming up through the clear water depths. A truly marvellous and memorable sight.

Yes! I was fresh back from Lake Nasser and at the beginning of May, out filming for TV again, shooting in Argyllshire, western Scotland, off shore from the picturesque town of Oban for my new *Dream Fishing* series. And filming this particular programme, doing battle with giant skate, I had been particularly looking forward to, because my 34 year old, pint-sized daughter Lisa was sharing in the action and most intent on landing one of the monsters.

When I initially rang experienced big-skate expert and skipper of 35 foot *Laura*

Dawn Ronnie Campbell, I asked how many days I would perhaps need to capture sufficient footage and his reply was. 'If you let me pick the best set of neap tides John, a couple of days should do.' Fortunately, Ronnie was slightly out, in that everything actually happened on day one, with myself hooking up to a real 'mother' of a fish, literally within half an hour of anchoring in 550 feet of water in the Firth of Lorne, less than 30 minutes out from picturesque Oban Bay. Unfortunately, this brute of a skate, akin to hooking up with an articulated lorry chugging along the M25, and which could well have topped that magical 200lbs figure, managed to slip the 12/0 hook, 30 minutes into the fight, just when I had managed eventually to prise its nose off the bottom (their suction is immense) and started to recover line. Boy was I sick.

Ronnie however didn't seem too perturbed. He certainly knows his stuff, this canny Scotsman, and I noticed the wry smile spread across his leathered face when an hour later my reel started screaming again. With tall, beautiful islands all around our anchored boat and families of seals covering the rocky promontories, it was difficult to imagine a more beautiful location for capturing British sea angling on tape, as I subsequently enjoyed a spirited battle with what was nothing like the size of my lost monster, while cameraman Paul Bennett changed position around me every 30 seconds or so to capitalise on a selection of angles. So important when it comes around to editing our programmes.

Up through the incredibly clear water (allowing us to capture excellent underwater footage) came my first ever common skate (a mere baby in Ronnie's books) an obvious male, with long claspers, which crewman and Scottish International angler Scott Gibson estimated from the weight for length chart (after careful measuring) weighed around 92lbs. Time has proven this to be a most accurate way of estimating a big skate's weight, and of course creates far less trauma than attempting (even in a huge sling) to hoist one up on the scales. The sheer, awkward size and shape of these fish being so difficult to deal with. I immediately noticed its huge, thick lipped, rasp-like mouth, used to swallow whole smaller specimens of its own kind like thornback rays, plus its staple diet of lesser spotted dogfish, spur dogs and crabs etc.

As both director and angler I was naturally over the moon, but there was much more to come because in the middle of playing my skate, Lisa had in fact also hooked up and 'big-time' with what was obviously a monster, by the look on her strained, but smiling face. When they suddenly power-dive straight back down to the bottom, it can be so demoralising, as all that line gained through exhausting, strength-sapping pumping, has to be recovered again. And a big fish might dive two or three times during an hour-long encounter, each occasion taking you right back to square one again. Talk about hectic sport. Any more action and our cameras could have barely covered what transpired, because nearing the end of Lisa's hour-long battle; yours truly hooked up yet again.

Now we had two whoppers on simultaneously. It was sheer, unadulterated pandemonium. From the get go, I had told Ronnie and Scott that I did not want a shoulder harness (laughs all round) and I was beginning to contemplate that maybe I should have known better at my age. But the old boy came through (the secret's in a steady, 'lift and pump' routine) and Lisa and I eventually boated giant common skate within minutes of each other following monumental encounters (both were females incidentally) of 190 and 182lbs respectively. Their huge, tooth-laden mouths easily capable of swallowing a rugby ball.

What a brace of fish and what a result. It was certainly 'job done'. It was far more than I had ever hoped. Lisa having stuffed her dad, again, good and proper. Her 190lbs specimen measuring seven foot two inches long by five feet four inches across the wings was in fact the heaviest specimen of both sea and freshwater species caught throughout the entire filming of my 15 part *Dream Fishing* TV series during 2006.

Did I lower a bait down again? Did I hear you ask? You have got to be kidding. The strain of playing three whoppers in one session was enough for this angler, who knows when he's had enough. Believe me.

Those interested in booking up a skate trip with Ronnie Campbell incidentally, are advised to do so well in advance. Telephone him on 01631 750213. M 07721 640024. Whilst in Oban we filmed a second programme on fascinating Lock Etive, a 20 mile long inland saltwater loch where Ronnie was in fact raised, after first filming the fish, seals and otters on shoe at the Scottish Sea Life Sanctuary beside Loch Creran. Certainly a number one visit for anyone touring the area.

Fortunately Loch Etive produced a wealth of dogfish, spur dogs and thornback rays, plus truly breath-taking scenery for the cameras, on a day that was so windy,

SIXTY YEARS A FISHERMAN

we would have otherwise never got off shore. So it was job sorted.

Our next destination or port of call as they say, was mighty Loch Awe, and while I rarely fish in British still waters between mid March and mid June, (what used to be the old close season) when Loch Awe pike fishing guide Keith Rowe, who lives beside the Loch in the village of Ford, recommended May as an ideal time for filming, I just couldn't resist the challenge.

A major feature of the Argyllshire countryside, and being some 25 miles in length, over a mile wide, with depths shelving to over 300 feet, this stunningly beautiful sheet of still water which is dotted with tree-clad islands, headlands and numerous pretty bays, and with a reputation for 'roughing up quickly', (as we were to experience) is in fact Scotland's longest freshwater loch. And while it is perhaps more famous for producing giant ferox brown trout to over 30lbs, the pike fishing on Loch Awe can prove fast and unbelievably furious with hard-battling, tail walking, breath-takingly-coloured and spotted fish, most prolific in the 10-15lbs range. Perhaps the incredibly clear, peaty water has something to do with their high metabolism. Who knows?

There are monster pike present of course and my guide Keith who has fished the loch for over a decade (Tel 01546 810371 for bookings) has taken some beauties to close on 30lbs. But with only limited time at our disposal to shoot a half hour programme, I had to be realistic and target numbers of moderate – sized fish to provide some exciting footage. And using freshly-killed rainbow trout dead baits, presented both static and worked with the ripple across mouth-watering bays beneath drift floats (sometimes with ospreys working overhead) we accounted for a plethora of speedsters. Which kept my two cameramen Paul Bennett and Steve Thorpe continually busy, providing unusually long and powerful fights?

In fact I cannot remember fishing anywhere, either at home or abroad, and I have pike-fished extensively in Canada's famous far north, where the pike fight for so long and so determinedly as on Loch Awe, repeatedly making run after run against the clutch. They have outboard engines for tails. Honestly. Despite 30lbs test braided reel lines on 6501 multipliers, coupled to my $2\frac{3}{4}$lbs test curve, 12 foot System pike rods, fights from fish to 15lbs were lasting between five and eight minutes apiece. I know this to be true because at night before dinner, as usual, I logged each tape to time code back in our hotel at nearby Kilmartin.

Loch Awe pike are also perfectly streamlined and proportioned, with huge fins. Which I guess is what provides them with such athleticism. In the words of 'Arnie'. I shall most definitely be back.

We were due to film tope fishing in North Wales with Charlie Bartlett and Dave Lewis out of Aberdovey at the end of May, but the weather turned foul during the two-day window of opportunity open to us. So coincidentally, having enjoyed a great day's fly fishing for trout at famous Lechlade Trout Fishery in Gloucestershire

with taxidermist mate Dick Brigham just a week after returning from Scotland, I immediately changed our filming schedule from tope to stalking brown and rainbow trout through the clear water of Lechlade Lake. Owner Tim Small and manager Geoff Davies pulling out all the stops to ensure we could capture the beauty of this fabulous two-lake fishery. And with both browns and rainbows into double figures, crashing about on a six weight outfit, I could not have asked for a more exciting replacement programme. I just loved Lechlade. How I wish I lived closer.

Following just an hour's flight from Norwich airport, the Flybe De Havilland turbo-prop touched down in Jersey, depositing the film crew and myself amongst some of the finest fishing within the Channel Islands. Yes, following some traditional June tench fishing (with beauties to close on 9lbs from a local gravel pit) I was filming again, organised with precision planning by Jenny Ellenger of Jersey Tourism, for my new series *Dream Fishing*.

It was great to meet up again with top Jersey skipper Dave Nuth and crewman Mark Andre, and we set off early the next morning on board 38 foot *Theseus 11* from St Helier marina, heading due west to a favourite conger mark. But first we had to secure enough fresh bait en route close to the famous 'Corbiere lighthouse' in the form of mackerel, which during the early light were stacked extremely near the surface, and came in five and six at a time on our sets of feathered jigs. I guess it's the boy still in me and all keen anglers for that matter, that makes feathering for mackerel so appealing, and it was hard to stop jigging and put the light rods away once we had fully filled a fish box. It was of course all great stuff for the cameras. Then it was time for the congers.

Situated around six miles from shore in 160 feet of water, Dave's mark seemed a curious choice for conger, in that the sea bed contained neither broken ground or rocks, nor any sign of a war-time wreck. Without question the pick of prolific conger habitats. But he certainly knows his stuff, and the honey-combed bottom obviously held immense attraction for numbers of eels in the 20-50lbs bracket, grabbing our mackerel flappers and cones literally within minutes of the 1lb leads settling on the bottom.

The beauty of presenting baits over ground where there is little chance of snagging up or an eel winding your terminal gear through rusting ironwork, is that sporting tackle can be used, and on just 20 and 30lbs test outfits, every single eel provided really great scraps, repeatedly diving back down into the depths again whenever they neared the surface, as they characteristically do, in reaction to the sudden increase of light. Their thick and powerful grey-brown backs and white bellies eerily visible as they spiralled up through the crystal clear water. Always a lovely sight.

Every so often a surprise would happen along such as a 20lbs tope, followed, several eels later, by a double figure Pollack. With such a melee going on down there, attracted by our carrot-sack of rubby dubby (cut up chunks of mackerel and sand eels) tied around the anchor chain, Dave made up a couple of really light rods presenting two, small-hook snoods baited with the heads of baby calamari, taken down by 8oz bombs. And in no time at all, we were enjoying the spirited scraps from big black bream in the 3-3½lbs category.

For a second programme bass and tope were our target species, and again, due to his immense knowledge of the seas around the island, Dave put us onto both species including some sizeable Bull Huss. So there was plenty of action for the cameras. What a great trip and what a great time being back out fishing with a good mate again. Incidentally, call Dave Nuth on 01534 858046, or 07797 728316 if you fancy enjoying what Jersey has to offer. We actually caught 17 different species during our weeks shooting.

At the end of June I enjoyed a fabulous week of filming striped bass and shark fishing over on the other side of the Atlantic off Montauk Point, Long Island in New York state, shooting footage for two episodes for *Dream Fishing*. It was in fact the fourth Brits Vs Yanks, Tag and Release sharking tournament held at Montauk Yacht Club, first conceived and extremely well organised by Christine Slater of Tailor Made Holidays who actually brought to the boat the largest blue shark of the three day event, guestimated by Chuck Mallinson, skipper of 40 foot *Joy Sea*, as being around 220lbs. This incidentally, equals our British record blue shark. But then inexplicably, blue sharks do tend to grow very much larger on the other side of the Atlantic. The all-time world record, caught off Montauk, weighed over 500lbs.

During the competition (with two Yanks and two Brits sharing each boat) in the heavy rips off Montauk Light house whilst catching fresh bait prior to drifting for sharks, and whilst drifting 30 miles out using 30lbs class gear presenting fillets of blue fish, big blue fish in the 8-12lbs bracket were very much in evidence. And on light tackle, free lining small mackerel chunks into the chum-line slick, they provided great action whilst awaiting a shark run. Unlike previous years however a glut of spur dogs all between 10 and 14lbs proved an absolute nuisance. Now I know most British sea anglers would relish a day catching specimen-sized spur dogs, but off Montauk they are classed as bait-robbing nuisances.

Also unlike the three previous tournaments, no one managed to hook into a Thresher shark. But Andy Danylchuk did account for a nice Mako. As expected, due to the late summer off Montauk this year, shark numbers were way down, though returns of up to nine and 10 blues to a boat made the tournament extremely competitive as usual, always with some noisy and lively chat in the poolside bar following each days drifting, and not until the final results came in at the end of day three, did we Brits find that we had beaten the Yanks for the third year running with a score of 9250 points to their 8050.

Highlight of my filming exploits however was interviewing the 'Monster Man', 80 year old Capt Frank Mundus, whose adventures were replicated over 30 years ago (by the character 'Quint') in that famous motion picture *Jaws*. What a guy, and what stories he had to tell about the huge white sharks off Montauk. Great stuff for cameraman Paul Bennett. It was indeed wonderful to meet up again with friends and to compare how our fishing lives had progressed since last June. And how lucky we all were with the weather. For on the morning the coach came to take our team back to JFK airport, the heavens opened with torrential thunder storms and the worst weather Long Island had seen for several months.

At the beginning of July the film crew and I had the privilege of filming at famous, 36 acre, Homersfield Lake situated beside the Upper Waveney which borders Norfolk and Suffolk, owned by two very good friends, Norman and his son Martin Symonds. Now Homersfield Lake is without question the most beautiful and prolific big carp water I have ever fished, with five large, landscaped islands and dense beds of beautiful red and white lilies at the house end. It holds an immense stock of thick-set monsters running to over 50lbs, with mid to upper 20's everyday targets, as I was to experience. The heat wave conditions however did make tracking them down (to walk, or in my case to 'stalk' all the way round the lake which covers a distance of over a mile) rather strength sapping. And although I did take a couple of 20lbs plus 'leathers' during the heat of the day by creeping about commando-style through the marginal undergrowth, with numerous refusals, only during the late afternoon as the sun started to drop, did they throw caution to the wind and show any real interest in my hook bait.

Casting into the strong southerly wind blowing lengthways down the lake from an awkward position amongst a marginal fringe of brambles, having catapulted free-helpings of mixers well upwind, I was able not only to watch the carp's reaction to my bait presented on a tiny (compared to the carp's mouths) size 10 hook, but also literally see the point at which to strike. And I lost out on several really huge specimens through nothing other than impatience. I simply struck before the fish, having inhaled the floater, got its head down beneath the surface again.

If a fish approached the floater diagonally from downwind and had to swim beneath the floating line, they would always refuse hook bait. So I became interested only in fish meeting it head-on. This in most cases resulted in a chance of hooking up. And to cut a long, extremely frustrating story short, where I genuinely had the chance of whacking into monsters over 40lbs (I pulled the hook out of one, incredibly long mirror that looked all of 14 inches across it's back) I did eventually connect with a stonking-great leather which pulled the spring balance down to over 27lbs, after one hell of a scrap. And of course this provided marvellous action for our two cameras.

With much of my time taken up both researching and filming, an offer from Martin Founds of Anglers World Holidays (tel 01246 221717 for information) to join him and Dave Lewis for a week in Northern Norway in July, could not have come at a more opportune moment. And I was more than happy, not actually having the time myself for research, because I first made programmes with Martin and Dave over 15 years back and trust their judgement implicitly. In fact their experiences with huge Norwegian cod in excess of 50lbs (Dave having now taken three over this magical weight) have become legendary in recent years. I'll even go further and state that it has totally resurrected the aspirations of British sea anglers who have sadly watched helplessly as their favourite fishing declined rapidly around the British Isles during this last decade. And I know Martin has every confidence that a British angler will one day top the ton.

That numbers of monsters well in excess of 100lbs leave the Barents Sea to spawn in the Norwegian Fiords, there is no doubt. The present national Norwegian rod-caught record standing at a staggering 93lbs. Just imagine the measurements of a cod that size? Whilst a leviathan of 105lbs was recently netted, coincidentally from the Joekelfiord area, bisected by the 70th parallel, and which Martin had arranged as our base.

These monsters of course are best targeted during March through to May prior to their spawning, but as Martin suggested that for settled weather, numbers of different species, and the delight of fishing in the midnight sun, but still with

LEFT

Holger Buricke and I show the stamp of haddock that are regularly taken on pirk's from the deep, clear water of Norway's magnificent fiords.

excellent chances of pirking up 30 to 40lbs cod, July was my best bet. So off we went. And he was so right. In fact I simply left Martin to arrange everything from the superb lodge-style accommodation at Tyrol House at the end of Joekelfiord, where Berger our host could not have been more helpful, to the flights from Heathrow to Oslo and then onto Alta, (just two 1½ hour flights) plus arranging two excellent and experienced local skippers and their boats.

Holger Buricke and his 27 foot *Tempest 750 Capelli Rib*, sporting a 200 HP Suzuki outboard which whisked us along at over 50 knots in the quieter waters of the steep-sided, snow-topped mountain, fiords. And Knute-Arne Mikalsen whose 35 foot boat *Skarungen* provided an excellent and most stable platform for filming in rougher conditions. Actually, sea fishing amongst these stunningly beautiful fiords, most of which offer calm conditions regardless of wind direction, in depths down to 300 feet in the clearest saltwater you have ever seen, was a completely new experience for me. And one not unlike the sea lochs of the Scottish Highlands, but without question, the most bountiful temperate, saltwater sport I have ever experienced. It must rate as the very best in Northern Europe.

Whilst pirking for coalfish with Holger for instance at an unbelievably prolific hotspot known as the Straumen (which simply means a force of water) where the waters of two fiords narrow and shelve down steeply just before a road bridge, I repeatedly watched my 2oz pirk, 20-30 feet beneath the boat above a kelp and gravel covered bottom being constantly attacked by small coalfish, before being inhaled by cod in the 5-12lbs bracket. A sight I had never before witnessed. Such is the clarity of water and sheer numbers of fish.

At this location, one of several we tried over a three day period (catching everywhere incidentally) we were merely light tackle, fun fishing for coalfish with double figure cod as bonus fish. One reason I stuck to 20lbs test braid and the 12lbs test tip of my (3 tip) Masterline, Tide Line system boat rod, for maximum enjoyment. But then every so often a whopper would grab hold of a small coalfish and go chugging powerfully around before coming off. Our trebles on the 2oz pirks being far too small to secure a hook up. On a couple of occasions, 30lbs plus cod actually followed smaller hooked cod right up to the surface. Being three feet in length, we were in no doubt whatsoever of their size. What a place. I have never before in temperate waters seen so much action from gulls and terns on the surface as tiny herrings and sand eels were being continually pushed up by vast shoals (we are talking acres here) of 2-4lbs coalfish. With very much larger coalfish and cod beneath the schoolies.

Having taken my fly rod along on Martins advice, I devoted a couple of hours one afternoon to purposefully catching coalfish on the fly for our two cameras. And didn't they go on an 8 weight outfit. How I wished I'd used it to catch those cod at the Straumen. Yes cod on the fly here, in addition to coal fish is indeed an everyday possibility. And with Atlantic salmon constantly running between one fiord and another from late July into August, and numbers of resident char in some of the off-fiord land-locked lakes, fly outfits from 7-10 weight with fast-sinking lines of several densities, will be amongst my kit when I return as I most certainly will.

A shrimp pattern that I usually use in shallow water for bonefish in warm tropical shallows certainly did the business with schoolie coalfish, being taken down to between 15 and 20 feet by my fast sinking, Hi D line. But I am sure any of the clouser minnow and deceiver patterns stacked in my fly box would have been equally effective. There are just so many fish about.

When Dave Lewis arrived half way through the week (he could only make the latter half of the week due to prior arrangements) we joined Knute on board *Skarungen* and having purposefully chosen a clear, sunny evening so we could appreciate and film 'the unique midnight sun experience', headed out of Joekelfiord into the mouth of Kvaenangen Fiord to fish a huge, mile-long reef known as the 'Amundsbaan'where, literally all night long, in depths varying between 100-170 feet, using 6-10oz pirks over the rocky, kelp-covered bottom, on 40lbs test braid with an 80lbs test mono rubbing leader, we really got among some lunker cod, specimen haddock into double figures, wolf fish, brosma, ling, redfish, and of course coalfish by the thousand, including individuals approaching double figures.

We were literally fishing 300 miles above the Arctic Circle, where from mid May till the end of July, darkness simply does not occur. It's a truly fascinating experience because it's like a sunny day all night long. And you can take a photograph without flash at any time.

By using multipliers with sensitive lever drags and large diameter spools for maximum line recovery, plus rods with forgiving tips, (as usual I found my Masterline 9½ foot Voyager rod perfect for the job,) we pulled out of surprisingly few fish.

It was all simply marvellous material for our two cameramen, Steve Thorpe behind the wide lense on board *Skarungen*, always within a few feet of me and linked with sound recordist Dave Runciman. And second cameraman Dave Allen on board *The 750 Tempest Rib* skippered by Holger, getting the reverse shots. The idea, as always, being to get the two boats drifting at a certain angle and a certain distance from each other for each cameraman to capture both Dave and I pirking or playing fish, without the other cameraman in shot. This proved a nightmare much of the time however because the lighter boat drifted faster and was always drifting into Steve Thorpe's frame. But that's fishing and filming for you.

Peter Trott of the Cornish Lure Company who specialises in pirks for fishing these fiords sent me a batch to try, and while they all caught fish,(would you believe I didn't loose one all week) I found the 'wiggler', a chrome lure sporting a huge, size 10/0 treble hook, particularly productive when jerked in an erratic manner.

Most hook-ups coming at the end of its fluttering descent, immediately before jerking it upwards again. And due to the level at which their prey, the coalfish were holding, hits could literally come anywhere between 20 foot down and the bottom. Talk about hectic and exciting pirking, if somewhat tiring.

Super strong split rings and swivels are of course imperative for targeting these big cod, as are huge 10/0 and yes, 12/0 trebles. Go much smaller and you hook up on too many smaller cod and coalfish all of which can actually get all three prongs of a 6/0 treble say, into their mouths. Bigger trebles definitely target bigger fish. Dave boating a long, lean monster of 36lbs and myself one of 34lbs, (my largest ever incidentally) amongst literally dozens and dozens of 20lbs plus fish. Three months earlier and 40lbs plus cod would have featured for certain, because all our big fish were spawned-out females.

Personally, I would love to have put in some time targeting a big halibut (they have been caught locally to over 200lbs) or gone for plaice which are regularly taken in the 6-8lbs category. But I was there to work (yes! making fishing programmes is work, just ask Martin or Dave) and at the end of the day we came away with two wonderfully fish-packed half hour episodes, so we were both more than delighted with the results, of beautiful big fish in truly awesome, breath-taking surroundings. What more can a man want?

No sooner had I returned from Norway in mid July, (how I wished I could have spent another week there) when another programme needed to be filmed. And this location I was very much looking forward to, the majestic River Wye. From its source amongst the mountains of mid Wales where trout and grayling predominate, through to the wide middle reaches, famous for salmon, shad, and a variety of coarse species, the majestic River Wye meanders on a southerly course through patchwork farmlands and steep gorges finally to empty its life into the Bristol Channel. It is arguably not only Britain's most picturesque river; it is also unbelievably prolific and delightfully challenging to fish. As fellow angling

SIXTY YEARS A FISHERMAN

writer Martin Bowler and I experienced having been invited to film for TV the wonderful chub and barbel fishing by The Wye and Usk Foundation, who issue day tickets to fish for salmon, trout and coarse fish along 80 miles of these two rivers from just above Builth Wells to below Hereford. The Foundations website is www.wyeuskfoundation.org or, you can ring the booking office on 01982 551520 to reserve a days sport.

Initially Martin and I tried the 'static' approach in the upper reaches immediately below Builth Wells, along the Rectory beat, which like much of the river is bedrock dominated with numerous mouth-watering, white water pools and long, smooth glides, ledgering halibut pellets over loose feed, and then long trotting the same runs with pellet and sweet corn whilst wading in midstream. Both methods produced, but a more mobile approach of casting upstream and rolling single hook baits such as a chunk of meat or large halibut pellet along with the flow, using minimal weight on the line, for a more natural presentation, was what those chub and particularly the barbel, really wanted. Not an easy technique, being continually on the move, for our two TV cameras to follow. So Martin and I were somewhat restricted, but managed to produce results amidst what can only be described as truly stunning scenery.

Virtually everywhere we caught nice chub in the 3-4lbs range, though we were informed that specimens over 6lbs are not uncommon. What I personally liked most in these upper reaches was the totally unspoilt surroundings and profusion of wild flowers colouring the steep, rocky bank sides. And it was just as beautiful as we made our way downriver through various beats into the wider, middle reaches around Hereford, where the specialist angler can add big pike to the list of species expected. Monsters over 30lbs are taken every winter from the Wye, and wouldn't a 30lbs river pike be something to aim for?

But on this trip we were specifically targeting barbel for my *Dream Fishing* series, and when we finally got a shoal feeding on loose fed halibut pellets, the action was fast and furious, despite the canoes which every so often come through your swim. I am afraid canoeists are very much a part of the River Wye Valley. But the barbel are obviously used to them, because we sometimes hooked up, using flat, 2oz leads to hold steady in the strong flow, literally within minutes of canoes passing through. Wye barbel are characteristically long and lean, and they fight like stink, helped of

BELOW

A still shot taken whilst we were filming chub and barbel fishing on the lovely River Wye for my *Dream Fishing* series. (Left to right, Pete Eveson, second camera. Steve Thorpe, main camera. Dave Runciman, sound. Myself with chub, and Martin Bowler.)

course by the strong current, and the string of beauties we caught, all between 6 and 9lbs, were the most exciting and hardest fighting I have ever caught. I would have dearly loved to fish some of the swims we didn't film later on in the evening. I'm sure double figure barbel were on the cards. But as I needed to log our day's shooting back at the hotel each evening, this was not possible. Nevertheless, another lovely and exciting TV shoot completed.

There can be few more picturesque spots in Wales, than the rugged and incredibly beautiful Pembrokeshire coastline, where the port of Milford Haven with its natural Fiord-like qualities affords the quickest route due west out to the edge of the gulf stream. And here, in depths of between 250 and 400 feet exist the best kept secret in British sea angling; shark fishing for both blues and porbeagles of a stamp equal only to those 'heady' Cornwall years back in the 1950's and 60's.

You want proof? Ok, here it is. How about a trip during August with old mate, and fellow angling writer Dave Lewis, on board Andrew Alsop's boat *White water 11*, whilst filming for Discovery Real Time TV. Even taking into account the slow and disciplined rigmarole of capturing the 50,000 Gannets on Grass Holm Island, plus mackerel fishing over the 'Barrels', on our way out to the sharking grounds, we still managed to boat no less than six big blue sharks on camera. Once our bags of oil-laced 'rubby-dubby' had been put over the side.

And when I say boat I mean exactly that. All six were expertly hauled into the boat by Andrew and his mate Simon Lewis, for unhooking and a clean release, having been hooked and played using barb less bronze, 10/0 hooks, on just 30lbs test outfits, which really allowed these long, and colourful sharks to show their true fighting capabilities. Stand-up scraps with these athletic sharks are surpassed by few other encounters within British waters. Believe me.

In addition, another two blues prematurely slipped our hooks, and both Dave and I were adamant that had we stayed on an extra hour or two, our tally would

BELOW

Whenever Dave Lewis and I team up for the cameras, in this case a 'sharking' programme for my Discovery *Dream Fishing* series, we always seem to do well. Like this brace of 100lbs plus blue sharks. Never before captured on film in British waters. (Top right is Andrew Alsop skipper of *White-water 11*. Bottom right is his mate, Simon Lewis).

have been well into double figures. But as it was, with four of our six blues topping 100lbs, the best at over 160lbs falling to Dave's rod, we had more than enough footage in the can by the time we returned back at the mackerel staging in Milford Haven for around 7pm. To enjoy a 'ruby' plus a bottle of red or two at the Taj Mahal restaurant once we had showered and changed.

Dave was adamant that our final encounter, a double hook-up of 100lbs plus blues, (which, like all the others sucked in fresh mackerel flappers) and an absolute rarity of a 'trophy shot' has never before been filmed on British TV. This was most pleasing to say the least, so holding up close on 300lbs of blue sharks for the camera's, provided a truly unique end to our adventure out from Milford Haven. I only wish I lived closer. But with a round trip mileage of just over 800 miles from my Norfolk home, skipper Andrew Alsop, (ring 01446 710815 for bookings) is never going to be sick of the sight of this angler.

Readers may be forgiven for thinking that I forgot my local fishing during such a hectic filming and foreign fishing year. But nothing could be further from the truth. Due to a lack of space I just haven't mentioned most of the domestic trips. One very much worth a mention though, because in just a couple of hours, I accounted for my then largest barbel ever, during an impromptu session along at a favourite River Wensum haunt. And how I wish I had a fiver for all the big fish that have come my way over the past 40 or so years as a direct result of reading the weather or, river conditions just right, and then capitalising on a very narrow window of opportunity. We are often talking mere hours here, when through perfect water levels, favourable barometric pressure, or ideal wind direction, perhaps even an amalgam of all three, everything seems simply ideal for big fish feeding aggressively. And of course there have been far more occasions when through work or family commitments I simply couldn't leave everything and get myself along to the water at that precise moment. But every so often, it all falls into place and a whopper comes along to be caught with surprising ease. Which on this occasion came about due to my driving over the river bridge and seeing the amount of water forcing it's way downstream as a result of torrential rainfall during the previous 48 hours, following virtually an entire summer of dangerously low water levels when most stretches were so heavily weeded, you could have trotted a 2BB float down anywhere, even in the mill and weir pools. Such was the lack of flow.

All thoughts of continuing to remove the thick roots of the common yellow water lily from the now ridiculously shallow margins of my two lake fishery, caused by the summer's drought were quickly put to one side, as was the promise made to my wife Jo of fixing fencing panels that had come adrift due to gales accompanying the rain. Instead I bundled my barbel gear, landing net and a bag of baits into the back of the estate and high tailed it along to one of my favourite swims at the tail end of a weir pool where, due to a good push of water coming through the five

foot deep, narrow run, I just new those old 'whiskers' would be up for a ledgered, and hair-rigged halibut pellet.

I had not however taken into account the sheer numbers of chub sharing the same swim, all good fish too in the 4-6lbs category, but by feeding them off further upstream with handfuls of 8mm loose fed pellets, there was time enough for a barbel to move over my bait. And if we are talking minutes here, I guess that no longer than 15 minutes elapsed before arriving and my rod wrenching around into an alarming curve as a big barbel inhaled the 15mm halibut pellet and powerfully motored across the flow and then downstream and across the river towards sunken willow branches, making me begrudgingly slacken off the multipliers star drag. Yes, and I've mentioned the fact numerous times, I just love playing sizeable pike, barbel and carp using a small multiplying reel. The slipping clutch is so beautifully smooth compared to even the most functional of fixed spool reels. And after stopping the fish from reaching the sanctuary of those willow roots by firm thumb control around the spool, and allowing it to make several more powerful runs across the river, each shorter than the previous, five minutes later there it was at my feet, and I was staring down into the mesh of the landing net at my then largest barbel ever from the river. All 14lbs 12ozs of it. An incredibly chunky specimen for September, with immense width across it's shoulders, and a couple of days later I took one of 9½lbs from the same five foot deep run, but had little time to spare thereafter in following up on the two barbel. I was off again, not filming, but to Africa with a party of Brits to catch tiger fish and catfish from the wonderful Zambezi River, fishing out of the renown Ichingo Chobe River Lodge, situated at the end of the 'Caprivi Strip' where no less than four countries meet at the junction of the Chobe and Zambezi Rivers. Namibia, Botswana, Zimbabwe and Zambia are the countries, and it is a totally unique location because at no other spot on this planet do so many countries converge.

As our 18 foot trolling boat came around a wide bend, half way around the narrow channel, a veritable galaxy of predatory birds could be seen, including greater egrets, black egrets, purple herons, grey herons, squacco herons, and cormorants, all having taken up prime ambush positions amongst the marginal mixture of rushes, tall reeds and beds of papyrus, beneath which dense fry shoals had gathered. Talk about a boiling pot of action, where I was also enjoying the close-up view of a lone marsh harrier quartering the margins not 40 feet away, far closer than I would ever expect to see one back home in my local Norfolk Broads, when 'wham', over went the tip of my rod, as line simultaneously screamed from the reel.

Following a dogged fight I finally boated a modest-sized sharp-toothed catfish (called barbel locally) of around 7lbs, not totally unlike our own wels catfish, although it has a long continuous, dorsal fin, which, by the horrendous wounds and tooth-marks along its greeny-brown mottled flanks, had recently been rather lucky escaping from the jaws of a crocodile, proving that to most occupants of the Zambezi River, death is never far away.

I carefully removed my Rapala, fire-tiger, J 13 plug from its wide jaws and returned it immediately. It shot straight back down to the bottom, seemingly none the worse for its second, potentially terminal encounter, within a few days. These particular catfish being very much part of the local people's diet, and highly prized in the food stakes. As there are no Vundu catfish (the largest predatory species in the Zambezi, reaching weights over 100lbs) upstream of Victoria Falls, where we spent our first of the eight day trip fascinated by the sheer majesty of one of the world's seven wonders, sharp-tooth catfish, which can occasionally top 50lbs, provide great sport in the upper reaches while spinning, trolling, or on small dead baits whether static – ledgered or drifted along with the flow, in addition to the legendary tiger fish, plus a whole bunch of weird and wonderfully coloured customers from predatory breams to the strange looking bottle nose.

Although the group took several catfish during our short stay, the most successful method being to dangle fish strip baits directly beneath the rod tip into small gaps amongst the mass of marginal grasses, largest of the week was a long, 12lbs beauty taken, ironically, from a deep eddy just in front of the Lodge before breakfast on ledgered chicken liver bait by Michael Wadham. Our largest tiger fish incidentally, a superb specimen of 14lbs, fell to the rod of Dave Evans from West Yorkshire. Rapala's Super Shad Rap in goldfish and fire tiger patterns, out-performing all others.

In October I had two weeks in Canada, escorting parties of Brits on behalf of Tailor Made Holidays. And strangely, it seems that wherever I've been fishing this past year, both at home and abroad, river and lake levels have been way, way down. So much so, it would appear a world-wide phenomenon. Back in April for instance I spent two weeks fishing for Nile perch on massive Lake Nasser in Egypt, where the lake had dropped to 10 feet below all previous levels, and when barbel fishing the River Wye near Hereford in July, the locals said it was the lowest they had ever seen the normally gushing river. My own East Anglian rivers and local pits have never recovered from the rain which failed to materialise last winter, and remain pathetically low, proving that old saying 'February fill dyke' to be so very true. Which simply means that if the rivers are not high and full up from rainfall and back to winter levels by the end of February, they will remain low all year because thereafter once the sap in trees and bushes starts to rise at the end of March, any further rainfall merely gets sucked up to feed the vegetation.

When I fished Africa's mighty Zambezi River for tiger fish in September levels were also unbelievably low, with next to no water coming over the usually thundering Victoria Falls. But I expected some resemblance of normality when visiting Canada's western seaboard where the Harrison River converges with the mighty 1000 mile long Fraser River, the worlds greatest, undammed, salmon-producing river (with a run of 50 million fish annually, comprising of no less than five species of Pacific salmon) is always full up and flowing faster than walking pace. But not this year. The level being at least four feet down, exposing huge banks of shingle over which thousands of salmon can usually be seen spawning. Again, locals cannot ever remember the river being so low, nor anywhere near so clear for the time of year.

Now what the implications of all these statistics mean, only time will tell. But it is kind of scary. Not that low levels totally ruined our fly fishing for chum, Coho and sockeye salmon, although the significantly higher water temperatures and reduced oxygen levels, did make our party work all the harder for what are normally readily, if not easily catch able fish, because there are simply so many occupying each pool or run. And by stepping down to lighter, less visible leaders and smaller flies, whilst wading stealthily, some nice fish came our way.

Tony Loizou accounted for several colourful sockeye's including a 10lbs beauty while his father Louis landed a huge Chinook of close on 40lbs, (one of four he caught during the week) which took a silver spoon. We also got amongst the giant white sturgeon for which the Fraser and Harrison Rivers are justly famous, which gorge upon not only salmon eggs amongst the gravel, but also on the carcasses of dead and dying salmon. These they easily hoover up with their under slung mouths, and with a healthy stock of monsters in the 100-300lbs category, these prehistoric-looking white sturgeon provide the most thrilling arm-wrenching freshwater sport in the world. Leviathans have been caught here weighing over 1000lbs, making the white sturgeon the planets most readily catchable river species. And the technique could not be more simple.

You ledger a golf ball-sized clump of fresh salmon eggs wrapped up in a section of nylon stocking (honestly) nicked onto a size 7/0 hook and two foot trace of 130lbs braid, with a running lead above the swivel, immediately downstream from a boat anchored in a deep, fast run selected by your guide. Mine being Fred Helmer who actually pioneered sturgeon fishing in the Fraser Valley. So I was in good hands. The reel line is also 130lbs braid and

BELOW

Experienced guide Tony Nootebos (left) displays a superb double figure sockeye salmon caught by Tony Loizou on fly from the clear water of the Harrison River in British Columbia.

SIXTY YEARS A FISHERMAN

alternate baits can range from the head end of a lamprey, to a fillet of salmon belly. But 'egg balls' are the most popular and usually the most effective.

Most guides working the Fraser use high powered 20 foot aluminium jet boats that can accommodate three anglers and hit speeds of 50 miles an hour. So they are not afraid of trying six or seven different locations in a days fishing (often several miles apart) if bites from sturgeon are not forthcoming within half an hour of putting the anchor down. During our weeks fishing several specimens in the 150-350lbs bracket were landed, providing my party of six British anglers with their longest fights and heaviest fish ever from a river. The monster of the week following a gruelling, hour long battle was finally beaten by Steve Revell from Hertfordshire and estimated to weigh in excess of 500lbs. It took all the strength of five men to haul the specimen up for a photo session. What a fish, that jumped no less than eight times. Immensely thick across the back with a girth of 48 inches it measured over nine feet long. Such fish cannot be lifted into the boat of course, and in order to take a trophy shot, it is carefully towed into the shallows.

Usually, the gentle, slowly tapping bite of the sturgeon occurs within five to 10 minutes, if fish are present just down from the boat. The secret then, being to slowly sleeve the rod from its rest (so the sturgeon doesn't feel the line momentarily tighten or slacken) and whack the hook home hard on the next firm pull. If successful this immediately results in the fish ripping much line from the reel and coming straight up to the surface for a glorious polaris-style leap. Something it may repeat several times throughout the fight. But then there are fish which you never see until totally exhausted. The best sturgeon fishing on the Fraser is between September and December.

After spending over a third of my life behind television cameras, I should perhaps by now, be prepared for any eventualities. Through exhaustive and painstaking research I endeavour to ensure that next to nothing can go wrong when the crew and I turn up on a prearranged morning (usually booked up months in advance) to start filming, whatever the weather. And due to variations in climate, air temperature plus river or lake conditions etc from one day to another; catching fish to order is difficult enough in itself. Believe me.

Contrary to popular belief, and as I've mentioned before, 'Wilson' does not have his swims prebaited for a week before hand. How I wished! Frankly, I would do whatever it takes to ensure some action for the cameras. But the simple truth is, most locations would simply not benefit me from any kind of pre-baiting anyway. How for instance do I pre-bait a still water trout fishery, when the trout I'm after have to be caught on artificial nymphs or dry flies? Or loose feed the blue water off the East African Coast for a days trolling? Come to that, could I heap maggots into each and every swim I intended to long trot for grayling on the day previous along Hampshire's River Test? Without concentrating the river's trout population just where I don't want them as a result. Not that I have ever considered prebaiting for species such as grayling or for techniques like long trotting anyway.

Ok, so on the rare occasions when it has been possible to introduce ground bait or loose feed into a bream, tench or barbel swim prior to filming the following morning because I arrived the night before. I have done so. But not with the overwhelming results some might expect. Besides, in the world of filming for TV, as I have already indicated, there are far more important influencing factors than whether I can pre-bait or not. Take our November filming trip to Thailand for instance to team up with my brother Dave who lives out there, to shoot the last episode of my 15 part series *Dream Fishing*. Because in no way could I have foreseen that 50 acres of marshes adjoining the five acre lake Dave and I were going to fish, were going to be filled in (with all the accompanying noise) for re-development, on the very morning we started filming. Or that subsequently, a line of 20, 30 ton lorries filled to the brim with aggregate, together with six bulldozers would all arrive and start work literally within half an hour of sound recordist Dave Runciman switching on our radio mikes, and continue all day long for the next four days. The resulting clatter was almost deafening, and it worsened on a daily basis as the machinery got closer to the lake, only stopping when 30 yards away at a series of marker pegs.

Neither could I have foreseen that brother Dave bless him, would ram a size 1/0, heavy gauge wire hook into the second joint of his forefinger way beyond the barb, just when we were starting to get into some heavyweight Swai catfish between 20 and 30lbs apiece, and filming was starting to shape up nicely. But an hour later Dave returned from hospital minus the hook having had the corresponding jabs, and we started giving those catfish hell again. It's all part and parcel of being a TV presenter/director, though sometimes akin to banging your head against a brick wall. Like it's great only when it stops. Or in my case, when we have finally finished for the day with sufficient useable material 'in the can' as they say.

What I also could in no way predict, was how, after carefully playing a huge (150-200lb range) Chao Phray, 'programme-making' catfish for fully half an hour on 40lbs test mono coupled to one of my powerful 11 foot voyager rods, that just when its runs were shortening and Wilson was starting to count his chickens, the braided trace would suddenly part six inches above the hook. You can see the look on my face in the programme, but not my throwing the same outfit into the drink when later on that day, and again after playing another monstrous fish carefully for over half an hour, (this time an arapaima estimated around 300lbs, Yes! 300lbs) managed to reach the sanctuary of a snag and the line parted. How about that for a day's work. Getting on for 500lbs of beautiful, exotic, programme-making monsters lost in the shape of just two fish. No wonder my hair is nearly white.

On the plus side, the 'Wilson brothers' did however account for some superb and hard-battling specimens which really did make great TV. Dave and I both hooked into and landed Thai Red Tail catfish of around 40-45lbs apiece using chunks of ledgered chicken and chicken livers, in addition to a dozen or more Swai catfish on float-fished bread flake, using the lift method of course. I then took a couple of 'PB's in the shape of a 7lbs plus, thick-lipped, giant Gourami, more commonly seen in the show tanks of British tropical aquarium enthusiasts, which has distinctively long (12-14 inches) pectoral beards, and a 20lbs plus Pacu which fought like a demon. This deep-bodied, piranha-shaped fruit-eater (though I caught it using rice paste) is just one of several exotic South American freshwater species which have been stocked into Thailand's commercial fisheries. The 20lbs plus, tooth-laden, Alligator Garfish which also hoovered up Dave's chunk of chicken liver and which tail-walked beautifully for the cameras, is another. What a strange 'scaley', crocodile-like body it had together with short jaws containing simply awesome dentistry.

But the real *piece de resistance*, was the exquisitely coloured, seven foot long arapaima, (with scales etched in silver, olive and deepest red, and fully 15 inches thick across the back) estimated at around 170lbs by Hong, the fisheries owner, taken by Dave following a truly monumental hour long encounter through tree's, vines, around posts and through beds of water hyacinth. Truly one of the most impressive and colourful of all our planets freshwater species, which was caught using the simple lift method, baiting with a lump of chicken. Float fishing at its very, very best, and definitely one in the eye for carp anglers who believe that big fish only succumb to bolt rig boilies.I mean, lift method, chicken? Could Dave's 170lbs arapaima be the largest fish ever caught using the lift method? I certainly think

ABOVE

And here is the monster. (Left to right, held by Hong, me and Dave). What an incredibly beautiful and exquisitively coloured fish. Thailand has so much to offer the travelling angler.

so. There is however a rather comical element to this particular shoot, (although brother Dave would perhaps not agree) in that whilst my trying to obtain stills for articles and this book (with cameraman Paul Bennett holding my Nikon D200) the arapaima suddenly lunged upwards, almost knocking Dave out. I put this clip over the credits at the end of the programme. And if you look carefully you will see Brother Dave being 'nutted' by his fish and knocked almost unconscious.

Once back home in the UK, I made the long drive up to Kelso in Scotland where the River Tweed joins the River Teviot at the famous Junction pool for a spot of salmon fishing. When I pulled back the curtains in my room at the Ednam House Hotel however, affording a panoramic view across Scotland's majestic River Tweed at Kelso, on the morning of what was supposed to be the first of three days fishing, my heart sank. Yet again, like so many times before, whenever good friend Con Wilson (no relation incidentally) invites me on a salmon trip, rain had blighted any decent chance of sport. And following a round trip of 12 hours driving over 600 miles from my home in Norfolk to Kelso and back, to then be subsequently fishing for just five hours out of three days, would perhaps seem a poor return for effort. But that's never the thought taken by those who love to fly fish for salmon. Half the fun is the banter and crack in the bar and throughout dinner every evening anyway.

Besides, how was I to know that after the three previous days which had produced returns of seven, 12, and 13 salmon to nearly 20lbs respectively, for our six man party from the famous Junction pool (arguably one of the most consistent of all Scotland's salmon beats) that torrential rain which fell during the latter part of my drive up, would overnight raise the river levels by fully six feet into raging torrents and render them the colour of strong, milky tea. Completely ruling out any action on day one. So I immediately popped along to the nearest bookshop for something to read and spent the day relaxing in the drawing room.

Nevertheless, as we gathered at the fishing hut on day two to meet up with the three ghillies, Gavin and the two Billy's, visibility-wise, The Teviot, miraculously actually looked almost fishable. So we decided to scratch about anyway using short Spey casts with heavy tube flies from along the eastern bank of The Teviot, working slowly downstream towards the junction despite the river still being three feet above normal level and running a distinctly peaty colour. And 'hey presto' yours truly hooked into a sea trout of around 3-4lbs after just a few casts, followed by another of similar size lost, and then a reasonable salmon which inexplicably rolled off the fly as it hit the surface. But that was my lot.

There then followed a lengthy lull before ghillie Gavin banked a cock salmon pushing 10lbs to save the day, which came to a fly of his own tying and put up an exciting scrap. The one and only salmon we could muster collectively from the three days. Because by the following morning, overnight rain had again swollen both rivers. Why does it always happen to me on The Tweed?

Back again at my Norfolk home, as always, it was 'heads down' time for editor Keith Judge and I at Anglia Television as we put the finishing touches to a year of filming, producing 15 half hour programmes of my *Dream Fishing* series. Adding the respective sound tracks to each programme and finally the sound dubs. Something I always enjoy immensely, though at this point I just cannot help remarking that is it not ironic, that 15 angling programmes of my *Dream Fishing* series (commissioned by Discovery TV) were shot using Anglia cameras and sound systems, by ex Anglia crew, presented by an ex Anglia presenter (me) and edited by an ex Anglia editor in Anglia Television studios in Norwich. And yet Anglia TV, or rather, Granada TV who owns Anglia, were not interested in actually making it? As a TV license payer and angler (which amounts to one in every 20 persons in the UK) frankly I think TV hierarchy sucks. Towards the end of 2006 just before Christmas I was once again provided with a wonderful accolade from readers of Britain's largest angling publication *Angling Times*, who bless them, in a 'legends' poll, voted me at the top of their all time 50 angling legends. I felt immensely proud.

With all the filming and editing over and done with, and around 150 half hour angling shows and specialist video's and DVD's completed in the last 22 years, I started the new year of 2007 in a very relaxed manner, pike and chub fishing during the coldest times. The then marketing manager for Masterline International Ltd, and my long time fishing buddy Bruce Vaughan who now resides on the west coast of Ireland, always

Long time angling
buddy Bruce
Vaughan holds
up a magnificent
brace of River
Wensum chub for
my camera. What
a high average size
these fish are now
caught at. Well
over 4lbs.

try and work a few hours fun fishing into our working schedule whenever he pops over to Norfolk to talk about new products. And as Bruce's favourite species is the ever-obliging chub, we popped along to a fast, winding stretch of my local River Wensum for a few hours, to find the flow incredibly strong, following several heavy downpours, but the colour absolutely perfect for chubbing with a visibility of around 18 inches, though surface debris consisting of leaves and twigs plus the occasional branch or two coming down, compliments of recent gales, made ledgering difficult as we were forever having to gently lift our quiver-tip rods from the rests in order to avoid rubbish catching our 6lbs test reel lines and dragging the hook baits round.

As usual, our approach of making up two bucket-loads of mashed bread in my kitchen sink before dawn broke, and then driving to the very top of the fishery, introducing three or four balls of mash into every swim we intended to fish, before even fixing our rods up, really paid off. The secret being that each and every chub in a dozen or more swims got not only to feed from the mash before we fished for them, but feed without the interruption of our casting and striking. So they were consequently far more willing to accept our bread flake hook baits and bite with real confidence, as we steadily moved down river from swim to swim. Taking a fish here and a fish or two there.

It's a lovely way for two mates to have a good natter whilst sharing a few hours or even an entire day's chub fishing, because Bruce and I invariably share each swim, and strangely, without ever tangling up. Mind, we have over the years used a most workable routine. Alternating who has the pole downstream position (we sit only a few feet apart anyway) every other move. One fishing close into the bank, and the other making long, exploratory casts up to 30 yards downstream.

How many did we catch? I honestly cannot remember. Though I do know that we failed to get bites in just the one swim and took chub ranging from 4-5lbs from all the rest. The heaviest falling to Bruce at a shade over 5½lbs. And didn't they each battle away in the strong current. Chub are such obliging fish which provide such great sport during these cold winter months; I really do not know what I would do locally without regular access to them in these days of minimal big-roach potential.

In addition to Norfolk chub and pike throughout the winter, I also travelled south to Hampshire with long time buddy Simon Clarke of the Catfish Conservation Group for some hectic trouting at Dever Springs (with rainbows to 8lbs) and long trotting for her ladyship the grayling. I just love watching the strong flow pull my wide-topped chubber float along and the centre pin's drum spinning fast. It's therapeutic almost. And with a maggot pouch around my waist, and just the 13½ foot rod and landing net to carry, I can and do, wander for miles. As usual my terminal rig consisted of a line of six AA, bulk shot set 12 inches above three maggots on a 14 hook, tied direct to the 3lbs reel line, ensuring the bait (with a BB shot half way between bulk shot and hook) drifted along close to the gravel bottom. But with the usually gin clear water of a River Test tributary that I was exploring, noticeably coloured from recent rains, bites were not forthcoming from the main runs. As was the case in every swim that Simon and I tried. We simply could not buy a bite from the fastest part of each mouth-watering and classical grayling swim, as expected.

Truth is, grayling simply hate chasing after items of food which in coloured water (there was but 10 inches of visibility) they simply cannot see until the last moment. And not until the float drifted virtually to a standstill in the filter lane on the inside of a particular bend in almost static water, did it slowly disappear.

I struck from a mixture of both instinct and total surprise, but probably not hard enough, to feel that lovely gyrating, head shaking response, four feet down close to the bottom, from what could only have been a big grayling, though the stretch Simon and I were fishing is a highly prised chalk stream trout fishery, where big brownies are common captures during a day's long trotting. Unfortunately, this particular fish, and the biggest in the swim often get the bait first, promptly shook itself off the hook. The next run through however after nicking on three fresh maggots and keeping my eyes glued to the float throughout it's 20 yard journey around the bend, produced an identical bite from exactly the same, slack spot on the inside of the bend. This time the little hook held fast (a size 14 does look tiny in the jaws of a sizeable grayling) and following a fabulous tussle of several minutes with my grayling crashing about heavily all over the swim, with it's sail-like dorsal fin cutting the surface every now and then, I thankfully, eventually slipped the net beneath an unusually long specimen weighing 2lbs 2oz. The largest I had ever taken in fact from this particular shallow, ever-winding tributary, which for the most part is less than three rod lengths across.

And to think, following that first hour of trotting a dozen or so known grayling runs, with little to show for our efforts I was even beginning to think my long, early morning drive from Norfolk down to where Simon lives near Farnham and then onto Andover, was becoming a fools errand. But we finished a simply marvellous day, with 20 grayling apiece, including several pushing 2lbs, by adjusting our thought pattern to where her ladyship wanted to feed on the day. It was as simple as that, and 'coloured' water made all the difference.

BELOW
Catfish Conservation Group Secretary Simon Clarke, shows one of the magnificent grayling we caught long trotting from Hampshire's wonderful River Test.

Towards the end of February, following a sharp overnight frost of minus 3 degrees, I certainly had no plans to go barbel fishing. Besides, my wife Jo and I were looking forward to having our three year old granddaughter Lana for the day. But when my daughter Lisa rang to say Lana had a sore throat and wouldn't be coming, fishing did suddenly seem a possibility. So just before noon I decided to walk our dogs around the lakes to see what the carp were up to during what had turned into a gloriously warm and sunny day. And was I glad I did. Just about every carp in our two lakes were up on the top sunbathing and moving about looking for food. So, reasoning that as barbel are nothing but river-carp anyway, despite that cold spell over night, something 'within', call it that old 'sixth sense' if you like, told me that for at least a couple of hours, (till the warmth of the sun left the water) there was perhaps a window of opportunity waiting along at a favourite River Wensum barbel haunt.

Less than 30 minutes later I was sat making my first cast to one side of the weir-pool's main flush. I gave the two 15mm halibut pellet boilies, hair rigged to a size 6 hook, with a PVA bag of small attractor, feeder pellets gently nicked on, around 20 minutes without so much as a chub pecking away, (always a good sign, chub can be a nuisance when targeting barbel in this part of the river) before recasting. This time, to the opposite side of the flush, and again, nothing after a further 20 minutes. So I placed my third cast (using an underarm flick to start the small multipliers spool revolving) way down the main flush to where the white water waves converged with the backflow. An area of rocking water which looks fierce, but of course things are much quieter below on the gravel bottom. In fact eight feet down along the bottom, the current is actually flowing in the opposite direction to what it is on the surface. A fact I discovered many years ago whilst scuba diving the same pool. And following perhaps a 10 minute wait, while enjoying watching a pair of oyster catchers in the water meadows on the opposite side of the pool, stumbling and running along as they do, I suddenly noticed out of the corner of my eye, and felt,(I hold the rod all the time when barbel fishing) the rod tip pull down violently, a distance of a foot, no more, but because it stayed there, I instinctively reacted by heaving the rod back solidly, and that wonderful feeling of throbbing resistance was immediately transmitted through my Masterline 11 foot, 1¾lbs test curve, Heritage rod, to my forearm, as something with real weight to it started chugging slowly across the pool.

Immediately I knew this was a big barbel. I had no option, with a 10lbs test reel line of even thinking about slowing such a fish down, so whenever it ripped across the bottom, the line cutting through white water waves on the surface, I allowed it to go, holding the rod up high to avoid snags on the bottom, and for several minutes it was virtually uncontrollable, and truly, lovely, lovely stuff. For let's be honest, such encounters do not happen along too frequently in British freshwater.

After around 10 minutes, though it could have been longer, following several

SIXTY YEARS A FISHERMAN

more powerful runs and a little head-shaking, I had managed to work my monster out of the pool's main current and into a huge slack, where it chugged around for a minute or so before (as they do, just like mahseer) rolling fully spent up to the surface to display its broad shoulders and immense length before sliding first time, thankfully, into my waiting net. What a fish, and what a size. My largest ever from the river by far, weighing a staggering 16lbs 13ozs. I immediately rang Jo at home to ask

ABOVE

My largest barbel to date. A 16lbs 13oz monster from my local River Wensum. An opportune fish if ever there was one, which came in February at mid day following a sharp overnight frost. A 'hunch' that paid off.

her if she would like to come and see the monster and perhaps take some nice photos. Which she did. And then we went home.

With the usual annual demonstrations and forums to be attended at the Five Lakes Carp Show in Essex, and the *Go Fishing* Exhibition at the NEC in Birmingham, March simply shot by, as did April with trouting sorties to Larkwood Fishery in Suffolk and John O'Gaunts in Hampshire, followed by yet another safari escorting a party of Brits to Egypt's massive and truly enigmatic Lake Nasser. And what a magnificent time my eight guests had, with good mate Marc Pickering from Birmingham taking the honours with a superb 120lbs Nile perch. Then it was May.

Chris Tarrant's long arm tantalisingly held the landing net out over the shallow, reed-lined margins as I drew what would have been my largest ever grass carp (a beauty looking well into the mid 20's) towards the sunken mesh, following an exciting, surface-thrashing scrap of longer than I expected. And don't they go berserk in water temperatures topping 80 degrees. But it just wasn't Wilson's day. The size 6 hook presenting four grains of hard maize on a long hair, followed by a 3oz semi-fixed, flat lead whizzed past my left ear like a bullet, while the fish shot off like a bat out of hell. Boy, was I sick, but we were enjoying a purple patch and confident more action was on the cards from massive Lake Hamilton, where our pre-baited maize had attracted not our intended target of big commons,(the state record is 53lbs) but large groups of big 'lawnmowers'. Chris having already landed a quartet of beauties between 22 and 30lbs in the space of just the previous two hours.

We had been invited along on a research trip at the end of May to Arkansas in the mid southern USA by old pal Martin Founds of Anglers World Holidays who's brother in law Frank Cooper made up the foursome, and in fact actually accounted for our first 'surprise' grass carp, weighing 2ozs over 30lbs.Which initially we had

put down to pure chance. But here we were a couple of days later, having caught small mouth buffalo carp from the Arkansas River at Dardanelle, plus several modest-sized grass carp into double figures in no less than four different lakes, really getting stuck into some whoppers in the clear water of a most picturesque lagoon off Lake Hamilton. The state record for grass carp here incidentally is a massive 80lbs.

With Tennessee and Mississippi to the east, Oklahoma and Texas to the west, Missouri to the north and Louisiana to the south, the 'Natural' state of Arkansas (as it's called) is the very heart of southern, middle America. With a population of less than three million and covering an area 280 miles long by 250 miles wide, over 60 percent of this modest-sized, stunningly beautiful state, comprises of forests, lakes and rivers which contain a staggering, 54 different species of freshwater fish. Even more staggering, especially for visiting carpers, is that with no less than 12 species reaching weights from 40lbs to over 200lbs (alligator gars) seven are in fact carp. Indigenous species are the buffalo big mouth and small mouth, and buffalo black, with imported grass carp, silver carp, big head carp and of course common carp. But the best part of it all, is that local anglers rate all carp species as rough fishes, along with bowfin and gar fish, and so rarely target any of them. Except, alas, with bow and arrow. Honestly!

Naturally, Arkansas carp do not immediately recognise boilies or halibut pellets as food, and so basics like bread or corn were the baits to start with. In our case it was hard maize mixed with wheat, sugar and boiling water, and left for several days in a big tub to ferment and start stinking. A bait incidentally, that has worked for me with carp species the world over in countries as far apart as Thailand, Morocco, India, Canada and Spain.

Our base was at the fabulous Mount Ida Mountain Harbor Resort beside Lake

Ouachita (pronounced 'Washitaw') which at over 50 miles long is Arkansas's largest man made lake, and here, apart from a couple of mid double commons and several channel catfish, our pre-baiting failed to produce, possibly due to their late spawning. But Chris and I did get out afloat on the lake after striped bass one morning with top guide Jerry Bean, where Chris caught a nice double on a live shad. But as Jerry catches 30lbs fish most weeks, with monsters of 40 and 50lbs there for the taking (all stocked annually by the state fisheries department, EA eat your hearts out) he was disappointed on our behalf. The best periods for big stripers apparently is in April and October when they really stack up after small shoal species.

There is such a wealth of exciting freshwater fishing in Arkansas, and lets not forget the fabulous cat fishing for channel, blue and flat head (the last two both topping the ton) our six day research trip, wonderfully organised by the tourist board, seemed like merely scratching the surface. But back to those lawn mowers of Lake Hamilton where I was longing to see one in the bottom of my net.

After pulling out of that earlier fish I moved one of my two rods to face the neck of the lagoon, because we were certain that fish were periodically entering from the main lake to feed upon our carpet of maize. 30 minutes later I missed a wonderfully slow drop back, and upon immediately recasting and tightening up, had the rod nearly wrenched from the rests as I was about to clip on the indicator. Something big had literally sucked in my maize on the drop and was fast ripping line from a firmly set clutch. This fish felt noticeably heavier than the one previously lost at the net, but it wasn't until it finally came into view in shallow water following a powerful fight which included several blisteringly fast and long runs, that we could see its immense girth and length. It looked all of 30lbs and some, and Chris almost had it in the net at the first attempt, but it spooked and shot off at alarming speed when its belly touched bottom. So fast that had I not slackened the clutch right off and had my forefinger on the spool to stop it slipping (something I subconsciously do with big fish when they come close in) the 12lbs mono hook length would have parted for sure.

After several anxious minutes I worked it back close in again, (there was no way I was going to loose this fish) where Chris duly obliged with the net. Being close on four feet long with an immense girth I knew

BELOW
No wonder Chris Tarrant and I are smiling. He's just managed to net a huge grass carp, following a wonderful scrap for yours truly, from picturesque Lake Hamilton. One of Arkansas's premier carp fisheries.

it was well over 30lbs, but when Chris hoisted it onto the scales and gasped 41lbs exactly, we were all amazed. What a fish. Almost double my previous personal best, coincidentally from my own two-lake carp fishery in Norfolk. And what a fabulous end to our Arkansas adventure.

Following some lovely early season tench fishing along at a favourite local gravel pit, which produced several chunky fish to over 8lbs, all on the lift method, it's now all change as the 30lbs class outfit lurched over in the rod holder as yet another blue shark (my sixth of the afternoon) had inhaled a large mackerel hook bait, to set the multiplier screaming like a stuck pig. Using a circle hook there was no need to strike as such, simply crank down fast to stretch the line fully, while yet another 150lbs plus blue powered away beneath the deep blue waves of the Western Atlantic from our boat *Masterpiece*, skippered by Mark Assogna, and I settled down to another exhilarating, arm-wrenching battle once the circle hook had found purchase in the corner of the sharks jaws. What hectic and marvellous sharking we were experiencing at the end of June, on this, our last day of the annual Brits Vs Yanks shark Tournament (one boat alone accounting for no less than 44 blue sharks) hosted by Montauk Yacht Club at the tip of Long Island, even though big, double figure blue fish were a nuisance (yes a nuisance) at times actually engulfing our shark baits. The Atlantic off Montauk is so bountiful not only with sharks, blue fish and striped bass but tuna and marlin later on in the summer. Water temperature during our trip being just 60-61 degrees.

Now while there can be few Briton's who haven't heard of the little town of Amity, police chief Brody, and captain Quint, each immortalised in that blockbuster, and unforgettable motion picture *Jaws*, which frightened the hell out of us all when it was first screened over three decades ago, much of Steven Spielberg's footage was actually shot at Martha's Vineyard and subsequently given the fictitious name of 'Amity'. But where it all really happened was further down the US eastern seaboard off Montauk (just two hours drive from New York incidentally) where

SIXTY YEARS A FISHERMAN

'monster man' Frank Mundus (alias 'Quint' played by the late Robert Shaw in *Jaws*) during the 1960's-80's actually brought in no less than eight huge great white sharks (more than any other man ever) weighing between 2000-4500lbs into the dock at Montauk from the western Atlantic fishing from his famous wooden boat 'Cricket 11(copied for *Jaws*),now over 60 years old incidentally, and berthed at Montauk marina, still seaworthy.

And whilst competing in the fifth Brits Vs Yanks catch and release tournament it was my great privilege to meet up once again with the monster man himself Captain Frank Mundus, now into his 80's, and without doubt the 'godfather' of shark fishing. He alone (sadly and inexplicably not recognised by author the late Peter Benchley who chartered Franks boat to research *Jaws*) is responsible for why anglers the world over, particularly Americans, love the challenge of shark fishing. Pre-Mundus, sharks were sadly classed as 'trash' fish over in the USA, where to this day common carp are still shot in bow and arrow competitions. That's the mentality problem which has trouble crossing the pond. How for instance the Yanks can happily and repeatedly pull out 2lbs small mouth bass or 4lbs walleye (our zander) one after the other all looking identical in size, yet decry the power-packed fight of a 20lbs common carp, enough to shoot it through the head with an arrow, to my mind defies any kind of logic. As they say 'only in America'.

Frank however, has a great sense of accountability, and realises that whilst his escapades with great whites could in no way be duplicated today due to conservation pressure, we could do much more for the overall conservation of sharks, (hence our catch and release tournament, the only one of its kind run off Montauk, probably in the whole of the USA) starting by using circle hooks, designed originally for commercial, saltwater long lining. He maintains that leaving an ordinary hook deep inside a shark, (as many are) results ultimately in a dead shark. Whereas with most sharks hooked using 8/0 or 10/0 circle hooks (actually I had one almost straightened and I'm still wondering by what!) which end up in the corner of the jaws even when the bait has been deeply swallowed, where if the trace close to the hook has to be cut (you cannot always risk life and limb carefully removing the hook from a thrashing fish whilst leaning over the gunnels of a heavily-rocking boat) the shark will survive and either shed the hook or it will 'rust off'. Gut-hooked fish however do not return to fight another day.

Sadly, due to fishing solidly out from Montauk for five consecutive days, I didn't meet up again with Frank till an hour before we caught the coach back from our base at Montauk Yacht Club to JFK airport. But our hours chat, as usual, made my trip, which saw us Brits for four years out of five now, 'kicking ass', and once again beating the Yanks on their home turf by 34500 points to 32750. And as 350 points were awarded for each blue shark, over the three day event, getting on for 200 blues averaging well over 100lbs were in fact caught, tagged and released,

(mako's and thresher's were conspicuous by their absence this year) all on just 30lbs test outfits. Tournament veteran Mark Williamson from Manchester boating the heaviest blue estimated at around 400lbs. Not bad sport considering the British record is just 230lbs. Why we never see any of these monsters over on this side of the pond however, is rather baffling.

Incidentally, the world record for blue shark stands at a massive 550lbs, caught off Montauk from Art Cortes's 38 foot boat *Half Back*, upon which I fished for striped bass and blue fish over the 'rips' off Montauk Lighthouse with Brits Mark Williamson and Paul Taylor on the day before the tournament started. This was an entirely different kind of fishing, trolling parachute jigs on a wire line at around two knots over the kelp-covered rocks in depths between 30 and 45 feet where the big stripers congregate. And the strength-sapping technique of continually working the jig by slamming the rod tip down every few seconds to simulate the action of a squid not only got our arms prepared for the sharking ahead, but produced double figure blue fish and several chunky 20lbs plus striped bass, the largest of close on 30lbs falling to Paul Taylor from Harlow.

Once the tide eased and the bass became less aggressive, we changed tactics to drift for fluke, which is a large, summer flounder, bumping our squid-baited, light tackle rigs along the sea bed using 4oz leads. And these mottled flatfish we caught to around 3-4lbs.

After the tournament, I put my last day to good use with a trip out from Sag Harbour on local guide and ex pat, Matt Miller's 23 foot *Parker deep Vee* boat, (pushed along at over 40 knots by 250 horses-it almost flies) after blue fish and stripers using light spinning tackle and a 9 weight fly rod. And if you think an 8-9lbs rainbow trout has an exceptional turn of speed, then you'll be amazed at not only the way they go zooming off, but the incredible stamina of both blues and stripers of the same size. Rainbows loose badly, believe me, and after taking more than a dozen of these two incredibly enjoyable species to double figures on surface popping plugs, shads, sluggo baits and with the fly rod, (deceivers and clouser patterns producing best) continually 'double haul' casting from Matt's drifting boat along the crashing waves of rips in a force 5 sea, I think I returned to Montauk even more tired than after the sharking. Matt can be contacted on www.matt@ montaukfly-light.com.

Those who have watched my TV programmes and flicked through my books and articles over these past 30 years will know that generally I do not play fish lightly.

Heaving into a living force at the other end of my line (ok! So I chuckle as well) is what really (amongst other things, hey I'm 65 not 95) turns me on and literally pulls my string. So why was I suddenly pussy-footing about and being ever so careful with a large lake trout hooked in the clear water depths of a remote Canadian lake? Well, situated around 300 yards southeast of Gull Island and doing two knots, Martin Founds steered our 16 foot aluminium boat to follow the contours of the drop-off which varied between 15 and over 30 feet. We had already initiated hits from lakers up to 10lbs using small copper spoons, when I instinctively changed over to a huge five of diamonds, yellow and red spoon sporting a barb less 6/0 single hook, which are mandatory in Canada. And after 10 minutes of pulling it along 40 yards behind the boat, my four piece Masterline travel spinning rod was almost wrenched from my grasp. It was immediately obvious that I was connected to one hell of a big fish, as 30lbs test braid evaporated fast from my 6500 multiplier, while Martin frantically wound in his lure to get on the cameras. The unseen monster had grabbed hold in just 17 feet of water, but was heading fast away from the shallow plateaux into the dark, mysterious depths of Wolf Lake.

Yes, it's nice to have good friends in the travel business. And when Martin Founds, owner and founder of Britain's premier angling travel service, Anglers World Holidays, first rang to ask if I fancied a trip across the pond to Canada's Yukon Territory to fish for giant lake trout and grayling in the clear, pristine, wilderness waters of Wolf Lake, I jumped at the chance.

Being able to research new locations for future TV programmes is always exciting, and it was actually due to Martin first taking me out to northern Canada 20 years back to sample the pike, grayling and lake trout of Nueltin Lake in northern Manitoba, that resulted in my filming three episodes of series five of my long running Anglia production *Go Fishing* in Canada. And here we were, once again back in Canada's fascinating far north.

Following flights from Heathrow to Vancouver, with an overnight stop in Whitehorse, capital of the Yukon, an hours float plane trip deposited us on Wolf Lake, (there are no roads) situated around 100 miles due east of Whitehorse. Now for those who have yet to sample the sheer vastness of Canada, it has 13 separate regions (like our counties)the most northerly three of which including the Yukon are classified as territories, with the rest called provinces. The Yukon itself is situated between the 60th and 70th parallels, with Alaska to the west, Canada's North West Territories to the east, and British Columbia to the south. In size the

ABOVE
Double figure striped bass and bluefish like the beauty I'm holding here, offer superlative sport on the fly, as ex-pat skipper Matt Miller proved to me whilst fishing with him out of Sag Harbour, Long Island. Screaming reels and unbelievably hard and lengthy fights on a 9 weight outfit are par for the course.

Yukon is similar to that of Spain (twice the size of Britain) yet has a population of just 30,000. Yes only 30,000 people, 20,000 of whom live in Whitehorse.

Famous in the late 1890's for the Klondike gold rush era centralised around Dawson, Life was indeed hard for early pioneers over 100 years ago, many having their possessions and lives taken away by perilous raft and boat journeys down the rapids of the Yukon River from Whitehorse to Dawson. Whitehorse, actually getting its name from the treacherous rapids of the Yukon River, from prospectors during the 1880's who saw a resemblance to white horse's manes in the spray churned up by the rapids.

A copy of the original stern wheeler boat, *SS Klondike 11* resides permanently on show beside the river at Whitehorse as a reminder of those gold rush days, which took just 36 hours to ferry prospectors and their provisions down to Dawson(its predecessor ran aground in 1936) but took four to five days on the return trip back upstream. Such is current force of the treacherous Yukon River, up which giant Chinook salmon run to this day. Being some 2000 miles from the Bering Sea off Alaska to the streams above Whitehorse, this is the longest salmon migration in the world. But it is the giant lake trout, lovingly called Lakers (they are actually a char) that attracts sports fishermen from far and wide to Canada's far north, where ice-out starts during May and ice-in (when everything freezes back over again for another long winter) during October. Because during the short summer in between, daylight lasts for 24 hours and the fishing is as good as it gets anywhere. Believe me. Better still, you get to share it with few others. It's like owning your very own chunk of this harsh and fascinating country during your stay. Quite literally, within hours of arriving and getting out afloat you experience a wonderful feeling of belonging, of bewilderment and wonder, as creatures only ever seen on wildlife TV like moose and caribou, beavers and muskrats, bald eagles, golden eagles, horned owls and ospreys, become daily sightings whilst you fish.

RIGHT

Getting real close up to wildlife like this moose and her calf in a true wilderness environment at Wolf Lake in the Yukon, is just part of the attraction. Huge grayling and giant lake trout, being the main target species.

SIXTY YEARS A FISHERMAN

Our hosts at Wolf Lake Lodge, Wes and Michelle Walker and their children, were waiting as our Cessna float plane put down beside their dock, following a marvellous hour-long flight across snow-topped mountainous vallies through which ran a continuous flux of streams, rivers and unfished lakes. There is so much water in Canada's far north (the North West Territories alone actually contain nine percent of the planets freshwater) most of it comprising of unfished and un-named lakes; it truly takes some while to get your head around it all. The remote yet comfortable complex of wooden lodges and restaurant/day room (unbelievably tasty and wholesome food for a wilderness environment) is just 100 yards from the dock where made up rods and reels are left overnight (no one else around remember) in the 16 foot Lund aluminium boats sporting 20 HP, extremely quiet outboard engines.

What a unique location they have at Wolf Lake, which measures 13 mile long by around three miles wide (that's the same surface area as Scotland's Loch Awe incidentally) surrounded along the margins and high up into the hills with a dense growth of Jack and Scots Pine, Red Willow and Spruce, poplar and cotton wood, plus a myriad of delicate, pastel-coloured wild flowers and lichens, with never more than 8-10 anglers fishing at any one time. I realised it doesn't get any better on day one when Martin and I set off going south to fly-troll for Lakers. We quickly picked up good concentrations of baitfish (grayling and white fish) on the finder at mid water with lakers below them, in depth bands between 16 and 30 feet. And our 9 weight outfits with Hi-D sinking lines and five foot, 15lbs test mono leaders presenting large flies tied on 2/0 and 3/0 barb less hooks (mandatory in Canada) trolled 30 yards behind the boats at between 1-2 knots, soon instigated action from powerful lake trout in the 4-14lbs category. The secret being to knock the engine into neutral for between 10-20 seconds every so often, particularly after marking fish on the finder, to allow our lines to take the flies deeper, with a strong 'pull-round' on the rod tips materialising as the fly suddenly rose when the engine was knocked back into gear. We reckoned our flies were working at somewhere between 10-12 feet down on the troll with hits coming at any time, whether marking shoals of bait fish or not.

It was noticeable, throughout our entire weeks fishing, that Martin's Hi D line (mine being a less dense sinker) produced far more hits, partly we deduced because his fly descended faster when the engine was knocked out of gear, but also because it in some way worked the fly more attractively. We changed flies regularly at first to compare results, switching from giant deceivers, to clousers to bunny leech patterns etc, with darker flies definitely attracting more attention in the amazingly clear, cold water. Water temperatures incidentally at various points around the lake varied from 48 to 54 degrees. But we always returned to the conclusion, that for fly trolling, the Hi D line was imperative. Also noticeable was that whenever we failed to connect as the rod tip bent round, because lakers were coming short and merely nibbling at the end of the dressing (we were using 4-5 inch long flies) holding a 12 inch loop of line against the rod handle (exactly as though fishing a salmon fly downstream and across) gave them more sucking time and resulted in bonus fish.

As for the fighting capabilities of these lakers, which are of course not a trout but the planets largest char (*Salvelinus namaycush*) I have simply never caught trout so powerful. I've been fortunate in taking lakers from all over Canada using a variety of methods, in Lake Kamistastin and the Kamistastin River in the wilds of Labrador. From Lake Nueltin in Manitoba, and from the Ferguson and mighty Kazan River systems in the remote region of the North West Territories. But, Wolf Lake lakers are really something else. Fighting with truly astounding stamina and power, far, far above their weight. Whilst playing my first laker for instance, which made several long runs and felt well into double figures, I was dumbstruck when it finally spiralled up through the crystal clear water towards the boat. It was as though someone down there had cheated me by swapping a mid double for a fish of just 6lbs. Honestly. And believe me when I say that lakers here under 10lbs are indeed considered small.

Whenever the lake settled to a flat calm in the evening as the sun started to set from half past nine onwards, modest sized lakers could be readily taken on dry fly close into the margins in just 3-8 feet of water. During one magical evening Martin and I were targeting sedge-chomping fish in a large bay amongst a truly stunning sunset, the sky a kaleidoscope of orange, yellow, purple and red, when a beaver left the margins to swim around the boat. What a memorable experience, made all the more exciting when a laker charged five feet across the glass-like surface to engulf my muddler in a violent swirl (they really react aggressively to flies being skated) presented on a 6 weight outfit and 6lbs leader. The very same outfit incidentally, that I love to use back home when targeting the double figure rainbows and browns of Hampshire's renown still water fisheries. But never have I experienced a rainbow (taken them to 16lbs) run out so much line (at least 60 yards of backing) or run so fast as that 5lbs laker. I took my last fish that evening, a veritable baby of about 3lbs (by far our smallest all week) that was feeding confidently upon spent sedges in the surface film. The time? A little after 1 o'clock.

I used exactly the same 6 weight outfit the following morning to target the magnificently coloured and most acrobatic, arctic grayling inhabiting the Wolf River, which exits from the lake's northwestern corner, to flow for 60 miles before it joins the Teslin River and lake system. Clarity in the fast currents of the Wolf River is just phenomenal, with equally phenomenal numbers of grayling averaging between one and 2lbs, with occasional monsters between 3 and 4lbs. I have simply never fished anywhere so prolific in quality-sized grayling, where depth varies between two and four feet over a hard gravel and rocky bottom. So everywhere is nicely wadeable.

Our guide, Matt Mossing, who hails from Sweden, suggested that large, buoyant dry fly patterns would score best. And he was so right. Casting upstream and across the flow, encouraging the fly to skate fast across the surface, were when most hits came. But I was unprepared for the size of flies these Wolf River grayling would take. Top pattern being the Chernobyl Ant, an extremely buoyant, outrageously large (over 1½ inches long – honestly) artificial made from layers of orange and red foam rubber, with thin, power gum legs. It produced drifting down in 'do nothing' mode. On the skate and when twitched back upstream erratically. Hot favourite on the river is the 'Ugly Bug', another large and super-buoyant fly tied from black rubber with rubber legs. And it too, instigated the most gloriously aggressive takes when skated across the turbulent surface. I found the most versatile pattern, invented by Hans van Klinken, was his 'Klinkhamer Sedge', a large bushy tying which produced strong hits on the surface, but worked with equal effectiveness even when totally waterlogged, drifted down several inches beneath the surface.

In nymphs, the lead-headed 'Peeping Caddis' when offered close to the bottom worked beautifully, as did my own leaded mayfly nymphs from back home. Though in hind sight due to sheer speed of flow, I should have doubled the lead wire tied in along the shank.

The flow was so strong in some of the three feet deep runs it was all I could do to keep my balance, but this provided some exhilarating fights despite my six weight outfit and 5lbs test leader. I'll maybe take a 4 or 5 weight next time for even more fun. Wolf River grayling are coloured differently to any I have caught elsewhere, with a decidedly 'golden' sheen along their flanks. Who knows, perhaps its due to the fact that there is gold in the surrounding mountains.

At lunchtime a dozen of our smaller fish were filleted and cut into chunks by Matt, rolled into heavily seasoned flour and tossed into sizzling lard covering the bottom of the largest frying pan I have ever seen (fully two feet in diameter) and

LEFT
Having rolled the fresh grayling (boneless) fillets in seasoned corn flour, Michelle Walker, co lodge owner and operator at Wolf Lake, drops them into sizzling lard, (to preserve the unique flavour of the fish) in the largest frying pan I have ever seen. While hungry mouths look on. Yep! Sure is tough in the Yukon.

cooked to golden perfection by hosts Michelle and Wes who had 'hopped' up the lake by float plane from the lodge five miles away (honestly) to join our cook-out. With hot freshly baked bread, bacon and beans on the side, they sure know how to fish and eat in the wilds of the Yukon. Maybe we had a few good tasting beers too.

At the southeastern end of Wolf Lake where caribou can be seen on the mountain sides and moose observed at ridiculously close quarters feeding upon curly pond weed and milfoil from the shallows at the entrances to numerous shallow, pike-filled bays and inlets, fly casting surface poppers, or working top water plugs and churners, will have you chuckling away like me all day long at the antics of small to medium-sized pike, tail-walking and cavorting about in and out of the weed beds and reedlines. It's floating line, predator fun fishing at its very best. The only addition to a standard 8 or 9 weight trout outfit being to add six inches of soft, easy- tie wire to the fly and join to a short, four foot 12lbs test cast, loop to loop, which then facilitates quick and easy fly changing. In fact I already have short wire traces tied to all my favourite pike fly patterns. And whilst those pike literally attacked anything churning the surface in the shallow bays and dykes entering Wolf Lake along its southeastern shoreline, bunny leeches and deer hair, long- tailed mice seemed to make them extra angry. Ok, big 'doubles' here are few and far between, but this doesn't matter as everything fights with amazing strength and stamina anyway. And it's all wonderful, often air-borne fun (these northern pike jump repeatedly) in the warm shallows.

Slowly, the shape of the monstrous laker rose begrudgingly foot by foot, continually shaking its huge head, through the crystal clear water, as Martin swapped his video for my stills camera, whilst I prayed the 6/0 barb less single would not be shaken out. I had been playing the monster now, heart in mouth, for fully 10 minutes during which time its power-packed runs got shorter and shorter. Then finally, it hit the surface in a shower of spray and head-shaking lunges, only to dive back down 20, 30, 40 feet again to the bottom. The size of its spade-like tail was enormous. And again, my heart skipped a beat. Truthfully, I cannot say that I completely enjoyed the battle due to being constantly aware that at any second it might slip the hook. But it didn't and following another five minutes of it chugging beneath and actually towing the boat, it finally hit the surface fully spent where Martin coolly scooped it into the net at the first attempt. And there it lay on the bottom of the boat, enormously deep in the flanks, in the absolute mint of condition for such an old fish (possibly over 50 years old) with not a blemish on either its body or fins. The pure white lines edging each of its pectoral, pelvic and anal fins, and intricate mosaic markings of pewter and cream along the flanks, depicting its char heritage. By far my largest lake trout ever. Over 40 inches in length and weighing a massive 33lbs.

Am I going back? You bet I am. And if I was a young man again (strangely, I keep

LEFT
Weighing 33lbs, this huge lake trout (a char really, just look at those intricate, mosaic markings) certainly made my weeks fishing with Martin Founds on Wolf Lake in the Yukon. It took a huge, five of diamonds spoon on the troll in 20 feet of water.

thinking this now that I'm 65) I would be clutching a one way ticket to Canada's remote, pristine, uncluttered wilderness, where the term 'nanny state' will I doubt ever be used.

If the couple of days at the end of August, spent carp fishing in the company of three good friends is anything to go by, television viewers have a real treat in store when the eight part angling epic, *Catching the Impossible*, beautifully made by Hugh Miles, finally hits our screens. Together with specimen hunter supreme, Martin Bowler who catches most of the whoppers, plus an assortment of various guests (yours truly included) and mate Bernard Cribbins, who not only catches, but narrates the programmes, Hugh and Martin have put together over these past four years, a truly monumental series, destined even to surpass Hugh's highly acclaimed *Passion for Angling* TV series. Which without fear or favour were in my and everyone else's opinion, the finest, most wild life-packed, innovative, inspirational and most wonderfully filmed of any angling programmes ever to grace our TV screens.

I would indeed love the weather to have been kinder when Hugh, Martin and Bernard arrived at my two-lake fishery, after all it was August. But Mother Nature knows best, and we just had to put up with whatever (including the kitchen sink) she threw at us while Bernard tried to tempt one of my carp into slurping down his floating dog biscuit, presented close in amongst an entanglement of leaves and branches, on a fly rod. Not, I might add the easiest of disciplines in overcast, decidedly nasty weather. But that was the plan, and we stuck to it religiously, not without each gaining a few more grey hairs along the way.

Due to the 'low' covering most of Norfolk during their stay, (which just about sums up our entire British summer during 2007) the carp were in a most unresponsive mood, coming up to suspiciously suck down a floater, only every so often. There was absolutely no chance of selecting a particular fish, which is

usually the delight of floater fishing, and after watching their reactions to our loose feed it became apparent that after taking just one or two floaters the carp would totally disappear. So Martin suggested, that we forget any kind of loose feeding, simply flick out the hook bait floater, an 11mm expanded biscuit super-glued to the shank of a size 10 hook, and wait till a carp appeared. Which is more or less what happened? That's Martins strength; he quickly homes in on what the fish want on the day. And after pulling the hook free from a huge golden orfe of fully 5lbs and shortly afterwards a big ghost koi, (all great footage for Hugh of course) Bernard finally wiped the smile from the face of my carp by solidly connecting with a superb, thick-set fish in one hell of a swim, where I feared that submerged tree roots and dense lily pads would tangle the 9 weight floating fly line. But no. Bernard was by now well up for this particular fish, suddenly becoming most aggressive, at the ripe old age of 75 would you believe, and piled on the pressure to stop it from snagging. So that several minutes later, I was to slip the net beneath his carp, a beautifully proportioned mid double figure common. The largest he'd ever taken on a fly rod incidentally. It was job done indeed.

Considering that sport was slowing down on the freshwater scene in mid September, with a myriad of leaves falling as we experienced our earliest autumn for many a year, things were surprisingly hectic. For starters, I was asked by Dream Flight and Sebastian's Action Trust in Berkshire to set up a days carp fishing for 14 year old John Jones, and his dad, (another John) from Swindon, who, having experienced a rare form of cancer and about to endure further chemotherapy, might just be up for a few hours of float fishing around my two-lake fishery here in deepest Norfolk. Which went great? And then at the following weekend, my old pal, Radio DJ Steve Wright (yes, of 'Wrighty' in the afternoon) was bringing his son Tom and his mate, musician Alex Claire, along, each hoping to get stuck into some of my carp. While 'Wrighty' sat there on the most comfortable reclining seat I own,

LEFT

Musician Alex Claire cuddles one of my carp, while DJ Steve Wright (he's got short hair these days) and his son Tom, cuddle Alex. What a morning's carping.

giving the occasional piece of advice (not that he knows anything about fishing) whilst reading *The Times*.

But let's return to the two 'Johns' from Swindon. Wisely, (as it turned out) I had decided to fix up each with a 'sleeper' rod presenting a ledgered 20mm boilie on a bolt-rig close up to a dense bed of yellow lilies fringing the opposite bank of my largest lake, directly opposite the house, not 30 yards out, whilst they took it in turns to catch roach on a simple float rig baiting with one or two kernels of sweet corn presented on a size 10 hook in around seven feet of water. Fortunately, these tactics worked an absolute treat, with lots of roach to a pound being caught, while each 'John' hooked into and landed following hectic scraps, double figure, beautifully scaled common carp. I could not have possibly, thanks to lady luck, planned their day any better. And I must admit to feeling more than a lump in my throat when the car carrying the two John's made its way up the drive on their way back to the M4 from my Norfolk home.

Then, on Sunday morning, it was 'Wrighty', and his gang, who always, and I mean 'always', gets lost between London and my Norfolk home. Ok, I know we live in seclusion in the middle of a woodland setting. But he has been fishing here for over a decade now, so how on earth he finds his way each day into the BBC studios has always amazed me. No fewer than four separate phone calls between Steve and I took place before his Range Rover came trundling down my drive, (as usual) a good hour late. But I've got used to this over the years. His son Tom, now 21 (in his early teens when he first fished my lakes) has developed into a keen 'carper' as has his mate Alex, so I suggested they too, fish 'sleeper' boilie rods whist enjoying the roach on float fished sweet corn. Little was I to know however, that

Alex would keep us laughing all day long at his outlandish actions upon hearing his bite alarm emit a continuous 'bleep'!

Being 20 feet away at the time, switching over one of my reels from right to left hand wind, (the reel handle is still in the lake) he dropped everything and ran like a man possessed towards his boilie rod, straight, waist deep, into the water of a growing-on pond adjacent to the lake, immediately ruining his cell phone. But he did eventually come spluttering to the surface to strike and subsequently land a nice mirror carp of around 12lbs. After lunch, (along at a local hostelry and paid for by 'Wrighty') Tom then took a nice double figure common to even the score. And when they all finally left at around 6pm, I can only assume Steve found his way back to London.

I just love fishing in the USA. Not only for the unashamed feeling of being an angler or hunter, (one in seven Americans fish, compared to one in every 20 Britons, so 'anti feelings' are simply not tolerated over there) but also for the multitude of wild, open places free to all who purchase their licenses which believe it or not, cost less than in the UK. The trip I made across the pond in May and now again in September, to research the fabulous carp fishing available in the mid, southern state of Arkansas (mysteriously pronounced 'Arkensaw') organised by buddy Martin Founds of Anglers World Holidays, simply blew our minds. The sheer volume of fishable water available in a state only marginally smaller in land mass than the UK, but with a population of less than three million, (yes, only three million) is simply staggering. There are in fact 20,000 miles of fishable streams and rivers, plus 600,000 acres of lakes, bayous, ponds, creeks and sloughs, all stocked by the state fisheries department (there are hatchery ponds everywhere) and open to all, many with wooden fishing platforms, tables and benches provided. In the state parks, cabins and boats may also be rented. Boat ramps and public slipways exist everywhere. How different to my local stretch of Norfolk's River Bure at Wroxham for instance (arguably the most popular and busiest spot in the whole of Broad land) where would you believe, there is no public slipway. Broads Authority take note!!!

All of Arkansas's large lakes are man made and vary in size between 10,000 and 50,000 acres. By comparison, the largest Broad in Norfolk, 'Hickling' covers just 400 acres; whilst Europe's largest man made Lake Rutland Water covers 3,500 acres. And if all this is insufficient to describe the enormity of it all, how about the fact that the levee (flood barrier) running beside the mighty Mississippi River, (which forms the state's eastern borderline) is actually longer than the Great Wall of China.

Moreover, the Mississippi is the planets fourth longest river at 3,700 miles long, while the Arkansas River is 1450 miles long. A resident annual fishing license for both trout and rough (coarse) fish costs just $17.00 (£8.50) A non resident annual license for both trout and rough fish costs $52.00 (£26) while a non resident seven day license for rough fish costs $17.00 (£8.50)

Over 60 percent of the state of Arkansas is heavily wooded. Its three national forests cover 2,648,825 acres. Arkansas is the only diamond-producing state in the US, and provides over 80 percent of the nations supply of bauxite ore, from which aluminium is made. Impressive stats indeed.

With so much water readily available, our problem on this second research trip was again, of course 'where' to start, though the lovely ladies at the tourist board, Mindy and Amber were immensely helpful, and again providing the experienced services of guide Jerry Bean, a resident bassing guide for both large mouth and striped bass, based on massive Lake Ouachita (pronounced 'washitaw') which has bays the size of Grafham and Rutland, and is situated due west of the states capital 'Little Rock'.

Naturally, with over 50 big and exciting freshwater species inhabiting the lakes and rivers of Arkansas, no less than seven being carp, we were more than spoilt for choice. But we had after all come for carp and needed to be selective. The state record for commons incidentally, is 53lbs and the potential for jumbo-sized grass carp is enormous. The state record being 80lbs. The record for silver carp is 39 ¼lbs and 83lbs for its big brother the big head carp. Added to these four non indigenous carp species are the Buffalo big mouth carp at 56lbs, the buffalo small mouth at 68½lbs and the buffalo black carp at 105lbs.

Tag on to the carp records, alligator garfish of 240lbs, striped bass of 64½lbs, brown trout of 40¼lbs, plus flat head catfish of 80lbs, blue catfish of 116¾lbs, and paddlefish of 80lbs, (the list just goes on) plus milder winters than the UK and long, hot summers with water temperatures into the 80's and even 90's, and this mid southern state (did I not mention a plethora of excellent Mexican restaurants?) is surely the best kept angling secret over on the other side of the pond.

On our first trip in May, following a long haul from Gatwick to Charlotte in South Carolina, just a short internal flight took us on to Little Rock, and then to our base at Ouachita Lake where our guide had not only baited some swims but prepared a huge chest full of 'stinking corn', which is hard maize mixed with a little wheat left to ferment for a few days having been soaked in boiling water and several bags of sugar added. In my experience carp love this 'stinking bait' the world over, which is both loose feed and hook bait (4-6 hard grains are presented on a long hair on a size 6-4 hook in conjunction with a 3oz in-line bolt rig) the mix having produced carp for me, often within a day or two of loose feeding, all over. Unfortunately, due to the immense size of Lake Ouachita, and that most of its 50,000 acres can only be fished by boat during the early summer (until levels are dropped drastically) we were compelled to move on having accounted for just a handful of commons into high double figures from one of Jerry's baited swims, plus a few blue and channel catfish. Other venues, particularly the Arkansas River

at Dardanelle, produced the strange-looking small mouth buffalo carp, which with its hoover-like mouth looks to all intents and purposes, just like a cross between a wild carp and a bream. And don't they fight too. Fish of just 7-8lbs easily taking line from a firmly set clutch on our 15lbs test, 2½ test curve carp outfits. Add a few various turtles for good measure (there are several species of these bait-robbing thugs from soft shelled to snapping monsters that could rip your hand off) and apart from watching ospreys feeding everywhere, that was about it on our first research trip. Very promising indeed and a second reconnaissance trip was planned for September.

After losing all our luggage and consequently not being able to fish on day one upon our return, Martin Founds, Matt Garfield and I quickly met up with Jerry Bean again, who (bless him) already had a batch of fermenting corn at our disposal. So we decided upon first revisiting the grass carp location on Lake Hamilton to see if our results back in May could be a regular thing. And I found out the answer within 20 minutes of loose feeding and setting up (in fact I was making up my third rod at the time) when away went the first rod and in came an extremely thick and fat grass carp of 34lbs. Matt unfortunately failed to hook up on his two runs, whilst my second run produced a real belter which felt huge but unfortunately, the mono hook link severed after a minute into the fight. It had been 'crimped' and had fractured a couple of inches above the hook. Turtles, or crayfish, no doubt.

We then headed north from Hamilton to 40,000 acre, Greers Ferry Lake, a

SIXTY YEARS A FISHERMAN

ABOVE
Look at the strange bream-like snout of this 15lbs small mouth buffalo carp, from Greers Ferry Lake in Arkansas. A species that grows to close on 70lbs and fights even harder than a common carp of the same size.

truly stunningly beautiful and huge mountainous water, where at Fairfield Bay Marina hundreds and hundreds of big, double figure commons plus the odd 20 pounder, tantalisingly wait to be fed in the crystal clear water (a daily tradition for visitors) beside the pontoon bridge next to a 'no fishing' sign on the dock. But as we were to discover, these were not the only fish around. After loose feeding a 12 foot deep area over on the other side of the marina and float fishing both bread flake and maize just a few feet out from a bank side pontoon, we enjoyed hectic sport during an afternoon and a morning session with several species including a couple of dozen commons to around 16lbs, small blue and channel catfish, bluegills, and small mouth buffalo carp to around 15lbs, and boy!, didn't they all shift in water temperatures into the 80's. Oh!, and Matt had three turtles. Strange thing was, just one run came to our ledgered baits further out concentrated over an area the size of a tennis court that had been heavily loose fed overnight with maize. Yet carp were regularly rolling over the bait on the surface in 18 feet of water.

Then the penny suddenly dropped, (and should have much earlier because I can recall my old mate the late Fred J Taylor mentioning the 'predatory' inclinations of American carp many years ago) when both Matt and I simultaneously watched, totally fascinated, as a pair of mid double commons moving fast about eight feet down suddenly charged up to the surface amongst the shoals of two inch long shad. And secured their meals in vicious, predatory swirls. We should have caught on much earlier, because each and every swirl showed predatory aggression. At least

Matt Garfield carefully slips the net beneath a thrashing grass carp at the beautiful 'Elms' plantation lake, for top Arkansas guide Jerry Bean, who probably won't dare tell his mates that he purposely fished for grass carp. Throughout much of North America all carp species are considered 'trash' fish. Strange, isn't it?

OPPOSITE

Hooked on just 10lbs line and a simple float rig, I'm endeavouring, by applying side-strain, to stop a huge grass carp from reaching the sanctuary of overhanging, submerged willow branches at the 'Elms' lake.

it explained why they were not interested in going down on our maize. Obvoiusly, in high water temperatures; carp are far more predatory than we ever see them in the UK.

We also fished the massive Arkansas River immediately below the weir in Dardanelle, but could not find a way of getting through the vast numbers of small mouth buffalo carp in the 5-12lbs range, to the commons that are obviously present, although I did miss a powerful run from a catfish (Jerry said it could have been a big 'blue') on the freshly cut head of a large shad. The 6/0 hook had turned 'point in' to the bait.

So once again we moved on, driving southeast from Little Rock to a wonderful plantation lake, dating back to before the civil war, in the town of Altheimer. A mysterious, rarely fished 16 acre, shallow lake over hung around two thirds of the margins by mature trees, aptly called 'The Elms'. And immediately upon arrival we were treated to the glorious sight of what appeared to be numbers of grass carp between 10 and 50lbs cavorting up and down the lake. Every now and then fry would scatter close to the willows overhanging the two large islands, and around the extensive beds of lilies. Their pads being fully 20 inches across. Jerry mentioned that the lake also held a good stock of large mouth bass (his favourite species) and invited me to accompany him in one of the canoes for a spot of lure fishing using spinner baits, before getting stuck into the carp. But would you believe, the first thing I hooked was a big grass carp looking all of 30lbs plus which after catapulting itself high into the air and making a couple of simply unstoppable runs on Jerry's little bait casting outfit, promptly went charging through a submerged bush and ditched the lure. We then went on to take some nice surface-thrashing large mouths

SIXTY YEARS A FISHERMAN

of between 2-4½lbs apiece (though why Americans prefer them to the significantly more exhilarating battle of a carp has always both puzzled and amazed me) before paddling back to shore and rigging up a float rig on my 10lbs test, all through action carp rod.

Just how many grass carp we four caught during the next day and a half's stalking around The Elms, I am not exactly sure. But it could not have been less than 50. The largest of exactly 40lbs falling to yours truly, (like all of them, which averaged double figures) on two grains of maize float fished just above the silty bottom. This being far more effective than presenting 'floaters'. And what an unbelievable scrap it put up on just 10lbs test line. Charging all over the lake, through sunken trees and bushes, sending up great clouds of dark, bottom silt, repeatedly making run after run. Incidentally, and this has always been something I do, fix your waggler to the line with a section of silicon tubing as apposed to 'locking shots' when seeking big fish. Losing a few floats when carp go charging through lilies or tree roots is one thing. Having the line snap when the float snags due to locking shots is simply unacceptable.

Our last location was massive Lake Chicot in the Mississippi delta where cotton field's stretch across the horizon for as far as the eye can see. At 20 miles in length it is in fact the largest Oxbow lake (once connected to the Mississippi over 500 years back) in North America, and the largest 'natural' lake in Arkansas. Being half a mile wide with cypress tree swamps and beautiful beds of lilies fringing the margins, this most impressive water, where big fish are constantly rolling out in the middle, must contain vast stocks not only of common and grass carp, both of which we took into high double figures on float fished and ledgered maize, plus a monster lost in a snag in just a couple of short sessions fishing from one of the wooden stagings, but of both silver and big head carp, small mouth and big mouth buffalo carp, plus three species of catfish growing to between 50 and over 100lbs. And lets not forget the turtles. What a place! We were of course on an overnight stop (using one of the comfortable state run fishing cabins) literally scratching the surface, but that's what research is all about.

In October it was back to Canada again where it's always nice to leave a fishing trip wishing you could make one last cast. Because then returning, is simply a forgone conclusion. Such were my feelings anyway, at the end of two glorious weeks fishing for salmon and giant sturgeon in the fast flowing Harrison and Fraser

SIXTY YEARS A FISHERMAN

Rivers situated in the foothills of the Rocky mountains in Canada's beautiful province of British Columbia. Friends Fred Helmer and Tony Nootebos, who run 20 foot jet boats out of Harrison Springs Resort, near Chilliwack, some 80 miles east of Vancouver, enabling visitors to get amongst the fish quickly, were as usual, like all their experienced guides, most courteous and enthusiastic. And the party of 12 Brits I was escorting on behalf of Tailor Made Holidays, (six for each of two consecutive weeks fishing) all bent on having their strings well and truly pulled, were fast into the action along the mighty Fraser system.

Using a variety of techniques from both shore and boat, from fly fishing to trotting artificials, and from spinning to trolling and bouncing spoons, we accounted for both Coho and pink salmon to around 10lbs. Colourful sockeye to 14lbs and hard battling chum salmon averaging into high double figures, with the largest a 25lbs monster falling to Dave Johnson using just a single handed 8 weight fly rod. The largest Chinook, a beast of over 40lbs was caught by Tony Wilkinson from Norfolk on a lure whilst fishing the Harrison River.

Catching and returning a dozen or more of the aggressive chum salmon between 15 and 20lbs on the fly using single handed 8-10 weight outfits and sink-tip lines (believe me when I say you don't want any more than a dozen in a day) is literally an every day occurrence here, where barb less hooked flies are mandatory. I did in fact take my 14 foot Spey outfit along, but soon went back to a single handed rod because it was simply more fun. What marvellous, arm-wrenching sport we all enjoyed amidst truly spectacular scenery, with the leaves of all the deciduous trees turning to yellow red and orange, whilst bald eagles, gulls, herons and turkey vultures gorged upon salmon along the shoreline not 100 yards away. Unlike our Atlantic salmon, all five Pacific species after spending between two to five years at sea run the Fraser system to spawn and to die. Though this might seem strange, it

RIGHT

No wonder Steve
Morris from
Hereford (third
from left) has an
ear to ear grin.
This nine foot
plus giant white
sturgeon which
took him half a
mile downriver
during an epic
three quarters
of an hour fight,
was estimated to
weigh in excess
of 400lbs. During
our weeks stay
incidentally, my
group of seven
Brits, accounted
for no less than
109 sturgeon,
with 38 of
them over that
magical 100lbs.

is nature's way of providing nutrients, from their carcasses, for young salmon fry when the eggs hatch.

Also feeding upon the dead salmon and upon their eggs, is the giant white sturgeon which reaches weights in excess of 1000lbs. It is thus arguably (some sturgeon never run to sea) the largest freshwater fish in the world. Such leviathans are of course rare nowadays, but one or two are still landed or lost each year to make such an encounter remotely possible, with numbers of lesser fish in the 200-400lbs bracket, actually considered weekly catches. In my mind this makes the Fraser River system totally unique? For I know of no where else on this planet anglers can visit for a weeks freshwater fishing in stunningly beautiful surroundings, stay in five star accommodation, and fish from 20 foot jet boats with experienced guides,(where all the tackle and bait is provided) and contemplate catching such monstrous fish.

In our first six days fishing for instance, and some of the time was taken up salmon fishing, seven anglers caught no less than 109 sturgeon, with 38 of them over that magical 100lbs. Several topped 200lbs. A 300lbs plus beauty fell to the rod of Alex Taylor, while Steve Morris from Hereford, following an arduous one and a half hour battle, hit the jackpot by eventually beaching an enormous sturgeon of 8 foot seven inches in length, estimated by his guide to be over 400lbs. A fish which twice during the fight leapt completely clear of the water, as they do, once mere feet away from the boat. In fact most sturgeon will jump at least once during the fight, very often, if held tight after setting the hook, at the end of their initial

run. And what a spectacle this provides (some fish jump several times during the fight) with a back drop of snow-covered mountains along the wide Fraser Valley.

Whilst the size of these monsters constitutes freshwater big-game fishing at its most exhilarating, guests enjoy every battle 'stand-up' style, using seven foot carbon rods matched to 100lbs test braided line on super-smooth lever drag multipliers. And here's the strangest thing of all, and which though I've been escorting Brits out to the Fraser now for seven years to fish for sturgeon, still amazes me. The bite from even a huge sturgeon sucking the bait in can be no more than a two to four inch nod of the rod tip. And if you strike at exactly the right time, all hell quickly breaks loose.

Towards the end of January 2008, having enjoyed some coldwater action with grayling along the River Test and some chunky rainbows to 9lbs from Dever Springs, I was so looking forward to kiss the chill of Britain behind for 10 days of glorious summer in South Africa, where following an 11 hour long haul to Johannesburg from Heathrow's terminal 1, and then an hours domestic flight to Richards Bay on the east coast, organised by Christine Slater of Tailor Made Holidays, our seven man party was greeted by, would you believe, cold, slanting rain and unusually high winds. Apparently, the end of a cyclone that had recently hit Madagascar. Unfortunately, this made for difficult beach fishing at St Lucia, our first location and a truly beautiful surf beach where several species of large sharks, guitar fish and rays are all usually considered daily catches by our experienced guide Dion Van Der Merwe, who has taken numerous bull and ragged tooth sharks here to over

With Brit Stan Povey looking on in awe, top South African guide Dion Van Der Merwe does his best to stop a huge bull shark from shredding his 45lbs mono reel line over a coral reef 300 yards out at Kosi Bay close to the Mozambique border. Unfortunately, the shark won.

400lbs. His tackle shop walls in St Lucia are simply crammed full of photographic living proof.

Using mackerel and squid bait however we did account for some unusual smaller species in the way of spotted grunters (a bass-like fish) bluefish and spotted guitar fish. Further up the coast just below the Mozambique border at Anton Roberts 'Amangwane camp' beside beautiful Kosi Bay, the weather improved vastly and we caught dozens of strange and colourful species from yet another spectacular surf beach including wave garrick, ladyfish, bonefish, threadfin salmon, cave bass and one of the most strikingly colourful of all sea species, a blue emperor.

But I shall personally always remember the size and sheer brute strength of the several monsters we lost using powerful 14 foot one piece carbon surf rods coupled to multipliers loaded with 300 yards plus of 30lbs mono and strong wire traces.

On our last evening beach fishing for instance, I connected with what was obviously a big stingray and for quite some while I really thought I was winning. Then quite suddenly, like all the other unseen monsters which for one reason or another we couldn't hold, most of which were obviously big sharks (probably bulls) the ray decided it was too close to the waves and simply headed due east across the Indian ocean into the twilight, in several lengthy, unstoppable surges, shredding my 30lbs line some 200 yards out on the reef. But I was not alone. Ken Sheath rather unluckily had an enormous giant trevally slip his mullet-baited two-hook rig when he piled on the pressure to stop it from reaching the same reef. While guide Dion ran over 200 yards along the beach (the shark would say he was towed) to stay in contact with a huge bull shark, having increased line strength to 45lbs test, but the end was still inevitable. We did however enjoy some spectacular boat fishing.

In fact several years ago whilst boat fishing off Mozambique along the East African coastline, I experienced the sickening feeling one afternoon of no less than three potential PB's, a giant trevally, a huge kingfish and a monstrous queen mackerel all bitten off by sharks during the fight. And all on a 12 weight fly rod outfit too. So it came as no surprise

LEFT
Yes! Hooked on drifted fish fillet over a deep water reef, this would have been my largest green job fish ever, had a shark not relieved me of most of it. Not an uncommon occurrence during our stay.

BELOW
Around one mile off shore from St Lucia along the rugged East African Coastline, boat anglers anchored up on shallow reefs often hook into giant guitar fish, also called shovel-nosed rays or sand sharks. Estimated at over 200lbs and though beaten and lying alongside, this monster was never coming into the boat after unhooking.

when boat fishing off South Africa's east coast, (close to the Mozambique border incidentally) when free lining whole mackerel, only to have what would have been a near 20lbs green job fish (a beautiful bass-like reef dweller) and yet another PB, taken by a shark. 10 minutes later, winding in a well hooked, beautifully conditioned, but sad looking head of around 7lbs, chewed off below the pectoral fin.

One of our seven man research party, Paul Dawson, actually got to play and bring one of the culprit sharks up to the boat, a bronze whaler of around 200lbs. But sightings of monstrous tiger sharks that came right up to our 17 foot boat drifting over a two mile long reef in between 150-200 feet of water, literally dwarfed Paul's shark. Our guide put these tigers at over 12 feet long and 800lbs. Boy, is there some wonderful shark fishing to be had along the South African coastline, plus spectacular game fish, not forgetting the most colourful and hard battling of reef dwellers. I literally lost count of the different species we caught after stopping at 30. Most of the smaller species averaging between 5-15lbs. So everything pulls your string, in these clear, blue seas, from the outrageously coloured tomato rock cod, to exquisitively marked moff grunters and yellow striped snappers.

Ken Sheath and I enjoyed a great morning's boat trolling for oceanic bonito and Dorado's off St Lucia with top guide Dion, despite launching his 18 foot cat directly into the surf. Not an experience for the faint hearted, I can tell you. I wrenched my left shoulder big time during the launching; it was a case quite literally of

either hang on or fall out of the boat (almost standing on its transom) as it crashes through that final big wave. In fact the South Africans beach launch in surf conditions that we at home would deem too rough for even casting into. This is why their 4x4 vehicles are fitted with both a tow hitch and powerful winch at the front, so they can 'push' their boats off the trailers straight into the surf. Upon coming in 'at full throttle' they then run the boat way up onto the beach and winch it up onto the trailer, the rear of which splits

and angles upwards till most of the hull is accommodated.

After a couple of hours trolling we finished the session anchoring up over an in shore reef for small sharks, grunters, and rock hind, all into double figures while one of the guys on another boat fishing the same reef brought a 200lbs sand shark (guitar fish) to the boat. Can't wait to go back on a trip Christine has planned for 2009.

For most of us unfortunately, 'red letter days' do not happen frequently enough, so allow me to recall a pike trip, when 'everything' went right for once after several consecutive mediocre sessions at the start of 2008. We angling writers experience 'blanks' too you know. Believe it or not. Actually, following over night lashing rain and strong winds, I wasn't intending to go fishing at all, and settled down in my office in front of the key board. But when I stopped to walk the dogs, I immediately noticed how mild it was, (around 10 degrees celsius) and somehow I knew that along at a favourite local gravel pit those southwesterly winds would be blowing hard into a particular deep, reed lined bay and really getting those pike moving.

At midday I made a flask of coffee and stashed the rods in the back of my Audi estate together with four packs of frozen smelt dead baits, and I was off. By a little after one o'clock I had a ledgered, popped - up smelt placed into the deepest part of the bay, with the line connected to a buzzer, while on a lightweight multiplier outfit I worked the margins beneath some overhanging willows with a wobbled smelt using a single swan shot on the trace to help it slowly reach bottom. One of my 'all-time' favourite techniques is wobbling dead baits.

After a couple of casts along came a greedy 4lbs jack, followed on the next cast by what I suspected was another jack. But half way in it woke up and materialised into a superbly shaped and thick set pike of exactly 22lbs. And didn't it scrap in the clear water, repeatedly making powerful runs. After returning it I wound in the popped – up bait and repositioned it the other side of the trees close to where I fancied working the wobbled bait. Now they say that intuition, or sixth sense, call it what you will, is a funny thing, because again, somehow I knew the action was far from over, and as I was watching the line whilst the smelt sank on just my second cast, it suddenly 'zinged' tight, immediately connecting me to something much bigger. I hardly needed to strike. But I did need the landing net when I saw the deep flanks of a beautifully marked and powerful pike that following no small amount of crashing through marginal reeds, swam promptly into the net and took the spring balance down to a shade over 26lbs.

Now two splendid, beautifully proportioned 20 pounders in one 'short session' would have been marvellous enough, but when the alarm connected to the line on my popped – up smelt started to scream a little while before I packed up, (having moved the rods 100 yards along the bank to be closer to the car) I knew, the very second I tightened up and struck, that this was one of those incredibly rare 'red letter days'. What did it weigh? Another 26lbs monster, that was closer to 27lbs. And no, it was not the same fish. By 4 o'clock I was on my way driving home, reflecting upon catching three pike over 20lbs in less than three hours fishing. Only the second time in British waters that I have taken three 20lbs plus pike during the same session. The first being way back from Norfolk's Blackhorse Broad during the 1980's. Though from the prolific waters of Canada's Neultin Lake in Northern Manitoba, I have twice caught three 20's on the same day. And on one of those I had four.

Fellow angling writer Dave Steuart and I go back a fair old time, to the early 1970's when we both wrote monthly contributions (Dave was in fact lead writer) for what many contemporary specialist anglers then considered (and still do incidentally) by far the best 'all-round' magazine of its day, (and now) *Angling* magazine, edited by Brian Harris. So just recently my wife Jo and I were both so pleased that Dave could make the long drive up to Norfolk from his home adjacent to Hampshire's marvellous River Test in Romsey (he can cast into the river from his conservatory) to stay with us for a few days for a spot of pike fishing at the beginning of March. Now I'm sure Dave won't mind me saying that he's only a year short of 80, and as such, I didn't fancy dragging him out, as is my usual routine, an hour before the crack of dawn, followed by an hours drive towing my boat to a favourite pike Broad, either off the Bure or Lower Waveney, to sit there all day in the cold. A spot of breakfast first after a leisurely get up, and then a short drive to a favourite local pit, would I thought be far more appealing.

As it happened the day was mild (around 50 degrees) with a bit of a chilly wind, and till lunch time when our only action had been a couple of dropped runs on static dead baits (tiny jacks) plus a 4lbs jack landed, I was convinced my decision had

been the right one. We had nattered continually about old times, Dave about the decline of salmon in the River Test, and myself about how cormorants have virtually destroyed the dace and roach fishing in most of my local rivers, But by four o'clock, still without a decent fish to speak of I was getting edgy, though assured Dave that that last hour of the day usually saw the bigger pike coming on the move. Then just as the light started to go, away went one of Dave's sliding floats, presenting half a mackerel on the bottom in 12 feet of water and over went his rod into a full, pulsating curve, as what was obviously a big pike charged to his left and rolled on the surface in a huge boil beneath an overhanging willow. Dave gave it some heavy side strain and following a couple of dives up it popped to the surface straight into the waiting net. A superbly proportioned pike which took the scales down to 26lbs. Dave's second largest ever.

ABOVE

I hope I'm still hooking into whoppers like this super, 26lbs pike when I'm approaching 80, like long time pal and fellow angling writer Dave Steuart from Romsey in Hampshire (we both contributed regularly in *Angling* magazine during the 1970's) when he spent a couple of days fishing with me in Norfolk. This particularly long specimen was his second best ever.

Shortly afterwards with the light virtually gone, one of my floats slid under and in came another superb fish of 23lbs, after we'd sat there for most of the day with diddly squit. But the next day's fishing proved even better.

With a couple of big pike in the bag, we shelved all plans for another pike session having done so well, and because my local River Wensum looked in such good trim, holding a smatter of colour with a strong flow, I suggested we try quiver-tipping a 10 foot deep back eddy of a local mill pool, where quality chub and bream plus the odd chance of a barbel or even a big roach were on the cards in such mild weather. Dave readily agreed and I knocked up half a bucket full of mashed bread (made from stale loaves) to compliment our thumbnail-sized fresh bread flake hook baits torn from the insides of a new white loaf covering a size 10 hook.

After introducing several balls of mash into the pool, way up into the flow so it came eventually to rest and feed the deepest part, we angled our 11 foot Avon quiver tip rods high up using two rests, in order to keep most of the line out of the strong backflow between where we sat and our ledgered baits 20 yards out, just

LEFT
Back-end fishing,
provided the
weather is mild
can usually
produce some
bumper hauls in
running water.
This near 9lbs
River Wensum
bream, being part
of a 20 fish catch
shared with Dave
Steuart, which
included roach to
2¼lbs, and chub
to 6lbs 9oz.

holding bottom with 3x 3xSSG shots, so we could encourage and easily interpret 'drop-back' bites. And just like the day before Dave was first on the scorecard with a huge roach weighing 2lb-4oz. What a marvellous surprise. But there was much more to come, due no doubt to sunlight filtering through the deep water and inducing everything in the pool to go on the rampage, following many days of subzero temperatures. And another four nice roach followed including one a shade over 2lbs for yours truly, the best I'd had from the river in several seasons. It was nice to know the cormorants haven't eaten them all. Though one or two swallows never make a summer, and predatory activity locally was indeed born out by horrendous scars on several of the fish in the bumper haul that we went on to catch, which included no less than 14 bream to over 8lbs and five chub to a huge 6lbs 9oz, my best ever from the river. The wounds on these magnificent fish were caused, yes! You've guessed, by otters.

Can you imagine a reverse scenario where the tables are turned and pike are responsible for biting chunks out of and killing otters? Well, wouldn't English Nature, the BTO and the good old RSPB all be up in arms, with a call for the culling of all big pike immediately? You bet they would!

The anal fin of my largest chub ever, was sadly almost chewed down to nothing. How I wish so-called 'do-gooders' would look at the 'biomass to predators' fish have to face in a stretch of river before introducing the most effective predator of all. Much of the Wensum already having been devastated from cormorants and to a lesser extent mink, during the past two decades. But I'm pleased to say despite all this, Dave actually got to experience what once upon a time, but now only rarely, the marvellous River Wensum could produce.

RIGHT

This roach I
was particularly
pleased with.
Weighing exactly
2½lbs and in
mint condition,
it was my largest
from the Wensum
for many a year,
due to the on-
going cormorant
predation which
has ravaged
the river for two
decades. But
I'm afraid one
swallow, does not
a summer make.

One week later at the end of the river fishing season, taking into account the fish Dave Steuart and I caught, I decided to long trot some favourite swims on my local River Wensum, which despite those nasty gale force winds from the southwest, was in fine trim and running with a steady flow and that all-important, 'tinge' of colour. And for the occasion wound 100 yards of fresh 3lbs test onto my Heritage centre pin. Trotting with the bait (which in my case was a thumbnail-sized piece of fresh white bread flake folded over a size 10 hook) just above or just tripping bottom is so much nicer at the end of the season when the river bed is clean and nicely scoured out. Virtually at all other times of the season these days, possibly due to the sheer amount of aggro chemicals leeching into the water throughout three decades of intensified farming, bumping bottom is not possible due to excessive weed growth, especially willow moss and blanket weed etc.

But during March, you can happily run a wide-topped, chubber-style float through most deepish and fast runs, carrying a bulk shotting of six AA's fixed 20 inches above the hook (with a no1 halfway between) and know that when the tip 'buries', it is due to a fish and not bottom. And to me, scything my 13½ foot rod back to pick up 20-40 yards of 3lbs test line, and then to feel on the fine tip that instant response of something sizeable shaking its head before charging off downstream, has and will always be for me, the most exciting feeling in freshwater angling. You can keep your big carp hooked at 90 yards, and even a big pike from a deep water gravel pit, because like as not, you'll actually be playing a good chub or big roach hooked on trotting tackle for very much longer anyway, having enjoyed a much higher skill level along the way in both hooking and eventually coaxing it into the net.

Such were my last couple of glorious experiences wandering the Wensum with half a bucket of mashed bread to use as loose feed and a fresh white loaf for hook baits. By trotting thumbnail-sized pieces, I went straight through the size barrier to the specimen-sized chub and roach I was seeking, taking in just two four hour sessions, numbers of fat chub to close on 6lbs, plus several surprise big roach with the largest, a beautifully proportioned and scale perfect specimen pulling the scales down to exactly 2½lbs. My largest from the river in many a year. No, the roach are not I'm sad to say on the 'comeback', though it would appear the cormorants have left me a few. And of the chub, bream and roach I did account for, sadly those roach were the minority species as expected. But didn't they look splendid, mesmeric almost, when I could see their sheer size and resplendent red fins during those last few anxious moments before slipping the net beneath, praying the hook would hold, my legs nearly went to jelly.

At the end of March I decided to spend Monday morning in the lounge at home reading to relax, following three hectic and demanding days at the *Go Fishing* show at the NEC in Birmingham, when the phone rang. It was fellow angling journalist Keith Elliot who had just returned from a Mahseer fishing trip to South India on the Cauvery River, (one of my favourite places on earth) with some sad, sad news. An old and faithful friend, guide Suban, had finally lost his battle with TB and had died. Now throughout my adult years I have probably shed more tears when burying loyal dogs than for fellow humans, (three separate 12 year old German Shepherds spring immediately to mind here) except for my mother and father who both passed away within six months of each other several years back. And then I didn't let loose and finally grieve on account of trying to be strong for the rest of the family, till months later. But when Keith put the phone down having been told by Suban's closest friend that he had always held me in the highest regard, I went out into the garden to tell my wife Jo and unashamedly cried into her arms like a baby.

Ironically, although I hadn't actually seen Suban for several years, I had in fact told a story about him at the NEC only a couple of days

before hand when on the forum with Des Taylor, and we were asked by compare Steve Parton of *Angling Times* to name the best anglers we had ever fished with. I chose angling guides because in many situations, especially in wild and dangerous locations abroad when you might only be there for a week, they are the people whose knowledge puts big fish onto your hook. And Suban was beside me when I connected with my first big Mahseer of the Cauvery River. Hooked on ragi paste bait from an evocative, wide bend in the river at a place known as Mosse Halla (which translates to 'crocodile rocks') the monster charged off downstream at incredible speed as they nearly all do, seemingly oblivious to the firmly set drag on my 10,000 multiplier and 40lbs test mono. Then as suddenly as it had come, it was off, and the

line fell back slack. It would appear I had done nothing wrong, so I looked at Suban and said 'it's come off', to which he immediately replied, 'hook gone, knot no good sir'. I thought, who does this little Indian think he is telling me I can't tie a hook on. But you know he was right, and I haven't felt so humbled since.

Suban simply tied on another 6/0 hook using a knot shown to him by a general in the Indian Army. A knot I have been using ever since which I call the 'Mahseer knot' which is so effective because under severe strain it 'stretches' as opposed to most blood knots which 'constrict' and then fracture, and in the unprecedented currents of mahseer rivers, this is its secret, if you wish to succeed by playing a 60-90lbs mahseer into submission following an hour long, arm-wrenching, gut-busting battle through rapids, through rocks and maybe half a mile downstream from where you first hooked it.

Fact is, a big fish can never be fought back upstream to where it took the bait. Such is current speed. You either go running after it, and Suban was always there to hold an arm up whenever I stumbled on slippery rocks, jump into the coracle should it be handy and set off down the rapids through a maelstrom of white water and boulders larger than a car, or even swim across the river whilst playing the fish, in order to get a better angle on it from the other bank. And every single time Suban was there looking after me. Carrying my camera bag high above his head whenever we waded out to fish from rocky fingers set amongst the fastest currents. A man of just 95lbs (for fun we actually put him on the scales in the weigh bag one day) with the skinniest legs and broadest smile you've ever seen. And a true giant of a man.

When good pal Andy Davison and I made our first trip to the Cauvery River, organised by the Wildlife Association of South India back in the mid 1980's we were driven to a makeshift camp at Gari Bora with a cook and provisions for our five week stay, which was when we first met our guides Bola and Suban who lived locally in Sangam Village. Whereupon the Jonga returned to Bangalore. We were well and truly on our own, in a beautiful, restful valley, and the only anglers with 14 miles of river to explore, but though we didn't know it then, in the very best of hands.

Being younger than Suban, Bola teamed up with Andy who is younger than me, which left Suban and I together. And that's how it always was during consecutive years for more than a decade. And everyone warmed to the 'always friendly' competiton element of who caught the biggest or most mahseer of the day. Upon arrival back one day at the sandy beach just below Gari Bora camp where the river is around 100 yards across, Andy asked Bola if he could cast his ragi bait across the river to land on the other side. And before long, there we all were like a group of kids trying to outcast each other. And yes, for those who have fished the same location, we each landed our ragi baits on the sand along opposite bank. On another day it was, 'could you swim across the river?' Now only that morning on the way back from fishing had we crept up on a huge croc lying on a sand bar not 200 yards downstream, to run off a few pics. But off Bola went, swimming across the river, which was in fact deceptively fast through the middle channel, followed by Andy of course, who is an exceptionally strong swimmer, followed by Suban and then a 40 something year-old Wilson (easily the older of the four) who 10 minutes earlier would have pooh-poohed the idea. And that I guess is how we came to fall in love with the Cauvery Valley and its mahseer, with more admiration for our guides than anyone we each knew, and has met since.

Incidentally, next to my feet below my office desk while I sit typing this is a nine year old West Highland Terrier called 'Bola', so named by my wife Jo for his fiery and fearless character. For when I took Jo mahseer fishing, Bola became her guide, and we spent a truly magnificent 10 days camped out at Haira in the company of Suban and Bola, accounting for numerous fish between 30 and 91lbs. But Jo still brings up the time when she was into a huge fish heading downriver fast, and which fouled up with my line caught in the rocks. Needless to say her line parted instantly. She was not a happy bunny! But she did land others to 45lbs. And that was in fact the last time Andy, Jo or I fished with both Bola and Suban together as a guide team. Suban left W.A.S.I. to join a Muslim fishing camp far downriver from Sangam where he remained guiding till his death and I didn't have the honour of ever fishing with him again. Though I did notice his moustache had

turned white when he appeared in the BBC's *Accidental Angler* Series featuring Charles Rangeley Wilson. (no relation incidentally). But he will forever be in my thoughts. Goodbye Suban!

I am always asked each year by the party of eight Brits I escort onto Lake Nasser, just how many perch they might expect to catch each day of their week's safari. Which of course is an impossible question to answer? But what I do say is, that most of them by the end of the week will no doubt have accounted for their largest freshwater fish ever (if they are new on the lake) in the form of at least one perch weighing between 30-50lbs, while some lucky angler will either have caught or hooked and lost a veritable buffalo. And do you know, in over 10 years I cannot remember when this hasn't happened. Buffalo, being the name we give to those breath-taking, decidedly hump-backed, monster perch weighing 100lbs and more. The fish of a lifetime no less, that makes trolling and shore casting artificial lures into the mysterious depths of Lake Nasser, (which is after all a flooded desert) such a unique experience. For in only a handful of other freshwater locations on this planet do you stand a realistic chance of hooking into such a monster?

But during my April trip on the Lake, (I have another safari this coming November) where we teamed up with my old friends Tim Baily (who runs 'African Angler' fishing safaris) and guide Mohammed, we went one better by accounting for no less than two buffalos, both of which actually came on the same morning whilst trolling a hot spot of sunken islands close to Abu Simbel in Egypt's southern half of the lake. Further south the lake (which of course is actually the River Nile) runs through the Sudan. The first monster of 110lbs came to the rod of James West from Romford, and the second of 120lbs, a particularly long specimen, grabbed a Rapala 'goldfish' Super Shad Rap plug trolled by Jason Mallalieu from Ringwood in Hampshire, and put up a long, most powerful scrap which included several 'nerve-shattering' leaps. But eventually, heart in mouth, Jason patiently steered his largest fish ever towards the boat and Mohammed's waiting arms, and the pair of them, as is characteristic on Lake Nasser with buffalos, got into the shallow water of an adjacent island so I could take a trophy shot.

Due to a full moon, when it is said that Nile perch with their superior sight (compared to their prey) hunt actively at night, we did find them generally unobliging. In fact on numerous occasions, wonderfully visible through the clear water, perch would follow our lures in half-hearted fashion, only to turn away at the last moment instead of grabbing hold. Sometimes soft, plastic and rubber lures can instigate hits when plugs do not, as I found one morning shore fishing when a beauty of 85lbs took a liking to a shad, providing a great and powerful tussle around a group of car-sized rocks at one end of a small island. Missed out on a slightly larger fish too a couple of days later, unfortunately, again in deep water close in beside a sheer cliff face. I rather suspect, due to the immense width across its back, that it could have been a 'buffalo'. But there we are. A great week none the less. Thanks Tim.

It must be almost impossible to have a bad day at Tim Small's Lechlade pretty two-lake fly fishery, extensively fringed by mature trees and reed beds, and hidden away in deepest Gloucestershire close to the River Thames. But not without trial and error in the accompanying heat wave conditions we were now experiencing during only the second week in May, which are never conducive to productive fly fishing. But this is the beauty of this particular day ticket fishery, (with evening, half day and full day tickets available from the on site tackle shop tel 01367 253266) because visitors have the choice of stalking the monster browns and rainbow trout stocked and caught to over 20lbs in eight acre Lechlade Lake where depths fluctuate between four and 20 feet, or fishing 20 acre Busheyleaze Lake situated across the other side of the A361 road which bisects the fishery. I did in fact enjoy some great action here at Lechlade Lake when filming an episode of my *Dream Fishing* series for TV, with both browns and rainbows into double figures. Boats and punts incidentally, are available on both lakes.

Due to the difficult conditions however, I must admit to choosing the easier option considering the blistering sunshine and gin clear water by first walking around Busheyleaze to see if any amount of fish were patrolling along the margins, and few were (although I did miss out on a couple of takes using buzzers) which meant that most of the fish had retreated into the extremely deep channel running through the centre of the lake. But few were rising despite the strong ripple that had developed within a couple of hours of my arrival, and so I took one of the boats out and tied up to a buoy out in the middle. I then put up a long leader of around 20 feet on my floating six-weight nymphing line, and added a 10 inch dropper six feet above the point. I then tied on a duo of size 12, black beaded buzzers and made a long cast directly down wind, waiting fully 30 seconds for the buzzers to descend into the cooler depths of the lake before starting a slow, figure of eight retrieve. Not 10 seconds into the retrieve, the line tightened firmly, and 'bang' I was into my first rainbow of the day, a superbly silver fish with a spade-like tail which must have been the better part of 4lbs, that I didn't even see for several minutes because it stayed deep and fought so strongly. What a great start, and after a couple more rainbows, all with outboard motors for tails, the point buzzer was inhaled by a beautifully proportioned brownie that lead me a real song and dance around the boat for several minutes. What fabulous sport in extremely difficult heat wave conditions?

I was actually in the area (a 500 mile round trip from Norfolk) to demonstrate at the two day Sportfish tackle show in Reading at the weekend on behalf of Masterline International Ltd. And decided to kill two birds with one stone, by having a couple of days fly fishing prior to the show. My second days fishing being on a beautifully kept stretch of the River Kennet. Now while Hampshire's River Test is considered by most fly fisherman to be the 'Holy Grail' of running water trouting, Royal Berkshire's Magical River Kennet must surely run it an exceptionally close second. Indeed, many anglers of 100 years ago when wild brownies in the Kennet were renowned for their specimen-reaching potential and craftiness, as angling authors of yesteryear regularly testified, would no doubt have even favoured this remarkable river. Being a larger river than the Test for much of its middle reaches the Kennet can still throw up monstrous brownies. In fact my largest ever UK river brownie which just topped the 9lbs mark came from the Kennet 10 years back, from a stretch between Newbury and Hungerford where sadly, two weeks short of the mayfly season, I now found myself wandering along in a most reflective mood with old friend and Kennet river keeper David Culley.

We talked about years gone by when the river held many more coarse fish than it does today, when great shoals of 2lbs plus roach could be clearly seen through the gin clear water in many of the deeper runs. And we reflected how mink (let out from farms by so-called 'do-gooders') have virtually wiped out that lovely little creature the 'water vole' during these two past decades. I used to love watching their busying around and comical goings on as they ran through tunnels amongst the marginal fringe of fox sedge, iris and sweet reed grass.

But what a privilege it was to be back again with a lightweight 5 weight outfit amidst fast, sparkling water, overshoot pools, glorious weir pools, ancient fishing huts, tussock sedges and cress-filled water meadows with every so often the fleeting glimpse of deer hopping over the tall grasses. Long may the hunting, shooting and fishing legacy, created and nurtured through magnificent estates, and subsequently handed down by our forefathers, continue to fascinate and inspire the next generation of countryside and field sport lovers. Regardless of the insipidly sad, politically correct, nanny state attitude we unfortunately now find ourselves wrapped up in.

David pointed out two good fish hanging just below the drop off from a long gravel run and I covered both several times with a small olive pattern. Without mayflies coming off as yet, those fish were not in any way aggressive. So I put up a tiny copper nymph, which the larger of the two fish inhaled from the surface film, literally before it had chance to sink. And what a marvellous scrap ensued. The ratchet of my little reel screaming like a stuck pig on each and every run it made downstream, till the elasticity in my eight foot carbon rod started to tell, and several minutes later I was able to bring it over the net held by David. A beautifully proportioned Kennet brownie of around 3lbs.

Though most fish on his four miles of Main River and tiny carriers are stocked, David was adamant that this particular brownie was a 'wild' fish. Its large fins and spade-like tail certainly suggested so. But either way we slowly made our way along the mainstream and then along three narrow, nicely overgrown carriers, taking a brownie here and a rainbow there, mostly on mayfly nymphs, and all weighing between 2 and 3lbs, before making our way back to the old fishing hut and main pool, where three anglers were already enjoying a liquid lunch. It was story swapping time.

I met long time buddy Simon Clarke of Catfish Pro at Stanstead Airport, and after a two hour flight to Zaragoza, we picked up the hire car and were heading along the AP2 road to Fraga, where we turned off towards the sleepy town of Mequinenza. Arriving about an hour and a half later. That's what I most like about

ABOVE
There is something truly magical about wandering along the banks of Royal Berkshire's River Kennet, and stalking superbly proportioned and spotted brown trout, using a tiny brook-rod outfit. I have river keeper and old friend Dave Culley to thank for my being there to enjoy what amounts to a piece of fly fishing history.

carp and cat fishing in Spain. I also like the spicey food and the Rioja mind. But in much less time than it would take me to drive either to Scotland or Wales from my Norfolk home, I can actually be fishing in Europe's premier big carp and cat fish capital, where the Rio's Segre and Cinca pour their water into the mighty Rio Ebro at Mequinenza. And unfortunately on this (extremely rare) occasion, the word 'pour' aptly fitted the river conditions, following three consecutive weeks of torrential rain. Our old mate and top guide on the river Gary Allen who used to work for the Bavarian Guiding Service in Mequinenza but now runs his own accommodation and personal guiding service (call his mobile on 0034667455863) from a commanding, elevated position high above the town, took us on a reconnaissance trip beside all three rivers close to the town, where the water was several feet above normal, full of debris including the odd tree, the colour of milky, yellow tea and thundering down completely unfishable.

But as Simon and I have learnt from past trips including filming for my *TV Safari* Series here a few years back, Gary always seems to find somewhere to produce some decent fish, and so we headed up country beside the beautiful Ebro valley to what locals call the 'upper lake', but which is actually the river, now immensely wide, deep and 'backed up' of course due to the huge dam at Mequinenza. Gary suggested that at the village of Chiprana the river would be less angry, less coloured and provided we could find somewhere to fish from the bank least affected by current surge and surface debris, into the middle of the river, both carp and cats were on the cards. And as usual he was spot on. Within an hour of arriving the following morning along heavily overgrown bank side skirting a peach orchard, and putting out two carp rods apiece, 50 yards into around 12 feet of water (the river being at least 250 yards across, but with the strongest flow and consequently all the surface debris on the opposite bank) all three of us were simultaneously into fish. What a place. Gary and Simon both landing beautifully proportioned commons of around 30lbs apiece following powerful scraps, while mine came off in a submerged bush as I fluffed around with the camera recording their action. 3oz in-line rigs baited with a single large boilie or 20 mm halibut pellet plus a PVA bag (made from 32 mm stocking) of smaller, loose feed pellets nicked onto our size 4 hooks, proving to be the perfect combination.

SIXTY YEARS A FISHERMAN

Action seemed to come in definite waves as different groups of carp moved over our loose feed, with waits in between of over an hour, on several occasions resulting in double hook-ups. But strangely, hectic sport, the like of which we have experienced on so many past occasions from this bountiful river never happened. Simon did catch a lone catfish of around 10lbs on one of his carp baits and I lost what could only have been a sizeable pussy which slowly evaporated over 50 yards of 15lbs test from my reel, (it was certainly no carp) when the hook inexplicably

pulled as I started to pile on the pressure. We had in fact expected more action from cats on our single 20 mm halibut pellet carp baits because this particular part of the Ebro is heavily and regularly baited with halibut pellets (by the 25 kilo bag full) specifically for the catfish, and has been for at least the last three years. To the extent that 100lbs plus pussies (as we were to experience) have now become every day catches for so many British anglers who visit the Ebro system, both in the upper lake and downstream at Mequinenza. But for day one in difficult river conditions and with the weather not being able to decide what to throw at us next, (we were continually taking our wet and cold weather gear off or putting it all back on again) our day's tally of 15 carp to 30lbs, easily averaging over 20lbs apiece, with several more shedding the hook amongst submerged shrubbery, was far more than we had expected when first clapping eyes on the hopelessly swollen lower river only the day before. Add regular sightings overhead of kites and vultures, swifts and swallows, and even a pair of golden orioles, and you can imagine that three very happy anglers returned to Mequinenza that evening.

The following morning saw us in the very same swim of course. There seemed little point in leaving feeding fish in a part of the river that was not only nicely fishable, but which also contained pussies. The fact that there was a great Chinese take away just up the road had nothing to do with it. Our cunning plan being to enjoy another day's carping, and then the following two days before flying home, after the cats. Which is exactly what happened, though day two, disappointingly, produced exactly, another 15 carp up to 26lbs (several being mid doubles) Gary accounting for half of them, despite fishing for less time due to driving into Chiprana at lunchtime to collect our Chinese food and a bottle of chilled white wine. The sweet and sour pork and barbequed spare ribs being particularly recommended. Again, the weather varied between cold rain and hot, sultry periods. To which we attributed our inexplicably slow catch rate. And we added serins and goldfinches, plus egrets and kestrels, which were continually mobbing crows, to the list of flying friends.

On day three we were back in the swim again, Gary having made up six catfish outfits (two each) comprising of powerful 10 foot rods and TLD 20 multipliers loaded to the brim with 130lbs braid. On the business end a pair of 25mm halibut pellets were secured on a double loop Dacron hair below one of Simon's 'Catfish Pro' thick wire, short shank BP (boilie and pellet) 6/0 hooks. Also onto the hook was fixed a 'stringer' of around 20 pellets threaded onto PVA tape. And above the five foot, 100 kilo test Cat-Link trace stopped by a bead and strong swivel, was a 'running' 1lb ball lead. With three 25 kilo bags of 25mm pellets for loose feed (yes I know this seems excessive but these big pussies clean up big time) Gary set about laying the baits way out into the river two at a time, and added an electric outboard motor and fish finder to his sturdy inflatable boat.

SIXTY YEARS A FISHERMAN

As there is of course no way of casting such heavy tackle (mandatory for fish which could weigh anything up to 200lbs) running the baits out in the boat while someone uses thumb pressure on the multipliers free spool is imperative. And in less than half an hour Gary had run all six baits some 150 yards out to rest on the bottom in a line going down river, in over 20 feet of water on the edge of the old river bed (where the cats were expected) and heaved in around each a good helping of halibut pellets. Back on the bank Simon and I put each rod vertically into the sturdy, steel holders and adjusted the lever drags on each reel (with the ratchets on) to only give line begrudgingly. Otherwise, the strong current would be forever indicating false bites. Not that there is ever any question about a catfish having inhaled the hook bait. The rod tip suddenly slamming over as though connected to a motorbike.

It was now a case of waiting, and as my two good mates had generously decreed that 'Wensum Wilson' (one of their 'nicer' pet nicknames for yours truly) could hit the runs till a big fish came along, I was sitting there like a gun slinger. Moreover, I actually connected solidly with the first run (cats do not hook-up so effectively as carp on what is more or less a 'bolt rig', so a certain amount of runs are missed) but it was a mere baby of around 30lbs. The next run produced a really good fish (easily over the ton) which following a powerful scrap and was coming in nicely (this auto biography was going to end on a whopper as I'd hoped) promptly shed the hook just 30 yards out. Served me right for counting my chickens.

I then went and missed the next two runs, which were a trifle 'juddery' and suggested small cats, but with number five, late in the afternoon, I whacked into big time, and it was wonderful to feel that awesome power of a fish taking line at will against the drag of a firmly set clutch. Especially when it's over 150 yards out. Big cats certainly pull your string, which I guess is what sends more and more Brits annually out to Spain, and for a good 10 minutes I built up quite a sweat hauling in the unseen monster. From its animal power and stamina this was the stamp of fish we had come to enjoy, as a huge head suddenly appeared on the surface not five yards out. It had remained close to the bottom till then. But following a couple of tail-slapping rolls I steered it towards Gary who quickly grabbed its lower jaw with both hands (gloved) and hauled it up onto the waiting, already wetted, giant unhooking mat. Like all we caught, carp included, due to the tea-coloured water, the fish was exceptionally pale, but nicely marked and powerfully proportioned. It looked well over the ton and in fact weighed 118lbs. Job done.

Unfortunately, Simon never got on strike that day because that fish provided the last run of the session. No doubt had we stayed till dark action would have improved. But we were not fussed and in holiday mood. So with a nice meal at a favourite restaurant on the cards back in Mequinenza, we left the pussies for another day. Our last day in fact, which started incredibly slowly.

Though settled in upriver at our Chiprana swim earlier than usual we sat there till half past three for our first run, and then had no less than five within a two hour feeding spell. Simon connecting solidly with his first run which obviously came from a ton-up fish. It fought extremely powerfully for over 10 minutes, making several gut-busting runs against the clutch till it was around 30 yards from the bank, which was when the line suddenly fell back slack. Simon wound in to find that the trace had severed a few inches above the hook. 'Ah well', he said, or something similar.

The second run, just 20 minutes later, produced almost a carbon copy of the first in that Simon was into yet an even larger fish which ran and ran against the clutch. For fully 15 minutes it lead him a real song and dance and as it begrudgingly came towards the bank it started veering to the right where dense, tall bushes grew out from the marginal flood waters. When it finally became stuck despite Simon wading out as far as he dare to impart side strain, Gary rowed out in the inflatable to grab the line and pull the great fish free from the branches. The first line he grabbed however was not Simon's, though it was as thick as his 200 Kilo Kevlar hook trace, but what appeared to be a dead-line (sadly, Britain is not the

only country suffering its 'angling' fish being killed to eat by Eastern Europeans) which somehow had become tangled with Simons fish. And when Gary pulled on the end its four hook rig (would you believe) caught on Simon's trace and acted like a disgorger. Whereupon the catfish, which Gary said looked all of 150lb plus, promptly came off. More unprintable expletives, this time from all three of us.

Run number three Simon missed completely, which due to its juddery, hesitant manner was probably from a small fish anyway. He even got the two hair rigged halibut pellets back. But number four was again from a whopper, and following a dogged, fairly short scrap (Simon by now was not about to lose another) an exquisitely coloured, yellowy cat topping the ton was heaved out by Gary, who (to quote an old footballing saying) has the safest hands in the business. Straight onto the scales it went, where the dial pulled round to 111lbs. Were we all over the moon or not?

No, there are no more monsters to come, although I was contemplating this happening when I struck run number five and the last run of our holiday, which resulted in our smallest catfish of the session. A kitten of less than 20lbs. Happily we motored back to Mequinenza and after finishing off a bottle of red and a pizza on the balcony outside Gary's accommodation with its mesmeric and panoramic view over the wide junction of the Segre and Ebro, now noticeably lower, less angry but nowhere near as yet, to being nicely fishable, we thanked our guide Gary for his experience, time and trouble in turning a four day trip into something memorable, as opposed to a disaster, before packing in readiness for our flight back to the UK the next day.

POSTSCRIPT

I certainly hope you the reader have enjoyed this 'extended' autobiography as much as I have indeed enjoyed re-living it all by recording such a varied selection of trips and memoirs during these past 60 years since I first tied a red worm around the middle with black cotton and half hitched on two feet above it a matchstick float, and became fascinated by the glistening stickleback that resulted. I've always endeavoured to live life to the full and have been extraordinarily fortunate in realising many personal ambitions and made some wonderful friendships along the way through this unique field sport we call angling, which has taken me all around the world to over 60 countries.

Sure, and I am sure you have gathered by reading between the lines that I'm concerned for the future of angling in this tiny environment we call the UK. There are far too many do-gooders, hypocrites, (I've already mentioned certain politicians) pseudo countrymen and modern alternatives around for my liking. I want kids to get out there come sun, sleet or rain and to get their wellies muddy for real. By following the legacy handed down from their forefathers of hunting shooting and fishing. Not through reality games and computerised learning. I want to retain our 'Island' mentality and standards. They are what once made our country great. Not water them down for changing by bureaucrats sitting in offices in Brussels. Which is what's slowly happening by our being part of the EU. I am English first and British second? I'm certainly not European and have no wish to be. Merely fish or holiday there occasionally.

The consequences of allowing the attitudes and cultures of others to affect our sovereignty is already rife in the summer of 2008 as I put this lengthy volume to bed, due to the nanny state this country currently finds itself in. And still without workable protection from the government departments whose mandate it is to actually protect our inland water ways. Unlike eastern Europeans for instance, most Britons choose to eat a chicken or turkey for Christmas lunch, not a boiled or roasted carp or catfish. We have grown up choosing to catch and return the freshwater species we love to catch. And we need vehemently to continue to protect our valuable inheritance. It is our life, our love, and what makes us what we are.

Good Fishing.

MY ALL-TIME BIG FISH LIST

217 fresh and saltwater species from 34 different countries.
Though I have in fact fished in 64 countries.

Freshwater – 101 Species from 12 countries

African Pike	2lb 0oz	Zambezi River, Zimbabwe
Alestes	5lb 10oz	River Nile, Uganda
Arapaima	130lb 0oz	Palm Tree Lagoon, Thailand
Awaka	3lb 0oz	River Nile, Uganda
Aruana	7lb 8oz	River Negro, Brazil
Barbel	16lb 13oz	River Wensum, Norfolk
Barbel (Southern)	6lb 3oz	River Ebro, Spain
Barbel (silver)	1lb 1oz	Zambezi River, Zimbabwe
Bass (Big mouth)	4lb 2oz	Dam, Morocco
Bass (Butterfly)	4lb 12oz	River Negro, Brazil
Bass (Paca)	6lb 0oz	River Negro, Brazil
Bass (Peacock)	13lb 0oz	River Negro, Brazil
Bicuda	2lb 6oz	River Negro, Brazil
Bream	13lb 14oz	Forgotten Lake, Norfolk
Bream (Pink Happy)	3lb 2oz	Zambezi River, Zimbabwe
Bream (Red bellied)	2lb 6oz	Zambezi River, Zimbabwe
Bream (Robustos)	4lb 8oz	Zambezi River, Zimbabwe
Brim	1lb 6oz	Goodradigbee River, Australia
Carp Buffalo,		
Small mouth	15lb 0oz	Greers Ferry Lake, USA
Carp (Carnatic)	5lb 0oz	Cauvery River, India
Carp-common	35lb 4oz	River Segre, Spain
Carp-crucian	3lb 14oz	Karlstad Lake, Sweden
Carp-grass	41lb 0oz	Lake Hamilton, USA
Carp-pink	8lb 2oz	Cauvery River, India
Carp-red	11lb 0oz	Cha-am Fish Park, Thailand
Carp-silver	9lb 3oz	Palm Tree Lagoon, Thailand
Catfish (Blue)	9lb 0oz	Lake Ouachita, USA
Catfish (Bullhead)	3lb 0oz	Red River, Canada
Catfish (Channel)	32lb 8oz	Red River, Canada
Catfish (Chao phray)	80lb 0oz	Bung San Ran Lake, Thailand
Catfish (Electric)	6lb 0oz	Lake Nasser, Egypt
Catfish (Flathead)	9lb 0oz	Rufigi River, Tanzania
Catfish (Mekong)	62lb 0oz	Cha-am Fish Park, Thailand
Catfish (Piraiba)	21lb 0oz	River Negro, Brazil
Catfish (Red tail)	75lb 0oz	River Negro, Brazil
Catfish (Thai Red Tail)	44lb 0oz	Palm Tree Lagoon, Thailand
Catfish (Sementendu)	60lb 0oz	River Nile, Uganda
Catfish (Sharp tooth)	18lb 3oz	Lake Kariba, Zimbabwe
Catfish (silver)	4lb 0oz	Cauvery River, India
Catfish (Squeeker)	5lb 0oz	River Nile, Uganda
Catfish (Swai)	31lb 0oz	Bung San Ran Lake, Thailand
Catfish (Upper Zambezi)		
Squeeker	1lb 10oz	Zambezi River, Zimbabwe
Catfish (Vundu)	95lb 0oz	Lake Kariba, Zimbabwe
Catfish (Wels)	120lb 0oz	River Ebro, Spain
Catfish (Yellow)	3lb 0oz	Cauvery River, India
Chessa	4lb 8oz	Zambezi River, Zambia
Chub	6lb 9oz	River Wensum, Norfolk
Dace	1lb 2oz	River Kennet, Berkshire
Dogfish-chub	4lb 3oz	River Negro, Brazil
Dorado (Golden)	18lb 8oz	Parana River, Brazil
Drum	9lb 3oz	Red River, Canada
Eel	5lb 2oz	Lakeside, Norfolk

Golden Orfe	6lb 6oz	Lakeside, Norfolk
Gourami	7lb 9oz	Palm Tree Lagoon, Thailand
Grayling	3lb 0½oz	River Frome, Dorset
Grayling (Arctic)	3lb 3oz	Kazan River, Canada
Ide (Golden)	4lb 12oz	Klaralven River, Sweden
Labeo	6lb 10oz	River Nile, Uganda
Mahseer (Black)	44lb 0oz	Cauvery River, India
Mahseer (Golden)	92lb 0oz	Cauvery River, India
Mahseer (Silver)	23lb 8oz	Cauvery River, India
Manyame Salmon	5lb 10z	Zambezi River, Zimbabwe
Murrell	6lb 10oz	Cauvery River, India
Nile perch	150lb 0oz	Lake Nasser, Egypt
Nkupe	5lb 5oz	Zambezi River, Zambia
Pacu	23lb 7oz	Palm Tree Lagoon, Thailand
Perch	4lb 10oz	River Great Ouse, Bucks
Pike	30lbs 13oz	Somerton Nth Broad, Norfolk
Pirhana	2lb 0oz	River Negro, Brazil
Puffer fish	3lb 0oz	Lake Nasser, Egypt
Roach	2lb 14½oz	River Wensum, Norfolk
Roach/Bream Hybrid	5lb 1oz	Wensum Pit, Norfolk
Roach/Rudd Hybrid	3lb 15oz	Forgotten Lake, Norfolk
Rudd	3lb 8oz	Elstowe Pit, Bedfordshire
Salmon (Atl)	10lb 6oz	River Bann, Northern Ireland
Salmon Chinook (Pac)	30lb 0oz	Harrison River, Canada
Salmon Chum (Pac)	25lb 0oz	Harrison River, Canada
Salmon Coho (Pac)	9lb 6oz	Harrison River, Canada
Salmon Pink (Pac)	10lb 2oz	Fraser River, Canada
Salmon Sockeye (Pac)	13lb 8oz	Harrison River, Canada
Shad/Twaite	1lb 13oz	River Wye, Wales
Sik	3lb 2oz	Klaralven River, Sweden
Sturgeon-giant white	300lb 0oz	Fraser River, Canada
Sauger	2lb 6oz	Red river, Canada
Tench	9lb 6oz	Wensum Pit, Norfolk
Tiger fish	14lb 10oz	Zambezi River, Zambia
Tilapia-Niloticus	7lb 2oz	Lake Nasser, Egypt
Tilapia- Three spot	3lb 6oz	Zambezi River, Zambia
Trout-brook	8lb 8oz	Kamistastin Lake, Canada
Trout-Brown	9lb 2oz	River Kennet, Berkshire
Trout-brown	11lb 0oz	Dever Springs Lakes, Hants
Trout-bull	3lb 6oz	Liluett River, Canada
Trout-cheeta	3lb 3oz	Avington Lakes, Hampshire
Trout-lake	33lb 0oz	Wolf Lake, Canada
Trout-blue-rainbow	11lb 12oz	Dever Springs Lakes, Hants
Trout-golden-rainbow	5lb 10oz	Chalk Springs Lakes, Sussex
Trout-rainbow	15lb 10oz	Dever Springs Lakes, Hants
Trout-sea	9lb 4oz	Morrum River, Sweden
Trout-steelhead	14lb 2oz	Copper River, Canada
Trout-tiger	5lb 8oz	Chalk Springs Lakes, Sussex
Zander	11lb 3oz	Middle level Drain, Norfolk

Amaco Jack	27lb 0oz	Islamorada, Florida, USA
Amberjack	78lb 0oz	Islamorada, Florida, USA
Antarctic rock cod	5lb 12oz	The Falkland Islands
Barracuda	33lb 0oz	The Seychelles
Bass	12lb 0oz	Suffolk Coast
Bass (Striped)	28lb 0oz	Montauk, NY, USA
Bastard Halibut	4lb 3oz	The Gambia
Black Bream	4lb 1oz	The Channel Islands
Black Jack	8lb 0oz	Barbados
Blue fish	12lb 0oz	Montauk, NY, USA
Bonefish	7lb 0oz	The Bahamas
Bonito	9lb 0oz	The Seychelles
Brill	7lb 8oz	The Channel Islands
Brosma	6lb 6oz	Norway
Casarva	12lb 0oz	The Gambia
Catfish-hardhead	31lb 0oz	The Gambia
Catfish-silver	8lb 0oz	Aden, The Yemen
Coalfish	17lb 0oz	off Rye, Sussex
Cobia	22lb 8oz	Islamorada, Florida, USA
Cod	34lb 0oz	Norway
Conger Eel	76lb 0oz	off Rye, Sussex
Crevalle Jack	12lb 0oz	Barbados
Dorado	43lb 0oz	The Seychelles
Flathead	7lb 0oz	Australia
Fluke-Flounder	3lb 7oz	Montauk, NY, USA
Garfish	1lb 10oz	The Channel Islands
Green Job fish	15lb 0oz	The Seychelles
Grunter-moff	9lb 0oz	South Africa
Grunter-spotted	12lb 8oz	South Africa
Guitarfish	35lb 0oz	Morocco
Guitarfish-spotted	8lb 0oz	South Africa
Gurnard-bronze	4lb 0oz	Montauk, NY, USA
Gurnard-red	1lb 6oz	The Channel Islands
Gurnard-tub	6lb 8oz	New Zealand
Haddock	12lb 0oz	Norway
Horse Mackerel	1lb 6oz	South Coast
Hound fish	6lb 0oz	The Seychelles
Jewfish	80lb 0oz	Islamorada, USA
Ladyfish	9lb 12oz	The Gambia
Limpopo Grouper	28lb 0oz	Mozambique
Ling	30lb 0oz	Denmark
Ling Cod	7lb 8oz	Canada
Mackerel-Common	2lb 2oz	South Coast
Mackerel-king	26lb 0oz	Kenya
Mackerel-Spanish	8lb 6oz	Barbados
Moon tail Sea Bass	11lb 0oz	The Seychelles
Moray Eel	12lb 0oz	Madeira
Mullet-grey thick lipped	4lb 2oz	Weymouth
Mullet-golden	2lb 2oz	Essex Coast
Mullet-thin-lipped	3lb 1oz	Christchurch
Permit	25lb 8oz	Islamorada, Florida, USA
Plaice	4lb 2oz	Weymouth
Pollack	18lb 12oz	South Coast
Pompano	1lb 9oz	Seychelles
Pouting	2lb-0oz	South Coast
Rainbow Runner	7lb 0oz	The Seychelles
Ray-eagle	65lb 0oz	Australia
Ray-small eyed	10lb 0oz	The Channel Islands
Ray-spotted	4lb 8oz	Dorset
Ray-sting	200lb 0oz	Barbados
Ray-thornback	11lb 6oz	South Coast
Ray-undulate	12lb 8oz	The Channel Islands
Redfish	3lb 0oz	Norway
Remora	5lb 0oz	Islamorada, Florida, USA
Rockhind	4lb 8oz	Seychelles
Rubber-lipped grouper	5lb 8oz	The Gambia
Sailfish	91lb 0oz	Mexico
Salmon-threadfin	20lb 0oz	The Gambia
Shark-Black tip	80lb 0oz	Fiji
Shark-Black-tipped	120lb 0oz	Mozambique
Shark-Blue	180lb 0oz	Montauk, NY State, USA
Shark-Bonnet Head	5lb 0oz	Islamorada, Florida, USA
Shark-Bronze Whaler	240lb 0oz	Namibia
Shark-Greater Spotted Dog fish	14lb 0oz	Weymouth
Shark-Hammerhead	300lb 0oz	Islamorada, Florida, USA
Shark-Lemon	300lb 0oz	The Gambia
Shark-Leopard	21lb 0oz	San Francisco, USA
Shark-Lesser spotted Dogfish	2lb 0oz	Weymouth
Shark-Mako	220lb 0oz	Montauk, NY, USA
Shark-Nurse	75lb 0oz	Islamorada, Florida, USA
Shark-Oceanic	180lb 0oz	Mauritius
Shark-Tope	49lb 0oz	The Channel Islands
Shark-Smoothound, common	18lb 8oz	Hayling Island
Shark-Smoothound, starry	21lb 0oz	Hayling Island
Shark-spotted Gully Shark	61lb 0oz	Namibia
Shark-spur dog	11lb 0oz	Ireland
Sheepshead	4lb 7oz	Islamorada, Florida,USA
Skate-common	182lb 0oz	Oban, Scotland
Snapper-Cubera	35lb 0oz	The Gambia
Snapper-Grey	11lb 0oz	Barbados
Snapper-Mutton	6lb 0oz	The Gambia
Snapper-Red	21lb 0oz	New Zealand
Snook	9lb 6oz	Barbados
Spotted Seatrout	5lb 0oz	Morocco
Sunpat	9lb 0oz	The Gambia
Tarpon	160lb 0oz	Islamorada, Florida,USA
Tomato Hind	6lb 0oz	The Seychelles
Trevally-blue spotted	18lb 0oz	The Seychelles
Trevally-giant	30lb 0oz	Kenya
Trevally-golden	15lb 0oz	Mozambique
Trevally-three spot	17lb 8oz	Mozambique
Trevally-yellow tail	16lb 8oz	Kenya
Trigger fish	2lb 4oz	Islamorada, Florida, USA
Tuna-big eyed	220lb 0oz	Madeira
Tuna-black fin	12lb 0oz	Mauritius
Tuna-blue fin	30lb 0oz	Australia
Tuna-skipjack	7lb 0oz	Madeira
Tuna-yellow fin	62lb 0oz	Kenya
Turbot	10lb 4oz	The Channel Islands
Wahoo	43lb 0oz	Kenya
Wave Garrick	3lb 0oz	South Africa
Weakfish-spotted	2lb 7oz	Islamorada, Florida,
Wolf fish	7lb 0oz	Norway
Wrasse-Ballan	4lb 0oz	The Channel Islands
Wrasse-Cuckoo	1lb 9oz	The Channel Islands

WHERE TO FIND...

The quotations in this book

The quoted verses are paraphrases of the Bible text, based on the following passages:

First mention of key people in this book

Aaron 94	Isaac 47	Naomi 164
Abraham 38	Jacob (Israel) 56	Noah 28
Adam 17	Jairus 350	Paul 466
Ahab 232	James 324	Peter 324
Ananias 468	Jesus 295	Philip 328
Andrew 324	Jezebel 232	Rahab 138
Bartimaeus 410	John 324	Rebecca 48
Benjamin (Ben) 75	John (Baptist) 317	Reuben 79
Bethuel 53	Jonah 264	Ruth 165
Boaz 169	Jonathan 200	Samson 156
Caleb 130	Joseph (NT) 284	Samuel (Sam) 173
Cornelius 463	Joseph (OT) 74	Sarah 40
Daniel 272	Joshua 130	Saul 183
David (171) 188	Judas 328	Solomon 221
Delilah 162	Laban 70	Thomas 328
Eli 173	Lazarus 418	Zacchaeus 414
Elijah 234	Leah 71	Zechariah 290
Elisha 251	Martha 418	
Elizabeth 288	Mary 284	
Esau 56	Mary (2) 418	
Eve 17	Mary Magdalene 446	
Gideon 151	Matthew 326	
Goliath 192	Miriam 94	
Hannah 172	Moses 99	
Herod 302	Naaman 248	